SIMPSON

IMPRINT IN HUMANITIES

The humanities endowment
by Sharon Hanley Simpson and
Barclay Simpson honors
MURIEL CARTER HANLEY
whose intellect and sensitivity
have enriched the many lives
that she has touched.

The publisher and the University of California Press Foundation
gratefully acknowledge the generous support of the
Simpson Imprint in Humanities.

Luminos is the Open Access monograph publishing program from UC Press. Luminos provides a framework for preserving and reinvigorating monograph publishing for the future and increases the reach and visibility of important scholarly work. Titles published in the UC Press Luminos model are published with the same high standards for selection, peer review, production, and marketing as those in our traditional program. www.luminosoa.org

# Ways of Seeking

ISLAMIC HUMANITIES

Shahzad Bashir, Series Editor

Publication of this Luminos Open Access Series is made possible by the Islam and the Humanities Project of the Program in Middle East Studies at Brown University.

1. *Forging the Ideal Educated Girl: The Production of Desirable Subjects in Muslim South Asia*, by Shenila Khoja-Moolji
2. *Witness to Marvels: Sufism and Literary Imagination*, by Tony K. Stewart
3. *God's Property: Islam, Charity, and the Modern State*, by Nada Moumtaz
4. *Placing Islam: Geographies of Connection in Twentieth-Century Istanbul*, by Timur Hammond
5. *Pious Labor: Islam, Artisanship, and Technology in Colonial India*, by Amanda Lanzillo
6. *Ways of Seeking: The Arabic Novel and the Poetics of Investigation*, by Emily Drumsta

# Ways of Seeking

## *The Arabic Novel and the Poetics of Investigation*

---

Emily Drumsta

UNIVERSITY OF CALIFORNIA PRESS

University of California Press
Oakland, California



Suggested citation: Drumsta, E. *Ways of Seeking: The Arabic Novel and the Poetics of Investigation*. Oakland: University of California Press, 2024.
DOI: https://doi.org/10.1525/luminos.178

Library of Congress Cataloging-in-Publication Data

Names: Drumsta, Emily, author.
Title: Ways of seeking : the Arabic novel and the poetics of investigation / Emily Drumsta.
Other titles: Islamic Humanities ; 6.
Description: Oakland, California : University of California Press, [2024] | Series: Islamic humanities ; 6 | Includes bibliographical references and index.
Identifiers: LCCN 2023029859 (print) | LCCN 2023029860 (ebook) | ISBN 9780520390195 (paperback) | ISBN 9780520390201 (ebook)
Subjects: LCSH: Arabic fiction—20th century—History and criticism. | Arabic poetry—20th century—History and criticism. | Detective and mystery stories, Arabic—20th century—Influence. | Modernism (Literature)—Arab countries—20th century.
Classification: LCC PJ7577 .D78 2024 (print) | LCC PJ7577 (ebook) | DDC 892.7/36—dc23/eng/20230807

LC record available at https://lccn.loc.gov/2023029859
LC ebook record available at https://lccn.loc.gov/2023029860

32 31 30 29 28 27 26 25 24
10 9 8 7 6 5 4 3 2 1

*for Adam and Levi*

مِن سَجايا الطُلول أَلّا تجيبا      فَصَوابٌ مِن مُقلةٍ أنْ تَصوب
فاسأَلناها وَاِجعَل بُكاكَ جَواباً      تَجِدَ الشَوقَ سائلاً ومُجيبا

—Abu Tammam

CONTENTS

# NOTES ON TRANSLITERATION, TRANSLATION, AND ABBREVIATIONS

For romanizations from Arabic, I follow the IJMES transliteration system with a few exceptions. I transliterate final *tāʾ marbūṭah* in nonconstructs as *-ah*, not *-a*. Where an English translation of a novel has been published, I use the transliterations of character names that appear there, except for Naguib Mahfouz's *al-Ṭarīq*; transliterations of names from that volume follow the IJMES guidelines. For Arabic book titles mentioned in the main text, I give the title of the published English translation followed by a full transliteration, with diacritics, of the Arabic title—for example, "Yusuf Idris' *The Sinners* (*al-Ḥarām*)." For book, article, and poem titles in Arabic for which no English translation has been published, I give the transliterated title with full diacritics followed by my own English translation of the title in parentheses—for example, "Yusuf al-Qaʿid's *Yaḥduth fī Miṣr al-Ān* (It's happening now in Egypt)." I keep full diacritics on transliterated Arabic book, essay, and periodical titles cited in the notes.

For romanizations from colloquial Egyptian Arabic, I use the system in Martin Hinds and El-Said Badawi's *Dictionary of Egyptian Arabic* with a few exceptions, as follows:

| Arabic Letter | Romanization |
|---|---|
| ء | ʾ |
| ح | ḥ |
| خ | kh |
| ش | sh |
| ض | ḍ |
| ط | ṭ |
| ع | ʿ |
| غ | gh |

I cite from published English translations of French and Arabic novels where available or appropriate, specifying where and when I have made alterations or offered my own translation instead. All other translations from Arabic and French are mine, as are any errors or oversights therein.

| | |
|---|---|
| *JAL* | *Journal of Arabic Literature* |
| *EI3* | *Encyclopedia of Islam*, 3rd ed. |
| *EI2* | *Encyclopedia of Islam*, 2nd ed. |
| MIT | Massachusetts Institute of Technology |
| *MK* | Naguib Mahfouz, *al-Muʾallafāt al-Kāmilah* |
| *D* | Tawfiq al-Hakim, *Diary of a Country Prosecutor*, trans. Abba Eban |
| *Y* | Tawfiq al-Hakim, *Yawmiyyāt Nāʾib fī al-Aryāf* |
| *E* | Driss Chraïbi, *Une Enquête au pays* |
| *F* | Driss Chraïbi, *Flutes of Death*, trans. Robin Roosevelt |
| *S* | Yusuf Idris, *The Sinners*, trans. Kristin Peterson-Ishaq |
| *Ḥ* | Yusuf Idris, *al-Ḥarām* |
| *YMA* | Yusuf al-Qaʿid, *Yaḥduth fī Miṣr al-Ān* |
| *H* | Jabra Ibrahim Jabra, *Hunters in a Narrow Street* |
| *ISWM* | Jabra Ibrahim Jabra, *In Search of Walid Masoud*, trans. Roger Allen and Adnan Haydar |
| *B* | Jabra Ibrahim Jabra, *al-Baḥth ʿan Walīd Masʿūd* |
| *Ṭ* | Naguib Mahfouz, *al-Ṭarīq* |
| *CT* | Naguib Mahfouz, *The Cairo Trilogy*, trans. William Maynard Hutchins, Olive E. Kenny, Lorne M. Kenny, and Angele Botros Samaan |
| *J* | Fathi Ghanim, *al-Jabal* |
| *WM* | Elias Khoury, *White Masks* |
| *WB* | Elias Khoury, *al-Wujūh al-Bayḍāʾ* |
| *L* | Sonallah Ibrahim, *al-Lajnah* |
| *C* | Sonallah Ibrahim, *The Committee* |
| *Z* | Sonallah Ibrahim, *Zaat* |
| *Dh* | Sonallah Ibrahim, *Dhāt* |
| *F* | Ahmed Saadawi, *Frankenstein in Baghdad* |

# Introduction

## *Toward a Poetics of Investigation*

Near the beginning of Naguib Mahfouz's *Cairo Trilogy*, a woman ascends to the roof of her house to tend to the plants and animals in the garden she has cultivated there. She waters the carnations, roses, and trellised jasmine vines, and she feeds the chickens and pigeons for whom she has built coops and cotes. The *Trilogy* is generally read as a paragon of Cairene realism, a bildungsroman focused on the intellectual development of its protagonist Kamal, often understood as a stand-in for Mahfouz himself.[1] This scene, however, focuses on Amina, the matriarch of the family whose lives the novel chronicles, and whom most accounts interpret as "the Egyptian mother of yesterday, enslaved and demeaned . . . incredibly naïve and outwardly submissive."[2] The text certainly supports such a reading. Mahfouz's omniscient narrator describes the rooftop garden as Amina's "favorite space of diversion in this vast world about which she knew nothing" and Amina herself as a "prisoner" of the great house, never leaving it except on rare occasions to visit her mother; even then, "the master always accompanied her in a carriage because he couldn't tolerate any eye falling upon his wife, whether she were alone or in his company."[3]

But let me invite you to look again at Amina in the rooftop garden she "created completely anew, from her own spirit,"[4] as she herself looks out on and understands her world. Her position in this scene is technically panoramic, her rooftop perch akin to the "objective" position of the viewing subject in Timothy Mitchell's theory of the "world-as-exhibition."[5] Yet the relation Mahfouz describes between the woman and the space around her is not exactly that of isolated, all-seeing subject to world-rendered-up-as-object:

> How happy she felt every time she scattered seeds or set the watering dish on the ground and watched the chickens race behind their rooster, their beaks assailing

> the grains with the speed and regularity of sewing machine needles, leaving tiny indentations in the dust like the pockmarks from a drizzle. How her heart opened every time she saw them returning her gaze with their tiny, clear eyes, inquisitive and questioning, cackling and clucking with a shared affection that made her tender heart vibrate like a plucked string. She loved the chickens and the pigeons as she loved all of God's creatures, and she made little noises to them, believing that they understood and responded to her. Her imagination imparted sentient, intelligent life to all animals, and sometimes even to inanimate beings. She was quite certain that these beings praised their Lord and were connected to the spirit world in various ways. Her world, with its earth and its sky, its animals and its plants, was a living, intelligent world. Its merits, furthermore, were not confined to the melodies of life; it supplemented and perfected them through worship . . .
>
> She went to the edge of the garden and stood behind the interwoven, coiling stalks, extending her gaze through the gaps in their greenery to the adjacent open space, unbounded by any limits. How she marveled at the minarets bursting skyward and leaving a profound impression, some so close she could see their crescent moons and lamps clearly—like Qalawun and Barquq—some in the middle distance, appearing to her as a single entity without distinguishing features—like al-Husayn, al-Ghuri, and al-Azhar—and some appearing only as specters on the distant horizon, like the Citadel and al-Rifaʿi. She studied them with devotion and fascination, love and faith, gratitude and hope . . . She turned away from the wall, overwhelmed by her contemplation of the unknown, both the unknown with respect to all people, the world of the unseen, and the unknown with respect to her in particular, namely Cairo . . . (*MK* 2:343–44)

Critics of Mahfouz have described Amina as an "emblem of the past," "illiterate, without any education except for an oral religious one" who "obviously" represents "a culture that . . . was not only almost totally religiously oriented, but happy to be so and unaware of an alternative." She is, finally, the "embodiment of a past isolated from reality and the true meaning of things," a truth and a meaning these critics locate squarely outside of pious practice or affect.[6] Approaching Amina from this perspective, the reader is invited to feel a mix of delight at her charming naïveté, pity at her captivity and coerced submission, and condescension at her ignorance about the world both within and outside her home.

To read in this way, however, is to overlook the alternative conceptions of "reality," "meaning," and "truth" that Mahfouz chronicles here. Looking at the passage again, we might instead notice the intricacy of the affects, attitudes, and sensibilities that are said to tie this subject to the world around her. Everything in Amina's world, from earth and sky to animals and plants, is endowed with a kind of life, and is linked in its own mysterious ways with the "world of spirit" (*ʿālam al-rūḥ*) and the "world of the unseen" (*ʿālam al-ghayb*). These are terms with Islamic resonances, yet here they serve not as theological concepts so much as everyday practices, conveying the sense that all beings—even pigeons, chickens, and jasmine vines—have a fundamental connection with an unknowable but all-embracing divine. Here humans communicate with animals in a mutually intelligible language of "little noises," just as elsewhere in the novel jinn "whisper" and awaken humans with their "warm breath" (*MK* 2:329). Here animals are not merely objects to be raised, slaughtered, and consumed, but "sentient, intelligent" beings who "praise their Lord" in their own way. Here the non-human is not mere passive matter waiting to be acted upon and transformed by the human, but both "animal" and "inanimate" beings have their own form of life. Although the scene takes place in the British colonial period between the two world wars, Amina's is not the "binary," colonial world of "reason versus force, intelligence versus nature, or the imagined versus the real,"[7] but a world of interconnected forces, all tied to the world of spirit through invisible "cords," "perfected and completed" (*yukammiluhā*) not by human industry and ingenuity, but by worship of God, *ʿibādah*—that is, the willed "obligation" or even "enslavement" of the human to the divine.[8]

Most importantly, Amina's panoramic view in this scene is not, for all its detail, panoptic. That is, she can only gaze out on the city through "the gaps in the greenery" of the jasmine and hyacinth beans, just as earlier in the novel she "peeked out through the tiny, round openings of the latticework panels" in a *mashrabiyyah* window to survey a midnight scene on the street below (*MK* 2:327). Amina does not seek out this high place to parse the significance said to reside in "the space opened up . . . between a human subjectivity and the world's inert facticity."[9] Far from attempting to master this unknown, this *majhūl*, by representing it in its totality, Amina remains with the partiality glimpsed through the cracks and crevices in the jasmine vines, and with the web of interconnected affects that the sight of these religious monuments prompts. Indeed, the passage is conspicuously saturated with the affective lexicon of Islamic piety, as Amina passes through "awe" and "terror" (*rawʿ*), "devotion" (*walāʾ*), "fascination" (*iftitān*), "love" (*ḥubb*), "gratitude" (*shukr*), "hope" (*rajāʾ*), "compassion" (*ḥanān*), "longings" (*ashwāq*), and "sadness" (*ḥuzn*). Amina, in other words, is less concerned with "reality" or the "true meaning of things" than she is with faith—*īmān*—and its semantic links to safety, security, and wholeness/perfection (*al-kamāl* implies both, and it is also the name of her son, the *Trilogy*'s protagonist Kamal). Mahfouz builds on the long-standing Arab literary figuration of cultural knowledge as an Edenic "garden" watered by numerous "narratives" (the Arabic noun *riwāyah* comes from the verb *rawā, yarwī*, "to tell," but also "to water, irrigate, give to drink"), a garden that is also a scene of knowledge.[10] He braids Islamic with secular symbolic vocabularies through the repetition of "the unknown" (*al-majhūl*), linking it both with the occulted world of the "unseen" (*al-ghayb*) and with the mundane world of Cairo itself. He saturates the landscape of Old Cairo with the holiness of al-Husayn ibn ʿAli—the grandson of the Prophet Muhammad famously martyred at the Battle of Karbala—but also with the holiness of Amina herself, who, Godlike, "created" (*khalqat*) an entirely "new world" (*dunyā jadīdah*) in her garden, but still "knows nothing" of the world outside it. He reveals the roof as an interstice between public and private worlds, infinite and limited time, seeing and not seeing, knowing and not knowing. Yet because he does so in the middle of a realist novel whose main import, we are told, is its chronicling of the modern, male, literary Arab subject's formation, Amina's alternative form of knowing, her relationship to truth, meaning, and the "unknown," has remained hard to see.

This book presents a history of knowledge that takes Amina's garden seriously as an epistemological space, together with many other scenes in which truth and meaning, seeing and seeking, are staged in unlikely, surprising ways across the archive of twentieth-century fiction from the Arab world. It builds this history not from the structures of seeing and knowing chronicled in colonial archives, but rather from the epistemological practices documented and dramatized in Arabic and Francophone fictions themselves. Throughout the twentieth century, Arab authors—who were, in many cases, the most prominent thinkers and philosophers of their times—persistently thematized knowledge production as a contested, contingent process that does not reveal so much as it constructs truth through a series of authorized effects and norms. The detective plot served as a particularly fruitful experimental structure for this purpose, not only because Sherlock Holmes, Arsène Lupin, and others have been a part of the Arab literary imagination since the late nineteenth century,[11] but also because, as Peter Brooks has written, detection represents "the narrative of narratives . . . its classical structure a laying-bare of the structure of all narrative" in which "what is at stake is a gain in knowledge, a self-conscious creation of meaning."[12] Building on and modifying the detective plot across historical periods and national contexts, the authors I examine in this study used fictional investigations to bracket and provincialize state-sanctioned, colonial, and academic truth-seeking practices. I argue that by staging tales of failed, framed, or derailed "investigation," authors like Naguib Mahfouz, Yusuf Idris, Jabra Ibrahim Jabra, Elias Khoury, Driss Chraïbi, and Sonallah Ibrahim dramatized how particular ways of seeking after truth (or rather, certain methods for producing it) were bound up with the operations of legal, juridical, and economic power at key historical junctures in the twentieth-century Arab world. At the same time, by exploring the older, less procedural or juridical resonances of a key Arabic term for "investigation" itself—that is, *baḥth*—these authors simultaneously revalorized alternative, metaphysical forms of seeking that are less focused on the knowledge itself than on the ethics cultivated in its pursuit.

What I call a "poetics of investigation," then, is grounded in the many meanings and translations of the Arabic term baḥth. Originally describing the action of an animal digging its paws or claws through the dirt, the most general definition of baḥth is "looking," "searching," "seeking," or "inquiring" after something. In the late nineteenth and early twentieth centuries, however, baḥth also became a preferred term for official "investigations" of various kinds—from police inquests to scholarly research projects and dissertations. The word *mabāḥith,* meanwhile, from the same root, has also come to refer, in contemporary times, to the dreaded "secret police" of military dictatorships. Yet, unlike another word for police investigation—*taḥqīq*—a verbal noun that, when rendered literally, means "the (re)establishment of truth (*ḥaqīqah*)," traces of less positivistic forms of seeking continue to cling to baḥth, from the Sufi mystic's never-ending search for the divine, to the quests undertaken by the heroes of popular romance.[13] This book argues that Arab authors figured the semantic instability of baḥth in literary form, staging fictional quests that are transformed from scholarly, scientific, or juridical "inquiries" into mystical, metaphysical "searches." Their novels framed and destabilized authorized procedures for producing knowledge in several key historical moments, while simultaneously offering alternative histories glimpsed through the eyes of characters normally excluded from these official processes. Even as various "experts" at home and abroad were producing knowledge about their societies, histories, and peoples, Arab authors were using the tropes of detective fiction, melded with a poetics of baḥth, to ask key epistemological questions: What is knowledge? Who has it, and how is it acquired? What forms of power and coercion does it enable, and how can these forms be neutralized or challenged? The answers they articulate take the form not of prescriptive solutions but of narrative structures—moments and scenes of knowing presented, like Amina's garden, as alternatives to the knowledge-producing mechanisms of colonial administrations and postcolonial states alike. It is thus crucial to write the history of these literary forms if we wish to understand how Arab subjects experienced the momentous epistemological transformations of the twentieth century on the level of everyday life.

Up to now, much of Middle East studies' approach to colonial history has focused on the mechanisms of representation and knowledge production that enabled the creation and implementation of colonial (and later, US neo-imperial) authority. One of the most influential paradigms in this regard is the "world-as-exhibition" effect theorized by Timothy Mitchell in *Colonising Egypt* (1988). Mitchell analyzed how the panoptic way of seeing staged at the 1889 World Exhibition in Paris both epitomized and helped authorize the continued European colonization of the Middle East and North Africa. Such exhibitions, Mitchell argued, facilitated their viewers' separation from the world around them, simultaneously producing a "subject" and a "world rendered up as object," and thereby portraying that world as ripe for possessing, reordering, and exploiting. Built on foundations laid by Martin Heidegger in "The Age of the World Picture" and by Michel Foucault in *Discipline and Punish* (1975) (also at the heart of Edward Said's *Orientalism* [1978]), Mitchell's theory of the "world-as-exhibition" also echoes art critic John Berger's earlier account of "the convention of perspective" in European Renaissance painting, from his similarly influential *Ways of Seeing* (1972). This convention, Berger argued, "centers everything on the eye of the beholder . . . like a beam from a lighthouse—only instead of light traveling outwards, appearances travel in. The conventions called those appearances *reality* . . . The visible world is arranged for the spectator as the universe was once thought to be arranged for God."[14] The problem of the all-seeing but unseen subject of theory has also plagued later critics in the field of literary studies. Samah Selim, in a recent critique of world-systems analysis, reveals how its practitioners' claims to universality through objective contemplation of the whole ("the world republic of letters") actually obscure the theory's own "scopic nature," such that "the 'world' in world literature is composed into an order by the detached, invisible, commanding gaze of the distant cartographer-turned-theorist."[15]

From Berger, Foucault, Said, Mitchell, Selim, and others, we have learned a crucial skill: to identify and criticize the colonial perspective that claims to see all, know all, act on the basis of this knowledge, and yet remain invisible, unmarked. How strange, then, that Mahfouz's Amina, standing in precisely the same panoramic position as Berger's bourgeois viewer, Mitchell's exhibition attendee, and Selim's detached and distant cartographer, should have such a different experience of the world laid out before her. From the pious Amina, and from countless other seers and seekers in twentieth-century Arab fictions, I argue, historians, sociologists, and other scholars of the Middle East can learn new methods of producing knowledge, ones modeled on the objects of our investigations, which often teach us ways to live with the *majhūl*, with the "unknown" world just beyond what we can see, as a kind of ethical check on our own scholarly practices.

The chapters that follow track specific narrative forms as they move through cultural networks stretching from Egypt to Lebanon, Morocco, Palestine, and Iraq. Whether showing how Arab authors mock the sociologists, detectives, "men of letters" (*udabāʾ*),[16] and other experts who serve as their protagonists, or observing as their narratives challenge the very notion of a well-bounded, identifiable, coherent subject of knowledge, my concern throughout *Ways of Seeking* is with narrative as a technique of power. How do novels know, I ask, and what do we learn from novels? What kinds of knowledge does narrative fiction create, and are these modes of knowing distinct from or identical to the knowledge-producing mechanisms of colonial administrations and post-colonial states? Can narrative fiction, as a representation rather than an enactment of knowledge production, stage, frame, and thereby contest its practices? Do novels see and know their characters omnisciently, thereby reproducing the panoptic gaze of modern discipline and summoning the reader into the position of Mitchell's "objective" subject or Berger's godlike "viewer"? Or is it possible for novels to record, transmit, and imagine less violent, less colonial ways of seeing, seeking, and knowing?

The question of narrative and power is, of course, not new. Many critics, particularly in English literary studies, have viewed novels—and detective novels in particular—as discourses producing societies of self-disciplining subjects in the modern era.[17] Foucault himself notes how "classic" detective fiction (on the model of Agatha Christie's works) neutralized crime writing by transforming it from a genre of popular sympathy for the condemned—often inspiring mass resistance to public executions—into "the quiet game of the well-behaved."[18] Franco Moretti similarly argues that the genre "resolves the deep anxiety of an expanding society" by reassuring its readers that "society is still . . . a unitary and knowable body,"[19] while D. A. Miller views Victorian novels as technologies for producing the novel reader as "liberal subject" and shoring up "the political regime that sets store by this subject."[20] In the opinion of many critics, then, fictions of investigation function not only to entertain their readers, but also to "reconcile [them] to the spectacle of the exercise of power."[21] Omniscient narration is a form of surveillance for these critics; it teaches readers to consider themselves forever watched, even in their most private moments, by all-seeing, unseen eyes.

Detective fiction is, certainly, about the ability to know and the power to narrate—the process of searching, uncovering, and reconstructing absent narratives, as well as using these narratives as the basis for punitive action. But the evidence I have gathered from twentieth-century Arab fictions of investigation makes me disloyal to those critical theories that equate narrative omniscience with police state surveillance. Rather, precisely because these novels allow their readers to see the operations of power from the point of view of their objects, they allow us to understand aspects of colonial, authoritarian, and military rule that historical sources do not. We may well be tempted to read *Palace Walk* (*Bayn al-Qaṣrayn*) in general, and the passage cited above in particular, as yet another instance of what Miller calls the "parallel" between "omniscience" and "social control."[22] Mahfouz's free indirect discourse lays bare Amina's innermost thoughts and feelings in that scene, prying into the most intimate spaces of her heart and mind, and forcing the reader into the position of a police officer compiling intelligence on this pious Muslim subject. But I would argue that Mahfouz's representation is savvier than this, precisely because Amina's Edenic garden is echoed in two later scenes from the *Trilogy*: the first a quite literal fall from the private garden into the public streets, the second a distant echo in the mind of the novel's young protagonist, Kamal, as he, too, ascends to a panoramic (but not panoptic) position over the city. In both scenes, Mahfouz deliberately contrasts Amina's pious, partial, affective experience of knowledge and the unknown with the instrumentalization of knowledge for the purposes of colonial surveillance and education.

The first of these scenes transforms Amina from a seer into a thing seen. At the prompting of her children, she decides to take advantage of her tyrannical husband's one-day absence from home to visit one of her most beloved religious monuments, the mosque and mausoleum of al-Husayn ibn ʿAli. After her visit to this emblem of the Islamic past, however, Amina quite literally collides with the modern Egyptian present: she is almost run over by a passing car on a busy street. As a crowd of onlookers helps her to her feet, she is less pained by her crushed shoulder bones than she is by the prospect of the incident's being written up in a police report. "The words 'police station' came as a blow to her and shook her to the core" (*MK* 2:412). The mere mention of the police drives Amina to ignore her wounds and get up at once, to prove to the policeman on the scene that she is all right. "She was so afraid that she no longer felt faint. The sight of the men staring at her horrified her, especially the policeman" (*MK* 2:412). Amina's horror derives mainly from her fear of being figuratively unveiled in the police report, and thereby publicly dishonored, according to the social conventions of her time.[23] But we can also read in her fear of the policeman's gaze an intuitive awareness of the colonial state's mechanisms of power, consolidated and exercised through the knowledge said to accrue in writing, in files—through being, in Émile Zola's phrase, "mise en carte," written up and laid bare in the ledgers of an all-seeing state.[24] By documenting for readers the panic, the fear, the recoiling that the very word for "police station" inspires in Amina, Mahfouz gives a glimpse of how the object of knowledge experiences its production. Where Mitchell's colonial exhibition rendered up the colonized world and all its peoples as objects, Mahfouz's work, as it follows Amina from the rooftop to the street, chronicles the terror of this experience from the perspective of the colonized. It records the process by which a private "garden" of faith, in which one affectively understands one's place in a larger, "sentient, intelligent world" of "interconnected forces," is transformed into a "report" or *maḥḍar*—literally, a "place where one is rendered present"—in the exclusive possession of the state.

But it is not only Amina who suffers a fall from the garden of Islamic knowledge in the *Trilogy*. Kamal, too, experiences the transition to modernity as painful and awkward, full of sadness and mourning for the emotional connections to pious knowledge that scientific empiricism has forced him to cut. In a central moment from the book's second volume, *Palace of Desire* (*Qaṣr al-Shawq*), Kamal takes a trip to visit the Great Pyramids in the company of his new aristocratic friends Husayn and Aïda Shaddad, the latter of whom he quite literally worships as his "beloved" or *maʿbūdah*, a word that resonates with Amina's form of Islamic worship (*ʿibādah*) in the garden several hundred pages earlier. By this point in the novel, Kamal has taken both literal and figurative distance from his childhood home in Bayn al-Qasrayn Street. He dreams of becoming a writer on the model of Nahda-era man of letters Mustafa Lutfi al-Manfaluti, and of learning "from his English teachers" at the Teachers' Training College "the meaning of confusing words like 'literature', 'philosophy,' and 'thought'" (*MK* 2:679). The transition is awkward, however, and Kamal continually struggles to fit in with Husayn and Aïda, who mock his tarboosh and short-cropped hair, his religious expressions and demeanor, his fervent nationalism, and his taste for genre fictions translated into Arabic. When Aïda asks if he's read any French novels, Kamal replies that he's read "some of Michel Zévaco's stories . . . those that have been translated into Arabic, anyway," as well as the fictions of al-Manfaluti and Oriental adventure stories by Rider Haggard.[25] "You won't be an author until you've mastered French," Aïda informs him in reply. "Read Balzac and Georges Sand, Madame de Staël, and [Pierre] Loti, then write a short story" (*MK* 2:679). Most of all, however, the Shaddad children mock the Old Cairo neighborhood where Kamal grew up, with all the popular beliefs, practices, and politics it imprinted on him. "You always attribute everything either to God or Saad Zaghloul," Husayn tells Kamal at one point.[26] "But of course that's how you are, since you're from the place where religion lives" (*MK* 2:676–77). Kamal's feast of whole roasted chickens, country cheese, local bananas, and oranges looks crude compared to the elegant cucumber sandwiches the Shaddads have prepared for their picnic, and he is "shocked and disturbed" to see the Muslim Aïda, whom he has transformed into the object of near-religious passion, drinking beer and eating ham sandwiches. "Don't be a Hanbali," she scolds him. "Ham's very tasty. Try it" (*MK* 2:684).[27] Bayn al-Qasrayn Street, as well as its proximity to al-Husayn's shrine, once a source of love and pride for Kamal, is now a source of embarrassment, as he longs for the affection of his Khedive-worshipping, ham-eating, Parisian-perfumed, Liberal Constitutionalist beloveds. Looking down on Cairo from the vantage point of Giza, Kamal wonders: "Where was Palace Walk amid all of this? Where was his mother, feeding the chickens beneath a trellis of jasmine?" (*MK* 2:676; *CT* 867).

As he did in *Palace Walk*, Mahfouz again mobilizes a panoramic gaze here—this time from the pyramids, that view sought after by European tourists and colonial adventurers alike—not to chronicle the subject's creation through its seamless separation from a world rendered up as object, but rather to narrate the awkwardness, the embarrassment, the "astonishment," and the "alarm" of Kamal's struggle to fully sever himself from "the place where religion lives" (*ḥayy al-dīn*) and enter the dispassionate, secular, European world of "literature, philosophy, and thought."[28] Mahfouz stages Egyptian modernity as a jumble of overlapping, out-of-joint beliefs, practices, and alphabets. When Husayn Shaddad jokes that they are performing a pious visitation (*ziyārah*) to the pharaohs' tombs, as one might visit the shrine of an Islamic saint,[29] Kamal picks up the thread of the paradox: "to recite the Fatiha in hieroglyphics" (*MK* 2:676). The modernization of Egypt's education system, transformations in class politics, and British colonial dismissals of faith, custom, and legend are here given not as large-scale structural changes marked by clear, definable ruptures, but as intimate experiences of affect and awkwardness, figured in the push and pull between Kamal's devotion to the pious practices of his mother, his disillusionment and loss of faith on discovering al-Husayn's head does not reside in its Cairo shrine, and his resultant desire for objective, scientifically verifiable "truth," with all the social status that access to such truth implies. To neglect the literary on the grounds of its imaginative distance from "real" historical sources is to miss out on this and other stories of messy, tangled affects and selfhoods in the complex narrative of Egypt's modernization.

Mahfouz was, in short, acutely conscious of the way colonial practices of knowledge production were transforming the inner lives of Egyptians like Amina and Kamal. That he laces the figure of Amina's rooftop garden through the *Trilogy's* many hundreds of pages prevents me from seeing that scene as yet another instance of narrative surveillance. Here and throughout this book, what I am calling the "poetics of investigation" mobilizes the semantic instability of baḥth to force a recognition of state power's historicity and contingency, and to open our eyes to other ways of seeing and seeking staged on the pages of Arabic fiction, to overlooked moments of unstable representation, unpredictable divisions between subject and object, meaning and materiality, knower and thing known. I trawl for the remains of nonhegemonic forms of knowledge scattered within Arabic novels themselves, even when these forms are presented as irrelevant, traditional, or outdated, and I reanimate them as key sites from which to construct an alternative, anticolonial history of knowledge in the modern Arab world. What if we thought of the novel as a space in which such moments, affects, and ways of seeing jostle for space and recognition, even as other voices deem them "traditional," "backward," or belonging to a "past world"?

True to the method of Amina's seeking, I have chosen to look more closely at traces, remnants, and echoes than totalities—to peer through the gaps in the greenery of the Arabic novel and construct a history of knowledge from what I found there. The corpus examined in the chapters that follow is thus selective rather than exhaustive: I dwell at greater length on fewer texts, highlighting the subtle moments, figures, and structures that a more broad-sweeping study of "the Arabic novel" might, of necessity, merely mention. As I returned to the well-trodden archive of modern Arabic fiction looking for narrative structures of investigation and knowledge production—detective or otherwise—I was surprised to discover how many fascinating epistemological plots and figures have been hiding in plain sight on the pages of otherwise exhaustively studied novels. My task, then, was not to uncover forgotten or neglected texts, but rather to reopen novels that have begun to molder in the dusty vaults of their labels ("realist," "socialist-realist," "post-67," "60s generation," "90s generation," etc.), with a spirit of openness and surprise, tracing how narrative forms that stage, satirize, and defamiliarize the modern era's sanctified forms of knowledge production have consistently crossed national borders and historical periods. The quest for knowledge—its perils and possibilities, its uses and misuses—has been a recurring theme in Arabic fictions throughout the twentieth century, in no small part because the scientific restructuring of knowledge was such a salient feature of colonial modernity. Yet this restructuring was fluid rather than seamless, and Arab fictions register this fluidity—the persistence of the metaphysical in the midst of the scientific—in ways that other archives often do not.

*Ways of Seeking* thus returns to the twentieth-century novel at a time when the field of Arabic studies is pushing away from this period in either direction—delving into the disremembered archive of the nineteenth century and the Arab Nahda, on the one hand,[30] and pressing ever further into the contemporary period and new media, on the other.[31] The excitement in the scholarly projects examining these periods has reinvested Arabic studies with a new, postnational outlook and a diverse range of theoretical tools; paradoxically, these tools have yet to be trained back on the twentieth century, whose once apparent hegemony is now a scene of neglect. There is still, I wish to argue, a good deal of historical and epistemological material that has been overlooked or reduced to political or biographical allegory in criticism on this period and these texts. Reopening these works as investigations—rather than representations—of specific historical junctures allows us to break them out of the referential and politically overdetermined narratives to which they have generally been confined. I offer up the forms of seeking dramatized in the fictions under consideration here as new scholarly and readerly methodologies. From these sources, we can better understand not only how knowledge has been produced by states, scholars, and governments about the Middle East, but how this production was contested by Arab thinkers and writers themselves, who interrupted the mellifluous functioning of intelligence-gathering mechanisms with their resistant practices of representation, edging every panorama with a *majhūl*, every totalizing theory with a figure who remains just outside its frame.

It is important to clarify that this book is not a comprehensive history of Arabic detective fiction. I am not concerned with simply identifying those Arab novels that neatly exemplify Western paradigms in the genre; nor do I delve into the history of Arabic pulp in any specific historical or national context.[32] Rather, while never losing sight of the historical and social circumstances of each work under consideration here, I am more interested in uncovering the forms of critique that specific characteristics of baḥth enabled for Arab writers across historical periods and national borders, and what their fictions might in turn enable for scholars of the modern Middle East in many disciplines. My aim, in the words of Gayatri Spivak, is "to make the traditional linguistic sophistication of Comparative Literature supplement Area Studies . . . by approaching the language of the other not only as a 'field' language."[33] From area studies, I draw the "quality and rigor" in studying "the language of the other" that Spivak identifies, but I work outside these disciplines' beginnings in a Cold War politics of management, manipulation, suspicion, and control. I argue that Arab fictions of baḥth themselves criticize such instrumental approaches to knowledge, inviting scholars and historians to occupy different, even multiple or ambivalent subject positions with respect to their textual and cultural objects.

Each of the chapters that follow focuses on a different connotation of baḥth as it has been staged in twentieth-century fictions from the Arab world. I move from a strict definition of baḥth as "criminal investigation" in novels by Tawfiq al-Hakim, Driss Chraïbi, Yusuf Idris, and Yusuf al-Qaʿid, to a larger orbit of novels that steer this term's epistemological insights in new directions: the missing persons narratives of Jabra Ibrahim Jabra and Naguib Mahfouz, the detective-dissolving mysteries of Fathi Ghanim and Elias Khoury, and the simultaneously epic-heroic and noir-inspired "questing" at the heart of Egyptian author Sonallah Ibrahim's *The Committee* (*al-Lajnah*, 1981) and *Zaat* (*Dhāt*, 1992). Each chapter also reads across the historical and political ruptures that have conventionally marked the so-called "development" of the Arabic novel throughout the twentieth century—showing, for example, how the politics of Yusuf Idris's sensation fiction in *The Sinners* (*al-Ḥarām*, 1959) resonate with those of Yusuf al-Qaʿid's postmodern, metafictional *Yaḥduth fī Miṣr al-Ān* (It's happening now in Egypt, 1974, hereafter *Yaḥduth*), despite the aesthetic break typically associated with the military defeat of the Arab Forces in the 1967 June War. Following the threads of baḥth woven throughout the Arab novel of investigation in this way deemphasizes common strategies of organization based on national origin or historical moment, prioritizing instead questions of literary form as a window onto social epistemology. Novels that dramatize investigation and the search for truth interrogate the present by revisiting the past, not as a lost utopia but as a reminder of other ways of being in the world. To neglect or ignore these moments of temporal eruption, as scholars and readers, is to be little better than the policemen, government officials, and hubristic intellectuals who are mocked and satirized on the pages of these novels.

Chapter 1, "The Detective as Conscript: Tawfiq al-Hakim and Driss Chraïbi on the Margins of the Law," begins the book with a consideration of baḥth in its strictest definition as "detection" or "police investigation." I focus on two texts concerned with the geographic and figurative peripheries of the nation and the law—the *pays* of Chraïbi's *Flutes of Death* (*Une enquête au pays*, 1981) and the *aryāf* (countryside) of al-Hakim's *Diary of a Country Prosecutor* (*Yawmiyyāt Nāʾib fi-l-Aryāf*, 1937). Though separated by national borders, language, and nearly five decades of history, both al-Hakim and Chraïbi wrote at times of political transition and disillusionment: the cynical tone of al-Hakim's *Diary* rhymes with the political mood of interwar Egypt, while Chraïbi's tragicomic treatment of Moroccan police brutality parodically responds to and criticizes Morocco's Years of Lead (*les années de plomb/sanawāt al-raṣāṣ*). These disillusionments imprint on the form of each novel in surprisingly similar ways. On the one hand, each text exposes the "backwardness" underlying modern processes of police interrogation and satirizes the hypocrisy of a modernity enforced through such violent means upon the bodies and livelihoods of peasants whom it claims, ironically, to "civilize." On the other hand, through surprising narrative eruptions, *Diary* and *Enquête* also explore the broken subjectivities of their protagonists, both native officers of the law who have undergone training designed to sever their affective ties to the communities they must police. These severances prove to be incomplete, however, and each novel—even as it criticizes the violence of official legal investigation—also explores the possibility of native alterities and solidarities, of subjects who remain inscrutable, indecipherable, and unconscriptable into the ledgers of the state.

Chapter 2, "Murder on the *ʿIzbah:* Spectral Legality and Egyptian Sensation Fiction, Yusuf Idris to Yusuf al-Qaʿid," continues in the vein of police investigation, but moves from the margins of the law and its official representatives to a zone of legal exception, the *ʿizbah* or "estate farm" in Egypt. Samera Esmeir has referred to the ʿizbah as a realm of "spectral legality," a space in which the arbitrary, sovereign form of power associated with khedival rule in Egypt not only survived, but was in fact constituted by the British-colonial implementation rule-of-law in the nineteenth century.[34] This chapter examines how reform-minded Egyptian fictions of the 1950s through the 1970s opened up the otherwise "spectral," silenced zone of the ʿizbah for public scrutiny, refocusing their metropolitan readers' attentions on the unregulated violence that continued to govern peasant life there despite the nominal implementation of land reform laws under President Gamal Abdel Nasser. Although they are conventionally read as belonging to discrete eras of Egyptian history, I illustrate how both Idris's *The Sinners* and al-Qaʿid's *Yaḥduth fī Miṣr al-Ān* use surprising shifts in narrative perspective to simultaneously assert the reader's complicity in systems of labor exploitation on the ʿizbah and invite them to view things differently, from the perspective of the laborers themselves. These novels' visceral, graphic descriptions of rape, birth, infanticide, and murder do much more than cater to popular tastes for melodrama. Their narration of sensation and scandal works to dispel the rhetoric of the "ordinary," the *ʿādī*, long associated with peasant suffering in Egyptian cultural production.

Chapter 3, "Bureau of Missing Persons: Metaphysical Detection in Jabra Ibrahim Jabra and Naguib Mahfouz," shifts gears from the sensational to the experimental, and from questions of law, justice, and sovereignty to questions of self, language, and subjectivity. Reading Mahfouz's experimental novellas and short stories from the 1960s alongside Jabra's *In Search of Walid Masoud* (*al-Baḥth ʿan Walīd Masʿūd*, 1978), I show how both authors crystallize the rhetorical indeterminacy of baḥth in literary form by causing the objective, rational, and empirical research methods their characters use to break down as soon as they take inscrutable figures like the eponymous missing Palestinian, the mysterious shaykh Zaabalawi, or the absentee father Sayyid Sayyid al-Rahimi as their objects. Both authors transform their detective-like narrators into mystics and poets despite themselves, such that at the end of each tale, the reader is sent back to the beginning, urged to maintain seeking and searching—rather than uncovering, seeing, and grasping—as modes of being in the world. And yet for all their desire to overcome the limits of their own subjectivities through unity with a perpetually absent, mystical figure, still the characters in these works ultimately remain trapped in the limits of their own atomized subjectivities. Whereas *Walid Masoud* represents an exception to Jabra's otherwise career-long devotion to the figure of the liberal individual floating free of petty political commitments, Mahfouz's "Culprit Unknown" ("Ḍidd Majhūl"), "Zaabalawi" ("Zaʿbalāwī"), and *The Way* (*al-Ṭarīq*), I argue, continue in new literary forms the asymptotic questing figured through the *shawq*—the "lovesick longing" often associated with mystic desire for the divine—in *Palace of Desire* (*Qaṣr al-Shawq*).

Chapter 4, "Effacing the Author, or the Detective as Medium: Fathi Ghanim to Elias Khoury," revisits the struggle to overcome the limits of the literary self but focuses on two novels that actually achieve some measure of success (at least, formal or imagined success) in the endeavor. Both Ghanim's *al-Jabal* (The Mountain, 1959) and Khoury's *White Masks* (*al-Wujūh al-Bayḍā'*, 1981) center on fact-finding investigations that ultimately eclipse the voices of their narrators and thereby allow others—specifically those historically marginalized by Arabic literary establishments—to speak in the space of the text. Garbage collectors, building caretakers, and Upper Egyptians take over the task of narration in these works (written in various registers, dialects, and accents of Arabic), as the authors stage their detective-narrators' gradual disappearance. The novels' very different historical contexts and settings admittedly yield different thematic concerns. Still, in both works, a police-like "investigator" (*muḥaqqiq*) stands in for the figure of the author, and his quest for the "truth" (*ḥaqq*) behind a given case ironically blinds him to the more pressing truths in the stories of the marginalized communities he has been sent to investigate. In such contexts, Khoury and Ghanim wager, the author-investigator's task is to eclipse his own privileged, literary voice and allow others to speak through him, altering and interrupting his narrative subjectivity with heterogeneous forms of popular expression. (Ghanim uses the Egyptian "narrative ballad," or *mawwāl*, while Khoury plays with the storied Arabic "proverb," or *mathal*.) The resulting texts ultimately teach their readers how to read less like a *muḥaqqiq*, like a "truth establisher," and more like a *bāḥith*, a "seeker" or listener invited to participate in the communal performance of a *mawwāl* or the transgenerational transmission of a *mathal*.

Where Ghanim and Khoury destabilize the rhythms of their narratives with popular voices, forms, and registers of speech in the hopes of democratizing or popularizing the Arabic novel, the Egyptian Sonallah Ibrahim, I argue, plumbs the depths of his era's isolation, alienation, and despair—the misery of individualism—as the negative image of possible future communalisms. This book's fifth and final chapter, "Epic Fails: Sonallah Ibrahim's Modern Myths of Seeking," examines the legacy of noir in two of Ibrahim's most famous novels, *The Committee* and *Zaat*. I read *The Committee* as an object lesson in Marxist critique: the "research method" (*manhaj*) developed by the unnamed narrator of that novella is concerned with both totality (what the narrator calls the "interlocking connections" between large-scale socioeconomic phenomena and individual experience) and futurity (the inexorable movement of history in favor of the poor and disenfranchised).[35] But while the narrator of *The Committee* fancies himself a working-class hero along the lines of Raymond Chandler's Philip Marlowe or the Arab popular epics' ʿAntarah ibn Shaddad, his attempts to confront the ruling classes fail because they are conducted in isolation from any kind of public. This concern with the "public," in both senses of this term (the commonly owned; the audience), spills over into *Zaat*—Ibrahim's epic of Egypt's neoliberalization under presidents Anwar al-Sadat and Hosni Mubarak—yet now serves, I argue, as a principle of composition rather than a thematic concern. That is, where the narrator of *The*

*Committee* shouldered the burden of "investigation," in *Zaat* it is the *reader* who is summoned to the task of apprehending Egyptian totality, asked to connect the political corruption, the public mismanagement, and the police violence reported in the novel's docufictional chapters with the tales of polluted food, social climbing, and alienation recounted in its narrative ones.[36] As the country's "self" or *dhāt* was suddenly and rapidly transformed, and as the terms of anticolonial nationalism were suddenly repurposed for an era of neoliberal privatization and Americanization, Ibrahim makes one last attempt at revitalizing the utopian, popular "public" of Egypt's nominally socialist, Arab nationalist era. He does so not by staging this public's imagined presence in fiction (as Khoury and Ghanim did), but by calling on readers to become that public—to step into the role of the investigator who understands the unbearable atomization, alienation, and isolation of the present as products of an unsustainable system of economic and social organization.

Wherever and whenever they thematize investigation, baḥth, or the objective, panoramic (or panoptic) gaze, Arab fictions become mimetic of research itself. In looking at characters who are themselves looking, we are reminded that, at every point in our scholarship, we too are engaged in acts of critical "seeing" equally as subject to the blind spots that form the intrigue of dramatic irony and epistemology in these novels. Noticing and analyzing the knowledge gaps in these and other characters' ways of seeing, we too—the readers, the scholars, the experts—are invited to reject approaches that assume a "view from nowhere," the unmarked Eurocentrism of abstract theory.[37] We are encouraged, instead, to look with "soft eyes," to remember the conditions limiting our own ways of reading and determining what we can see.[38] These reminders are crucially important in the field of Middle East studies, I wish to suggest, because in the field's rush to deduce and analyze totalities elsewhere, and then to present these realities as narratives to readers in the United States and other metropoles, it can overlook the many resonances and possibilities embedded in small places—in a single word like baḥth, for example, and the methodological, epistemological lessons it offers. "Soft eyes" are equally as important in comparative literary studies, where the demand that scholars adhere to theoretical lexicons imported from continental philosophy can cause us to overlook the idiomatic in the languages we study, to let a theory of baḥth remained unelaborated.

I do not mean to overstate the significance of the fictional works I examine by making them identical with actual challenges to material, social, and economic conditions, but I do aim to highlight within these fictions an unwillingness to be marshalled into a modernity policed by a politics of knowing and control. Nearly every novel in this book features a madman or a shaykh, a mystic or a seer, a friend of God or a poet who stands opposite the rational detective, revealing the supposedly exceptional modern quest for truth as yet another asymptotic approach to unsolvable mysteries. Considering the form of fiction allows us to see more clearly the forms we ourselves invest with authority in the pursuit and exposition of scholarly knowledge, meaning, and truth. Every panorama is hemmed with a border of *majhūl*; Arab authors engaging with "investigation" as plot device, narrative structure, and allegory of reading constantly remind us of this truth. From them, we can learn to revalorize the search, the puzzle, and, by extension, "theory" more generally, as an asymptotic process rather than a totalizing rubric. We can learn—like Amina—to live ethically with the unknown, to prioritize baḥth over *taḥqīq*, the humility of searching over the hubris of attaining and explaining truth. This is a lesson that extends far beyond the academic communities of Middle East, Arabic, or comparative literary studies. By revealing how Arabic fictions mirror the very practice of reading back to their readers, we can animate and enliven texts that many of us might assume to be utterly "distant" or "other" to our own experience, seeing the literary as "our teacher as well as our object of investigation."[39] The obstacles, setbacks, and comic failures encountered by the seekers in these works estrange us, as readers, from the practices of truth- and meaning-making that we might normally take for granted. As Arab authors reveal the mechanisms of power undergirding the specific truths and knowledge systems governing their own times, so too they teach us to look behind the scenery of our own epistemologies, to see "our" world as a construct of such mechanisms, equally as much as "theirs."

1

# The Detective as Conscript

## *Tawfiq al-Hakim and Driss Chraïbi on the Margins of the Law*

In theory, the Egyptian Tawfiq al-Hakim and the Moroccan Driss Chraïbi make strange bedfellows. The former is best known as the pioneering modernizer of Egyptian theater, the latter as the author of *The Simple Past* (*Le passé simple*), a novel whose critique of both French cultural imperialism and Arabo-Islamic patriarchy rocked the Moroccan cultural scene during that country's struggle for independence from the French protectorate.[1] Less known, however, is each author's career as a writer of detective fiction. In the world of Arabic literary studies, al-Hakim's 1937 *Diary of a Country Prosecutor* (*Yawmiyyāt Na'ib fī al-Aryāf*) has already been recognized as an example in the genre,[2] and Chraïbi's series of novels from the 1980s featuring the wily Moroccan Inspector Ali also, for the most part, obey the rules of engagement. Writing in different languages and different national contexts, separated by almost fifty years of history, al-Hakim and Chraïbi might seem like an odd pair with which to begin this study. What, then, does reading them together yield?

For one thing, both al-Hakim's *Diary* and Chraïbi's 1981 *Une Enquête au pays* (*Flutes of Death*, hereafter *Enquête*) were written at times of historical and political disillusionment in Egypt and Morocco. Interwar Egypt was a particularly bleak political landscape for reform-minded thinkers like al-Hakim. Fewer than twenty years earlier, in March of 1919, mass demonstrations had united Egyptians behind an independence movement with the populist hero Saad Zaghloul as its figurehead. It was a formative moment for writers of al-Hakim's generation, one in which an end to Britain's thirty-seven-year protectorate seemed near. The Egypt of al-Hakim's 1937 *Diary*, however, looked vastly different. A series of agreements and capitulations, including the Anglo-Egyptian Treaty of 1936, had failed to effect

Britain's complete withdrawal from the country.[3] What began as the "revolution of 1919" had quickly "transmuted into a domestic, Egyptian political struggle" between the Wafd—Zaghloul's party—which demanded complete and unconditional independence, and the Liberal Constitutional Party, which sought to stabilize relations with the British and "restore public order" in the wake of ongoing mass demonstrations.[4] Isma'il Sidqi, who served as prime minister from 1930 to 1933, had revised the constitution and redrafted electoral laws to suppress suffrage and bolster the authority of King Fuad's palace, thereby "ushering in the most repressive period of government Egypt had ever known."[5] The reforms championed by Wafd leaders—free elections, free press, and freedom of assembly—had been coopted and manipulated by Sidqi's cynically named "People's Party" (Hizb al-Sha'b), which, among other forms of repression, conscripted peasants and political prisoners to shout chants in support of government-backed candidates in the elections of 1931.[6] In short, everything the Wafd had stood for in 1919 seemed a farcical caricature of itself by 1937, including the secular, modern legal system in which al-Hakim was employed at the time.[7] It was a period in which, as the public prosecutor who serves as the narrator of *Diary* puts it, "'justice' and 'the people'" were little more than "phrases whose only purpose is to be written on paper and delivered in orations, like many other words and abstract concepts that don't really exist."[8] There is a cynicism to *Diary*, in other words, that is alien to al-Hakim's earlier, more famous, and largley Romantic-nationalist novel *Return of the Spirit* (*'Awdat al-Rūh*). It is what Egyptian critic Ghali Shukri has called a work of "critical realism" in which "Egypt is not merely an eternal, metaphysical idea," as in *Return*, but rather "a reality filled with tragedy and shame."[9]

The Moroccan political situation to which Chraïbi responds in *Enquête* was similarly bleak, but for different reasons. When the Parisian publishing house Seuil brought out this first of Chraïbi's Inspector Ali novels in 1981, reports of King Hassan II's massive human rights abuses in Morocco were just beginning to reach the international community. It was the peak of what would subsequently be known as the "Years of Lead" (*les années de plomb* in French, or *sanawāt al-raṣāṣ*, in Arabic),[10] which were generally said to begin with Morocco's independence from France in 1956 and to end with the death of King Hassan II in 1999.[11] Forced disappearances, political imprisonments, arbitrary detentions, torture, and murder at the hands of the judicial police (*police judiciare*) were among the many brutalities faced by thousands of Moroccans who voiced opposition of any kind—"Marxist, Islamist, nationalist, Sahrawi, feminist, Amazigh/Berber activist"—to the regime of Hassan II.[12] The most detailed accounts of torture in Morocco's secret detention centers didn't begin to reach the Moroccan public until the late 1990s, with the death of King Hassan, the release of thousands of former prisoners, and the consequent (albeit incremental) decrease in former prisoners' fear of speaking and writing publicly about their experiences.[13] Nevertheless, throughout the 1970s and 1980s, even as Chraïbi was penning his satirical novels from the relative comfort of exile in France, the French press was circulating a slow but steady stream of letters and testimonials smuggled out of prisons and torture centers in Morocco, documents testifying to physical torture, psychological abuse, and death at the hands of the Moroccan police.[14] While writing *Enquête*—a novel centered on two police officers—Chraïbi would certainly have been aware of the horrors inflicted on his countrymen by their own police forces. As in interwar Egypt, "democracy," "justice," and "legal reform" were little better than facades erected by the Moroccan regime in this context. Like *Diary*, then, *Enquête* lampoons officers of the law, revealing their self-claimed defense of "progress" and "civilization" to be little more than a mask for authoritarian violence.

In addition to the similarities between their respective historical and political contexts, however, al-Hakim's *Diary* and Chraïbi's *Enquête* also illuminate and speak to each other for another reason. Both novels center on the misadventures of what I am calling the "detective as conscript," the native officer of the law caught between two ways of seeing, seeking, and being in the world: the communal, colloquial one of his native upbringing, and the isolating, official one of his legal education and police training. The detective at the heart of each novel has been forcibly severed from the community around him, compelled to occupy the position of investigating subject and to transform those around him into the mute, inert objects of his investigation. Yet, as this chapter will illustrate, in both novels the severance is incomplete. The ontological split between narrating subject and narrated object is not rigid but porous, and it is never fully realized in either text.[15] Rather, despite each character's police training, still his contact with rural others—the fellahin or peasant-farmers in al-Hakim's "countryside" (*aryāf*) and the *paysans* or Amazigh tribe in Chraïbi's remote Atlas Mountain "village" (*pays*)—causes images and echoes of his pre-police self to bubble to the surface of his memory. Each narrator consequently experiences his legal training not as a process of enlightenment and acculturation but rather as a violent severance or cutting, a quite literal amputation from the body politic, on the one hand, and an incomplete graft of Western "civilization," on the other.

The specificity of the rural elsewhere summoned by the novels' respective titles makes them notoriously difficult to translate into English. The "country" or "countryside" that Abba Eban's *Diary of a Country Prosecutor* might evoke for English-language readers likely differs greatly from the vast farmlands of the Nile Delta summoned to the minds of Egyptian readers by al-Hakim's *aryāf*. Likewise, the French *pays* has connotations for French readers that are lost even in the literal translation "An Inquest in the Countryside," to say nothing of Robin Roosevelt's *Flutes of Death*.[16] Like baḥth, the French *pays* connotes a number of contradictory meanings, from the hyperlocal "village, canton, province" to the much larger "nation, country, homeland," as in *mourir pour son pays*, "to die for one's country."[17] For immigrants to France, *le pays* can also mean "homeland" or "country of origin," often referring to previously colonized territories of the French Empire, and thereby implicitly equating formerly colonized nations with quaint, simple "villages" stuck in a romanticized past. The *pays* in Chraïbi's title is thus simultaneously a "backwater," a "village," and the entirety of "Morocco" itself. The author has returned to "his country" (*son pays*) to write the novel, just as Chief Mohammed and Inspector Ali, the novel's protagonists, must journey from the city to the "village" (*pays*) for their investigation. The same is true for al-Hakim, who both physically, for his job in the state legal apparatus, and imaginatively, via his novel, returns to the *rīf* after a period of education abroad in Europe.

Each novel thus offers a meditation on the messy, tangled subjectivity of a newly enfranchised native class in interwar Egypt and in post-Protectorate Morocco, subjects acculturated in cities but born and raised in rural places. In al-Hakim's case, this social group is the *effendiyya*: the teachers, doctors, architects, lawyers, and judges—many of them from poor or rural backgrounds—whose self-styled modern identities shaped the country's new state institutions and its emergent nationalist discourse.[18] But unlike contemporary authors of the period, like Yahya Haqqi, al-Hakim refuses to end his tale with the seamless melding of native authenticity and Western-style modernity that is the hallmark of the effendi.[19] Rather, with his characteristic dark humor and dry wit, al-Hakim dramatizes the spectacular failure of imported Western legal systems and procedures when practiced in the Egyptian *rīf*, while at the same time allowing supposedly irrational, backward others (such as the semi-mad, poetry-spouting Shaykh Asfur and the mysterious peasant girl Rim) to not only shape the plot of the novel but also to exercise a hold over truth, albeit a different form of truth than the one sought after by state-mandated procedures of legal, police, and forensic detection.

Chraïbi, meanwhile, focuses on the intermediary class of government functionaries who emerged in the wake of French colonialism—Moroccan inspectors, officers, deputies, commissioners, servants, secretaries—and who, in his words, seemed "forever caught between the new masters of the Third World and the people."[20] Inspector Ali embodies this intermediary class of functionaries standing between the "police chiefs" at the very top of society and the rural, Amazigh others at the very bottom. By simply continuing to exist, by refusing to recognize or acknowledge the officers who attempt to "know" them through police interrogation, Shaykh Asfur, in *Diary*, and Hajja, Raho, and the entire Aït Yafelman clan in *Enquête*, mount a passive resistance to the unsuitability, at best, and inhumanity, at worst, of the supposedly more humane modern legal and juridical regimes in each context. They refuse to become the objects of the state's aspirational all-knowing gaze; and the legal officers, al-Hakim's Prosecutor and Chraïbi's Inspector Ali, find themselves caught between different forms of truth—different methods for creating and legitimating it—both of which they understand, and neither of which has a complete hold over them. I use the phrase *forms* of truth deliberately here, since in all cases, al-Hakim and Chraïbi wed specific narrative forms to specific truth effects. Al-Hakim's prosecutor is forced to measure the distance between the formulaic, state-mandated language of the legal case files he must produce by the ream, which dull his mind, and Asfur's quasi-gnostic poetry, which stirs vague flickers of recognition in his soul; Chraïbi's Ali knows from the outset that his superior officer's interrogation tactics are doomed to fail when used on the Aït Yafelman, yet he is caught off guard by the glimmers of recognition that draw him to Hajja, the clan's matriarch, as a stand-in for his own mother and the tales she told him as a child.

Despite the echoes of alternative forms of truth that percolate into their conscious minds, however, neither al-Hakim's prosecutor nor Chraïbi's Inspector Ali is ultimately able to fully return to the community from which his legal training has alienated him. *Diary* ends with the prosecutor throwing up his hands in resignation, consigning unsolved case files to the dustbin of Egyptian history in a tone of "bitter mockery" (*sukhriyyah*, a term that will later be important to Yusuf al-Qaʿid's take on the *rīf*) and sarcastically proclaiming to his associate: "There! Are you happy now? That's it, we're done, we've solved all the crimes!" (*D* 134; *Y* 192). Likewise, at the end of *Enquête*, despite having been overcome by his memories of an alternate, Amazigh creation myth that his mother told him as a boy, Ali ultimately becomes only what the villagers expect him to be: "a solemn, thoughtful, efficient being. A real chief" (*E* 214). Neither al-Hakim nor Chraïbi privileges the "middle way" of Ismaʿil in Yahya Haqqi's famed story, "Umm Hashim's Lamp."[21] For them, the middleman—prosecutor, native policeman—is always a conscript in conflict.

Borrowed from anthropological theory, the notion of the "conscript," as I am using it here, begins with Stanley Diamond's "conscripts of civilization" and makes its way through Talal Asad's "conscripts of Western civilization" before arriving at David Scott's "conscripts of modernity."[22] The idea, throughout, is that colonized or enslaved individuals who take up European Enlightenment discourses to demand "secular, democratic, independent states responsible for their own national development" (in Asad's reading of India) or liberation and natural rights (in Scott's reading of C. L. R. James's Toussaint Louverture) do so not in acknowledgement of those European discourses' innate moral or civilizational superiority but simply because the violent impositions of colonialism and the modern state have limited the choices available to them.[23] They are not, in Diamond's formulation, volunteers into modernity's project but conscripts to its order, which has obliterated the epistemological, social, and political choices previously available to them.[24] Understanding modernity in the Foucauldian sense described by Scott—as "a positive structure of power, a historical formation of certain constitutive and productively shaping material and epistemological conditions of life and thought"—allows us to turn the focus away from individual agents (even agents of resistance) and onto the social, historical, and material circumstances conditioning their actions.[25] Chraïbi's Inspector Ali and al-Hakim's prosecutor "could not choose *not* to be modern" (or Western, or West-looking); rather, their worlds had been "coercively reorganized by the material and epistemic violence of a modern regime of power and forcibly inserted into a global order in a state of subordination and dependence."[26]

As they recognize and dramatize the constrained options available to their protagonists, however, al-Hakim and Chraïbi also take advantage of fiction's imaginative capacities to leave open the possibility of subjects at the margins of the nation and the law, figures who remain illegible to and undocumented in the ledgers of the modern state. Both the Aït Yafelman, in Chraïbi's text, and the murder victim's sister-in-law Rim, in al-Hakim's, escape the prying eyes of the police and the author both, disappearing from the public eye and from the text of the novel itself. In this way, both al-Hakim and Chraïbi also address what D. A. Miller has called the "entanglement between the nature of the novel and the practice of the police," the link between the documenting, identifying, surveilling tactics of the state and those of novelistic discourse.[27] Yet, unlike the authors examined in Miller's study, al-Hakim and Chraïbi—as colonized or formerly colonized writers—recognize the link between laying bare the everyday lives of their peasant characters and producing knowledge about them. Their novels thus self-consciously dramatize this tension between realist authorship and police work. Even as they stage their protagonists' entanglement in the web of conscription and detection, they allow certain characters to flee from the novel's all-knowing gaze. When Inspector Ali returns to the Atlas Mountains at the end of *Enquête* as "Chief Ali," the Aït Yafelman have disappeared. And when called on to authorize an autopsy of Rim's body at the end of *Diary*, the prosecutor simply declines to carry out this act of cutting open and laying bare. Neither *Diary* nor *Enquête* attests the actual existence of figures outside modernity's reach; rather, simply in imagining the possibility of "primitives" unconscripted into the violent epistemic reordering of social and individual life, al-Hakim and Chraïbi register their protests to that order, loosening its hold and allowing their readers to imagine, if only in fantasy, its relativity, its contingency.

By withholding solutions to the mysteries they dramatize and by focusing instead on the divided subjectivity of the postcolonial detective himself, both *Diary* and *Enquête* teach their readers a new way of seeking after truth. These novels do more than merely reflect the historical and social situations that produced them. By dramatizing those eras' methods for producing and legitimating truth, and by staging these methods' failure when confronted with alternative, "native" forms of truth-making, *Diary* and *Enquête* demonstrate their awareness of how novel writing—an occupation of the intellectual class—can participate in state surveillance, but also how it can provincialize, bracket, and thereby destabilize (if not dismantle) the state's monopoly on truth. They do so by interrupting the narrative flow of the realist novel with inscrutable mystical poetry, matrilineal myth, and other unruly literary forms.

## PERFORMING THE AUTHORITY TO KNOW

One of the central ways that both *Diary* and *Enquête* frame and interrogate the production of truth is by dramatizing the investigative hubris of their detective-protagonists. The prosecutor in *Diary* and Chief Mohammed in *Enquête* view themselves as much more than detectives. To them, "investigation" (baḥth/*enquête*) is more than a method for solving mysterious crimes. It is, rather, a way to deduce truths about the world in which they live and the people who populate that world. They transform legal power into metaphysical and philosophical authority, using their observation of clues to uncover truths lurking deep within the human soul. Their performance of detection thus becomes a performance of the authority to know. Yet both texts also satirize this tendency among conscripted officers of the law, mocking the hubris of the newly enfranchised native class and revealing the barbarism lurking behind the detective's civilized exterior.

*Diary* begins when its narrator—an unnamed figure referred to only as "the prosecutor" (*al-nā'ib*)—is awakened in the middle of the night to investigate a shooting in a remote village.[28] The victim turns out to be a man named Qamar al-Dawla Alwan.[29] At first, the prosecutor assumes this will be a case like hundreds of others, unsolved and unsolvable, thwarted by multiple forms of peasant recalcitrance and marked *ḍidd majhūl*, "culprit unknown." However, midway through the prosecutor's suspect interrogations, the village's wandering holy man Shaykh Asfur offers this cryptic, poetic clue: "Seek out women, there you'll find / the cause of all turmoil" (*Y* 20). Following the shaykh's advice despite himself, the prosecutor is led to a new suspect: Rim, the victim's sister-in-law. As soon as the prosecutor sees her, he is struck by her mysterious beauty. Suddenly, the case of Qamar al-Dawla takes on a different significance: "There was now nothing on my mind except the image of that girl in her black frame, and her secret which I had so far failed to uncover. Her secret was the key to the entire case, and I was impelled to unearth it by an urge quite unconnected with my work. I also wanted to know" (*D* 31; *Y* 26).

This "desire to know" and "uncover" Rim's secret—a desire that exceeds the bounds of his professional training—motivates the narrator throughout the rest of the book. It is no accident that it was inspired by a snippet of poetry uttered by the wandering holy man Shaykh Asfur, that saintly "friend of god" whom the police bring along on every investigation,[30] "a strange man who wanders aimlessly by night and day, sleepless, eternally humming the same songs, mouthing stray words, uttering predictions which win the credence of simple folk" (*D* 18; *Y* 8–9). Oddly, Shaykh Asfur also seems to be addicted to mystery, in whatever form it takes; it just so happens that, in the modern setting of al-Hakim's novel, there is no mystery more thrilling than the "police incident" (*ḥādithah*, pl. *ḥawādith*). "Nothing gives the man more pleasure than going out to investigate incidents [al-khurūj ilā ḥawādith] with the Legal Officer and the police. Whenever he hears the horn of the Ford van blowing in the distance, he follows it wherever it goes, like a dog following its master to the chase" (*D* 18; *Y* 8). Left out of Eban's English translation is the police officers' call to Shaykh Asfur: "Get in, Shaykh Asfur! [There's been] an incident [*ḥādithah*]!" (*Y* 8). The "incident" or "occurrence" is both a crime and a tear in the normal fabric of life. True to his status as a friend of God, the shaykh is called to follow every unexplained phenomenon. And true to his status as an effendi, the prosecutor is called to co-opt the shaykh's popularly accepted form of knowledge—the poetic, mystic, endless questing of *ma'rifah*—and transform it into his own, authorized, established form of knowledge, *'ilm*.

The prosecutor's pursuit of Rim's mysterious truth, however, is endlessly thwarted by the annoyances of rural life and the backwardness of rural people. Indeed, as a Cairo-educated interwar rural reformer, al-Hakim's narrator constantly measures the sights, sounds, and smells of the countryside against a European standard and finds the former sorely lacking. He complains about being stationed in a rural outpost far from the "lights, noise, and cabarets" of Cairo, in this place where there are no buildings except the "little hovels" in which the fellahin live "like worms," and whose "dusty brown color was suggestive of mud, manure, and the dung of cattle" (*D* 53). He also laments what he calls "deficiencies of character from which the Egyptian peasant suffers, in addition to his many bodily, mental, and social ills"—deficiencies that, to the narrator's mind, make the peasant incapable of grasping the "up-to-date regulations and procedures" governing modern, positivist law (*D* 103, 101). He describes rural Egyptians as plagued by "sheer incapacity and diffidence arising from a long tradition of slavish work at agriculture" (*D* 104). They "can hardly be relied upon for judgment or discernment of any kind" as witnesses in legal cases, since "their eyes have been consumed by trachoma since childhood and [their] mental faculties have been left to decay under the rule of so many governors of all races" (*D* 100). He ultimately compares them with "monkeys," "worms," and "chameleons" (*D* 51, 81, 53, 110).

These and other unsavory moments of essentialism in *Diary* have led many critics to denounce al-Hakim's contemptuous attitude toward the Egyptian lower classes (especially the fellahin), both in *Diary* and in his other fictional and nonfictional writings.[31] Many have even read *Diary* as an autobiographical text, and thus also understood the prosecutor's opinions about the fellahin as veiled expressions of al-Hakim's own views.[32] From their diffident, passive natures to their base, animalistic characteristics, the fellahin are decisively *other* to the narrator of *Diary*, as they were—in a different way—for Muhsin, the narrator of al-Hakim's earlier novel, *Return of the Spirit*. Yet despite the shift in tone between these two works, there is something common to both al-Hakim's earlier pharaonic nationalism and his more dehumanizing brand of essentialism: both perform a very particular, specialized mode of knowledge production about the countryside and its inhabitants.[33] The village, its harvests, and the particular "character" of the fellah—these are things *to be known*, and to be known by experts with specialized training like the legal officer himself. The legal officer must not only read stacks of mind-numbing case files; he must also "read" the peasants who surround him, diagnosing their bodily, mental, and character deficiencies and—most importantly—recording them in his diary, the very *Diary* we are reading. The diary, in turn, becomes a place "to speak freely" not only about "crime" and "[one]self," but also about "*all living beings*" (*D* 14, emphasis added), to record truths about the village that only a refined man of letters like the prosecutor can piece together. And yet his desire for solitary moments in which to record his reflections—to let his pen "roam through dream-pastures"—is endlessly thwarted by the constant demands of his work (*D* 69). Reading about such trivial cases as "the exchange of abuse between Sitt al-Dar and her neighbor Kataif," "situation reports about a donkey which had run away from outside a house," and about "a sycamore branch which fell on the head of Haj Habbab's goat" is, the prosecutor informs us, taking a toll not only on his "poor physique and frail constitution" but also on his "sensitive temperament" and "refined sensibilities" (*D* 125, 60). In a humorous intertwining of form and content, the Arabic phrase for "refined sensibilities"—diqqat al-ḥass wa riqqat al-shuʿūr—has the lilt of rhymed prose (*sajʿ*), which itself has historically appealed to a particular kind of refined literary sensibility.

*Diary* thus proves to be less a record of Tawfiq al-Hakim's personal opinions about the fellahin or his work as a country prosecutor and more a metafictional commentary on what I call ways of seeking—on seeking after and finding (or not finding) truth, as well as the various procedures involved in this search and the forms of power it is used to authorize. Al-Hakim transforms the novel into a dramatization of reading and writing as processes, thereby framing and destabilizing the truth effects of both. Rather than investigate murders, identify culprits, and generally perform his role as a public servant, the prosecutor must instead spend his days replying to petty grievances filed by countless peasants employing countless public scribes (*ʿarḍaḥāljiyyah*), who turn a profit from the peasants' illiteracy and the new legal order. He therefore deems "official" writing excessively formulaic but still recognizes it as a necessary ill if he wishes to secure his job and the social status that comes with it. "The Report is the be-all-and-end-all in the eyes of higher authority," he notes. "It is the only evidence testifying to the accuracy and skill of the Legal Officer. Nobody worries, of course, about the mere apprehension of the criminal" (*D* 21; *Y* 12). Seasoned by his elders in the profession, the prosecutor now cares more about the length, structure, and form of his report than he does about the victim himself, remembering the criticism he once received from a superior officer after turning in a solved case of murder written up in merely ten pages. "Next time we will be more careful about the weight!" he remembers affirming to the incredulous superior. Now, years later, the case of Qamar al-Dawla is no different: "The victim no longer concerned us, now that we had crammed our Report full of his particulars, so we left him wallowing in his blood" (*D* 22; *Y* 13).

In contrast with official writing, which he knows ultimately goes nowhere and does nothing, it is by writing about the peasants in his diary (and in *Diary*) that the prosecutor performs his ability—indeed, his authority—to know them. At several points in the novel, this ability to know exceeds the merely legal and extends into the realm of the human itself. The legal profession, the prosecutor writes, is constantly "placing before us human souls whose uncharted territories [*majāhilahā*] we are supposed to explore, and whose innermost secrets we are supposed to expose" (*D* 64; *Y* 78). Here, again, is that "unknown territory," that *majhūl* we encountered with Amina on her Cairo rooftop in Mahfouz's *Palace Walk*, the same majhūl who will be listed as the "unknown culprit" in endless unsolved case files marked "ḍidd majhūl," a legal shorthand with metaphysical connotations in Arabic. (It is also the title of a short story by Mahfouz, which I read in chapter 3.) The prosecutor is a soul explorer, a secret uncoverer, a penetrator into occulted worlds; he moves beyond merely observable facts in an attempt to deduce and express "the truth about the feelings lurking in the depths of the human soul" (*Y* 23). Despite his complaints about the fellahin and the rural setting to which he's been banished, then, the legal investigator relishes the opportunity to observe, analyze, and gather new facts about the victims and defendants in his cases, deciphering the realms of the mind and the soul. Al-Hakim consciously and conspicuously dramatizes this relish, linking it with literary writing itself.

Nowhere is this hubris of decipherment clearer than in the following passage, where the narrator admonishes his young assistant about the nature of legal observation, deduction, and knowledge:

> I pointed out to my assistant that our profession was full of material for study and observation, so that as long as he lived he ought not to go about with his eyes closed. A Legal Officer is a little king in his own tiny sphere: if he understands everything in this kingdom, observes everything, studies people's natures and instincts, he can thereby come to know that larger kingdom which is his own country, and even understand the wider world of humanity itself. (*D* 104; *Y* 143)

Here it is clear that the legal officer has no concern for the actual, day-to-day lives of the fellahin under his jurisdiction. To him, the peasants are mere objects for "study and observation" (al-baḥth wa-l-mulāḥaẓah), perhaps even test subjects for projects of social improvement.[34] To study people is to know them, and to know them is to exercise a certain sovereignty over them—to transform oneself into a "little king" (*ḥākim*) and the objects of one's gaze into a "kingdom" (*mamlakah*). Hercule Poirot himself, when asked about his profession, replies arrogantly, "'I am a detective,' . . . with the modest air of one who says, 'I am a King.'"[35]

In this admonishment from the prosecutor to his young assistant, I read not a veiled expression of al-Hakim's own attitudes toward the countryside and the fellahin but a parodic stylization of the refined, modern effendi and his voracious drive to know.[36] Al-Hakim writes power back into the relationship between the effendi and the fellah, the enlightened author and the rural objects of his knowledge. Even as the rest of the novel inundates the reader with unsavory characterizations of the fellahin written in the narrator's voice, the peasants—as Samah Selim argues—interrupt this hegemonic discourse with their own colloquial objections, their own linguistic forms of resistance.[37] But the prosecutor's language also interrupts itself and stammers, troubling its own claims to authority. The passion for "study" and "observation," which he attempts to inculcate in his young assistant, is laced with a covert acknowledgement of these processes' entanglements with power and monarch-like dominance, inherited from Europe and practiced by a newly enfranchised native intelligentsia. Through this covert acknowledgement, al-Hakim reveals the extent to which power and its exercise in the Egyptian countryside is a performance, a kind of legal drag. I use "drag" deliberately here, since various other peasant characters also recognize power as a contingent performance enhanced by and premised on attire.[38] When the wives of the police chief and the district judge publicly exchange insults from the roofs of their houses, for example, in a scene of comic insult or *radaḥ*,[39] each dons her husband's official attire to "enrage her rival." "You don't have any escort worth mentioning, just a shabby old rag-and-bone man with dyed hair,"[40] the wife of the police chief shouts while wearing her husband's cap and uniform, complete with crown and star; "but the police chief has a post full of guards and soldiers under our command." The judge's wife, in response, descends to her husband's room, dons "his official red sash over her dress," and returns, shouting: "You certainly have command of a couple of miserable guards. But who else is there in the whole town who can lock people up and hang them and say, 'The court has decided' . . . ?" (*D* 62–63).[41] Like drag performers, these women recognize a radical contingency in the exercise of juridical power over life and death, "in the face of cultural configurations of causal unities that are regularly assumed to be natural and necessary."[42] Their performance may not, in itself, constitute a political revolution, but it does call into question the *reality* of juridical power, making it unclear how to distinguish the real from the unreal. "And this is the occasion," Judith Butler writes, "in which we come to understand that what we take to be 'real,' what we invoke as naturalized knowledge . . . is, in fact, a changeable and revisable reality."[43]

It is Shaykh Asfur, however, who perhaps most obviously parodies the prosecutor's sincere vision of the legal officer as a "little king." After emerging from a "thicket at the edge of a field"—itself a figure of dense unknowability—to join the legal officer, the police chief, and the others headed to the scene of the crime, he "got into the Ford van with the air of a man entering a Rolls Royce, first plucking a twig . . . and carrying it as though it were a royal scepter" (*D* 18; *Y* 9). Once the small town's preeminent keeper of mysteries and penetrator into the unknown, Shaykh Asfur has been stripped of his social power by the imposition of the modern legal system, which had to displace his forms of knowledge as irrational if it wished to establish a monopoly over truth. Al-Hakim, true to his vision of modernity's messy, incomplete, uncomfortable transplantation into colonial Egypt in *Diary*, maintains Shaykh Asfur's presence as a persistent reminder of the old meanings of words like *majhūl* ("unknown"), *ḥaqq*/*ḥuqūq* ("truth" but also "rights"), baḥth, and other terms incompletely co-opted by and conscripted into the new legal system, rather like the prosecutor himself.

Driss Chraïbi, too, is concerned with the arbitrariness of power's outer trappings among a newly enfranchised native intelligentsia—in his case, a whole class of "chiefs" who, despite the departure of the French, "only had a single politics: to keep everything for themselves, to keep chewing away on their 'chief-ness'" (*E* 131; *F* 91). Chraïbi situates Inspector Ali within an intermediary class of government functionaries who, in the post-colonial situation, stand somewhere between these "chiefs" and the "slaves" at the bottom of the social ladder: "The French had gone, but the slaves stayed behind—porters, domestics, secretaries, little intermediaries forever jammed between the new masters of the Third World and the people" (*E* 131; *F* 91). Where al-Hakim's parody of the effendi-*cum*-prosecutor parodically stylizes this figure's performance of the authority to know, Chraïbi's parody of the "new masters of the Third World" is directed squarely at Chief Mohammed in *Enquête*. The chief does everything systematically. He sees himself upholding logic, coherence, and even thinking itself against the lawless and "primitive" Aït Yafelman clan. "To think, to cogitate cleanly, firmly, to shield the spirit of initiative against the winds and the tides, against the primitiveness of this countryside [*bled*] and its infernal heat—this was his lot" (*E* 147; *F* 101). More than merely "thinking" (*penser*), the chief "cogitates" (*cogiter*), invoking the Latin of the European Enlightenment and the Cartesian "cogito, ergo sum" to give his thoughts dignity and legitimacy. Indeed, his frequent recourse to Latin rhetorical terms—including "sine qua non," "curriculum vitae," "*in petto*," "*primo . . . deuxio . . . tertio . . . quarto . . .*" "*illico presto*," "*ex abrupto*," "ad hoc," and so on—are but one piece of his fervent display of enlightened rationality (*E* 148, 163, 89, 151–52 passim). He upholds these methods against the "primitive" logic of the Imazighen—the "lullabies bathed in legends that crude, uneducated grandmothers once sang" (*E* 161). The chief even wants his thoughts to operate like the administrative paperwork of the state, "laid out in order of importance, classified in different-colored folders" (*E* 159; *F* 108).

With his reverence for administrative procedures, the chief also views police work as the peak of civilizational achievement, far exceeding any other form of cultural production or civil service. Unlike factory laborers, schoolteachers, deputies, or even ministers, police chiefs "have the cerebral faculty to really think, cogitate, and conceptualize" (*E* 96–97; *F* 65), according to the chief. He aims to structure his own interrogation of the peasants into four movements like a "classical symphony" (*E* 97; *F* 65). Here, too, as in *Diary*, the detective does much more than merely collect clues and solve mysterious crimes. His investigative work becomes almost identical with the ability to know and understand the human and the unseen. Chraïbi's parody of Chief Mohammed is quite explicit here, whereas al-Hakim's framing of the intellectual-*cum*-legal officer is more subtle. In both cases, however, the police officer is a tongue-in-cheek stand-in for the intellectual class as a whole, which performs its authority to know the peasants it investigates, interrogates, and objectifies.

Yet in both texts, this very same "authority to know" quickly dissolves when it takes a rural, subaltern populace as its object. For all his praise of Western-style bureaucracy and civilization, as well as his belief in the greasy shine of *officialité* (officiality or official-ness),[44] still the veneer of logic, organization, and progress that Chief Mohammed carefully crafts in *Enquête* rapidly dulls under the influence of conversation with the Aït Yafelman. In their very simplicity and ignorance, these "paysans" repel the chief's conventional tactics for commanding submission, and this imperviousness nearly drives him mad. To conduct his investigation in secret, for example, the chief speaks only in French with his subordinate Inspector Ali, assuming (correctly) that the Aït Yafelman understand nothing of this colonial language. Yet the Aït Yafelman, far from being intimidated by the chief's superior knowledge, instead describe his French as a kind of sickness, a "raclement de la gorge" (raspy throat), a "râlement" (hoarseness) induced by demon possession (*E* 45–47). In his frustration, the chief loses all semblance of "civilized" behavior:

> The chief was falling apart, little by little, despite himself, overcome by a *force majeure*, abandoned by civilization's trappings, its taboos and interdictions, professional duty, and even the super-ego so dear to Freud; he was shaking, stomping his feet, and hammering the ground with his boots . . . The chief of police flailed his arms like an epileptic windmill and babbled in all the languages known to him: in his mother tongue, in French, in English, in poker-game American, beerhall German, in Wolof, in all the civilized languages whose insults he had perfectly assimilated. He was like the Third World man who, aside from some cultural refuse, had absorbed from the West all the detritus of its values and gotten some armaments in the deal. He was evidently a long way from any form of ratiocination, and could do little more than low like a cow . . .
>
> —Curses upon your pagan race! . . . I'm going to screw you, whore and daughter of a whore! . . . Oukc'est mon fusil que ch't'écrabouille les claouis à coups de crosse? I'm going to blow your balls off you son of a bitch! . . . Bugger off! . . . Kleb des chiottes! . . . Schweinhalloufhund! . . . Banderkatolikouyyoun! . . . . (*E* 46; *F* 32)

Here the chief's behavior and speech are governed not by Cartesian logic, symphonic harmony, or the prohibitions of Freudian "superego," but by "anarchy" and "force majeure." "Civilization" quickly devolves into "colère" (rage) and even "coprolalie" (coprolalia) (*E* 89).[45] Even as the chief consistently demands correct speech from his subordinate, Inspector Ali—"esplique, articule, cause français" ('splain it, articulate, speak French), "arrête de t'exprimer en bouillie et en purée" (stop spouting broth and purée), "parle correctement" (speak correctly), "tu ne fais que 'charabier'" (you do nothing but spout gibberish), and so on—his own speech quickly devolves into obscenity (*E* 43, 95, 18, 100). He invokes the police practices of the West in the name of law and order, but the only elements of the Occident to which he can truly lay claim are its "cultural refuse." Very quickly, discursive thought becomes a bestial "lowing."

Crucially, Chraïbi uses language—and specifically the linguistic cacophony and ridiculous portraiture displayed above—to lay bare the violence behind the chief's conventional methods of obfuscation. Chraïbi not only interrupts the standard French of *Enquête* with interjections in formal and colloquial Arabic (*fuṣḥā* and *dārijah*) throughout; he also disrupts the idea of "standard French" *itself* by compiling a veritable lexicon of French words for mispronunciation—words with which the language has historically policed its borders.[46] With its numerous terms for accented and "incorrect" pronunciations of French—not only by formerly colonized peoples, but also by those who now fall within the ambit of hexagonal French identity (Bretons, Alsatians, Provençaux, etc.)—Chraïbi's language also dismantles the idea of pure French.[47] In this context, we could point in particular to the word *charabia*, one of the chief's many insults for Ali's incorrect French (*E* 18). From *charrar*, "hissing" or "stuttering," in the Auvergnat dialect, the term is originally borrowed from the Spanish word *algarabía*, "gibberish" or "babble," which is itself borrowed from the Arabic *al-gharbiyyah*, "Western language," referring to the North African dialects of Arabic, which are substantially different from Eastern dialects and thereby virtually incomprehensible to Eastern Arabic speakers.[48] With these and other terms, Chraïbi exposes the French language itself as already unstable and self-interrupting, imbued with derivations from numerous dialects and Mediterranean languages, including an Arabic that makes its way from North Africa to Occitania through Spain. The irony, of course, is that *charabia* was originally an *Arabic* word used to mock a *Western—gharbī*, that is, North African—way of speaking Arabic, not the other way around.

Language's inconsistency with itself is also at the heart of a key scene in al-Hakim's *Diary*, in which the prosecutor's "desire to know" is revealed not as a superior level of civilized inquisitiveness but as a violent, merciless drive, a kind of butchery. At one point in the novel, the prosecutor remembers the first autopsy he ever witnessed in the countryside—an ultimately unsuccessful one that failed to uncover the bullet in the body of a shooting victim. Through the subtle integration of terms from Egyptian Arabic,[49] al-Hakim breaks down the supposedly rigid divide between the scientific methods and procedures of the forensic pathologists and the "savage," "backwards" practices of the "medical barbers" whom these pathologists have supposedly replaced:

> With both hands, [the forensic pathologist] removed all the brains that were in the skull until he had emptied it like a clean, metal bowl. He then divided this brain into four parts and gave one to each of his assistants, ordering them to look carefully for the bullet. So they began to knead this substance, which is said to be the source of all human eminence, until they had reduced it to a liquid paste like *muhallabiyyah*.

> "This is the human brain!"
>
> I whispered these words to myself, and the caution that had seized me at first began to disappear, bit by bit. My nerves hardened, and my feelings relaxed. There awoke in me a strong curiosity (*ḥubb istiṭlā'*) and a desire to have the entire body opened up before me so that I could look inside it . . .
>
> We had to get results, come what may. Here was a murdered man—surely there must be a bullet. The doctor set to work in real earnest and some impatience, running his scalpel all over the body. I stood behind him, watching and saying:
>
> "Cut here! Tear him open!"
>
> I was seized by a strange fever and lost all human feeling. "Show me his lungs!" I started shouting to the doctor. "Show me his intestines! Show me his gall-bladder!" etc. etc. The doctor did not hesitate for a moment; he made an incision from the chest to the lower abdomen and took out the heart, then the intestines, dictating all the while . . . "Despite careful examination, no bullet was found." . . .
>
> As we finished the operation and departed, I was astounded by the reversal that had occurred in my soul. I, a man of genteel sensibilities, could see this butchery, this dismemberment—indeed, even demand its continuation—without so much as trembling! And what a disillusionment it was! . . . No—we ought never to see ourselves from within. (*Y* 170–71)

For a scene that is supposed to be the pinnacle of science and forensics, al-Hakim's autopsy is surprisingly full of Egyptian expressions. The narrator compares the dead man's skull to a "metal bowl" (*sulṭāniyyah*) of the type used to serve stewed fava beans, and the word he uses for "kneading" or "smearing" the brain is the Egyptian verb *yulaghwaṣūn*, as though the brain were food in the hands of a messy child. Finally, when all is said and done, the brain comes to resemble *muhallabiyyah*, a popular rice pudding. Al-Hakim reveals these supposed "men of science" as little better than the peasants they deride as lowly, primitive, backward creatures. The scientists are sorcerers conjuring miracles, ravenous knowledge seekers cleaning out their soup bowls, children smearing and kneading the human brain like rice pudding.

Whereas the acquisition of knowledge about the human body "from the inside" might have delighted the prosecutor earlier in the text (remember: "if the Legal Officer understands everything in this kingdom . . . he can thereby come to know that larger kingdom which is his own country, and even understand the wider world of humanity itself"), in this scene the prosecutor experiences the same "drive to know" as a form not only of "disillusionment," but also of violence, "butchery" (*jazar*), "dismemberment" (*taqṭī'*), even as a "strange fever" and a "loss of all *human* feeling." His "hardened nerves" and "relaxed feelings" impel him, ironically, to greater violence, just as the doctor's fierce insistence on logical cause and effect ("Here was a murdered man, surely there must be a bullet!") drives his botched autopsy forward. The side of mankind that our narrator has seen "from the inside" is thus not only the inner organs of the murdered man. It is also the "inside" of his own rational intellect—the violent impulses hidden beneath his "genteel," "civilized" exterior (*raqīq al-ḥass*). "Human beings," as the German philosophers Max Horkheimer and Theodor Adorno famously wrote, "purchase the increase in their power with estrangement from that over which it is asserted."[50] Knowledge of nature—this "curiosity" or, literally, "love of discovery" (*ḥubb al-istiṭlā'*), which overcomes the narrator in this scene—is a form of domination over it. This explains why, at least for Horkheimer and Adorno, "Enlightenment is totalitarian," because—in language that echoes al-Hakim's bodily imagery in this passage—it "amputates the incommensurable."[51] In this scene, the prosecutor recognizes himself as a (narrative) subject endowed with a domineering, "feverish" drive to know and the extent to which his "curiosity" is not a naturally occurring superior disposition with respect to the world,[52] but a learned fascination with investigating and uncovering, cutting open and laying bare.

Both al-Hakim and Chraïbi thus reveal the "barbarism" lurking behind the refined and civilized sensibilities of the prosecutor and the police chief alike—and, by extension, behind the supposedly refined and civilized legal system imposed by colonial modernity in both contexts. Not only do their investigative tactics ultimately fail to arrive at the truth, but the parodic dramatization of these tactics' disintegration frames the operations of power, dethroning those native, metropolitan officials who assume superiority over their rural others. Instead of cultivating sympathy for the police officer, then, as in the conventional police procedural, both al-Hakim and Chraïbi transform the cop into an object of ridicule—a lowing, flailing idiot; a dismemberment-crazed butcher. They make visible the violence that legal and juridical claims to objectivity portray merely as a matter of banal but necessary procedure for arriving at truth. At the same time, neither Chraïbi nor al-Hakim completely tears down or lambasts the native-son-turned-officer. On the contrary, central to the intrigue and suspense of both texts is the detective's status as an incomplete conscript in whom there still lurk the traces, however vague or indistinct, of filiation with the communities he has been trained to police.

## INCOMPLETE CONSCRIPTION

In dramatizing their protagonists' status as native detectives in colonial legal systems, both *Diary* and *Enquête* turn once again to language. Specifically, each protagonist is caught either between two different languages (French and Arabic) or between multiple registers of the same language (colloquial Egyptian and formal, technical Arabic). Thus, in Chraïbi's text, Inspector Ali's upbringing as the child of impoverished public oven workers, combined with his training as a would-be soccer player, his experience as a street thug, and his subsequent transformation into a police inspector, have made him a veritable polyglot, having "a slang vocabulary capable of making even a Moroccan's hair stand straight on end" and "singing the *Internationale* in Arabic as well as he could the Palestinian national anthem, or the Polisario rally" (*E* 121; *F* 85). Likewise, in the same autopsy scene from al-Hakim's text examined above, the narrator understands the colloquial Egyptian wailings of women in mourning as well as he does the technical, scientific terminology of the forensic pathologists conducting the examination. The conscripted detective's status as awkward intermediary is thus also staged through his incomplete assimilation to any single language or register, as he stands suspended between two modes of expression, the first an alienating formal education that has nevertheless granted him access to higher social status and greater material gain, the second a well-loved but irrecuperable familial, communitarian, even pious vocabulary and identity. In both works, the heteroglossia of the novel form invites simultaneous recognition and distance on the part of readers familiar with the spectrum between the colloquial and the formal. The medical, legal, and police argots meant to supplant the irrationality and backwardness of the colloquial, oral, folk forms are once again revealed to be barbarous in their own ways, having alienated the native detectives from their national brethren and, ultimately, also from themselves.

For an illustration of these linguistic dynamics in each text, let me return briefly to *Diary* first, to a slightly earlier moment in the same autopsy scene examined above. The prosecutor describes how the shooting victim's family has wrapped him in a shroud and carried him from the field where he was found back to their house, "surrounded by women wailing, shrieking, and befouling their faces with mud" (*D* 119; *Y* 167). These same women look on as the medical and legal professionals cut open their male relative in the courtyard of their own home:

> The doctor passed the scalpel over the dead man's head and dictated to the clerk: "Scalp removed" (by which he meant the scalp of the head, of course).
>
> At this we heard the shrieks of the women . . . Amidst the confused sounds I discerned a warm, high-pitched voice which ripped at my heart: "Oh Father, oh tree in whose shade we once sheltered!" [Yaa shagara wi-midallilnaa yaa buuyaa!]
>
> It was followed by another voice, equally as high-pitched and warm, mixed with sobs and bitter tears: "Oh Father, and after your last meal of the fast!" [Ya-lli kunta khaarig bi-suḥuurak fii baṭnak yaabaa!] . . .
>
> [The doctor] went on dictating:
>
> "Bullet wound four centimeters long."
>
> He groped for the bullet, but without success. Taking a saw from his tool case, he began to saw the skull at the forehead, to make an opening in the head, but he was unable to break through. So he took up a small hammer from among his instruments and began to knock on the saw, as though he were opening a box of sardines. One of the women heard this sound and, looking through the roof, beheld this hammering on the head of the father of the family and the master of the household. She buried her face in her hands, exclaiming, "The name of God protect him!" (Ism-alla ʿalayh!)
>
> This expression shook me and I found something strange in its effect. This old woman still thought her man was there in all his human personality, just at the moment when I began to doubt it. (*D* 119–20; *Y* 168)

Here the prosecutor is torn between the technical, official Arabic register used by the doctors, which he understands perfectly well, and the fervent, colloquial language used by the female relatives of the murdered fellah, which "rips at his heart" and "shakes him" to the core. He parenthetically explains that the pathologist's expression—*farwah*, which can mean "pelt," "hide," or "fur" in Arabic—refers in this context to *farwat al-ra ʾs*, the "scalp," thus illustrating his knowledge of the scientific, anatomical uses to which Arabic terms with older resonances have recently been put. At the same time, the moaning of the women affects him emotionally—it is no accident that this language is feminine and colloquial, the language of the private home as opposed to the public sphere. It may be tempting to read the women's complaints in this scene as a kind of traditional, female, Islamic piety diametrically opposed to the secular rationalism of the doctors. Yet Khaled Fahmy's social history of autopsy in nineteenth-century Egypt invites us to view things differently. Perhaps the women's mourning "should not be judged as a reactionary response . . . to the proven benefits of modern science," but rather "should be seen as representing the reaction of common people to the encroachments of the modern state on private life," encroachments that "[were] most deeply felt in connection with death, when the dead ceased to belong to their families and communities and, instead, were appropriated by the state, which decided how, when, and where they were to be buried."[53] The prosecutor is caught between the women's desire to claim, mourn, and bury their relative on their own terms, and the medical professionals' scientific desire to locate the bullet, solve the mystery, and thereby not only fulfill their professional purpose but reconfirm their monopoly on truth. In light of the way the autopsy is conducted, the women's cries start to seem less like a case of hysteria to the prosecutor and more like a form of protest against the dehumanizing practices of the modern state.

If this scene from *Diary* offers a short and partial glimpse into the minds of those outside the state's ambit, Chraïbi's *Enquête* focuses at even greater length on elaborating what I call an "autochthonous alterity," a fantastical, imaginary alternative subjectivity bound neither to the ledgers of the state nor to the practices of Islamic piety, but one that is built on a timeless attachment to the primal elements of earth and sun. Raho and Hajja, the patriarch and matriarch of the Aït Yafelman family, embody this alterity, this "cult of the earth" most explicitly in *Enquête* (*E* 40). "Transmitted to Raho," the novel's omniscient narrator reports,

> from generation to generation, across religions and cultures, as though all human enterprises were sieves allowing what was essential in life to filter through despite themselves, there was the antique tradition where the elements dominated: earth, water, air, fire. Everything else was ephemeral. (*E* 82–83)

The "cult of the earth" is transmitted "par voie orale" (orally) and has little need for written language at all. In this way, Chraïbi resolves (at least superficially, fictionally) the vexed question of "language choice" in postcolonial Maghrebi writing, inventing a world and a worldview in which written language is altogether irrelevant.[54]

Nowhere in *Enquête* are the features of Chraïbi's fantastical, autochthonous alterity clearer, however, than in one of the novel's final scenes. The Aït Yafelman have just killed Chief Mohammed, and they now have their sights set on Inspector Ali. Raho commands Ali to bury the chief, informing him that a council of village elders will soon decide whether to kill him or spare his life. As Ali digs, the villagers around him play a chilling "hymn of the dead" on drums and "desert flutes" (*naÿ*), and this music summons forth timeless memories in him. Despite his best efforts to suppress them, "he vaguely recognized the profound and 'earthy' inflections that he had once loved so well. Where, and in what past existence had he heard them?" (*E* 198). Flashes of memory have already interrupted his investigation earlier in the novel: he sees elements of his own father in Raho, and of his mother in Hajja.[55] Yet the novel culminates here when the memory of a story his mother told him as a child interrupts and overcomes both Ali's mind and the text of the novel itself. The tale is an alternate creation myth transmitted matrilineally for generations. It recounts the story of "the earthly life of men," from a time before religion, civilization, and the state, "long, long ago, before time itself" (*E* 211). In this time before time, human beings were the original inhabitants of a paradise on earth, while the gods of the sky were a wicked and vengeful tribe. The gods so coveted the earth that "*they had depleted the stars . . . burned up the moon and the sun*," and, having nothing left in the sky for themselves, came down to earth intending to exploit it and enslave its inhabitants. To do this, they brought with them "*what they called the law*," embodied in the holy books of the Jews ("*des Youdis*"), the Christians ("*des Nazaréens*"), and the Muslims ("*le Coran des islamiques*").[56] They enslaved mankind first to these pieties, and then to the concepts of "progress" and "civilization." Very quickly, these "gods" come to resemble the Maghreb's many centuries of colonizers:

> *And thus it was that [the people of the earth] began to work for their masters like slaves, building houses and cities, making machines and more machines of which they had no need. And their descendants continue on and on, taking pains and exhausting hopes in the void. It will never end. Because the gods boiled our minds, they mixed their language of lies and magic with ours, they erased our memory of ancient times . . . so much so that the man of this earth will never be happy with his lot. And, when they perceived that their books were worn out like dry figs and that they could no longer get anything from them, or next to nothing, then they invented another stratagem: progress, civilization.* (*E* 207)[57]

From invaders belonging to various monotheistic religions with their holy books, to the scientists, technicians, and politicians of colonial and postcolonial modernity, the people of the sky, in this tale, have severed earth's inhabitants both from the earth, their "*mère nourricière*" (*nourishing mother*), and from each other.

Simultaneously environmentalist, anticapitalist, and mystical, this alternate, matrilineal myth of origins—as it surfaces involuntarily in Ali's mind—offers him a way out of his police training and into the autochthonous world of the Aït Yafelman. He spends the rest of the night attempting to reconnect with this myth of origins, and to prove his innocence in the hopes that the villagers will spare his life.

Yet, although the considerable amount of space devoted to this alternate creation myth in *Enquête* seems to promise the possibility of its return in Ali, Chraïbi ultimately withdraws that possibility. Neither the memory of his mother's tale nor his trickster's facility with words end up saving the inspector from the Aït Yafelman.[58] Instead, only his insistence on the durability of *paper* in the hands of the government convinces the Aït Yafelman to spare his life. "Sure, agreed," he insists in one last ruse, "they could dismantle the old buggy into bits and pieces and sell them all over the Sudan . . . And of course they could bury the corpses, his and Chief Mohammed's . . . But how would they eliminate the papers at Headquarters, down there, in the capital of the cops and the government? Documents and mission orders die hard" (*E* 212; *F* 141). The ruse eventually works. Soon after, the Aït Yafelman gather around Ali, asking him what he will do to "eliminate the government's papers." And he, "such a joker in life, such a variety artist in his everyday language (and in his mind)," transforms from the novel's trickster into the original target of its satire: "He knew what they expected him to be: a serious, sensible, efficient being. A true chief" (*E* 214–15). The possibility of returning to the Aït Yafelman's "culte de la terre" has been eclipsed.

This ending should perhaps come as no surprise, however, given how thoroughly Chraïbi records and documents this autochthonous alterity on the pages of *Enquête*. Through omniscient narration and free indirect discourse, the narrator of *Enquête* has given the reader not merely a glimpse but an expansive and detailed blueprint of Raho's and Hajja's views on the world. A great deal of the novel's narrative energy has been dedicated to recording, chronicling, and enumerating these views. And thus it seems these characters were never truly "illegible," never truly "outside" state discipline to begin with. Chraïbi recognizes and acknowledges his own authorship as yet another form of surveillance. The novel's omniscient narrator explicitly satirizes the inhuman procedures and practices of the postcolonial Moroccan state, yet through the very act of novel writing, he also self-consciously constitutes the Aït Yafelman as objects of knowledge. Raho and Hajja are deeply and intimately known, put on display by none other than Chraïbi himself. The success of Chraïbi's "enquête" for nonreified forms of identity is thus also its failure: it has uncovered the tales that might have otherwise remained buried in Ali's memory, yet in exposing these tales to the light of a reading, intellectual public (or, in the chief's preferred phrase, "des *insectuels*"), it has also become the very document, the very kind of "mise-en-carte" to which it sought an alternative.[59]

The situation is much less tangled in al-Hakim's *Diary*. The reader is never invited to imagine the prosecutor relinquishing his position of legal authority and rejoining the fellahin; there is no matrilineal myth of return here. Nevertheless, like Chraïbi, al-Hakim does maintain a fantasy of inscrutability and alterity to the prosecutor's investigative tactics, incarnated in two specific characters: the mysterious peasant woman Rim (the murder victim's sister-in-law), and the quasi-mystical friend of God Shaykh Asfur. Rim frustrates the prosecutor's ability to know and expound on fellahi life in particular and on humanity in general. In many ways, she is a prototypical country beauty, the central actor in a national romance much like her predecessor, the titular character of Muhammad Husayn Haykal's 1913 *Zaynab*, or her many successors, including Zohra, the inscrutable heroine of Naguib Mahfouz's 1967 novel *Miramar* (*Mīrāmār*). She is the feminized figure for the nation whom the novel's narrative subject is trying to know and possess as object.[60] But the prosecutor's fascination with her is motivated less by love or lust than by her defiance of his investigative tactics, her sphinxlike resistance to being known. He is convinced that she is hiding a "secret" that will be "the clue to the entire case" (*Y* 26). The precursor of many future inscrutable Egyptian peasant girls, she also prefigures J. M. Coetzee's barbarian woman as viewed through the eyes of his imperial magistrate: "So I continue to swoop and circle around the irreducible figure of the girl, casting one net of meaning after another over her . . . What does she see?"[61]

Before the prosecutor in al-Hakim's *Diary* can uncover Rim's secret, however, her corpse is found in a nearby irrigation canal. It is yet another mystery for the prosecutor to solve, but this time he uncharacteristically resists attempting to uncover the truth behind the case. Rim offers him the remembrance of a time when he might have reflected on her mysterious beauty not as "the key to a case," something to be instrumentalized in the pursuit of knowledge, but rather as "a sweet creature," a "marvelous image" (*Y* 172–73). She is not, like the other fellahin, an object for observation, study, and social improvement, but what Mohammad Salama, writing of a different feminine figure in al-Hakim's oeuvre, describes as "a receding telos, a pursuit and never a fulfillment."[62] As the prosecutor returns to Rim's file to write "the usual formulation" at the bottom—"We order an autopsy of the corpse"—he suddenly "becomes aware of the horror in these words—yes, for the first time I found them horrible" (*Y* 173). Ironically, Rim, the novel's great inscrutable figure, is the only character who allows the prosecutor to see the "atrocity," "horror," and "heinousness" (*faẓāʿah*) embedded within his desire to "uncover," "reveal," (*istijlāʾ*) and "penetrate" (*nafdh*) the secret she conceals, reminding him of the first-ever autopsy he experienced, before his years in the legal profession hardened his sensibilities (*Y* 26). Indeed, as he realizes in this passage, it is a horror that the dry, bureaucratic, "official" language he is constantly scribbling on the pages of legal reports is specifically designed to conceal. In the end, Rim's "secret" dies with her, escaping the prying eyes of the prosecutor, his report, and the reader of *Diary* all at once. Like the Aït Yafelman in *Enquête*, Rim holds out the promise of a subject whose truth cannot be deduced through the state's formulaic legal procedures. Her truth lies elsewhere, in the pursuit itself, rather than in its fulfillment.

Shaykh Asfur embodies yet another form of native resistance to state-mandated ways of seeking. Like Rim, Asfur also holds the "key to the case" of Qamar al-Dawla, but in his own way. "There's no doubt that Shaykh Asfur now knows all the secrets of the case," the prosecutor thinks to himself at one point, after realizing Rim has escaped from the police chief's custody with Asfur's help. "But will he ever reveal anything to us? He himself is a locked mystery . . ." (*Y* 78). That Shaykh Asfur's ways of seeking are related to but distinct from police detection is evident from his intimate friendship with the police: he accompanies them on hundreds of investigations to track down criminals. "He was almost regarded by the police as one of the family" (*Y* 87). Fearing for his professional and social status, the prosecutor repeatedly worries that Asfur knows more about the novel's main mystery than he does, and indeed it is Asfur who provides the major clues in the case of Qamar al-Dawla, hinting through his poems that the prosecutor should "seek out women," thus drawing him to Rim, and later implying, through a poem about hunting for fish—"the first one was a slippery cod / the next a turbot fair / the third, a creature graced by God, / became the sailor's snare"—that the case involves multiple murders (*Y* 84). Asfur turns out to be right: Qamar al-Dawla's shooting was preceded by the strangling of his wife, whose body was dumped in the canal several months ago (a story the prosecutor confirms through yet another comic scene of exhumation and autopsy at a local cemetery), and it is followed by the murder of none other than Rim, his wife's sister, whose presumably drowned body is also found in the canal at the end of the novel. The prosecutor, in other words, is not wrong about Asfur: the mad shaykh knows the mystery behind the case, but his allusive, poetic way of speaking defies the truth-seeking methods used by representatives of the modern legal system like our narrator.

The relationship between the two forms of truth is epitomized in a key scene of interrogation between the prosecutor and the shaykh. Approaching the edge of his frustration, the prosecutor demands of Asfur, "'Who are you?' The man looked at me like he hadn't understood the question. I repeated it to him with violent emphasis. 'I'm . . . I'm Asfur,' he replied. 'I glean grains above the earth and worship the Lord below it [Alquṭ al-ḥabb fawq al-turāb, wa-aʿbud al-rabb taḥt al-turāb]" (*Y* 83).[63] The seeming illogic of these words belies their rhetorical richness in Arabic; as with all of Asfur's utterances, the form has its own meaning. The morphological parallelism between the two pairs of clauses (alquṭ al-ḥabb, aʿbud al-rabb; fawq al-turāb, taḥt al-turāb) highlights the antithesis in the meaning ("above the earth," "below the earth"), just as the paronomasia between the rhyming *ḥabb* and *rabb* also underscores their contrasting meanings (the humility of gleaning grains, the worship of an all-powerful God). There is meaning to these words, but it is not the meaning sought by the prosecutor's formulaic legal questions, "Who are you?" and "What is your profession?" Through his poetic reply, Shaykh Asfur advises the prosecutor to look for great significance in humble places, and to not become too arrogant about his social power as a legal officer, since it is often the grain-gleaners—that is, poor, mad beggars like Asfur—who draw closest to God and, by extension, a more all-encompassing truth. Asfur's language itself resists the logic of the state and its authorized practices for producing truth while at the same time offering another, more metaphysical truth, couched in the figure of the fisherman, whose work hunting fish is not unlike the detective's hunting answers (or the Sufi's hunting unity with the divine). Asfur is "that 'secret' giving us glimpses of the occulted world," and each "remains a perpetual, eternal puzzle we can never fully grasp . . . ."[64]

By engaging with persistently inscrutable figures like Rim and Shaykh Asfur, Raho and Hajja, the conscripted native detectives at the center of Hakim's *Diary* and Chraïbi's *Enquête* become disenchanted with the modes of investigation and objectification in which they have been trained. They recognize the extent to which their investigative tactics of "seeking," "investigating" (*enquête*), "uncovering" (*istijlāʾ*), and "knowing" (*ʿilm*) have forcibly and violently severed them from the objects under their investigation—namely, the others who might have constituted a community, a public. And thus both narrators, suspended between worlds, implicitly understand the bleakness of their narrative individualism, the desolation and isolation of a "refined sensibility." In al-Hakim's scenes of dissection and disinterment, and in Chraïbi's scenes of primordial involuntary memory, in the prosecutor's repeated attempts and failures to "decipher" Rim and Shaykh Asfur, and in Chief Ali's failure to find the Aït Yafelman when he returns to their *pays* in the final chapter—in all these moments, I read a simultaneous provincialization of the state's knowledge production and a validation of the supposedly "backward," "uncivilized" practices it claims to replace. Even if both novels also recognize and acknowledge the irrecoverability, possibly even the unreality, of those practices, they still invite them into the text as a potentially destabilizing, disruptive force. Even as they acknowledge, with Foucault, Miller, Mitchell, and others, that there is no "outside" to modern power, they still gamble that it is worth imagining a line of escape, even if only as an irrecoverable trace, an undissected body.

## CONCLUSION

Responding to very different moments of political disillusionment and rural suffering, both al-Hakim and Chraïbi turn to detective fiction. They do so not to offer distraction or "mere entertainment,"[65] but rather—quite the contrary—to draw their readers' attention ever more urgently to the legal and juridical obfuscations that have made this suffering possible. The central character in this drama is the conscripted detective, the native officer of the law who, despite his police training, nevertheless feels a continued affinity with those he must police, even if returning to their ranks is also impossible for him ("he cannot choose *not* to be modern").[66] Incompletely conscripted, these detectives stand in less as figures for the reader than as figures for the author, and particularly for the Arab author working in a colonial or postcolonial context.[67] Al-Hakim and Chraïbi find themselves caught between the desire to investigate poverty and reveal injustice and political corruption at its root, on the one hand, and the knowledge that the man of letters—the effendi, the *insectuel*, and, by extension, the prosecutor, the chief—in his hubristic claim to represent the real, is little better than a cop. In their hands, the Arab poetics of investigation restructures the novel as a space for imagining other potentialities of the subject—not a logical, all-knowing detective, but a comically defeated cop, thwarted by the pesky persistence of practices on the margins of the modern, which draw their vitality from alternative claims to history and memory. Their detectives are forced to cultivate a relationship with the *majhūl*, the unknown, unknowable realm proper to mysterious beauties, mad shaykhs, and earthy autochthones.

By dealing with questions of epistemology, al-Hakim and Chraïbi intervene in intellectual debates that, at the times of their respective writings, extended far beyond the pages of novels and literary magazines. The place of postcolonial Moroccans in the independent nation's police apparatus; the prestige or nonprestige of different languages, classes, and ethnicities in the national community; the similar levels of brutality encountered in the French-colonial and royal postcolonial regimes—these were all questions of great urgency at the time of Chraïbi's writing, and he plays with the linguistic certainties that French and Moroccan readers might have taken for granted. Al-Hakim also engages fictionally, imaginatively, and critically in debates about legal, juridical, and medical transformations to Egyptian governance, while at the same time refusing to consign earlier forms of knowledge and seeking to the dustbin of progressive history. Al-Hakim and Chraïbi dramatize modernity not as the triumphant fusion of native authenticity with Western science but as an incomprehensible, arbitrary imposition of violence for the rural others whom the law takes as objects of reform, improvement, and humanization. For al-Hakim and Chraïbi, the "investigation" or baḥth structure at the heart of the detective plot offers an opportunity to explore the fragmented, self-interrupting identity of the colonized or formerly colonized investigator—a stand-in for the real-life intellectual class in both contexts. For the authors in the next chapter, by contrast, the genre offers the potential for a new politics of literary form—one which forges communal action through the judicious deployment of scandal, shock, horror, revulsion, and other affects associated with "sensation fiction."

2

# Murder on the *ʿIzbah*

## *Spectral Legality and Egyptian Sensation Fiction, Yusuf Idris to Yusuf al-Qaʿid*

Your laws are but of two classes; the one makes criminals, the other punishes them . . . Let those whom the law protects consider it a protector; when did it ever protect *me*? When did it ever protect the poor man?

—EDWARD BULWER LYTTON, *PAUL CLIFFORD*

Hunger is a nonbeliever.

—ARABIC PROVERB

Both Tawfiq al-Hakim and Driss Chraïbi borrowed the conventions of detective fiction—already familiar to reading publics in 1980s Morocco and 1930s Egypt—to dramatize the contradictory web of affiliations in which the colonized legal officer finds himself. Neither the mystery of Qamar al-Din's murder, in al-Hakim's novel, nor that of the antigovernment rebel's return from Algeria, in Chraïbi's, is solved, yet each book in its own way reveals the disconnect between the investigator and the rural populace he has been charged with investigating. The peasants and the Aït Yafelman resist the modern state systems that attempt to render them legible, and they do so not by forging political or militant collectivities, but simply by refusing to recognize the authority of any legal doctrine or officer of the law. Whereas this nonrecognition frustrates the chief in Chraïbi's novel and the judges in al-Hakim's, causing them to view the rural subalterns as uncivilized, backward others, Ali and the prosecutor remain ambivalent, incompletely severed from their rural, popular roots. They not only recognize but are affectively moved by their countrymen's protests against the state's incursion into their lives, and these recognitions destabilize their highly cultivated status as knowing, investigating subjects. For all their social critique, however, both *Diary* and *Enquête* ultimately withhold the possibility of transforming this relationship of power between the narrating self and the objectified, rural other. Their detectives only end up reconfirming their status as *vrais chefs* (true chiefs).

Other Arab authors, by contrast, turned to crime fiction for a very different purpose: as a public forum in which to simultaneously expose the injustice of the law and to advocate for specific social, political, and economic reforms—to "invite real, or realistically squalid, crime into the house of fiction," as Martin Priestman puts it, thereby creating "a new kind of scandal within the walls of literature itself: the scandal of indifference."[1] This was an especially common use of the genre in mid-twentieth-century Egypt, following the Free Officers' Coup of 1952, which brought with it dreams not only of economic and political restructuring but also of attendant transformations to the nation's social order. The divide between Egypt's metropolitan elite and its rural underclass of landless farmworkers was arguably felt more acutely than ever in this historical moment,[2] as reflected in cultural productions from the period. The Egyptian countryside, once romanticized as a space of timeless continuance, was now opened up and revealed as a space of exploitation and corruption, on the one hand, and popular resistance and struggle, on the other.[3] The classed dynamics of rural labor in particular became the topic of many authors' explorations. The peasants were no longer a teeming, indistinguishable, timeless mass, but were woven into a complex web of socioeconomic relations involving small landowners, permanent and seasonal wage laborers, sharecroppers, small-time estate officials, and others.

Murder in particular—as a plot conceit and narrative structure—offered many authors precisely the level of scandal, horror, and outrage they wished to incite in their readers. By promising the drama of a murder plot, authors like Yusuf Idris and Yusuf al-Qaʿid—whose crime novels are the focus of this chapter—used the shock of peasant murder to open up a space that had been closed off from the public and the law for nearly a century, a space where the coercion and exploitation of peasant labor had long escaped regulation and become an unspoken, accepted matter of course: the *ʿizbah*.

A specifically Egyptian political, economic, and social formation, the *ʿizbah* (pl. *ʿizab*) is a "country estate consisting of a manor house and laborers' dwellings surrounded by farmland," or else, in more recent times, a "hamlet which was formerly such an estate and which is under the jurisdiction of the *ʿumdah* [local mayor] of a village."[4] Often described by historians as a quasi-private, quasi-public "realm of exception,"[5] the ʿizbah, in twentieth-century Egyptian cultural production, was a palimpsest-like space in which traces of both Ottoman and British colonial power persisted despite the changes brought by postcolonial nationalist rule. The agricultural regulations, managerial staff, and relations of production on the ʿizbah, first designed to shift Egypt's agrarian economy from subsistence to cotton and sugar monoculture farming in the nineteenth century, would persist well into the twentieth, even after the nominal implementation of land reform laws under Gamal Abdel Nasser in 1952.[6] In this sense, the ʿizbah was a zone of what

Samera Esmeir calls "spectral legality," a space in which arbitrary, sovereign power persisted despite its supposed eradication through the colonial implementation of the rule of law.[7] Far from regulating the use of violence and forced labor on the ʿizbah, colonial law instead privatized this violence, selling off lands owned by the Khedive and his family members to pay European creditors, and thereby placing these lands outside "the reach of the law's regulatory powers" and "purify[ing] the *concept* of the law from the business of labor management on the estates."[8] Esmeir reveals the sovereign rule persisting on the ʿizbah less as an "exception" to the law and more as the manifestation of "multiple zones of spectral legality" continuing on within the regime of modern law.[9] Yet, as Esmeir also points out, there were two areas in which state law *did* intervene in the affairs of the otherwise exceptional, private ʿizbah during the colonial period. The first was agricultural inspection and regulation, to ensure that farmers were producing and laboring at maximum capacity. The second—appropriately—was murder.[10] Since the colonial period, cases of murder and violent crime had invited the Egyptian public eye into the silenced realm of the ʿizbah, providing the pretext for an investigation of the otherwise unchecked corporal punishment, political imprisonment, labor exploitation, poverty, starvation, and disease that characterized peasant life in this space.[11] It is fitting, then, that murder on the ʿizbah should also serve as a premise for the reform-minded fictions of the post-1952 period.

This chapter focuses on two Egyptian crime novels set in the contested rural territory of the ʿizbah. The first, Yusuf Idris's *The Sinners* (*al-Ḥarām*, 1959), though written and published after the Free Officers' Coup, is set just before it, while the second, Yusuf al-Qaʿid's *Yaḥduth fī Miṣr al-Ān* (It's happening now in Egypt, 1974), is set in the very different historical conjuncture of Anwar Sadat's presidency (1970–81). During this time, the implementation of an "open-door" trade policy or Infitah (*infitāḥ*) and capitulation to American financial and military interests brought about the effective demise of Nasserist étatism and the deepening of social inequalities, particularly in the countryside.[12] This political, economic, and social shift was epitomized, for many Egyptians, in the triumphalist rhetoric surrounding President Richard Nixon's visit to the country in June of 1974, only one month after the House Judiciary Committee had begun impeachment proceedings against him. Nixon's visit forms the background of al-Qaʿid's *Yaḥduth*, and it is to this event that the "it" of the novel's title partly refers. Although these novels are normally read as belonging to discrete eras of Egyptian history—the first a novel of Nasserism, the second a work of Infitah-era protest—I argue that there is a continuity, rather than a rupture, between Idris's and al-Qaʿid's projects (and indeed, between both novels and al-Hakim's *Diary*). Like the authors of Victorian Newgate fictions before them, both Idris and al-Qaʿid wager that scandalous, shocking events, if innovatively (and, in Idris's case, viscerally) narrated, can alter a reader's way of seeing, jolting her out of complacency and into a state of agitation that (the authors hope) can be turned to political purpose. Al-Qaʿid and

Idris transform fiction into a form of incitement, and they do so through a very specific narrative structure.

Initially, in both novels, the reader is forced into what I call "seeing like an effendi": the portrait we receive of the countryside is focalized through the eyes of landowning, upper-class characters, and it thus offers an exaggeratedly dehumanized portrait of the ʿizbah's laboring underclasses, from its landed fellahin to its landless day laborers and seasonal migrant workers. Through this initial narrative positioning, both novels subtly accuse the reader of complicity with (or, at least, tacit consent to) the exploitative and immiserating relations of production on the ʿizbah. With the revelation of a scandalous murder, however, the reader is invited to view things differently, this time from the point of view of the supposed criminal, who is, in both cases, a poor and landless farmworker. This process of narration and renarration construes crime not as an innate proclivity of rural peasants (a notion common in the field of Egyptian criminology at the time)[13] but as a social construction, the product of long-standing but ultimately mutable material and cultural conditions. Peasants become criminals, Idris and al-Qaʿid wager, not through inherent vice, but rather—as both Paul Clifford and the Arabic adage have it—because they have been impoverished by man-made laws governing social policy, because poverty makes people hungry, and because hunger will drive people to do anything, even beg, steal, or kill, to survive. For characters like Idris's Aziza and al-Qaʿid's al-Dubbaysh ʿArayis, "sin is not a moral, but a social phenomenon," and "being honorable is not a matter of choice."[14]

In lifting the silence on the ʿizbah and exposing it as the local Egyptian space where global social and economic inequalities play out, Idris and al-Qaʿid delve into a previously unexamined "criminal" underworld to cultivate popular sympathy for the peasant victims of private greed. Yet, unlike their Victorian counterparts in "sensation fiction," these Egyptian authors' purpose is not to shore up the necessity of the detective police force at home and a corps of colonial administrators abroad;[15] instead, it is to dispel what I am calling the rhetoric of the *ʿādī*, the language of "ordinariness" or "normality" that surrounds peasant immiseration on the ʿizbah. In their fictions, "investigation" (*baḥth*) is not only a compelling narrative structure that creates suspense through the promise of a clarifying ending; it is also an imperative, a necessity incumbent on any cultural producer to break the national silence surrounding the conditions of peasant life on the estates. While Idris's agricultural inspector-*cum*-detective works to uncover the true story behind the mysterious murder of a newborn baby, Idris himself, through a series of intertwined plots, shows how cultural concepts like "the forbidden" (*al-ḥarām*), "shame" (*al-ʿīb*), and "honor" (*al-sharaf*) allow the upper classes to shore up the social order by equating poverty with immorality, making dishonor the exclusive province of the poor. As the novel's Arabic title—*al-Ḥarām*—indicates, Idris's aim is to "expose the real meaning of 'the forbidden,' 'shame,' and 'honor' in the Egyptian countryside,"[16] showing how "those who fling these words at others are also those who sin the most."[17] Through a similar technique of narration and renarration, in which investigation becomes a gradual exposure of class-based hypocrisy, al-Qaʿid, too, "brings out what is silenced and absented from Arab reality more generally," revealing how even the Nasser-era socialist organizations designed to support migrant laborers on the estates (e.g., the Arab Socialist Union, the Organization for the Protection of Migrant Workers, etc.) began betraying their public function for private gain in the neoliberal era of Anwar Sadat.[18] Writing their murder mysteries with a social purpose, both Idris and al-Qaʿid, while responding to different moments in modern Egyptian history, use scandal and sensation to take on the rhetoric of the ʿādī and the specter of sovereignty on the ʿizbah. By thematizing investigation and, by extension, reading itself, each novel—in its very narrative form—compelled its Egyptian readers to reconsider what they thought they knew about the *rīf* and the people who live, toil, and die there.

## HISTORIES AND FICTIONS OF THE ʿIZBAH

To understand the social relations governing peasant life on the ʿizbah, readers would do just as well consulting Egyptian film and fiction as they would turning to historical accounts. Indeed, because official archives tend to focus on the testimonies of the estates' managers rather than those of its laboring underclasses,[19] Egyptian fiction has served as a vital alternative record of peasant life and experience in this space. Writing of legal reforms throughout the nineteenth century and how they shaped life on the ʿizbah, Timothy Mitchell describes "acts of confinement, regulation, and supervision of the population" instituted by the governments of Muhammad ʿAli and, later, Khedive Ismaʿil,[20] disciplinary measures aimed at "putting villagers in their place," "fixing the rural population" onto the *ʿizab* and "inducing them to begin producing cotton and other commodities for European consumption."[21] This "fixing" of the peasants in place had long-lasting effects, which are reflected even in late twentieth-century Egyptian fiction. The narrator of al-Qaʿid's 1971 novel *News from the Meneisi Farm* (*Akhbār ʿIzbat al-Manīsī*), for example, describes how the estate's small-time farmers "belong to the land in one way or another, and remain on it regardless of changes in its ownership."[22]

The dynamics of sovereign power on the estates are likewise as central to Egyptian ʿizbah fictions as they are to historical accounts of this space. Samera Esmeir describes how, by the early twentieth century, "under the private legalities governing the estates, the landowner was the sovereign king of the island," giving "a sense that the peasants were totally abandoned by the world outside."[23] Timothy Mitchell also describes the proprietor of the ʿizbah as "an absolute master . . . accountable to no one . . . [who] could imprison, expel, starve, exploit, and exercise many other forms of arbitrary, exceptional, and if necessary, violent powers."[24] Compare these historical accounts with Idris's fictional description of Fikri Effendi, the "agricultural commissioner" (*maʾmūr al-zirāʿah*) of the estate farm in *The Sinners*:

> He was the master of all this property and the absolute ruler of everything it held. This *abʿādiyyah* or *taftīsh*—or, as it was sometimes called, this *dāyirah*[25]—comprised more than two thousand acres of the finest soil, and everything on it—people, houses, machines, livestock, and crops—was under his control. He was the sovereign lord of all this . . . He could even slap, punch or kick, if he wished . . . and no one could challenge his rulings.[26]

Where the English translation might bring to mind Esmeir's "sovereign king" ("master," "absolute ruler"), the Arabic—huwwa mālik hādhā al-mulk wa-l-āmir al-nāhī fīh—resonates with the oft-repeated Qur'anic phrase regarding those who "encourage what is good and forbid what is evil" (al-āmir bi-l-maʿrūf wa-l-nāhī bi-l-munkir), suggesting that the workers on Idris's farm estate perceive Fikri Effendi's authority to be as unshakeable as divine law. In the absence of official records documenting the unregulated violence against peasants on the estates throughout the late nineteenth and early twentieth centuries, fictions like *The Sinners* offer unofficial substitutes.

Finally, in *News from the Meneisi Farm*, al-Qaʿid's detailed description of farm estate administration closely parallels Esmeir's account of the ʿizbah's exemption from state oversight. In Esmeir's words, the sale of the Khedive's estates to private, often European, owners at the end of the nineteenth century "also resulted in releasing the central authorities of the state from the administration of vast areas of land" such that "the estate community interacted with market and state actors [solely] through the mediation of estate management."[27] Although it is set nearly fifty years after the period Esmeir examines, *News from the Meneisi Farm* gives a similar sense of the peasants' abandonment to the sovereign will of estate management. A section titled "Concerning Hajj al-Meneisi, the Elder," the owner of the estate, notes that "this land belongs to him. Each individual cultivates a piece of land, [but] they do not deal with the Cooperative Agricultural Association. [The Hajj] deals with it on his own . . . He sells the crops and settles their accounts . . . They do not appeal to their Member of Parliament or to the village Chief for assistance, because the Hajj takes care of everything . . . Throughout the farm's history, no outsider has ever been acquainted with its interior affairs."[28] Likewise, although the farm in *News from the Meneisi Farm* is said to "lie within the boundaries of Demisna village," still it "is totally independent from it . . . [The ʿizbah] has its own, private watchman who reports neither to the Mayor, nor to the Chief Watchman, nor to the police headquarters at Niklat al-ʿInab . . . Indeed, they do not follow Demisna in any way, and the Governor has no authority over them."[29] Given the secrecy and sovereignty that had governed life on the ʿizbah for so long, the task for mid-century authors like Idris and al-Qaʿid was to work as social historians, to expose this space by laying out the specifics of its social organization and its exemption, as privatized land, from government regulation.

Here a word about that social organization might be helpful, as the names and titles of the managerial class on the ʿizbah have imprecise English translations yet important implications. Although the estate owners were the ultimate authorities on these lands, they often did not live on the premises and only visited infrequently. In their absence, the *maʾmūr*—in my rendering, the "commissioner"—occupied the topmost level of estate management, alongside the *bāshkātib* or "secretary," who recorded and controlled the estate's finances with the help of a cadre of "undersecretaries" or *katabah* (sing. *kātib*). Beneath this class of administrators was a second tier of *khiwālah* (sing. *khūlī*), "overseers" who coerced peasant labor in the fields with canes, whips, and sticks. On Idris's twentieth-century farm estate, there is a further "middle class" of *usṭawāt* (sing. *usṭā*, a word borrowed from Turkish), of what we may call "drivers" or, more generally, "skilled laborers," those who can supervise the use of agricultural machinery. The stratum immediately beneath these skilled laborers is occupied by the fellahin, the farmers who live on the estate and either own or rent their portion of land from the owner himself. Lowest of all in this class system are the migrant or seasonal laborers (*ʿummāl al-taraḥīl* or *tarḥīlah*), who are brought in for the most menial and painstaking task on the farm estate: extracting cotton worms and their eggs from freshly sprouted cotton plants. These seasonal laborers are at the heart of Idris's novel.

After immersing the reader in the nightmarish world of landowners, clerks, and agricultural overseers—with depictions of the farmworkers as a teeming, animalistic herd—both Idris's *The Sinners* and al-Qaʿid's *Yaḥduth* turn around a crucial, hinge-like shift in narrative perspective designed to incite the reader's shock and indignation at a social system that impoverishes rural farmworkers and then criminalizes them for the poverty it itself has caused. Each novel creates this shock in a different way. Idris holds the reader suspended in the mind of the effendi class for the first half of *The Sinners*, only to reveal—in a shocking, graphic scene that tears through the text's midpoint—the kind of pain, shame, and suffering endured by the ʿizbah's lowest classes, its seasonal migrant laborers. Al-Qaʿid, meanwhile, confronts and accuses the reader from the very beginning of the novel by addressing her in the second person, on the one hand, and by refusing to play by the conventional rules of detective fiction, on the other. The Egyptian critic Ghali Shukri has thus referred to Idris's novel as "the second daughter of al-Hakim's *Diary of a Country Prosecutor*" (after ʿAbd al-Rahman al-Sharqawi's *Egyptian Earth* [*al-Arḍ*]). He argues that Idris transforms al-Hakim's "critical realism," which "condemns the constitutional laws that allow [an] unjust form of social organization to persist," into "revolutionary realism," which moves beyond mere representation "to explanation and analysis," and which "doesn't merely express a desire for change, but also lays out the path toward that change."[30]

If Idris's text narrates "murder on the ʿizbah" as a way of subtly implicating and then confronting the reader with the unchecked violence committed against migrant laborers, al-Qaʿid's does so as an insistent reminder of the desperately precarious lives of Egypt's poor and landless despite the triumphalist rhetoric surrounding Richard Nixon's 1974 visit and the Infitah more generally. Their fictions of baḥth, far from offering a pleasurable escape, challenge their readers to confront the rural realities so often silenced in colonial and nationalist discourse alike—realities in what al-Qaʿid calls "the *other* Egypt, the Egypt of the countryside and the teeming fellahin."[31]

## SEEING LIKE AN EFFENDI

Like any good detective novel, *The Sinners* begins with the discovery of a body. After performing his early morning ablutions, one of the ʿizbah's night watchmen spots a small white bundle on the banks of an irrigation canal. On closer examination, the bundle turns out to be the corpse of a newborn baby. Shocked and appalled, the guard reports his discovery to the estate commissioner, Fikri Effendi, who proceeds to investigate, thereby becoming the "internal focalizer" of this first half of the novel—that is, in Gérard Genette's terms, the narrator of the novel's first half says only what Fikri Effendi knows (with a few exceptions or "paralepses").[32] The commissioner immediately suspects the Gharabwa, the migrant laborers brought to the estate during the cotton season to pick worms from the plants' freshly sprouted buds. "It must be one of them," he proclaims. "They're Gharabwa and sons of bitches" (*S* 10). Like most of the estate's residents, Fikri Effendi views the migrant workers as an unclean, immoral, even inhuman, mass—"wretched people who wear ragged clothing and have a strange smell." Their existence is quite different from that of the "respected farmers" (fellahin) who live and work on the estate year-round. Though only slightly better off than the Gharabwa, these farmers—like the estate's managerial class—nevertheless deride the migrant workers as "miserable human refuse" (*S* 11–12).[33]

The movements of these seasonal laborers and their presence on the estate are determined by the specifics of cotton planting and harvesting. To bring them in at the appropriate time of year, Fikri Effendi must work with labor contractors in the western delta provinces of Tanta, Monufia, and Gharbia ("which one does not matter since Fikri Effendi is acquainted with many villages and many contractors"). He refers to these interchangeable, impoverished towns as "anthills" (*ʿishsh al-naml*, literally "ants' nests") because they are so densely populated, and because, as soon as he arrives with the promise of semisteady work, however scantly remunerated, "the numerous ants emerge from their holes," ecstatic at the possibility of earning a few piasters (*S* 12–13; *Ḥ* 19).[34] The metaphor of the ants is only one in a series of figures the narrator uses in this first half of the novel to describe the Gharabwa, all of which equate them with animals or commodities to be transported and exchanged. The trucks specially licensed for transporting the Gharabwa, for example, are "just like the special licenses for transporting bags of rice and livestock" (*S* 13), and they carry hundreds of Gharabwa men, women, and children with their overflowing foodstuffs "in a solid, teeming mass, so tightly packed you can hardly tell a man from a woman or a boy from an earthenware jar" (*S* 14).

Even after they arrive on the farm, the Gharabwa continue to be described as "a single, dense, dark-colored mass." The smells in their camp are indistinguishable from one another, and smells of cooking (frying oil, fish, matured white cheese, lentils, and onions) blend with smells of cleaning (soap, phenol) "in a strange and pungent whole, to create a distinctive odor which . . . the peasants call 'the migrant workers' smell." (*S* 15). In the eyes of the fellahin, as with Fikri Effendi, the Gharabwa are without distinguishable features, without gender, without humanity. "The gray-haired old man was a laborer, and so was the little boy. You couldn't see the difference between a man and a woman among them" (*S* 22). The third-person narrator of *The Sinners* thus presents the migrant workers to the reader through the eyes of the fellahin and the effendi alike. The descriptions are exaggerated, designed to shock and scandalize a Cairene reading public unfamiliar with working conditions on the rural ʿizab. Idris makes clever use of internal focalization, forcing readers to confront their own preconceptions about migrant workers. Readers become commissioners themselves, simply in the act of reading.

Accustomed to viewing the Gharabwa as an animalistic herd, Fikri Effendi is disturbed by the notion that one of these nameless, faceless laborers is, in fact, the murderer of a newborn infant. He cannot believe that in order to sniff out this criminal, he is going to have to look at the migrant laborers differently. "Normally, he thought about them only as hired laborers, farmhands who picked off worms, harvested cotton, and dredged drainage ditches . . . They were all the same: feet cracked from hunger and walking barefoot, calloused by the unyielding earth; thin, sunburned hands; and grim faces whose sorrow you couldn't tell from joy." Although he is certain that the murderer is among them, he still has trouble believing that in this "human herd," there are "Gharabwa women capable of having babies, legitimately or otherwise." To conduct his investigation, "he was compelled . . . to start looking at the migrant workers from a different angle" (*S* 22; *Ḥ* 37).

The important thing here is that we, too, as readers of *The Sinners*, are being "compelled to look at the migrant workers from a different angle." Through his narration—and through the Egyptian national silence surrounding the "spectral" space of the ʿizbah—Idris's readers have also "gotten used to seeing" the Gharabwa as an amorphous heap of human refuse. Now, however, alongside Fikri Effendi, they are being forced to consider these seasonal laborers "from a different angle." Idris places his educated readers in the mind of the effendi-detective, subtly accusing them of having similarly dehumanized and neglected the nation's migrant workers. His storytelling, however, will soon retrain us in a new way of seeing—one shaped not by the prejudices and obsessions of the ʿizbah's managerial class, but by dense, visceral descriptions of the everyday realities and sufferings of the migrant worker. Before we can get there, however, Fikri Effendi must solve the crime that served as the novel's original premise.

Ironically, it is only when he gives up his criminal investigation and reassumes his position as the estate's chief cotton commissioner that Fikri Effendi manages to sniff out the woman responsible for the infant's death. As it turns out, this otherwise "sovereign lord" of the estate farm lives in mortal fear not only of his human superiors—the "agricultural inspector," or *mufattish*, and the estate's owner—but also of the seemingly divine force of a natural enemy: the cotton worm. Every year, when the season comes to "combat the worm while still in the egg," Fikri Effendi—like all commissioners on large Egyptian ʿizab—goes through a time of "terrible testing" and "wears himself to the bone" in the fields, "leaving before sunrise to scout all the cotton fields, sniffing the air and fearing that, God forbid, his senses would pick up the scent of worms." "What he feared most," we are told, "was a lull in the battle" (*S* 57).[35] He has a lot at stake in the worm's eradication: if the eggs hatch and ruin the cotton crop, he will lose not only his job, but his entire life, since, "like most estate commissioners and managers, Fikri Effendi . . . had no house, no community, and no place to call his own" (*S* 57–58). Where conventional methods of detection like the police lineup fail Fikri Effendi elsewhere in the novel (as they failed al-Hakim's narrator before him),[36] his enduring fear of the cotton worm and the methods he has developed to combat its spread all arrive to help him solve the mystery. As he himself says early on, "all he had to do was look [the laborers] over and try to pick out the worm from their midst" (*S* 28). His most effective investigative tools are not those of the police detective, in other words, but those of the cotton worm detector in chief.

After a spike in worm eggs is reported midway through the novel, Fikri Effendi goes to inspect the fields on foot, to ensure that all the Gharabwa are working at maximum capacity. On his mission, he discovers a small shelter among the stalks, with a woman lying beneath it. The commissioner thinks he has sniffed out the culprit behind the cotton worm's rise: a lazy migrant worker. But he is actually on the brink of solving the novel's original crime—the case of the dead newborn on the canal bank. He interrogates one of his overseers, Arafa, about the woman's identity, and why she is sleeping instead of working. Arafa can only reply with a colloquial expression meant to shield the effendi's ears from such a gruesome story: "This is Aziza, Mr. Commissioner, sir . . . The tale's not fit for your excellency's ears [ʾism-alla ʿalaa maqaamak yaa saʿaadat al-beeh]" (*S* 61; *Ḥ* 85).

If, as readers of *The Sinners*, we spend the entire first half of the novel discovering the social order of the ʿizbah through the eyes of its managerial class, Arafa's aphoristic reply announces—both to the bey and to the reader—that we are about to rediscover the Gharabwa through their own eyes. *ʾIsm-alla ʿalaa maqaamak* thus functions as the colloquial hinge around which the entire novel turns.[37] The case of the dead newborn is now narrated to us from a new perspective—that of its mother and its murderer, a seasonal farmworker named Aziza. Back in her home village, Aziza lived with her husband Abdallah and their three children. With "no land to farm and no land to rent," Aziza and Abdallah "depended for their livelihood on seasonal migrant work." Describing their impoverished life,

Idris's language also takes on a tone of bare subsistence, as if in imitation of the sparseness it describes: "They got by [*ʿāshā*] . . . They collected their wages from Hagg Abd al-Rahim the contractor in the cotton season and lived on it for the rest of the year. They got by through force and trickery, sometimes on cheese, other times on dry bread and salt, but they got by, and that's all there was to it [*was-salaam*]" (*S* 66–67; *Ḥ* 92–93). Not only does the third-person narrative voice veer into colloquial Egyptian in this passage—for example, in the line "he worked for a daily wage . . . one day there was work, the next ten there wasn't" (yawm fiih, wa ʿashara maa-fiish); the repetition of the one-word sentence "*ʿāshā*" (they got by), the subsequent zeugma ("they got by through force and trickery, sometimes on cheese and other times on dry bread and salt"), the bare simplicity of the final "*was-salaam*"—all of these syntactic elements combined represent a major shift in tone, language, style and perspective from the earlier chapters in the novel focalized through Fikri Effendi and other members of estate management.

Yet, because Aziza and her husband live in such abject conditions, it is "inevitable" that Abdallah will get sick (*S* 67; *Ḥ* 93). Like many rural Egyptians living near standing water, he contracts the parasitic disease bilharzia, which leaves him unable to work and Aziza in charge of caring for him and feeding their three children. Thus, when Abdallah one day requests a sweet potato, Aziza does everything in her power to track one down for him, thinking it a kind of medicinal craving. As she trespasses on the field of a local farmer, she comes across the landowner's son. Although the man initially helps her track down a few remnants of sweet potato in the dirt, he ultimately assaults her, confining her to one of the holes they have dug and raping her. Not wanting to "drag her name through the mud" with the revelation of this scandal as it is happening, Aziza freezes in the ditch, unable to act or even cry for help. More than anything, what she feels, and fears, is *faḍḥ*—that is, causing a scandal, or making a scene. "You knew it was wrong and shameful [ḥarām wa ʿīb]," she chides herself later, referencing the titles of two Idris novels, "but you didn't resist him as you should have, fearing scandal [*al-faḍīḥah*]" (*S* 73; *Ḥ* 205). Here, as elsewhere in his work, Idris illustrates how thoroughly cultural conventions of morality are transformed into socioeconomic cudgels to keep the poor in their place. Aziza spends very little time fretting over her violated body; her concern is primarily with what people will think.

Although memory of the rape initially plagues her, Aziza is soon able to push it from her mind, since, in Idris's colloquial phrasing, "nothing erases a person's memory so much as the persistent search for something to eat [luʾmat il-ʿeesh]" (*S* 71; *Ḥ* 98). And yet, despite the persistent call of hunger—both her own and that of her family—Aziza soon realizes that she has become pregnant from the rape. She tries to terminate the pregnancy the only way she knows how, with "stalks of Jew's mallow, turning the handmill on her stomach, jumping from the roof," even "beseeching God to save her," but, as Idris's wry narrator puts it, "none of her prayers was answered, and what happened instead was something even more bitter: the cotton season arrived" (*S* 72; *Ḥ* 99). Note that the Arabic for "the cotton season arrived," *jāʾa al-mawsim*, includes no mention of "cotton." Idris knows what his readers know: that, as another Idrisian title has it, "cotton is king" in Egypt.[38] The pregnant Aziza ships off to the ʿizbah.

At first, the demanding physical labor of the fields helps Aziza forget about the rape and the pregnancy both. In another Idrisian zeugma: "Forgetting and remembering were but a small part of the many things that beat upon her in successive waves: the sun . . . the day with its summer heat, sweat, and thin bamboo switches whose blows were felt clear to the bone" (*S* 72). Soon, however, one form of labor must give way to another. The contractions begin while she is still at work in the fields, and she struggles to conceal the pain. She manages to finish out the day's work and make it back to the Gharabwa camp, but at night the contractions increase in frequency and intensity. She sneaks away to give birth by the side of the canal, making sure not to forget "the egg she had borrowed or the half-burned piece of dry willow stick." It is here that Idris segues into the novel's most graphic and sensational scene, which is worth quoting at length:

> Putting the dry willow stick between her teeth, she squatted on the ground. As each successive wave of pain surged within her, she sank her teeth to their roots in the dry wood and squeezed a handful of moist earth from the canal until, its moisture gone, it became hard, and she flung it aside.
>
> Nor did she forget what she must do. As soon as the baby's head appeared, she broke the egg, and smeared herself with its slippery contents in the hope of helping the head to slide out.
>
> And finally the baby came . . .
>
> It slipped out all at once, and as though her soul flowed out with it, she grew a little dizzy, and then lost consciousness for a moment. It was only a short moment, but when she came to, she heard, she truly heard, a soft cooing sound. It was the baby, without a doubt. Then, all of a sudden, it cried. A cry that seemed to her as if it filled the whole world and could be heard by everyone.
>
> She had not prepared herself for that moment. She had thought only about ridding herself of the evil swelling that had exhausted her for so long . . . Now that she had freed herself from it, it was crying and threatening her with a bigger scandal than ever . . . She reached out a trembling, unsteady hand, and it fumbled with the living, human mass until a finger, automatically, found the mouth . . . mouth . . . the real mouth of a suckling infant . . . The child suckled her finger for a moment. A brief moment, but it electrified her. A strange, violent feeling flowed from that small fleshy cave to her finger, her arm, and then her whole body . . .
>
> But all this took no more than a moment. Afterwards the child cried. Her hand went swiftly back to close its mouth. The small opening tried to free itself from the fingers laid across it, and their pressure increased . . .
>
> All at once, Aziza came to herself and found her hand pressed tightly over the baby's mouth. At the same moment, she sensed that the child was still, too still. And in a hoarse, frightened, trembling voice, she cried:
>
> "Oh my God" [*yaa lahwii*]. (*S* 74–75; *Ḥ* 102–3, translation modified)

Idris doubtless drew on his professional training as a medical doctor to conjure this scene.[39] He is known in Arabic letters as a master of defamiliarizing description, particularly in graphic scenes involving sex and the body. Indeed, as Ghali Shukri notes, sex, gender, and politics are almost always linked in Idris's work.[40] Aziza's story is likewise constructed to create shock. Teeth sunk to their roots in a willow stick, handfuls of mud squeezed dry and flung aside, a hand pressed over the newborn's "fleshy cave" (*jaḥr laḥmī*) of a mouth—we are clearly meant to taste, feel, touch, and sense this scene. Idris spares no taboo around birth as a physical process, as *labor*.[41] All of a sudden, we have been jolted from the effendi's detached, dehumanizing perspective to Aziza's visceral, all too human one. Fikri Effendi, our stand-in detective, has solved the case of the newborn's murder, yet the truth turns out to be even more unsettling than the mystery. To cover up the scandal, and to continue earning six piasters a day, Aziza has endured rape, virtual enslavement, birth, infanticide, and puerperal fever, all alone and in secret, in a desperate effort to survive. Idris's description of this reality is nothing less than a confrontation. We may no longer see like an effendi. We must now feel like a laborer.

In this way, *The Sinners* explores the possibilities of storytelling as a social tool, and it does so both formally and thematically. Just as it invites the reader to view the Gharabwa "from a different angle" by eclipsing Fikri Effendi's voice in the second half of the novel, so too Aziza's tale functions thematically as the catalyst for an unprecedented mixing between the ʿizbah's landed fellahin and its landless migrant workers. This mixing begins with the farm children who, after playing with the Gharabwa, discover that "the other boys' faces were all different from one another's and they did not all look alike as they had thought before" (*S* 85). The change then spreads to the adults as they congregate around Aziza, who has become violently feverish after her ordeal—a puerperal fever that eventually kills her. "It was around the shelter and Aziza's sick bed that the farm people and the migrant workers became acquainted . . . . The farm people discovered that the migrant workers had villages too, and that like them they knew about farming and worked the land . . . Likewise, they . . . had complaints about their boss, and reasons to complain about the commissioner, the administration, and the estate [ʿizbah]" (*S* 100). Aziza's story has shown the fellahin that the Gharabwa are not simply a dark, teeming, animalistic mass, but a collection of individuals, each with their own story. At the same time, the story has also built class solidarity between both groups, forming them into a class-conscious collectivity numerous enough to challenge the sovereign rule of estate management. The story of Aziza thus forges a common struggle, both within the diegesis of *The Sinners* (between the fellahin and Gharabwa) and beyond the pages of the novel (between the implied metropolitan reader and the laboring rural underclasses).

Yet the hope is short-lived. When the novel was first published in 1959, the coming of "revolution" and the "Agricultural Reform Law," narrated in its "Epilogue," were said to fulfill in material form the class-bridging promise offered in

Aziza's story. The landowner sells the estate land and everything that goes with it to the farmworkers, and he "even razed the mansion," effacing the last traces of the previous regime (*S* 113). With the novel's republication in 1977, however, Idris made several revisions to the text's original parable-like ending. In this new version, the narrator notes that the landowner only sold the land "so that the [land reform] law would not apply to him," and he describes the "new landowners" as merely "nominal," placing the word "landowners" itself in parentheses.[42] These changes certainly reflect Idris's disillusionment with the actual results of Nasser's 1952 land reform laws, which were, as Timothy Mitchell argues, less a flagship project of the new regime than a ruse to secure popular support for its takeover.[43] Reading according to the conventional narrative of the Arabic novel's "development," therefore, we might interpret Idris's edits as yet another instance of post-1967 disillusionment and "self-criticism," a cynical reflection on the naïveté of Nasserism and pan-Arabism following the crushing defeat of the Arab forces in the June War.[44]

I would argue, however, that even the 1959 edition of *The Sinners*—the one without Idris's disillusioned revisions—ends ambivalently, with no sure promise that either Aziza's story or the agricultural reform law have indeed brought justice to the ʿizbah. Even as land reform does away with the estate's mansion, stables, administration, commissioner, inspector, workmen, guards, and day laborers, still, we are told, "some" of these new landowners "began to grow bigger, become rich, and hire laborers," while others "grew smaller, became poorer, and put themselves out for hire" (*S* 113). It is as though a natural process is resuming, revolution being supplanted with counterrevolution. And even before this description, which comes from the novel's rather pat "Epilogue," one wonders whether Aziza's story has really made such a difference to life on the ʿizbah, when the sounds of the truck carrying her corpse away in secret are said to be "borne on the winds and slowly absorbed into the huge masses of darkness crouching on the breast of creation," replaced by the voices of the estate's overseers yet again, shouting at the line of toiling migrant laborers: "Get down lower, boy . . . lower, girl" (waṭṭī yā walad . . . waṭṭī yā bint) (*S* 109; *Ḥ* 149). Far from unifying the Gharabwa with the fellahin in the common cause of demanding justice, Aziza, her body, and her tale have been reabsorbed into the darkness and the night, and the Gharabwa have returned to the cotton plants, their backs stooped over in nameless, faceless lines. What kind of change have Aziza's life, death, and posthumous story actually wrought in this novel? And what, following Idris's implicit metafiction in this text, can *The Sinners* itself hope to accomplish?

The novel is not unambiguously hopeful; nor does it view political or legal solutions as the most effective agents of social transformation. Land reform, after all, will not affect the culture of shame and scandal that hushed Aziza into silence and suffering. It is only by interrogating these cultural concepts and practices, relativizing them through new representations, as Idris does here and throughout his work, that revolution can reach the level of the social. Narrative structure, then, is not merely a choice designed to achieve a particular artistic effect, but a social act in *The Sinners*. Having been forced to confront their effendi-like sensibilities in the first half of the novel, Egyptian readers are subsequently thrust into the "undignified," "scandalous," *ḥarām* life of the migrant worker, compelled—by the novel's form itself—to feel the pain of rape and forced birth. It is not Aziza who has sinned, but the "heretical class society" that is at fault, and thus, "there is nothing to save the poor from the forbidden, shame, and sin except the eradication of poverty."[45]

## SEEING LIKE A DEVELOPER

Like *The Sinners*, Yusuf al-Qaʿid's *Yaḥduth* concerns a murder on the ʿizbah, and, like Idris, al-Qaʿid exposes the exploitative social relations in this realm of "spectral legality." Yet, unlike Idris, al-Qaʿid never allows his readers to fully occupy the mind of the effendi class. There is little in the way of free indirect discourse in his novel. Instead, the author enters into a direct, explicitly metafictional relationship with readers from the very beginning, addressing them in the second person and presenting them with a series of primary documents (testimonies, interviews, and reports), which come to form the text of the novel itself. The narrator of *Yaḥduth* is thus also an author, and he frequently intervenes in the narration to jolt the reader out of complacency, preventing her from fully subscribing to the village officials' views by exaggerating them, on the one hand, and by pointing out, in copious footnotes, their numerous lies and falsifications, on the other. Instead of saving the surprise of the murder's explanation for the end of his detective novel, al-Qaʿid reveals it in the book's first several pages, thus initiating what I call his poetics of confrontation. He refuses to offer readers the entertainment and escape of a detective novel. Instead, he explicitly tells them that he wants to "torture [their] consciences" by exposing them to the scandalous cheapness with which officials treat peasant life in the provinces (*YMA* 174). He will do this through multiple exaggerated and parodic stylizations of official speech and of the Infitah-era rhetoric of economic and social "development." Finally, where Idris's critique of the social system that enables peasant misery on the ʿizbah extends only to the officials who manage the estates (and, metafictionally, to the readers themselves), al-Qaʿid also implicates another figure from the Egyptian social order in this shared guilt—none other than the author himself.

Before examining the finer points of al-Qaʿid's poetics of confrontation, a brief summary of this complexly constructed novel is in order.[46] Set in a number of villages and towns in the Egyptian province of Beheira (in the western Nile delta just south of Alexandria), the events recounted in *It's Happening Now* take place in June 1974, on the eve of President Richard Nixon's visit to Egypt and tour of the countryside by train. In conjunction with this visit, a shipment containing large quantities of food aid from the United States arrives in the village of al-Dahriyyah. The chairman of the village council (who remains nameless throughout the novel) is instructed not only to distribute the aid, but also to ensure that each recipient understands their portion as "a personal gift . . . sent by President Richard Nixon, international man of peace" (*YMA* 23).[47] But the chairman soon finds himself unsure of how to distribute the aid most equitably. He consults his "lifelong friend" the doctor, who suggests it should be given only to the pregnant women in al-Dahriyyah—not because this seems fairest, but because it will put the doctor in control of the food and allow him to distribute it only to his best-paying clients, pregnant or not. In exchange, he hopes these clients will lend him enough money to build a private clinic for himself, even though, as a footnote from the author-narrator informs us, his contract as a public servant in the nationalized Egyptian health system strictly forbids such an enterprise (*YMA* 31).[48] The chairman, meanwhile, sees himself in a dream catapulted into the prestigious position of governor of nearby Alexandria, thanks to the overwhelming success of the welcoming celebration he is about to organize for Nixon. Blinded by a combination of ambition and superstition, he agrees to the distribution plan proposed by the doctor, and they push it through an easily manipulated village council meeting.

Meanwhile, the landless "agricultural workers" (*ʿummāl zirāʿiyyūn*, sing. *ʿāmil zirāʿī*) of al-Dahriyyah soon hear about the arrival of the food aid, and one man in particular—his name, we later learn, is al-Dubbaysh ʿArayis—comes up with a plan to trick the authorities and secure food for his impoverished family, even though his wife Sudfah is not pregnant. (The names are significant here: *dubbaysh* means "rough-cut," as a stone, or "crass," as a person, and *ṣudfah* is "coincidence," "happenstance.") He straps some old bits of rag and hay to her belly, covers her in a long robe, takes her in to the doctor's office, and is immediately given a portion of the aid. However, word of the trick soon reaches the doctor, and, together with a battalion of police officers, he storms al-Dubbaysh's house to take back the food. In retaliation, al-Dubbaysh confronts the doctor in his office, screaming at him and eventually knocking him unconscious. He is arrested shortly thereafter, and the chairman transfers him to the prison in the regional capital, al-Tawfiqiyyah, under the care of another "lifelong friend," the "respected officer." In the middle of the night, al-Dubbaysh suffers a severe beating at the hands (it is implied) of the police. The officer quickly has him transferred to the regional hospital, but al-Dubbaysh dies almost immediately. Not wanting to shoulder the blame for the farmworker's death, the officer ensures that he is buried in an unmarked grave, and the doctor, chairman, and officer then meet to decide how to handle the case. Either they can assert that al-Dubbaysh was an enemy of the state organizing a protest of Nixon's visit and thereby threatening national security (a plan they refer to as "D.E.," or "Dubbaysh Existed"), or they can attempt to prove that al-Dubbaysh never existed at all, and thus avoid the possibility that authorities above them will continue to investigate the case (a plan they refer to as "D.N.," for "Dubbaysh Never Existed") (*YMA* 123). In the end, they decide to follow the latter plan, which only works because the farmworker was so poor he lacked even the most basic documentation to prove his existence. Soon after, a mysterious visitor arrives in al-Dahriyyah from the regional capital (it turns out he was a nurse at the hospital where al-Dubbaysh died), and it seems for a moment as if plan "D.N." will be foiled: the visitor informs al-Ghilban ʿAbd Allah, a friend and fellow worker of al-Dubbaysh's, that there has been a conspiracy to cover up al-Dubbaysh's death. Al-Ghilban subsequently informs Sudfah, then gathers a group of farmworkers who vow to obtain justice for their friend. Yet because they cannot produce any written documentation definitively attesting to al-Dubbaysh's existence, their efforts to avenge him, find his grave, and obtain state compensation for his family ultimately prove fruitless.

These events, however, are not revealed to the reader in the neat, chronological manner in which I have narrated them here. Rather, they are disclosed gradually, through citations from the various primary documents collected in al-Dubbaysh's case file. Furthermore, al-Qaʿid purposefully spoils the ending of the "mystery of the dead farmworker" in a passage of explicit metafiction from the novel's very first pages.

> Normally, the conventions of the profession would dictate that I should conceal the fact of the farmworker's death from you. It would be much more interesting if I told you about his mysterious nocturnal disappearance and we followed the adventures of the Officer's search [baḥth] for him everywhere, only to discover in the end that he had died . . . But I've disclosed my secret and exposed my plan. Still, I don't want you to forget about the farmworker's death. In fact, I'll remind you of it every step of the way throughout this novel. (*YMA* 16)

The author-narrator "Yusuf al-Qaʿid" is more interested in confronting readers with the violent realities continually transpiring outside the text than allowing them to escape within it. Meanwhile, the biographical author Yusuf al-Qaʿid refuses to turn the reading of crime fiction into a pleasurable parlor game of decipherment. Unlike the conventional mystery author, he refuses to maintain a monopoly on knowledge, judiciously disclosing only fragmentary bits in order to "secure the reader's interest in [the] novel and ensure that he runs along breathlessly behind the words" (*YMA* 15). On the contrary, al-Qaʿid refers to these narrative strategies as "weapons" and vows to relinquish them in the title to the novel's second chapter, "The Author Surrenders his Most Important Weapons to the Reader" (*YMA* 15). Like al-Qaʿid's other novels, then, *Yaḥduth* "makes the novel itself into an object of narrative contemplation."[49]

By spoiling the mystery in advance, al-Qaʿid frees readers from the task of decipherment and forces them to confront instead the exaggeratedly dehumanizing rhetoric used by the village officials, on the one hand, and its large landowners, on the other. This rhetoric is readily apparent in the primary documents collected in al-Dubbaysh's case file, which comprise the novel's first several chapters.

The doctor, for example, frequently refers to the farmworkers for whom he is supposed to care as "half-human, half-animal creatures" who are hardly worth his time (*YMA* 20, 38). The testimony given by the estate owner on whose land al-Dubbaysh was working the day of his death goes even further. In a chapter sardonically titled "A Feudal Lord of the 1975 Variety Wonders, Why do the Poor Covet What the Rich Have?" this landowner affirms that on the day al-Dubbaysh "disappeared," he had "twenty-three and a half laborers" working his lands, and then explains this rather odd calculus thus: "Well, there were twenty men, two old men, and five children. Old men and children are paid half-wages. So the total was twenty-three and a half" (*YMA* 66).

Littered throughout the first half of *Yaḥduth*, the exploitative, dehumanizing language of officialdom and the landed upper classes reaches its apex in the final chapter of book 2, "The Lifelong Friends' Last Meeting." The officer, doctor, and chairman get together at the doctor's villa to decide what they will do about the al-Dubbaysh Affair, now that the officer's investigation is over. "Thanks to the officer's cunning," the narrator notes, "the whole issue [of al-Dubbaysh's death] had passed them by without doing any harm, and it was in fact transformed into a rare moment of human friendship among three men whose bad luck and empty pockets . . . had thrown them into a hell called the countryside [*al-rīf*]" (*YMA* 121). It is here that these "lifelong friends" will decide to claim that al-Dubbaysh never existed (plan D.N.). Although the chairman expresses some initial reservations—"What will people say?"—the officer reassures him as follows: "What people? Al-Dubbaysh was born to die. He's been dead since the day he was born . . ." The three then proceed to toast "the living dead man, al-Dubbaysh ʿArayis" (*YMA* 124, 128). What concerns the officer, however, is that some "revolutionary agitators" in the village will discover the case and cause a ruckus. Now it is the doctor's turn to reply, which he does while laughing: "You're in the Egyptian countryside in 1975. Political acts? Nooo [*nūūūū*] . . . Objective understanding? Nooo . . . Freedom of assembly? Nooo . . . Class consciousness? Nooo . . ." (*YMA* 125).[50] Given how severely the farmworkers have been treated at the hands of the state, the officials need not fear any collective action or revolutionary agitation from them. What Timothy Mitchell calls a "culture of fear" has subdued them into silence.[51]

The doctor, officer, and chairman, in their last meeting, are banking on the hope that the villagers of al-Dahriyyah will turn al-Dubbaysh into a legendary figure like al-Zanati Khalifah, Abu Zayd al-Hilali, or al-Adham al-Sharqawi—the popular heroes of famous Egyptian narrative ballads—rather than view him as the victim of official state violence.[52] As it turns out, the officials' hopes are fulfilled, for as the narrator informs us in the novel's first chapter, "with the coming of night, al-Dahriyyah forgot the story of the farmworker . . . Some said he was a poor man and a victim, while others said he deserved what happened to him and more, that water will never flow uphill, and that not even al-Adham al-Sharqawi or al-Zanati Khalifah could have gotten away with saying that the mule was in the pitcher, as the saying goes" (*YMA* 12).[53] Here al-Qaʿid's narrator does not applaud but overtly criticizes the oral narrative forms and languages proper to the countryside and the fellahin. The peasants absolve themselves from taking any action against their daily oppression by continuing to believe in such heroes' future arrival.[54] In al-Qaʿid's satire, colloquial Arabic and popular narrative forms like the *mawwāl* and the *sīrah* are not necessarily a subversive or subaltern language that, simply by virtue of being unofficial, challenges or disrupts the formal Arabic of state discourse. Folk narrative forms do not contrapuntally contest; rather, they only reinforce discourses of power, transforming murder into a timeless tall tale.[55]

There is one character, however, who will go on to seek justice and retribution for al-Dubbaysh ʿArayis's death. Fellow farmworker al-Ghilban ʿAbd Allah assembles a group of landless laborers who turn to a series of official organizations seeking acknowledgment of al-Dubbaysh's murder and compensation for his wife and children. (Like the name "al-Dubbaysh," which means "rough-cut," the name "al-Ghilban ʿAbd Allah" can be translated—tragicomically—as "the poor man who worships God.") Yet al-Ghilban and his band will only be disappointed by the various institutional representatives they consult, from the secretary general of the Arab Socialist Union (ASU) and chair of the "Office for the Protection and Care of Migrant and Day Laborers' Rights," to the "basic unit" (*wiḥdah asāsiyyah*) of their local union. The narrator of *Yaḥduth* knowingly casts al-Ghilban and the reader into this nightmarish world of nameless bureaucrats, affirming that "because the majority of characters you've met in this novel have been nameless, we'll finish out the few remaining pages in the same vein" (*YMA* 143). Since the readers already know the circumstances surrounding al-Dubbaysh's arrest, disappearance, and death, they are once again freed from the task of decryption and forced to confront the dismissive language used by these officials, even those who, as professed socialists and labor union leaders, are supposedly on the workers' side. This time, however, al-Qaʿid takes aim not at the landowners and *effendiyya* who were also the target of Idris's satire in *The Sinners* but at the triumphalist rhetoric of "development" surrounding Sadat's economic reforms and Nixon's visit to Egypt in 1974.

This satire culminates in a chapter titled "When al-Dubbaysh was Turned into an Investment Project," in which al-Ghilban and his band pay a visit to the town's *ʿarḍaḥāljī*, a "professional self-employed writer of applications and petitions" to the central government.[56] This particular public scribe, however, "travels to America every summer, and thus has a more realistic viewpoint on things" (*YMA* 160). Rather than lodge the farmworkers' complaint against the government in writing, thus serving his traditional role as helpful intermediary, the ʿarḍaḥāljī suggests instead that they file a lawsuit against President Nixon himself, since "he's the one who caused this whole thing, from 'knock-knock' to 'see ya later'" (*YMA* 159).[57] When al-Ghilban protests that he, his group, and al-Dubbaysh's family combined couldn't come up with the money for such a lawsuit, the ʿarḍaḥāljī suggests they bring in a rich financial backer for the project, who, in exchange for his investment, will receive three quarters of the total profits. If they succeed in making ten thousand Egyptian pounds off the lawsuit,

> "you could turn al-Dahriyyah into a touristic village . . . We'll turn the age of the free market to our benefit and find an American investor to supply 49% of the project's capital. After that there are thousands of things we could do. Al-Dahriyya is a treasure. We could start a cannery, look for oil, or extract mineral water from the earth. We could start a carpet factory in cooperation with Iran and sell the products to Europe, or we could build cabins and chalets on the riverbanks for tourists to spend their vacations near the mighty Nile River."
>
> The young man spent a long time discussing ways to profit off of al-Dubbaysh ʿArayis's murder. (*YMA* 161)

In the simultaneously dystopian and all too real world of *It's Happening Now*, the ʿārḍaḥāljī is seeing not "like an effendi" but "like a developer." He is selling the landless farmworkers precisely the same kinds of projects that American development agencies like the United States Agency for International Development (USAID), the International Monetary Fund (IMF), and the World Bank sold to the Sadat regime starting in the mid-1970s. In theory, these projects of "decentralization" and "privatization" were meant to democratize government by empowering local, provincial, and village officials and thereby—it was assumed—increasing the economic opportunities available to small farmers.[58] In practice, however, these kinds of projects—canneries, tourist villages, petroleum extraction, and so on—merely entrenched (and, in many cases, increased) preexisting inequalities between the rural upper classes and the working poor, who, "in the absence of a minimum wage, and under a system of patronage, policing, and surveillance in rural Egypt that prevented [them] from protesting against or organizing to change their condition," had been left "with no resources but their labor."[59] Al-Qaʿid's character al-Dubbaysh is the quintessential product of this new social order. His "main distinguishing feature, from the moment he was born, was that he was one of those men who doesn't own an inch of land." His only real possessions were "his two arms and his strength" (*YMA* 96).

Al-Qaʿid's critique of US-financed development projects specifically and of the era's neoliberal ethos more generally are woven throughout this third and final book of *Yaḥduth*. Even before introducing readers to the ʿarḍaḥāljī, the author-narrator parodies the rhetoric of American consumerism saturating Egyptian media at this time—only one year, it should be noted, after the United States had backed Israel against Egypt in the 1973 October War, which killed between five and ten thousand Egyptians. "Witnesses sold [al-Dubbaysh's life] as cheap as dirt," the author-narrator writes, "in exchange for promises that would never be kept . . . The American president, come from across the Atlantic! He is the only man in our world capable of solving all the problems of the Middle East . . . Cairo will become a city of canned beef [*biloobiif*], Alexandria hills of fine white flour, Port Said will be filled with mountains of televisions, cars, tape recorders, refrigerators, washing machines, and water heaters" (*YMA* 155). The landless peasant's life, it is implied, might have been spared, if only local officials and villagers had not been so preoccupied with preparations for Nixon's visit and all the private profit it was meant to signify: for the officials, ambitions of promotion; for the villagers, an open market for new, imported commodities. "The seventies," as al-Qaʿid once said in an interview, "only offered individualistic solutions that did not create opportunities for communal development or national projects to improve society in general. They essentially killed off the notion of civil society."[60]

Alongside washing machines, televisions, and tape recorders, "peace" was another commodity sold to Egyptians on the pages of the national newspapers and in speeches made by both presidents throughout their tour. In a speech given at the presidential palace in Cairo on June 13, 1974, for example, Nixon affirmed that the goal of his visit was twofold: "to achieve economic advancement in all areas, for the good of your people . . . and to achieve a true, just, and lasting peace." According to Nixon, each of these goals was dependent on the other. "We cannot achieve advancement without achieving peace, and without advancement and hope, there can be no peace."[61] Both the speeches and the newspapers that reproduced them contributed to this association between Nixon, US capital, "development," and peace, and the promises of privatization drew massive crowds of supporters, both on the pages of the newspapers (where various government agencies and private corporations paid for advertisements in support of Nixon and Sadat, as in figures 1 and 2) and in the streets of Cairo and Alexandria (figures 3 and 4). One enterprising television shop in the well-to-do Cairo suburb of Heliopolis even offered a discounted rate on "American-made" RCA televisions "in honor of President Nixon's visit to Cairo" (figure 5).

The promise of peace was thus made contingent on Egypt's consumption of American products and its implementation of economic policies favorable to American business. By contrast, in al-Qaʿid's studied satire of capitalist triumphalism, and in his ʿarḍaḥāljī's method for transforming violent death into private profit, there is a combination of despair and outrage at the idea that murder could be so thoroughly swept under the rug without popular protest. At the end of the chapter, al-Ghilban quietly withdraws from the scene, "leaving [the farmworkers] to build the palaces of their hopes and dreams from the blood of al-Dubbaysh, whose location was still unknown to anyone in al-Dahriyyah." Arriving at home, he asks himself: "What's happened to this country [ʾil-balad garaa-l-haa ʾeeh]?" (*YMA* 161). Al-Ghilban is not the courageous hero who will lead the farmworkers in an uprising against their capitalistic masters but the victim of a nightmarish bureaucracy. What he offers is only a gesture of indignation; yet, for the first time in the novel, the everyday colloquial language in which it is uttered stands in sharp relief against the public scribe's and the two presidents' overweening, dehumanizing language of profit.

الأهرام - ١٣/٦/٧٤ - ٥

في ٦ اكتوبر ٧٣، العاشر من رمضان ، ومع القرار التاريخي للرئيس المؤمن

محمد أنور السادات

ومع كل الثقة بالنفس والإيمان، عبرت الجيوش العربية وحررت وغيرت وجه التاريخ، وبدأ مع هذا عهد جديد باستعادة الشعب العربي والمقاتل العربي ثقته بنفسه في الحاضر والمستقبل، وبدأ العالم كله يشعر بالوجود العربي والإرادة العربية في استرداد الأرض وحقوق شعب فلسطين. ومن هذا المنطلق ومن أجل السلام ومن أجل الحق والعدل

يرحب

شعب الإسكندرية

بالرئيس الأمريكي

ريتشارد نيكسون

ويبايع بطل العبور القائد المؤمن الرئيس

محمد أنور السادات

داعيا الله أن يحقق على يديه آمال شعبنا ، والله ولي التوفيق ،

أمين الاتحاد الاشتراكي

المهندس عيسى شاهين

محافظ الاسكندرية

عبد التواب أحمد هديب

FIGURE 1. Full-page statement of support for Nixon by the "people of Alexandria," signed by the city's mayor, ʿAbd al-Tawwab Ahmad Hudayb, and the chair of the Arab Socialist Union (ASU), ʿIsa Shahin, *al-Ahrām,* June 13, 1974.

WORLD WELFARE

OUR FIRST INTEREST IS DIRECTED TOWARDS WORLD WELFARE

THE MODEL OF CO-OPERATION BETWEEN EGYPTIAN AND U.S. AUTHORITIES IN CLEARING THE SUEZ CANAL GIVES A CLUE TO THE RANGE AT WHICH OUR TWO COUNTRIES CAN BUILD A TRUE FRIENDSHIP, AND SINCERE COLLABORATION FOR THE SAKE OF WORLD WELFARE.

WE OPENED A NEW ERA IN WORLD RELATIONS, AND GAVE AN EXAMPLE OF CO-OPERATION BETWEEN PEOPLES IN THE INTEREST OF WORLD PEACE

WE HOPE TO REALIZE ALL OUR OBJECTIVES AND REACH LASTING PEACE IN THE REGION OF THE MIDDLE EAST

PRESIDENT
MOHAMED ANWAR EL SADAT

THE MINISTRY OF HOUSING AND RECONSTRUCTION IN THE ARAB REPUBLIC OF EGYPT, TAKES A GREAT PLEASURE, AFTER THE COURSE OF HISTORY HAS BEEN CHANGED, AND THE ARAB PEOPLES REGAINED THEIR SELF-CONFIDENCE FOLLOWING THE DECISIVE AND HISTORIC DECISION TAKEN BY THE DEVOUT

PRESIDENT

MOHAMED ANWAR EL SADAT

ON THE GREAT DAY OF OCTOBER 6, AND THROUGH WHICH BOTH EGYPT AND SYRIA AND THE REST OF THE ARAB PEOPLES RE-ASSURED THEIR RIGHT IN LIBERTY AND PEACE FOR THE SAKE OF REGAINING THEIR TERRITORIES, AND RE-ESTABLISHMENT OF THE LEGITIMATE RIGHTS OF THE PALESTINIAN PEOPLE,

TO WELCOME EGYPT'S DISTINGUISHED GUEST:

PRESIDENT

RICHARD M. NIXON

AND HONOR, IN HIS PERSON, THE AMERICAN PEOPLE, ASSURING THAT VICTORIOUS EGYPT WILL CONTINUE TO BEFRIEND ALL THOSE WHO SEEK HER FRIENDSHIP, GREATLY APPRECIATES THE U.S. CONSTRUCTIVE ROLE, REASSURES THE WHOLE WORLD THAT SUEZ CANAL WILL ALWAYS SERVE WORLD PEACE, AND WELCOMES MUTUAL CO-OPERATION, UNDERSTANDING AND RESPECT FOR THE INTEREST OF JUSTICE AND PEACE.

رفاهية العالم

إن اهتمامنا الأول هو الرفاهية العالمية وأن المثل الذى ضرب فى عملية تطهير قناة السويس بين السلطات المصرية وبين الولايات المتحدة الأمريكية يعطى البرهان على مدى ما يمكننا أن نشيده من صداقة خالصة وتعاون مخلص لمصلحة الرفاهية العالمية .
إننا فتحنا عهداً جديداً فى العلاقات العالمية وضربنا مثلا على تعاون الشعوب من أجل مصلحة السلام ، ولنأمل أن تتحقق جميع أهدافنا وأن نحقق سلاما دائمًا للمنطقة

الرئيس محمد أنور السادات

ويسعد وزارة الإسكان والتعمير بجمهورية مصر العربية

بعد أن تغير وجه التاريخ واستردت الشعوب العربية والجيوش العربية ثقتها بنفسها بعد القرار المصيرى والتاريخى الذى اتخذه

الرئيس المؤمن

محمد أنور السادات

يوم ٦ أكتوبر العظيم ، وأكدت به مصر وسوريا وكافة الشعوب العربية حقها فى الحرية والسلام من أجل استرداد الأرض واستعادة حقوق الشعب الفلسطينى

أن تحيى ضيف مصر

الرئيس ريتشارد نيكسون

وتحيى فى شخصه الشعب الأمريكى وتؤكد أن مصر الظافرة تصادق من يصادقها وتقابل بالتقدير الدور الأمريكى البناء وتؤكد أن القناة فى خدمة السلام . وترحب بالتعاون والتفاهم والاحترام المتبادل من أجل الحق والسلام .

FIGURE 2. Full-page statement of support for Nixon and al-Sadat from the Cairo Ministry of Housing and Reconstruction, *al-Ahrām*, June 13, 1974.

FIGURE 3. Sadat and Nixon greet crowds in Alexandria, with a welcome banner by the ASU (photograph no. 7268211, June 12, 1974; Nixon White House photographs taken January 20, 1969—August 9, 1974, "President Richard Nixon with Egyptian President Anwar Sadat, Waving from a Motorcade Driving through Alexandria, Egypt," National Archives Catalog, https://catalog.archives.gov/id/7268211).

19 JUL 1974
7-COPY

الأهرام

Al-Ahram

١٢ صفحة

٢٠ مليما

دار « الأهرام »

رئيس مجلس الادارة : محمد عبد القادر حاتم

رئيس التحرير : احمد بهاء الدين

# استقبال شعبى ورسمى كبير لنيكسون فى القاهرة

## السادات : ليس هناك طريق آخر الى السلام الدائم بغير حل سياسى للمشكلة الفلسطينية

## نيكسون : العالم مدين لشجاعة السادات وحكمته لما احرزناه من تقدم السلام حتى اليوم

استقبلت القاهرة امس الرئيس ريتشارد نيكسون استقبالا شعبيا كبيرا عبر عنه الرئيس الامريكى فى اول كلمة القاها امام الرئيس انور السادات قائلا : لقد تأثرت من هذا الاستقبال الذى لقيته . لقد شاهدت مئات الالوف فى الشوارع يحيوننى من أعماق قلوبهم ، ولقد جعلنى ذلك ادرك مايجب علينا تجاهكم وتجاه الاجيال المقبلة .

وقد تصافح الرئيسان السادات ونيكسون بحرارة فور نزول الرئيس الامريكى من طائرته ، وكانت أول جملة قالها الرئيس السادات : انه ليوم عظيم لبلدينا . ورد نيكسون قائلا : فعلا أنه ليوم عظيم .

### الطريق الوحيد للسلام الدائم

### بداية عهد جديد فى علاقاتنا

### جلسة محادثات مغلقة بين الرئيسين

٢٥ مليون جنيه

FIGURE 4. "Large Popular and Official Welcome for Nixon in Cairo," *al-Ahrām*, June 13, 1974.

FIGURE 5. Advertisement for a sale on American RCA televisions. "On the occasion of President Nixon's visit to Cairo, the al-Nasr Television Company announces its production of a quantity of American R.C.A. televisions, from 19–23 inches. Now sold at the Najmat Ramses Shops in Roxy Square (Heliopolis), 188 Ramses St. (Ghamra), 86 Sikkat al-Wayili St. (al-Qubbah Bridge), and the Ramses Building in Ramses Square," *al-Ahrām*, June 13, 1974.

Al-Qaʿid's satire also extends to another, unlikely suspect in the case of al-Dubbaysh ʿArayis, however—the author Yusuf al-Qaʿid himself. Al-Qaʿid acknowledges that in transforming al-Dubbaysh's story into a mystery novel, he runs the risk of exploiting the farmworker in much the same way as the feudal landowner, corrupt officials, and ʿarḍaḥāljī do elsewhere in the text. It would be, as he writes in the last chapter of *Yaḥduth*, "to transform the corpses of the destitute into cars and bottles of whiskey"—to turn a profit from the suffering of the poor by transforming their stories into village fiction, by now a well-established, if not the premier, form of Egyptian cultural production (*YMA* 170). At one point in the novel, al-Qaʿid even stages himself realizing this conundrum, when the author-narrator—now a character in the novel named "Yusuf al-Qaʿid"—enters Sudfah and al-Dubbaysh's house for the first time. "I laughed at myself in bitter mockery [*sukhriyyatan*]," the narrator notes (echoing Tawfiq al-Hakim's "bitter mockery" in *Diary*), "as I realized that I am one of those people who earn their livelihoods from other people's pain" (*YMA* 88). Like Idris's tale of "murder on the ʿizbah," *Yaḥduth* also teeters between hope and despair, clinging to the ideals and intentions of Nasser-era social reforms while exposing the violent rural realities of their merely nominal implementation.

In the end, as in Idris's *The Sinners*, it is unclear whether either the biographical author Yusuf al-Qaʿid or the fictional character "Yusuf al-Qaʿid" effects change merely through the narration of murder on the ʿizbah. In the chapter chronicling the "lifelong friends' last meeting," the doctor reminds the officer and the chairman that "there is a man from the village who writes novels and works in journalism," and he worries that this author will spoil their plan. The chairman, however, quickly brushes this worry off: "I don't think his presence in the village poses any danger. He's come here like a tourist, wearing tinted glasses and dressed in pants like an effendi. What can he really do anyway? Even if he were the editor of a newspaper, writing about the death of al-Dubbaysh would spoil coverage of Nixon's visit in a way that would anger the authorities in Cairo" (*YMA* 126). Raised in the village but educated and acculturated in the city, al-Qaʿid, like Idris, places his own anxieties about his ambivalent social position in the mouths of these fictional officials. Has he really been transformed into an unthinking, unseeing effendi, a narrative subject turning the suffering of his countrymen into the object of a representation, rather than doing anything to change it? Or can literary representation contribute to social change, if only by focusing on exposure, scandal, and sensation?

These questions crystallize in the final passage of *It's Happening Now*, when the narrator breaks the novel's frame to address the reader directly yet again:

> Let me remind you, and it won't be the last time, that al-Dubbaysh ʿArayis was killed. All I ask is that you recognize that there are many more people dying every moment. But at the same time, I beg you not to see al-Dubbaysh ʿArayis' murder as something ordinary [*amran ʿādiyyan*] . . . What happened is not ordinary, and its transformation into something normal, recurrent, and everyday reiterates a treachery that must be confronted (*YMA* 174).

Like Idris, al-Qaʿid recognizes that the "culture of fear" in which most Egyptian farmworkers live depends on the *normalization* of violence, its transformation into something ordinary, *ʿādī*, everyday. And, like his predecessor, al-Qaʿid wagers that shock may be the only way to dispel this resigned acceptance. His poetics of confrontation thus extends beyond the (semi)fictional world of *It's Happening Now* and onto the pages of the novel's paratexts, specifically the critical introduction he wrote for the book's fourth edition (and the first to be published by an Egyptian press) in 1986. There, al-Qaʿid describes some of the questions he faced from friends and colleagues before bringing out this new edition: What would he do about the word "now" in the title? And the verb "it's happening" in the present tense? Why not rename the book "*It Happened in Egypt in 1974*"? To justify his retention of the original title, al-Qaʿid returns to the rhetoric of the ʿādī:

> I looked around me, reviving the eyes of my distant childhood in order to see with the greatest possible degree of shock and contemplate everything we have come to

> understand as customary in an unaccustomed way. I tried to look at my country as though I were seeing it for the first time . . . and I discovered that the "now" of 1974 is the same "now" of 1986, that the age of American domination is long, and that the American sideshow continues in Egypt even today. The twelve years that have passed in my country [since the original publication of *Yaḥduth*] have made the exceptional into the ordinary, the temporary into the permanent, and the unacceptable into something that not only remains but . . . is very close to being accepted, so accustomed have we grown to it.[62]

Al-Qaʿid's poetics of investigation thus falls somewhere in between socialist-realist commitment and modernist formal experimentation. Like the committed realists, al-Qaʿid wants to "shock" his readers into outrage, portraying "everything we have come to see as customary" (*al-umūr al-ʿādiyyah*) in an "unaccustomed way" (*bi-ṣūrah ghayr ʿādiyyah*), and thereby dispelling the facility with which the oppressed internalize their oppression as a "normal" (ʿādī), phenomenon. But, like his contemporaries in the 1970s, al-Qaʿid is also wary of all the "readymade," "worn-out" words saturating Egyptian media at the time of his writing (*YMA* 87).

Like other writers responding to the hypocrisies of Sadat's presidency, al-Qaʿid's work seethes with outrage yet recoils from triumphalism and fabrication. He refuses to tell a pat story of collective protest and triumph over the rich, not because he wouldn't support such an event but simply because "this isn't what happened," and it's not "what's happening now" in Egypt. "The most salient feature of Yusuf al-Qaʿid's testimony," the Egyptian novelist and literary critic Mustafa Bayyumi writes, "is that it distances itself equally as much from superficial, Romantic visions and dreams as it does from readymade Leftist doctrines and sayings."[63] Somewhere in between the effendi and the farmworker, the international developer and the migrant laborer, al-Qaʿid—like Idris before him—crafts a form of detective fiction in which even the reader, even the author himself is shown to be a kind of criminal. In both novels, the reader is invited to look again, with different eyes, at the criminality and inherent vice of the poor. The very structure of the novels invites this reexamination of the ordinary, this training in learning how to look, then look again. It is, in fact, a lesson in historical materialism, in learning to view the given world as mutable rather than inevitable, the contingent product of human actions rather than the necessary outcome of incomprehensible forces, and thereby open to change. The result is a pair of Egyptian crime novels that question the very premises of "investigation," "truth-seeking" (*taḥqīq*), and "realism" presumed by effendi, developer, police officer, and author alike. They do not confuse writing fiction with social transformation, but they implicitly believe in narrative's ability to transform the nature of knowledge, as well as how—and by whom—it is used.

## CONCLUSION

I have dwelled at length on these two understudied novels to illustrate how their continuity of purpose gives the lie to the conventional narrative of political event leading to aesthetic rupture in Arabic fiction. Both Idris and al-Qaʿid are concerned with offering, in fiction, a previously unwritten social history of the ʿizbah, exposing the continued immiseration of the migrant workers, small farmers, and wage laborers who live there despite successive waves of national reform, from the social-scientific boom of the interwar period all the way through the "structural readjustments" of the 1970s and 1980s. Idris makes use of his medical training, rural upbringing, and penchant for shocking description to scandalize his readers, jolting them out of the effendi's subjective position and into the viscerally embodied, violent reality of the migrant laborers' experience. He transforms the rural objects of the national gaze into subjects of intensely felt sufferings. Al-Qaʿid, meanwhile, "tortures the reader's conscience" by spoiling the mystery in advance, exaggerating the dehumanizing rhetoric of the ʿizbah's managerial class and satirizing the triumphalism of the Infitah. In both cases, crime is the occasion for exposure, for a reexamination of accepted, normalized realities and conventional definitions. The criminals and perpetrators in both texts turn out to be the victims of much larger crimes, perpetrated by police officers, landowners, union leaders, agricultural inspectors, and others at the regional, national, and international levels—extending even to Richard Nixon himself.

On yet another level, however, readers of these texts are also forced to confront the "effendi-like" sensibilities that tend to govern the practice of literary critical reading itself. Both authors deny their readers the position of the detached, all-seeing subject who transforms the countryside into either an "object of development" or a source of thrilling, scandalous entertainment.[64] These novels, in other words, demand a different reading practice from their readers, one in which reading about the Egyptian countryside is no longer an act of quiet reflection on the simple, earthbound lives of rural others. It is, rather, a confrontation with the bare, sparse, hungry realities of the ʿizbah laborer and an exposure of the poverty at the root of crime in the countryside. This new poetics of prose yields ambivalent outcomes in both texts: the prison guards responsible for al-Dubbaysh's murder are never prosecuted, and the Gharabwa go back to laboring in the fields as Aziza's body, and story, are reabsorbed into the night. Still, in both novels, crime and its investigation (baḥth) become the occasion for uncovering and exposing the interconnected forces maintaining the current social order on the ʿizbah. Crime creates a rupture, a scandal, a temporary disturbance in the functioning of power. Idris and al-Qaʿid capitalize on this disturbance, this small rent in the fabric of the Egyptian social order, to hint at power's instability, its susceptibility to change.

3

# Bureau of Missing Persons

## *Metaphysical Detection and the Subject in Jabra Ibrahim Jabra and Naguib Mahfouz*

The question is the story itself, and whether or not it means something is not for the story to tell.

—PAUL AUSTER, *CITY OF GLASS*

Such suffering is part of the cure!

—NAGUIB MAHFOUZ, "ZAABALAWI"

Up to this point, I have focused on the peregrinations of "classical detection" as conducted by investigators both official and unofficial, private and public, in select fictions from Egypt and Morocco. This chapter and the one that follows, however, begin a new section on the uses of the "metaphysical detective story" in works from Lebanon, Egypt, and the Palestinian diaspora.[1] These are texts that, in the words of Patricia Merivale and Susan Elizabeth Sweeney, "subvert traditional detective-story conventions—such as narrative closure and the detective's role as surrogate reader—with the intention, or at least the effect, of asking questions about mysteries of being and knowing which transcend the mere machinations of the mystery plot."[2] Like Edgar Allan Poe, Jorge Luis Borges, Paul Auster, and others examined in Merivale and Sweeney's study, Arab authors, too, have frequently zeroed in on the element of mystery, puzzle, or enigma (*lughz*) at the heart of detective fiction, using the unknown, missing story of the crime as a metonym for the great unknown or the absent, occulted world (*ʿālam al-ghayb*), with all the religious connotations these words imply. In novels and short stories that predate the postmodern works of writers like Paul Auster, Umberto Eco, and Thomas Pynchon—sometimes by decades—Arab authors also assume a "flamboyant yet decidedly complex relationship to the detective story," using the mystery plot to question elements of classical detection, including "the hermeneutic strategies of rendering meaningful those signs which are unintelligible to others . . . the epistemological method of discovering truth by questioning sources of knowledge; and the adept detective's triumph over the dangerous Other."[3] Just as Poe depicts C. Auguste Dupin's ratiocinative powers as an astounding, awe-inspiring form of divination,[4] so too the authors of Arabic metaphysical detective fiction summon the lexicon of mysticism to draw attention to the search itself, rather than the truth it uncovers.

This chapter brings together works by two writers known more for their status as litterateurs and intellectuals than for their experiments with metaphysical detective fiction. The first, the Egyptian Naguib Mahfouz, has gained fame as the Arab world's first and only Nobel laureate in literature to date, recognized mainly for his *Cairo Trilogy* (1946–52), which I discussed briefly in the introduction. As Mahfouz became increasingly associated with his realist masterpiece, being hailed as "the Dickens/Balzac/Zola (take your pick) of Cairo," his later experiments with form, genre, and voice, particularly in the novellas and short stories from the 1960s, languished in obscurity, especially where Western readers of his works in translation were concerned.[5] Yet these novels stage an important shift in Mahfouz's narrative poetics. Why did this great realist chronicler of Egypt's modern history suddenly turn to novels of crime and seeking? And why are Sufi characters, themes, and lexicons so central to these later novels, short stories, and novellas? Sasson Somekh has argued that "Egypt could have had its foremost detective writer in Mahfouz," and many others, including the author himself, have acknowledged Mahfouz's lifelong interest in detective stories.[6] Other critics have noted the important role that Sufi themes and concepts play across his oeuvre, particularly in the novellas and short stories of the 1960s.[7] Yet no scholar has attempted to analyze these two features—the Sufism and the noir, the spiritual and the detective-style seeking—together.

The second writer, Jabra Ibrahim Jabra, is best known as a Renaissance man of Arabic letters, a prolific essayist, poet, painter, translator, art critic, and novelist whose vast oeuvre chronicles both his own experiences as an uprooted Palestinian and the debates of an entire generation struggling to understand the place of the intellectual, the legacy of the Nahda, and the value of modernity and tradition in a postwar, post-colonial Arab world. *The Ship* (*al-Safinah*, 1970) is arguably Jabra's most famous novel; polyphonically narrated by a series of Iraqi, Palestinian, and Italian characters as they float through time and space on a cruise ship crisscrossing the Mediterranean, it firmly established Jabra's reputation as the Arab world's foremost novelist of ideas.[8] Yet Jabra's later novel, *In Search of Walid Masoud* (*al-Baḥth ʿan Walīd Masʿūd*, 1978),[9] borrows equally from the mysticism and the mystery at the heart of metaphysical detective fiction, beginning as it does with the disappearance of the titular Palestinian character and staging its characters' ongoing and ultimately fruitless "search" to discover the truth behind that disappearance (what Tzvetan Todorov calls the story of the crime).[10] The novel itself, then, is both the open-ended "search" for Walid Masoud conducted by all its characters, on the one hand, and the systematic "research project" or "study" that its sociologist frame narrator, Dr. Jawad Husni, vows to write about him, on the other.[11] In between, we tend to learn more about the characters doing the searching than we do about the absent Palestinian,[12] but we also learn a good deal about what it means to "search" more generally, what tools various characters with different backgrounds marshal to conduct their searches, and how the unsolvable mystery defies those tools and thereby calls their effectiveness into question. Whether engaging with the scholarly methodologies of psychology, sociology, and history, the ancient practices of astrology, tasseography, and hunting, or the artistic practices of oil painting and poetry writing, the characters in *Walid Masoud* dramatize what it means to seek knowledge in different ways, and what it means to have one's methods overturned by a particularly enigmatic object.

What brings the Egyptian master of realism and the Palestinian doyen of intellectuals together? Both Jabra and Mahfouz experimented with a specific form of metaphysical detective fiction, which Merivale calls the "gumshoe gothic," the story that engages with "Missing Persons, rather than Dead Bodies," and in so doing subverts from the very beginning the function of forensic evidence at the heart of classic detective fiction. These stories "deal with . . . a person sought for, glimpsed, and shadowed, gumshoe style, through endless labyrinthine city streets, but never really Found—because he was never really There, because he was, and remains, missing. One was . . . only following one's own self."[13] In Mahfouz's novels and short stories, as well as in Jabra's, there is a gumshoe but no criminal; likewise, the "triadic multiplicity of detective, criminal, and victim is reduced to a solipsistic unity," as the search to know and understand an Other merely sinks the detective further into his own subjectivity.[14] Mahfouz and Jabra use the plot-level search as a figure for the seeker's loss of confidence in his own identity, his boundedness as a subject, and his ability to know others.

Yet there are several ingredients to the Arabic metaphysical detective stories I read in this chapter that distinguish them from their Western counterparts. They share with Poe and others a skepticism concerning the hard distinctions between science and religion, logic and mysticism, ratiocination and divination that gained traction in Europe during the nineteenth century. But, as writers engaging with the physical, institutional, and epistemic violence of colonialism, their critique is aimed not only at the West but also at the modernizing project of the Arab Nahda—the "awakening" or "revival" from cultural decline (*inḥiṭāṭ*) that began in the nineteenth century. Through military, administrative, juridical, and educational reforms gleaned from educational missions to Europe and the translation of European scientific publications and textbooks, Nahdawi intellectuals—an emergent bourgeoisie or *effendiyya*—sought to "meet the challenges raised by national independence movements in provinces of the Ottoman Empire, and to catch up with the increasingly powerful West."[15] Mahfouz's skepticism about the Nahda's cultural and intellectual project is evident as early as the *Cairo Trilogy:* the journey of its protagonist Kamal away from faith and toward secular literary "enlightenment" is shown to be painful and fraught with perils. Jabra's skepticism about the same project, by contrast, is harder to discern. His voluminous essays on topics in Western aesthetics (especially British Romantic poetry), his signal translations of key English literary works, and his criticism's continual focus on the importance of visionary individualism all paint the portrait of a latter-day Nahdawi, modernizing Arabic literature and culture through a healthy dose of well-translated English literature and criticism. I argue, however, that the poetics of Jabra's *In Search of Walid Masoud* tell a different story. As a succession of narrators try and fail to grasp the truth about their absent Palestinian friend, a series of authorized disciplines and methodologies for deducing truth inherited from the Nahda are also shown to fail. At the same time, Walid's own papers and documents reveal a history of dabbling in Christian mysticism, and the characters' contacts with him—whether in person or on paper—increasingly come to resemble experiences of mystical ego death. The metaphysical detective novels of Mahfouz and Jabra, in short, target the same Enlightenment as Poe's short story, but in its transplanted form as the Arab Nahda, whose repercussions—including a sense of civilizational inferiority, a rejection of centuries-long literary traditions, and a devaluation of popular forms of religion and cultural practice—lasted long into the twentieth century.

In another crucial difference from Western metaphysical detective stories, the elusive and enigmatic figures pursued in Arabic "missing persons" narratives were not completely unknown to their initial Arabic reading audiences; they were, rather, recognizable character types drawn from premodern and popular Arabic literature and culture. Poe purposefully designs his man of the crowd to be paradoxical and unclassifiable, simultaneously ragged and rich, carrying both "a diamond and a dagger."[16] Mahfouz's elusive shaykhs, by contrast—especially Zaabalawi, in the eponymous 1961 short story, Sayyid Sayyid al-Rahimi in *The Search* (*al-Ṭarīq*, 1964), and even Shaykh Mutawalli ʿAbd al-Samad in the *Trilogy*—would have been recognizable to Arab publics as "friends of God" (*awliyāʾ Allāh*, sing. *walī Allāh*), much like Tawfiq al-Hakim's Shaykh Asfur in *Diary of a Country Prosecutor* (see chapter 1). Mahfouz seizes on the same kind of resistant unknowability figured by Poe's man of the crowd, but he ties this unknowability to a specific figure in the Egyptian cultural imagination. By modern standards, the friend of God is considered a vagrant, a charlatan, a swindler, sometimes even a drunk or drug addict, but by much more long-standing social conventions, these very qualities bring him closer to God, and he thereby imbues the atmosphere around him with holiness and transcendence—spiritual cures for modern ills. Jabra's Walid Masoud would also have been recognizable to Arab reading publics as a figure for the miraculously productive, visionary Palestinian intellectual, simultaneously embodying all the metaphysical symbolism of the early Christian "desert fathers" (as well as Jesus himself) and the related qualities of the fedayee: self-sacrifice, asceticism, conviction, elusiveness, shape shifting, otherworldliness.[17] In sum, it is not that the enigmatic figures in Mahfouz's and Jabra's works "refuse to be read";[18] it is that they embody truths to which modern ways of seeking have become inhospitable.

But what kind of truth do Zaabalawi, al-Rahimi, Masoud, and other missing persons in Arabic metaphysical detective stories embody, if not the truth offered up by scientific analysis? I have found one possible answer to this question in Friedrich Nietzsche's "On Truth and Lies in a Nonmoral Sense," and in Paul de Man's reading of one key sentence from that essay: "What, then, is truth? A mobile army of metaphors, metonyms, and anthropomorphisms—in short, a sum of human relations which have been poetically and rhetorically intensified, transferred, and embellished, and which, after long usage, seem to a people to be fixed, canonical, and binding. Truths are illusions which we have forgotten are illusions."[19] Interrupting Nietzsche's sentence before it can arrive at its pithy final formulation, de Man's analysis highlights the difference between metaphor and metonymy, on the one hand, which imply "that truth is relational" and allow for "the possibility of definition by means of infinitely varied sets of propositions," and anthropomorphism, on the other hand, which "is not just a trope but an identification on the level of substance." Anthropomorphism "freezes the infinite chain of tropological transformations and propositions into one single assertion or essence . . . no longer a proposition but a proper name."[20] Just as Nietzsche sees in the "concept" the sedimented and worn residue of a once vibrant and living sense perception, so de Man sees this same movement from truth to falsity reenacted in the rhetoric of Nietzsche's sentence itself. "Truth is a trope; a trope generates a norm or value; this value (or ideology) is no longer true. It is true that tropes are the producers of ideologies that are no longer true."[21] The truth that Zaabalawi, Sayyid Sayyid al-Rahimi, and Walid Masoud represent, then, could be described as the truth of metonymy and metaphor, of infinitely varied propositions before they have hardened into a proper name.

But there is another, perhaps more apt, answer to the question I posed above. Both Nietzsche's essay and de Man's reading of it deliberately suppress the divine implications of an "infinite chain of tropological transformations,"[22] which, in another time and place, might simply have been called "God" and, in certain Islamic traditions, might also have been called "language" or, specifically, the Arabic language, the language of the Qur'an. The quests for "missing persons" in Mahfouz's and Jabra's narratives, then, might be better equated with the narrator al-Harith ibn Hammam's continual search for the "eloquent rogue" Abu Zayd in al-Hariri's *Impostures* (*Maqāmāt*). Al-Harith wanders from town to town searching for "some inspiring oratory," following what Michael Cooperson has called "a thwarted reflex of a spiritual search," much like Christians in late antique Egypt would seek out the Desert Fathers in search of "a word," meaning "a memorable summation of some spiritual precept."[23] Abu Zayd, meanwhile, is both a master of disguise and a masterful manipulator of words; he uses the Arabic language for the very worldly purpose of "swindling money out of the gullible narrator," but in so doing, he transports the narrator and anyone else who happens to be present to the peaks of marvel and awe.[24] "The most economical explanation for [Abu Zayd's] vaporous indeterminacy," Cooperson writes, "is that he is Arabic itself . . . He is the language of God in the world of men. And that language is so powerfully in excess of material reality that it overwhelms the agreed-upon relationship of word and object."[25] Melding Cooperson's reading of al-Hariri's *Impostures* with Merivale's theory of the gumshoe gothic, we might say that in the works of Mahfouz and Jabra examined below, the characters' painstaking searches for and fleeting encounters with the mysterious figures they seek also overwhelm the agreed-upon relationship between person and identity—between the possible infinity of their humanity and the proper name, address, and identity card to which modern regimes of truth have confined them.

The term *metaphysical* thus suits novels like Jabra's *In Search of Walid Masoud* and Mahfouz's *The Search*, since these works paradoxically revive questions of religious tradition and faith even as they conform to Georg Lukács's characterization of the novel as the "epic of a world abandoned by God."[26] Their narrators may momentarily experience mystical self-loss and ego death through their pursuits of and encounters with mysterious others, but in the end they remain atomized individuals caught up in their own concerns who are thereby cut off from any kind of collectivity. The fleeting feeling of simultaneous ego death and infinitude they experience is, if not illusory, at least unproductive, part of an endless cycle of pursuit represented in the form of the narratives themselves, which all end precisely where they began—with the narrator's resolution to "find" the mysterious Other, thus sending him "back to the same old vortex."[27]

The theory of the metaphysical detective novel has helped me identify and delineate the features of a trend I see across Arabic works of fiction from several national contexts but, to be clear, I am not arguing that these Arabic fictions exemplify an essentially Western paradigm. Part of what I read in these works by Jabra and Mahfouz is a reinscription of the history of pious, mystical "seeking"—Islamic or Christian—into the novel concerned with an unsolved, infinite search. I find in their works not the failure of the Nahda and its modernizing projects but a chronicle of the coloniality in those projects' aspirations, as well as their encounters with older, local, and popular practices of truth making and truth using—in other words, local epistemologies inconsistent with the objective aspirations of secular philosophy and science. I read these novels, therefore, not as a validation of native irrationality against Western rationality but as explorations of the irrationality and contradiction on which the Enlightenment and Nahda projects were themselves premised, by means of an engagement with and exposure of the tropological, rhetorical, and figurative qualities in supposedly rational, scientific approaches to truth. Mahfouz and Jabra do not destroy or "move beyond" the figure of the Arab intellectual but they do frame and destabilize his hubris, and this framing in itself allows readers to imagine other subjects who, in fleeing the textual labyrinth, might make a new postcolonial reality.

## FORMING INTELLECTUALS: JABRA AND THE POLITICS OF VISIONARY INDIVIDUALISM

Where *Walid Masoud* constitutes, in my reading, the exception to the rule of Jabra's otherwise near-religious devotion to the figure of the visionary, Romantic individual throughout his career, Mahfouz's *Cairo Trilogy*, and particularly *Palace of Desire* (*Qaṣr al-Shawq*), when read against the grain, proves to be as skeptical of Nahdawi intellectual hubris as the later novellas and short stories of Sufi noir. This section offers a history of Jabra's lifelong commitment to the Arab intellectual as visionary individual and the politics behind this commitment; the subsequent section will examine Mahfouz's career-long skepticism of this figure and his sense of the losses entailed in its formation.

As an essayist, poet, artist, and translator, Jabra has come to epitomize the figure of the intellectual for many subsequent Arab writers and intellectuals. An Assyrian-Palestinian of extremely humble origins,[28] he emerged during the 1950s and 1960s as one of the Arab world's most recognized and prolific thinkers. Raised mostly in Bethlehem, Jabra subsequently graduated from the Arab College in Jerusalem, read English at Cambridge University, returned home to teach at the Rashidiya secondary school in Jerusalem, and—after the 1948 Nakba drove him into exile—proceeded to become a professor at the Teachers' Training College in Baghdad.[29] Through no small feat of self-cultivation, Jabra transformed himself over the course of his life from a barefoot schoolboy roaming the fields outside Bethlehem into one of the Arab world's preeminent scholars, critics, and literary innovators. By the time Elias Khoury wrote his Palestinian epic *Gate of the Sun* (*Bāb al-Shams*) in 1998, the association of Jabra with intellectual refinement had become a given of modern Arabic literature and culture. "I love Jabra," that novel's narrator confesses, "because he writes in an aristocratic way, with well-chosen, beautiful sentences. It's true that he was poor as a child, but he wrote like a writer."[30]

Jabra's early role as intercultural thinker and champion of visionary individualism can be observed in his numerous essays from the 1950s and early 1960s—essays and lectures on such topics as British and American Romantic and Modernist poetry,[31] the "free verse" movement (*al-shiʿr al-ḥurr*) in Arabic,[32] and Iraqi fine art,[33] as well as his own paintings and translations of foundational works such as Faulkner's *The Sound and the Fury*, Shakespeare's *Hamlet*, Beckett's *Waiting for Godot*, and Whitman's "Song of Myself," to name only a few.[34] His passion for the British Romantics during this period goes some way to explaining why he continued to carry the torch of visionary individualism at a time when pan-Arabist, socialist, and "committed" aesthetics were sweeping the Arab world. In the 1957 essay "al-Ḥurriyyah wa-l-Ṭūfān" (Freedom and the flood), he spoke out against commitment (*al-iltizām*) as the primary criterion of aesthetic judgment in modern Arabic literature. Committed literature, in his view, "is focused on politics more than it is on the human being [*al-insān*], and it focuses on abstract collectivities rather than individuals." For this reason, it "simplifies and fragments the key question of literature," which, "as we can see from our study of poetry, theater, and narrative from ancient times to the present," is not that of the collectivity but that of "the human being."[35] This and other essays from Jabra's oeuvre hew toward the "personalism" in modernist Arabic aesthetics that Robyn Creswell has connected with Charles Malik, the American University of Beirut professor, and his mentee, the Lebanese poet and critic Yusuf al-Khal, one of the co-founders of *Shiʿr* magazine, to which Jabra was a frequent contributor. "Personalists argued for the spiritual dignity of the human person, threatened by the rival materialisms of capitalism and communism," Creswell writes, and "for Arab modernists too, the person is a hero of negative liberty, a lyrical 'I' that floats free from the claims of all ideological collectives."[36] This apoliticism was and is, of course, its own form of politics, as Creswell also shows—a feature of late modernist and early Cold War liberalism seeking to establish an international consensus of "militantly anti-Communist, aggressively internationalist, spiritually engaged" intellectuals and cultural producers "chiefly concerned with negative freedoms."[37] "Al-Ḥurriyyah wa-l-Ṭūfān" and other essays from the 1950s and 1960s illustrate how thoroughly Jabra's *explicit* poetics aligned with this late modernist, anti-Communist liberalism.[38]

Jabra's defense of the visionary individual is nowhere clearer than in his novels from this period, particularly *Hunters in a Narrow Street* (1960).[39] Written in English, it chronicles the experiences of a young, Cambridge-educated, Christian Palestinian exile named Jameel Farran as he copes with the experience of the 1948 Nakba and adjusts to his new life as an English professor in Baghdad—a social, cultural, and political landscape as "other" to him as it probably was to the first English-language readers of Jabra's book. Jameel's past life in Palestine echoes through his current reality in his new city; as he remembers the catastrophic events of the Nakba, readers of *Hunters* are also told a history that, at the time the novel was published, was scarcely being written in English. The charming Jerusalem love story unfolding between Jameel and Leila Shahin is suddenly interrupted by "violent explosions," which jolt readers out of romance and into history:

> Jewish terrorists had been killing the British for several years, blowing up government offices, army barracks, officers' clubs. Now they had started on the Arabs. United Nations [*sic*] had recommended splitting Palestine in two, and the terrorists were determined to achieve the bloody dichotomy. Barrels of T.N.T. were set off in market squares, killing about fifty people at a time, and now it was the beautiful white and rose stone houses of the Arabs they were after. (*H* 8–9)

This same history will bring Jameel's love story to a gruesome end: following the Jewish terrorists' destruction of the Shahins' house, Jameel discovers his beloved's severed hand protruding from the rubble, "with the engagement ring buckled round the third finger" (*H* 10). The image is clunky and melodramatic, like much of *Hunters*, but it drives home the novel's condemnation of the Nakba and the Western regimes that enabled it.

The novel goes on to stage the many debates of Arab modernity—West versus East, tradition versus modernity, custom versus innovation, desert versus city, art versus technology, and so on—among the poets, intellectuals, students, activists, bourgeois characters, and even the rare foreigners among whom Jameel finds company in Baghdad. The commitment- and Communist-minded poets Abdul Kader Yassin and Kareem serve as foils for the liberal, visionary individualism touted by Jameel and his Bohemian poet friends Adnan Talib and Husain Abdul Amir (*H* 77). Towfiq al-Khalaf is the Bedouin cloak- and cartridge belt-wearing incarnation of the desert Arab, a mouthpiece for the traditionalist argument that Arab authenticity lies in the desert, that "civilization means deterioration," that art and bourgeois love are "the poisonous exhalation[s] of the vast swamp that so-called civilization is," and that the only remedy is to live "the genuine way of Arab life," which, for al-Khalaf, is characterized by riding camels, sleeping in tents, and reviving the oral culture of the ancient Arabian peninsula (even though he comes from a wealthy metropolitan family and holds a law degree) (*H* 82–85). Faced with the same problems of postcolonial modernity, Imad Nafawi, a conservative upper-class professor and tyrannical father-jailer to Jameel's young student and love interest Sulafa, prescribes "mosques and police stations, the fear of God and the fear of authority" as "the only medicine for our sickness" (*H* 102). Above all, it is the customs of sex, gender, marriage, and love that loom largest in the plot of *Hunters*. Jameel denounces the cloistering of young women like Sulafa, and he is horrified by the honor killing of the young servant Azima by her brother in the novel's sixth chapter. "We live in cities and yet we follow the law of the desert," Adnan explains in response to Jameel's shock at Azima's murder. "We're caught in the vicious meshes of tribal tradition" (*H* 46).

Yet despite the obstacles he faces—the prospect of an arranged marriage between Sulafa and Towfiq al-Khalaf to settle a tribal dispute, the love triangle he creates with Sulafa's aunt Salma—it is Jameel who ultimately emerges triumphant, his love for Sulafa vindicating the earlier loss of Leila and, more importantly, marking the first signs of the old Arab social classes' demise, as they, along with the "backwards" customs they represent, perish. "Rubeidi was slipping," Jameel notes in the novel's final chapter. "A whole order of things was slipping" (*H* 230). As he waits for Sulafa to turn twenty-one so that she can elope with him, and as the novel's other characters "impale themselves on rows of political and social swords," Jameel calmly observes "crows and kites [flying] over the palm groves of a slowly refurbished land" (*H* 232). Like these birds, Jameel—the Palestinian Christian humanist, the Arab English professor, the "savior," the "successful peace negotiator" (*H* 196, 203)—flies free of the pesky "political and social swords" that trouble his Iraqi friends, committed to nothing but romantic love. His act of removing Sulafa from the conservative social customs of traditional marriage is his contribution to this slow refurbishing, this push toward modernity—or so the novel implies.

Like "Freedom and the Flood" and other essays from this period in Jabra's career, then, *Hunters* explicitly champions negative liberties, the "freedom from" political commitments, social customs, and religious beliefs that allows exilic intellectuals like Jameel to soar above the restraints of tradition and collectivity. *Hunters* also contains a telling monologue about the role of Christianity in Jameel's enlightened subjectivity—one worth quoting at length for the echoes it will find in Jabra's later characterization of Walid Masoud. While remembering the immediate aftermath of the Nakba, Jameel recalls a conversation with his priest. "I can't understand the West," Father Isa says. "It is supposed to be Christian. Look what it is doing to Christians and to the land of Christ." Jameel responds by asking the Father how exactly he thinks about Jesus Christ.

> Father Isa was alarmed . . . "My son, I don't know what you mean by your question. He is the Lord of Light, the Redeemer, the Comforter—"
>
> "Very good, father. But I think of Christ as a man walking our streets with a haggard face and beautiful hands. I think of Him standing barefooted on our cobbles and calling all men to His love and His peace. I think of Him here, in these very streets and hills and houses and hovels. For me Christ is a part of this place. But how do you suppose they think of Him in the West? Do you suppose our Christianity is like theirs? When they sing of Jerusalem do you think they mean our own arched streets and cobbled alleys and terraced hills? Never. Christ for the West has become an idea—an abstract idea with a setting, but the setting has lost all geographical significance. For them the Holy Land is a fairy land. They have invented a fanciful Jerusalem of their own and made it the city of their dreams . . . What does it matter to them if our houses are destroyed, if a thousand Leilas are blown to bits and our city gates are turned into shambles? They've stolen our Christ and kicked us in the teeth . . .
>
> "For fifteen hundred years Christianity has been exclusively European. What have we, Arabs, Asiatics, Levantines, to do with it? We originated it, but the Greeks and the Romans took it away from us. All we have left of it is an antiquated set of rituals to which we have contributed nothing in a thousand years. What creative, civilizing part has our Christianity played in the midst of a Moslem world? . . . We have never enjoyed the full benefit of belonging to our fatherland—don't you hate the term 'religious minority,' the survival of which is always to indicate the tolerance of the 'religious majority'?—nor have we distinguished ourselves by the creation of some great or even different civilization out of our different faith. Europe has always been afraid of the Moslem East, but the Christians in it, always looking out towards Europe until their necks have ached, have earned no more than its benign contempt. That is why the West will let Jerusalem fall into ruins under the hoofs of Zionist terrorists." (*H* 16–18)

Several positions on Arab modernity, Christianity, and Palestinian history intertwine here. First and foremost, Jameel offers a clear condemnation of the West, not only for its status as colonizer but also for having "stolen *our* Christ" and transformed him from a real-life, everyday Jerusalemite into "an abstract idea," completely removed from his proper geographical setting and community—that is, Palestine. Jameel similarly condemns Western Christianity's abstract understanding of the Holy Land as a "fairy land," the "city of their dreams." By the second paragraph, however, it is also clear that Jameel accords a special transformational, "creative," and even "civilizing" role to Christian Arabs, even if they have thus far failed to fulfill that role in modern history. His condemnation of "Arab, Asiatic, Levantine" Christians for having become mired in "an antiquated set of rituals" is laced with the conviction that it is Christian Arabs who have the most potential as agents of transformation in the Arab world. That Christianity originated in Bethlehem and Jerusalem is no accident for Jameel Farran; it is the landscape itself that imbues the place with transformational potential. Like Jabra refusing the denomination of "refugee,"[40] Jameel refuses the denomination of "religious minority" for Levantine Christians. And, like Jabra's passionate defense of individual expression in "Freedom and the Flood," Jameel's politics in this passage also align with the Christian theology-influenced liberalism of Malik, whose call for Western revolution was in fact "a call for the West to rediscover itself in the East as the historical fountainhead of Christianity."[41] For Jabra as for Malik, Eastern Christians, and Palestinian Christians in particular, have a special role as mediators between East and West. They are the leavening agents capable of absorbing, translating, and implementing the best, most "civilizing" features of Western modernity without compromising Arab authenticity or alienating their Arab confreres.

Many of these same ideas find their echoes in *Walid Masoud*. In the chapter titled "Walid Masoud Remembers the Hermits in a Distant Cave," the titular Palestinian character narrates his young fascination with Christian hermits. "It is the pious hermits who came closest to being prophets," he remembers the priest instructing him, including Saint Jerome, Saint Anthony, and Simeon Stylites (*ISWM* 86). When Walid's young friend Sulayman invites him to put these ideas into practice by running away from the monastery and taking up residence as hermits in a cave outside Jerusalem, Walid happily agrees, seeing this adventure as the fulfillment of what he calls his "mysterious dreams." In those dreams, he tells Sulayman, "I see myself flying in the sky like an eagle, soaring and swooping through the valleys . . . If we go and become hermits, can we change mankind, change the world?" (*ISWM* 87). As they did for Jameel Farran at the end of *Hunters*, birds stand for negative liberty in this chapter of *Walid Masoud*. To soar free from all political commitments is to achieve the potential to "change mankind, change the world." During their adventure, however, the boys are sorely disappointed to discover that God does not in fact send down bread and water to sustain them, despite their fervent prayers. Instead, it is an old man on a donkey who comes to find them

(*ISWM* 98–99). The priests, their parents, and the entire monastery school ultimately chastise the children for their young and naïve act of faith. It is presented in the text of *Walid Masoud* as both an example of Walid's Christian piety, even as a young boy, and of the holiness that inheres in the lands around Bethlehem and Jerusalem themselves.

This experiment with hermitism is reprised in the novel's sixth chapter, "Walid Masoud Writes the First Pages of His Autobiography." There, Walid recalls the notion of rebellion, the desire to "change the world into love," that so preoccupied him as a child in Jerusalem. As in the story of Jesus, Walid's desire to change the world is inspired by the poor and humble Jerusalemites around him, people who on feast days would pray, "forget their poverty," and mill through the busy streets, "laughing, crying, and arguing with each other." "Whenever I conceived of the earth changing," the older Walid now writing the autobiographical pages remembers in a famous passage, "I'd feel a pleasant shudder deep down inside me. It wasn't the way politicians bring about change . . . but that of rebels not yet familiar with theories and revolutionary planning; and the kind of change such rebels aspire to has no connection at all with mere change in governmental systems and class conflict" (*ISWM* 131). Once again, "change" here goes far beyond secular, worldly systems of economic and political governance. It is, rather, what Walid calls "absolute love and freedom," which compels the rebel to "reject laws and customs that were found to be incompatible with [it]." And once again, the bird returns as a figure for negative liberty. "It was as though I had to be rid of everything, of every relationship, and float like an unknown bird in unknown heavens; and, within the setting of my isolation from everything, I would actually, paradoxically, be in touch with my love of everything" (*ISWM* 131). Walid Masoud here continues and extends the vision of intellectual freedom articulated by Jabra in his anti-*iltizām* essays, but the fictional character adds a christological dimension absent from Jabra's nonfictional writings. "I soon realized all this would involve suffering . . . The rebel, then, has to be crucified as well, and his victory will be in his crucifixion" (*ISWM* 131).

In common with Jameel Farran, Walid, in these pages from his autobiography, links transformational, civilizational change with the landscape of Palestine itself. If Jesus forever altered the course of history, he seems to assert, it is at least in part because he came from this place, these mountains, these hills. Walid "retained [the] obscure sense that those mountains of ours contained forces that could change the world" (*ISWM* 131). In fact, this character reiterates Jameel Farran's view that it is precisely *because* Christianity has been uprooted from the geography of Palestine and transplanted to Rome that the religion has lost its "creative, civilizing" power. After studying for some time at the Santa Maria Dolorosa monastery in Milan, Walid realizes that Italy will not allow him to "find the logic that would justify my dream, the dream I hadn't been able to understand in the cave in Wadi al-Jamal," site of his childhood hermitage. Where what he had envisioned was "to change the profundities, those things whereby mankind would be created anew," he discovers that the institution of the *Roman* Catholic Church has transformed Christianity into "a means of maintaining the world as it is, not changing it" (*ISWM* 139). Amid the marching and military displays of Mussolini's newly recruited fascist armies, "this Arab boy from Palestine" envisions a different kind of change. "The Messiah didn't use weapons," he reminds an Italian friend who has urged him to join the armies if he is so committed to change. "Look what He managed to do with just twelve poverty-stricken disciples . . . In two or three centuries He changed the world. But then the aging Roman Empire came along, and took over Christianity and absorbed it. So change came to a halt" (*WM* 139). The roots of change—and, by extension, of modernity and modernization—are Christian, for Walid Masoud, just as they were for Jameel Farran. But they are also Christian-*Palestinian*, linked to the physical landscape where Jesus was born, lived, and preached among the poor. "Here I was in a strange country," Walid says of Rome, "where I couldn't respond to the people and their problems, only to the pictures, statues, and music, because I felt that they all pointed to my country, to Bethlehem, Jerusalem, and Tiberias, to Palestine with its plains and mountains and springs" (*ISWM* 140). According to Walid Masoud himself, Palestinian Christians, by virtue of their very marginality, their so-called "minority" status, possess a powerful potential to change the Arab world, to free it from the customs and history that hold it back, just as Jameel freed Sulafa from her father's tyrannical cloistering in *Hunters*.

Yet there is a crucial difference between the way this Eastern-Christian liberal individualist ethos is presented in *Hunters* and the way it surfaces in *Walid Masoud*. The former novel is narrated in the first person by the very character who holds these views. Jameel Farran controls the entire narrative, and at its end he emerges as triumphant as any Romantic hero. In *Walid Masoud*, the narrative situation is quite different. The novel is polyphonically narrated by numerous characters and includes testimonies from Walid's Iraqi friends Jawad Husni, Ibrahim al-Hajj Nawfal, Maryam al-Saffar, Tariq Raouf and his sister Wisal Raouf (the first auditors of his mysterious tape-recorded monologue), as well as others written by Walid himself as draft chapters in his autobiography. Still other chapters are narrated by family members and friends from Palestine, including Issa Nasser, a Palestinian carpenter who knew Walid as a child in Bethlehem, and Marwan Walid, Walid Masoud's fedayee son.[42] Taken as a whole, and given the numerous references to folders, papers, correspondence, and journals left in the custody of its sociologist frame narrator Dr. Jawad Husni,[43] the novel's structure suggests that what we have in *Walid Masoud* are not the private meditations of the characters who originally listened to Walid's tape-recorded final monologue at a garden party held by the architect Amer Abd al-Hamid,[44] but rather a selection from the various primary sources compiled by Jawad. The book is not only a "search for" Walid Masoud but also a "study about" him (the dual meaning of the word *baḥth* in the novel's title).[45] What we are told about Walid is thus "really threefold," as

Vladimir Nabokov reminds us: "shaped by the teller, reshaped by the listener," and "concealed from both by the dead man of the tale."[46]

In light of this formal conceit, we must remember that the "pages from Walid's autobiography" that elaborate the details of his liberal individualist ethos are explicitly *framed* by the novel's larger narratives of disappearance and searching. They are merely a few sheets among the "seas of paper" that fill Dr. Jawad's office with "their own form of silent roar" (*B* 364). "Silent roaring" is a fitting description for the writings of a liberal, humanist intellectual in an era of politically committed aesthetics. Where *Hunters* proclaims, *Walid Masoud* frames. While several characters are ultimately convinced that Walid did indeed run off to join the fedayeen (and many critics have followed them in this conviction),[47] it is impossible to know what exactly happened to Walid—whether he actually joined the fedayeen, achieved his vision of change, or wrested any reality from his youthful dreams of flying as free as a bird. We cannot know for sure if Jameel's prophecy will be fulfilled by Walid's action, if "an entire order of things" does indeed end up "slipping," or falling, through the diplomatic interventions of the visionary Palestinian (*H* 230). This uncertainty, I wish to argue, is precisely the point of *Walid Masoud*, and what distinguishes it from Jabra's earlier fictional and nonfictional works.

If *Walid Masoud* is not the same sort of paean to Palestinian Christian, liberal humanist individualism as *Hunters in a Narrow Street*, what is it? How, if at all, does *Walid Masoud* revise or frame Jabra's earlier convictions, and what does this framing achieve? I would argue that any analysis focused only on the character of Walid Masoud—particularly as an autobiographical parallel for Jabra himself—misses a crucial aspect of this text. Walid Masoud is not a stable entity; he is not, in de Man's words, a "proper name." He is, rather, a series of tropological associations, "an infinitely varied set of propositions."[48] He is, thus, a figure for truth itself, in the dialectical movement between material and abstract, empirical observation and scientific concept. Attempting to solve or decipher the mystery of his disappearance deflects attention away from the actual material collected in *Walid Masoud*: a chain of testimonies, papers, poems, paintings, letters, and memoirs that could, theoretically, stretch into infinity. There is, indeed, an element of infinity to *Walid Masoud*, since its frame narrator Dr. Jawad ends the novel precisely where he began, by "promising more" (*ISWM* 276). "Now I'll begin my study in earnest," he writes in the novel's last paragraph, as though the book we have just read were merely a draft or sketch, one of an infinite number of possible manuscripts.[49] Infinite, too, are the novel's reflecting mirrors, since, in writing about Walid Masoud, these characters only ever seem to unearth truths about themselves.[50] Jawad compares his research with "traveling inside mirrors" (*ISWM* 277; *B* 365). When Walid's onetime rival Kazim Ismail accuses him of being the scion of a "hidden" or "extinct" aristocracy, "a bourgeois individual who uses humanism as a cover to hide his own class's fears of downfall," his sister Samira reminds him with a laugh that "if Walid had said the same thing to me about you, I might have believed it" (*ISWM* 49).

*Walid Masoud* is a dramatization not so much of the pleasure in solving, then, as the rapture of seeking. Every character who comes into meaningful contact with Walid seems to have a mystical story about the encounter. Ibrahim al-Hajj Nawfal, an art critic and occasional leftist from an upper-class Iraqi family, describes how, at their first meeting, Walid "looked like a hermit; there was something monkish about him" (*ISWM* 236). In an oft-quoted passage, Ibrahim paints Walid as a Christlike redeemer of the Arab world from ignorance and stagnation, "the kind of Palestinian who rejected, pioneered, built, and united (if my nation can ever be united) . . . a scholar, architect, technocrat, rebuilder, and violent goader of the Arab conscience." The English translation, though excellent, loses the tropological, enumerative grammar of the Arabic original, which strings together a series of morphologically rhymed active participles (*asmāʾ afʿāl*, sing. *ism fāʿil*) to create Ibrahim's portrait of Walid:

فوليد انما هو ذلك الفلسطيني الرافض، الرائد، الباني، الموحّد (إذا كان لأمتي أن تتوحد)، العالم، المهندس، التكنولوجي، المجدّد، المحرّك للضمير العربي بعنف. (*B* 322)

Described elsewhere in the novel as an "activist" (in both Arabic, *al-rajul al-fāʿil*, and transliterated English, *al-aktīfist*) (*ISWM* 267; *B* 349), here Walid literally becomes a series of active participles: of first-form verbs (*al-rāfiḍ, al-rāʾid, al-bānī*), followed by second-form verbs in the same structure (*al-muwaḥḥid, al-mujaddid, al-muḥarrik*). His most important task, we are told, is "to foster the new spirit based on knowledge, freedom, love, and a revolt against looking back—all this as a means of achieving the complete Arab revolution." In Ibrahim's eyes, Walid becomes a "self-sacrificing" prophet, a saint (*ISWM* 244). Another character observes that whenever Ibrahim visited Walid's house, "he looked as though he'd been on a pilgrimage to a saint's shrine (*ziyārat waliyy*) or met some legendary hero" (*ISWM* 49; *B* 68–69). The portrait Ibrahim paints, in other words, is colored by his own romantic notions about exilic Palestinians; it is not a faithful representation but a mediated perception.

Maryam al-Saffar, meanwhile—one of Walid's many lovers—also describes her contact with Walid as a kind of mystical experience.[51] The chapter she narrates focuses on a particularly climactic moment during their first romantic encounter at Walid's house in the mountains outside Beirut. After a night of lovemaking, Maryam suddenly jumps up and runs from the bedroom into the exterior garden. Barefoot and naked, she circles the trunks of trees, cuts her feet on sharp stones, and eventually grabs a heavy rock, which she lugs inside the house and presents to Walid. "My pagan body," she recalls, "unsheathed before the wildness of the star-studded night, pierced all things, and all things in turn pierced it. What was this passion? Annihilation? Or being, an utterly violent being?" (*B* 227; *ISWM* 170). Maryam's scene in the highly symbolic "garden" leads to a mystical, "pagan" loss of the self—indeed, the self's "annihilation" (*talāshin*, "becoming nothing")—as it merges with the "things" around it in a chiasmus whose form intertwines with its meaning ("pierced all things, all things in turn pierced it"; yanfudh fī al-ashyā' kullahā, wa-tanfudh al-ashyā' kullahā fīh). The addition of the "stone" or "rock" also symbolically ties this particular mystical experience to Jerusalem, which Jabra describes elsewhere in his oeuvre as a "city of rock" and site of the Dome of the Rock.[52] Loving Walid brings Maryam—significantly named for the Virgin Mary—into ever-closer contact not only with the concrete, tangible, rocky territory of Jerusalem but also with a quasi-mystical experience of the world and all its inanimate "things." The young Wisal Raouf, another of Walid's lovers, describes a similar ego death and infinity in her romantic encounters with Walid: "I used to be aware of myself as a separate entity, as something affected by forces external to it with which it wasn't merged in any way. Yet, with Walid came the peculiar discovery that I was totally merged, transforming, meshing, and emerging as a completely different person from before . . . Time and again, the illusion came to me that Walid was actually me" (*ISWM* 199).

Nowhere is the absent Walid's mystical and supernatural effect on others clearer, however, than in the chapters narrated by Jawad Husni. Our frame narrator begins his "study" by relying on his training as a sociologist, collecting evidence in the form of oral testimonies, letters, and documents, "trying to take all the elements back to square one, to compare part with part, to establish where the gaps are, to look for the lost pieces to fill them" (*B* 364–65; *ISWM* 277). Yet he soon realizes that the methodological and rhetorical constraints imposed by his discipline are far from adequate to his purpose. "What am I supposed to write?" he exclaims at one point. "Don't you know that the sociological point of view rots the imagination at the root? For ten years they train you to view man as a societal phenomenon, and then there you are at the end of it all, totally incapable of looking at him as a discrete, unique person, whose strength of character lies in his mind, in the cells of his brain" (*B* 82; *ISWM* 61). The visionary individual defies the logic of quantitative, sociological, historical analysis. In the end, even as Jawad resolves to finally write his "study," he also questions whether he'll ever reach a conclusion. "Can there ever be a definitive conclusion about any event in life, let alone a man's life as a whole?" (*ISWM* 288; *B* 378). As with any mystical quest for truth and unity, "definitive conclusions" are beside the point. Working on his book-length study of Walid thus becomes more than merely an intellectual, professional, or academic pursuit for Jawad; it is an almost religious passion, one that requires monastic solitude and, every so often, rewards him with moments of ecstasy and rapture:

> When I enter my office alone, I shut the door and exclude my family, my friends, and people in general. The universe is united in a small room, as densely packed as a forest, surging in waves like the sea. I'm at one here too; I ignite, I'm fired, I circle in rotating heavens like a piece of the sun that's broken off. I feel my way through an unknown universe at once horrifying and wonderful. Yet, the only way I can express any of all this is through a feeble phrase here and an even more feeble phrase there . . . When were words bits of chaff, of flame, of rapture, like those that would come

> to me during the trances that thrust me around and dashed me in pieces just so as to reassemble me, then smashed me in pieces once more, so as to reassemble me once more, and so on ad infinitum? (*B* 364–65; *ISWM* 277)

Jawad finds a simultaneous "oneness" and "dashing-to-pieces" in his study, a mystical destruction of the self not in the sublimity of nature but in reading and solitary study. Yet the natural world is not entirely absent from this scene. Jabra's poetic use of the cognate object (*mafaʿūl muṭlaq*) invites the natural elements of "sea" and "forest" into even closer contact with Jawad than the English similes in the above passage let on: Yatawaḥḥad al-kawn fī ghurfah ṣaghīrah, muktaẓẓah iktiẓāẓ al-ghābah, māʾijah mawjat al-baḥr—literally, "Existence is at one in this room packed with the packedness of a forest, waving with the waviness of the sea." As a productive and sought-after destruction of the self combines with a feeling of oneness with the universe, Jawad's contemplation of Walid's life and work transforms him from a self-serious sociologist to a rapturous quasi-mystic. Walid lives here in the "ad infinitum," in the "infinite chain of tropological transformations" before it has frozen into an anthropomorphism, a proper name.[53]

Reading *Walid Masoud* as a metaphysical detective novel, a "missing persons" narrative, reveals its exceptional status among Jabra's extensive oeuvre. The novel does not dramatize the triumph of exilic liberal humanism, as *Hunters* once did, so much as it stages that ethos's ties to the pursuits of Christian mystics and holds it just outside the grasp of characters and readers alike. At a historical moment in which Arab intellectuals and cultural producers were looking for definitive answers (to the mystery of the Arab forces' defeat in the June War, among other things), *Walid Masoud* reenchants the search with the otherworldliness of dreams, memories, and mystical annihilation/permanence (*fanāʾ/baqāʾ*). Yet the novel is also conscious of its status as a closed circle, a vicious cycle, an inescapable Möbius strip. Ibrahim al-Hajj Nawfal nicely captures this problem in the chapter he narrates:

> I noticed something about Walid. Theoretically, his mind was wide open, and he refused to adhere to any one intellectual school (such as Marxism) that would assist him by channeling his energies in increasingly integrative directions. Instead, he imposed on his thinking a circular motion, which may have taken him up in a spiral toward some noble goal, but which also failed to provide him with a complete springboard for all his powers. He seemed very much like a bird with huge wings, flying around in a big hall and eventually bumping against the ceiling unable to break through to the sky beyond. (*ISWM* 237)

Atomization and isolation are the flipside of the liberal-humanist coin. Ibrahim tempers and reinterprets the figurative significance of the bird that elsewhere in Jabra's oeuvre symbolizes aesthetic autonomy and negative liberty. The bird does not transcend political and religious commitments but merely collides with itself in vicious circles. The visionary individual striving to "change mankind, change the world" is also alone in his tree. This critique of atomized subjectivity also surfaces in a passing description of the passengers from *The Ship*: "Transistor radios in every hand blared out all kinds of music—each one a tiny world of its own, establishing its individuality and its incompatibility with everything else."[54] So too are Jawad, Maryam, and Walid tiny worlds of their own, incompatible with everything else. The mystical pursuit is not a line but a circle; the labyrinth of the visionary Arab modernizer has no exit.

## FROM *PALACE WALK* TO SUFI NOIR: MAHFOUZ'S MISSING PERSONS

In contrast with the differences between *Hunters* and *Walid Masoud*, which mark a shift in Jabra's politics of literary form, I argue that all of Mahfouz's works, from the *Trilogy* through the philosophical quest novellas and stories of the 1960s, give form to the skepticism and loss entailed in the departure from faith and the subsequent search for nondivine truth. While the later novels may break with the realist style of the *Trilogy*, the struggle and search for truth in the absence of faith, amid a slew of conflicting philosophies and seemingly random occurrences, remains the same across the middle part of Mahfouz's oeuvre. This section will look first at Mahfouz's more explicit "missing persons" narratives from the 1960s—specifically, the short stories "Culprit Unknown" (*Ḍidd Majhūl*) and "Zaabalawi" (*Zaʿbalāwī*) from the 1962 collection *God's World* (*Dunyā Allāh*) and the 1964 novel *al-Ṭarīq* (*The Way*)[55]—then illustrate how these works serve as continuations of, rather than divergences from, the mystical, asymptotic truth seeking dramatized specifically in the second volume of the *Trilogy*, *Palace of Desire* (*Qaṣr al-Shawq*).

Of all Mahfouz's writings, the short story "Culprit Unknown" most closely follows the conventions of a detective story. Narrated in the third person limited, it begins with a detective, Muhsin ʿAbd al-Bari, facing down both a gruesome murder and a puzzling crime scene. The body of a retired teacher, Hasan Wahbi, has been found brutally strangled in his bed overnight, in the well-to-do neighborhood of Abbasiya. Yet nothing else is out of place: no valuables missing, no broken windows or forced locks, no signs of struggle. Detective Muhsin tries his best to follow the empirical principles of his profession: "This had definitely been a crime, without a doubt," he thinks to himself, "and every crime has a criminal" (an affirmation of cause and effect reminiscent of Tawfiq al-Hakim's prosecutor at his first autopsy: "Here was a murdered man—surely there must be a bullet").[56] Detective Muhsin reminds himself of the steps usually followed in a police investigation: identify the motive, interview potential suspects and witnesses, and develop some conjectures, "trying to resist his own subjective reactions as much as possible" (*MK* 3:142). Even after a thorough forensic investigation and an exhaustive series of interviews and interrogations, however, he comes no closer to solving the mystery. "The man's murder was a puzzle that boggled the mind" (*MK* 3:144).

Feeling defeated "in a way he never had before," he tries to distract himself by reading. "He loved reading Sufi poetry," we are told, "especially the work of Sa'di, Ibn al-Farid, and Ibn al-'Arabi," a pastime so rare among police officers that he "tended to hide it even from his best friends." When he is eventually forced to label Hasan Wahbi's murder file "case closed, culprit unknown" (*ḍidd majhūl*), his readings in Sufi texts give him a new perspective on this formulaic legal phrase. "'Unknown!' he said to himself... 'This really is the great Unknown!'" (*MK* 3:144). In "Culprit Unknown," therefore, echoes of the infinite and divine continue to resonate in Arabic words like "unknown" (*majhūl*) that have lately been used for more mundane juridical purposes. It is only because he reads Sufi poetry that Detective Muhsin picks up on this multivalence, "the language of God in the world of men ... so powerfully in excess of material reality that it overwhelms the agreed-upon relationship of word and object."[57] This same multivalent "unknown" recurs later in the story, when another body is found strangled in bed, with no signs of struggle, no evidence, and no discernible motive for the crime. Detective Muhsin finds himself "facing down the same murderous puzzle that had defeated him only a month earlier . . . staring straight into the unknown, with its silence, strangeness, mystery, cruelty, absurdity, and bitter mockery" (*MK* 3:144).

Like descriptors of the "unknown," bodies also accumulate as the story continues, but there is no discernible connection between the victims, no specter of a motive, and no progress toward knowledge on the part of Detective Muhsin. Abbasiya is gripped by terror, perplexed by "the nature of this danger that advanced indiscriminately and took people by surprise, without distinguishing between old and young, rich and poor, male and female, healthy and sick, or between a house, a tram, and the street" (*MK* 3:147). It slowly becomes apparent that the criminal is death itself—that is, the mystery, unpredictability, and inevitability of death in life. True to the conventions of the metaphysical detective story, the roles of killer, victim, and detective start to blur together for Detective Muhsin 'Abd al-Bari. "I'm the real victim of all these crimes!" he thinks to himself at one point; then, in the very next paragraph, he says, "The only suspect in this case is me!" (*MK* 3:147). Even his pregnant wife's kind words fail to comfort him; he begs her to leave the neighborhood, fearing for her safety and peace of mind. Facing down his despair, Detective Muhsin is once again

> seized by a desire to flee into the world of his Sufi poetry, where there was quiet and eternal truth, where all lights dissolve into the higher oneness of being [*waḥdat al-wujūd*], where there was comfort for the troubles, failures, and futility of life. Isn't it amazing that both a worshipper of Truth and a ferocious criminal could belong to the same life? We die because we waste our life in petty concerns. There is no life, no deliverance for us, unless we aim for Truth [*al-ḥaqq*] and nothing else. (*MK* 3:147)

Sent on a worldly quest for the "truth" (*ḥaqīqah*) behind a series of murders, armed with nothing but the empirical, procedural tools of police "investigation" (*taḥqīq*, "truth-establishment"), and colliding endlessly with the failure and inefficacy of these tools, Detective Muhsin seeks comfort in a different form of truth—eternal Truth, to be found in the "oneness of existence" (*waḥdat al-wujūd*), a phrase specifically associated with the writings of Ibn al-ʿArabi,[58] whom Mahfouz's narrator mentions explicitly as one of the protagonist's favorite writers. For Ibn al-ʿArabi, the term *wujūd* captures both the essence and the existence of God; it is "a philosophical term equivalent to the name 'Allah.'"[59] Its presence in this passage thereby makes it difficult to translate. *Wujūd* does mean "existence," and it has been used in the Arabic philosophical tradition in contrast with "essence" (*shayʾiyyah* or "thingness," for Ibn Sina) and with the "nonexistent" and the "possible" (*al-maʿdūm* and *al-mumkināt*, for the Muʿtazili school).[60] But *wujūd* is also the nominal form of the verb *wajada*, "to find," so that *wujūd* also means "finding," and something that is *mawjūd* is "found"—as one might "find" a killer. Ibn al-ʿArabi's ultimate goal was to illustrate the paradoxical idea that all things are one with God, but that God transcends all things. On the one hand, created things are "radically dependent, mere manifestations of God's true being"; thus God is identified with existence itself.[61] On the other hand, God is also associated with nonexistence, since the things God has not yet created are "at first contained within Him as non-existent and then brought forth" through *nafas al-Raḥmān*, "the breath of the Merciful," a phrase from the hadith implying that "creatures are released or breathed forth after being pent up or constrained, held back from existing."[62]

The presence of Ibn al-ʿArabi's metaphysics makes "Culprit Unknown" highly dialectical: existence is always coupled with nonexistence, and death with life. Mahfouz literalizes the paradoxes of this metaphysics with a plot twist: amidst all the murder around him, Detective Muhsin's wife gives birth at a nearby hospital. After returning to the world of his investigation, the detective feels "something like vertigo," as the Sufi lexicon invades his worldly murder investigation yet again:

> Life extinguished by an unknown noose, becoming nothing. But it was something, without a doubt, something precious. Love, poetry, and a newborn child. Hopes whose beauty knows no bounds. Existence in life . . . just existence in life [*al-wujūd fī al-ḥayāt*]. Is there a wrong that needs righting? When would it be righted? The vertigo intensified, as when waking suddenly after a deep sleep. (*MK* 3:147–48)

Detective Muhsin ʿAbd al-Bari and all the residents of Abbasiya are plagued by the mystery of inexplicable death, which claims lives without any humanly discernible logic, and which cannot be arrested or prosecuted. Yet Detective Muhsin himself witnesses the very process of creation described by Ibn al-ʿArabi: his newborn child goes from "non-existence" to "existence," inhaling the "breath of the All-Merciful" even as the rest of his life is consumed with anonymous victims making the opposite, inexplicable journey into death. Retranslating Mahfouz's passage with this theological lexicon in mind, we might instead write, instead of "existence in life," "*God* in life . . . nothing more than God in life," the everyday miracles and terrors of life and death. Far from seeking justice for a series of gruesome murders, Detective Muhsin is coming to terms with the mysteries and paradoxes of God's simultaneous existence and non-existence in the world we know as human beings. And far from writing a thrilling detective story, Mahfouz is in fact writing a philosophical, metaphysical parable.

If "Culprit Unknown" is a metaphysical parable parading as a detective story, "Zaabalawi," from the same volume, is just the opposite: a tale of questing explicitly saturated with the lexicon and themes of Sufism yet equally critical of the police, specifically of the spiritual "sickness" caused by the policing of modern subjectivities and identities. Plagued by what he calls "that sickness for which no one has a remedy," a sickness which causes "all paths to close before me" and "despair to surround me," an unnamed first-person narrator sets out to find Shaykh Zaabalawi, a man he heard about in a popular song from his childhood and remembers his father describing as a "true friend of God" (*MK* 3:155)—that is, "a holy person, often a paragon of virtue [or] miracle worker memorialized in hagiography and shrine visitation."[63] Like a good gumshoe, the narrator embarks on a series of visits that lead him from the palaces of Cairo's Garden City to the crumbling façades of Umm al-Ghulam and al-Tambakshiyyah, alleyways and neighborhoods around Islamic Cairo. Throughout this journey, the city of Cairo itself becomes reanimated and reenchanted, just as, for the sometime detective fiction writer G. K. Chesterton, the detective's urban pursuit once transformed "every twist of the road" into "a hieroglyph" or "a finger pointing to . . . the meaning of the mystery."[64]

Beginning with Shaykh Qamar, a judge in the religious courts who now has an office in the well-to-do neighborhood of Garden City (popular with foreigners since it was built—and named—by the British), the narrator of "Zaabalawi" then consults a "neighborhood shaykh" in Islamic Cairo, who encourages him to "seek help from his rational mind" and proceeds to draw out a detailed map of the neighborhood around al-Husayn Square. The shaykh stresses the importance of looking carefully in "cafés, recitation circles, mosques, prayer rooms, and around al-Husayn's tomb [al-Bāb al-Akhḍar]," since Zaabalawi "could be mixed in among the beggars in these places, and you'd never recognize him" (*MK* 3:156). However, it is only when he leaves his "rational mind" (*al-ʿaql*) behind and plunges into the world of art and artists that the narrator begins to draw closer to Zaabalawi. A calligrapher named Hassanein describes the shaykh as a "man of mystery" whose presence permeates everything he has ever drawn (*MK* 3:157), while an oud player named Shaykh Gad fondly remembers Zaabalawi inspiring one of his most famous melodies with a line of poetry by famed Egyptian Sufi poet of love and wine, Ibn al-Farid (*MK* 3:158). The quest reaches its climax in the narrator's encounter with Hagg Wanas al-Damanhouri, "a man of private means," who he is told to look for at a local bar. After finding him, the narrator realizes he is "in the presence of a hardened drinker" (*MK* 3:158); in fact, the Hagg refuses to discuss Zaabalawi unless the narrator shares a bottle of wine with him. (That mysticism transcends sect or creed for Mahfouz is evident from this character's name, which implies unity between the Muslim honorific "Hajj," the Coptic Christian saint's name Wanas, and the land of the Nile delta itself—the regional capital Damanhur.) The narrator drinks with the Hagg to the point of passing out, falls into a dream, then awakens surprised to find that his hair is wet. "Did someone see me in this state?" he asks Hagg Wanas in embarrassment, using the Sufi term *ḥāl* for "state" or "condition."[65] "Don't worry," the Hagg assures him. "The man who saw you is a good one. Haven't you ever heard of Shaykh Zaabalawi?" (*MK* 3:158–59). Only on losing his conscious mind does the narrator approach—without ever attaining—his cure.

"Zaabalawi" has been widely described as a kind of Sufi quest narrative, and it is not difficult to see the narrator's "visits" to various secular, religious, and artistic authorities as a series of stations or stops (*mawāqif*, sing. *mawqif*), or alternately "states" (*aḥwāl*, sing. *ḥāl*) on the path toward annihilation and enlightenment in divine permanence.[66] Less often discussed, however, are the story's numerous references to Zaabalawi's fraught relationship with the police. Several characters accuse Zaabalawi of "charlatanism" (*al-dajal*) and advise the narrator to seek his cure with a (real) "doctor" (Mahfouz uses the Arabized English word *duktūr*) (*MK* 3:156). The musician Shaykh Gad also describes how Zaabalawi used to be easier to find, since he "lived in a place that people knew" and occupied a social position "akin to that of political rulers." Now, by contrast, "the world has changed," and Zaabalawi is instead "chased down by the police on accusations of charlatanism" (*MK* 3:157–58). Once considered holy, Zaabalawi is now not only mad but also criminal—and criminally elusive—just as in "Culprit Unknown," the police hunting for the serial murderer concentrated their suspicions on "outcasts, deviants, and madmen, as is the fashion these days" (*MK* 3:146).

The rather lengthy description of the narrator's final dream in "Zaabalawi" has also, surprisingly, remained off the radars of Mahfouz's critics; yet the sudden appearance of the "police" at its end merits further attention (*MK* 3:159). After drinking three glasses of wine, the narrator describes losing first his "will," then his "memory," and then any sense of the "future." He falls out of worldly time and ultimately loses his sense of identity and self. Yet, as he awakens, the self comes barging back in, accompanied by none other than the police:

> There was an extraordinary sense of harmony between me and my inner self, and between the two of us and the world, everything being in its rightful place, without any conflict, irregularity, or discord. In the whole world there was no reason for speech or movement, for the universe moved in a rapture of ecstasy. This lasted but a short while. Then I opened my eyes, and consciousness struck me like a policeman's fist. (*MK* 3:159)

What the dream seems to have facilitated for the narrator is a kind of mystical ego death. He has lost his sense of separation, as a self, from the world around him. "Harmony" comes not only from being at peace with one's own "self" or "soul" (*nafs*) but also with "the world"—that is, the "lowly, mortal" world, *al-dunyā*, as opposed to the infinite "hereafter," *al-ākhirah*. There is no need for movement or speech because it is not humans who move the world of "being"; rather, it is "a rapture of ecstasy" that does so. And yet, when the narrator of "Zaabalawi" leaves the world of the dream and regains consciousness, it is the "police" who arrive as a simile, and it is the "policeman's fist" that violently puts him back in his place as a subject. Whereas the protagonist of "Culprit Unknown" sought to "find" (*wajada*) a mysterious serial killer, and this seeking expanded his sense of what it means to be "found" (*mawjūd*) and what exactly constitutes "presence" or "existence" (*wujūd*) in a world where death and life not only coexist, but coconstitute one another, the narrator of "Zaabalawi" seeks to *lose* himself through healing contact with a "friend of God," a figure whose holiness and grasp on truth are related to his changingness, his defiance of the fixed addresses and identities mandated by modernity (and maintained by the "policeman's fist"). Unlike Zaabalawi, however, the narrator escapes the prying eyes of the state only fleetingly, in a *ḥāl* brought on by the drunken loss of the self but ended by the "policeman's fist." The story ends where it began: with the narrator's conviction that "yes, I must find Zaabalawi" (*MK* 3:160). Neither the reader nor the narrator ever truly "find" Zaabalawi in this story; he is not a stable entity, not a "single assertion or essence," but a figure for truth as trope, "an infinite chain of tropological transformations and propositions" that no closed text, no short story, can locate, contain, or define.

Published in 1964, two years after the collection which included "Culprit Unknown" and "Zaabalawi," *al-Ṭarīq* reads like an extension of these short stories, as it follows yet another anguished male protagonist, Sabir, on an ultimately failed search for his father, a man named Sayyid Sayyid al-Rahimi.[67] Mahfouz overtly thematizes the semantic instability of the word *baḥth* itself between the novel's beginning and its end. In the first chapter, just before she sends Sabir off to search for his father, his mother—an Alexandrian madam named Basima ʿUmran—recalls long periods of contemplation in prison during which she realized that it was not her profession but her approach to mothering Sabir that caused their joint ruin. She "loved her son with all her strength" and used her ill-gotten money to buy him a lavish home, sheltering him from the seedy underworld of her work. But what she once saw as protection she now realizes was mere coddling, preventing Sabir from carving his own path—*ṭarīq*—through life. "I convinced myself that it's not right for me to insist on keeping you, protecting you, because it's not in your best interests . . . The government took you away from me the day they confiscated my money; I no longer have the right to possess you either" (*Ṭ* 11). In trying to shelter Sabir from what she considered an immoral and sinful life, Basimah has, ironically, only further mired him in that life, since she prevented him from acknowledging and working through its realities, leaving him subject to the rumors and derisions of others, which he subsequently internalized as the truth about himself. Basimah sends her son to "search" for his father in this context:

> "Don't judge me. Instead, get ready to search [*li-l-baḥth*] for him . . "
> "To search?!"
> "Yes, I am talking about a man to whom I was a wife thirty years ago, but now I no longer know anything about him . . "
> "Mother, what is the meaning of all this?"
> "The meaning is that I'm directing you toward the only way out of your dilemma."
> "Maybe he's dead."
> "And maybe he's alive."
> "Should I waste my life searching for something before knowing for sure that it exists [*wujūdih*]?"
> "But you won't know for sure that it exists unless you search." (*Ṭ* 12)

As in "Zaabalawi," Basimah prescribes "searching" or "seeking" (*al-baḥth*) as the cure for Sabir's spiritual illness, his obsession with the lowliness from which his mother tried and failed to protect him. For Sabir, "seeking" is a waste of time unless it leads to "finding"—*wujūd*—which, as we learned from "Culprit Unknown," is also, for Ibn al-ʿArabi, "a philosophical term equivalent to the name 'Allah.'"[68] For Basimah, however, the value of the search is not in the "finding" (*wujūd*) or the "God" with which it presumably ends but in the potential for cultivating Sabir's independence. "Under his protection," she promises him, "you'll find respect and dignity, and he will liberate you from the shame of relying on any other creature to set up a life of hustling and crime for you. In the end, you'll attain peace of mind" (*Ṭ* 16). These three terms—respect, dignity, and peace of mind—become the bywords of Sabir's journey throughout the rest of the novel.

In a way, Basimah was right: "searching" for his father quite literally leads Sabir to "peace of mind"—specifically, to Ilham, the young woman at *The Sphinx* newspaper who helps him place a wanted ad in search of al-Rahimi. Only she—this "inspiration," as her name implies—has the power to dislodge his otherwise "fixed ideas about the opposite sex," a group he views, thanks to his experience in the Alexandrian underworld, as "a series of savage, seductive creatures seeking unprincipled passion" (*Ṭ* 43). Even though this was very much his habit with the girls in Alexandria, Sabir doesn't want to undress Ilham in his mind. "Stripping her naked was not wise," the narrator tells us in free indirect discourse,

> because her magic did not reside in any particular location; it radiated like moonlight, and it had an unknown dimension on which his hopes hung as on the abode of his father. He would not realize his happiness with her as he had with the others, that is, through acrobatics and rapacious words, scandalous acts and barbarous, insolent playfulness. She was something rare. And in just a few hours, she had revealed another nature within him, given things a new flavor [*dhawq*] he had never tasted before. (*Ṭ* 43–44)

The "unknown" from "Culprit Unknown" and *Palace Walk* resurfaces here—in the "unknown dimension" (*jānib majhūl*) of Ilham's "magic"—as does a connection between this woman and Sayyid Sayyid al-Rahimi. Both promise Sabir an exit from the prison of the identity he has built for himself, assuming that, because his mother was a prostitute, he too is destined for a life of crime and hustling. Mahfouz's Arabic is again alive with Islamic polysemy too: "tasting" (*al-dhawq*) is another word from the Sufi lexicon, "one of several terms often employed as a virtual synonym for unveiling [*al-tajallī*]" in Ibn al-ʿArabi,[69] and often theorized as a prelude to or "foretaste" of *wajd*, the overwhelming experience of divine presence.[70] It is not so much a life *with* Ilham as one modeled after her example that offers Sabir the promise of "respect, dignity, and peace of mind" he associates only with Sayyid Sayyid al-Rahimi. "She is like his father in the way she sees him, and in being a dream difficult to realize. As for Karimah," the young wife of the octogenarian ʿAmm Khalil, who owns the Cairo hotel where Sabir stays, "she was a living extension of his mother in the pleasures and crimes she inspired" (*Ṭ* 90). He says to Ilham what he cannot say to himself: "It seems to me that I didn't come to Cairo to look for Sayyid Sayyid al-Rahimi, but rather to find you. Sometimes we run toward a specific destination, then on the way [*fī al-ṭarīq*] we stumble on something we soon come to believe is the true destination" (*Ṭ* 86).

Still, although he implicitly acknowledges both Ilham's "rarity" and the "other nature" she has "revealed" in him (*kashafat*, a synonym for *tajallī* in Ibn al-ʿArabi's work), and although he recognizes her, early on, as the "true destination" of the baḥth on which his mother sent him, Sabir cannot accept the goodness of this alternate path, because it contradicts with the image he has built of himself. The depraved identity he has created becomes a prison for his otherwise infinite soul:

> Just as he hid his polluted nature under a façade of strength, so too he hid it by violating good morals to make his past the rule, rather than the shame-filled exception of his life. For this reason, Ilham, even if she had risen like a fire in his life, had also stirred up his fears and his convictions, shaking the foundations of the world he had built for himself and in which he felt secure. In truth, he could only forget his torment in Karimah's fire, kindled in the darkness after midnight. (*Ṭ* 74)

Sabir clings to his passionate relationship with Karimah and agrees to be the protagonist in her murder plot because it confirms his "fixed ideas" about himself: that he is fit for nothing but a life of crime, that he is from slime and to slime he must return. If Ilham is a "clear sky promising safety," Karimah is "a heavily clouded sky, warning with its thunder, lighting, and rain, but also the sky of beloved Alexandria" (*Ṭ* 85), the familiar rather than the great unknown. Like Sabir, Karimah has "wallowed in the mud for a long time, and they understand each other even when they are far apart" (*Ṭ* 88). He rejects the path he has found in Ilham—precisely the "peace of mind" his mother envisioned for him—to fulfill his own prophecy about himself.

Sabir's plot-level "search" for his father, then, represents the first meaning of baḥth that Mahfouz mobilizes in *al-Ṭarīq*. But in the novel's last chapter, the author also activates another resonance of this word when Sabir, who has spent the entire book engaged in one kind of search, becomes the object of another: the "investigative report" (baḥth) one magazine conducts with "a group of distinguished thinkers" regarding his case (*Ṭ* 166). In this report,

> a university professor discussed the unequal marriage between ʿAmm Khalil and Karimah, considering it the real root of the crime. A journalist said that poverty was the culprit, since it had tempted Karimah's first husband to sell her to her second; he described Karimah as a martyr of class warfare and its distinctive characteristics. A social services professor criticized Sabir's upbringing in the embrace of a madam and the traces this past must have left in his psyche. A psychology professor claimed Sabir was afflicted by a father-love complex and that his criminal drive could be explained in two important ways: first, he found in Karimah a substitute for his mother, so he fell in love with her, and second, his sociopathy drove him toward vengeance, so he murdered the hotel owner as a symbol of power and attempted to confiscate his money just as the government had confiscated his mother's. A shaykh and man of religion said that the question was, at its core, one of lost faith. If Sabir had spent one tenth of the time he spent searching for his father searching for God instead, God would have destined him for all he aspired to attain from his father, both in this world and in the hereafter.
>
> Sabir read all these comments in fatigue and confusion, then dismissed them with a shrug of his shoulders. "But nobody has found out whether Karimah was telling the truth or lying," he said to himself, "or whether al-Rahimi exists, or not." (*Ṭ* 167–68)

Mahfouz here offers us something other than a play on worldly and metaphysical seeking like those we encountered in "Culprit Unknown" and "Zaabalawi": this second baḥth is a commentary on reading and literary analysis themselves. He knows, even as he writes, that his stylistic pivot from epic realism to metaphysical allegory will occasion a series of academic experts to weigh in with their chosen metanarratives. University professors, journalists, Marxists, psychologists, and men of religion all come under fire in this passage, not so much for the falsity of their methodologies as for the conviction with which they practice them, the confidence with which they turn the explanation of truth into a profession. In the wake of its publication, many literary critics offered up precisely the readings of *al-Ṭarīq* that Mahfouz parodies here. Rasheed El-Enany assumed the position of the "shaykh and man of religion," arguing that "Sabir's search for his father on the realistic level is nothing short of mankind's search for metaphysical truth (or the Father who is in Heaven) on the symbolic level," and thus the reader is tasked with moving, unidirectionally, from "the characters and events grounded in reality" to "the higher level of meaning."[71] Mahmud al-Rabiʿi, meanwhile, posed as the "psychology professor" when he underscored the parallels between *al-Ṭarīq* and *Oedipus Rex*.[72] But in performing their knowledge and expertise, both Mahfouz's fictional experts and his real-life critics ironically dodge the actual questions at the heart of Sabir's case, which are both ontological and epistemological. Was Karimah lying, or not? And, more importantly, "does al-Rahimi exist or not?" Or, alternatively, "had anyone ever found al-Rahimi, or not" (in kāna al-Raḥīmī mawjūdan am lā)? Here, again, is Ibn ʿArabi's word for "existent things," *mawjūd*, entities "which exist on any level or in any world which is envisaged."[73] In seeking to "explain" the mystery of Sabir's behavior, in other words, these "men of thought" fail to find the truth.

Instead of pathologizing Sabir or identifying al-Rahimi with one or another transcendent meaning, we might turn instead to the more literal meanings of the text: the descriptions Mahfouz *does* provide of this mysterious figure. In this same final chapter, we are told that Ilham hires a lawyer named Muhammad al-Tantawi to defend Sabir in court. On their second meeting in prison, al-Tantawi brings Sabir news of al-Rahimi. It comes secondhand—from a curious figure whom the lawyer introduces as his neighbor in Heliopolis. "Have you ever heard of the journalist who used to sign his daily column 'the Age-Crossing Journalist'?" he asks Sabir, then answers his own question: "Of course not, he stopped working twenty years ago . . . He used to be my teacher in law school, and he's one of the most learned people I know when it comes to the sharia" (*Ṭ* 172). It turns out that this mysterious, blind journalist—this expert in both secular and Islamic law—knows al-Rahimi, or at least "knows" him in the way the calligrapher Hassanein and the musician Shaykh Jad knew Zaabalawi. The journalist tells al-Tantawi, and then al-Tantawi tells Sabir, that al-Rahimi "had only one pastime in this world: love" (*Ṭ* 173). When Sabir asks al-Tantawi if his journalist friend ever heard al-Rahimi speaking about his marriage to Basimah ʿUmran and how she subsequently left him, al-Tantawi replies: "In the life of a man like al-Rahimi, people are as numerous as days; you can never know who was the one leaving, and who was the one left behind" (*Ṭ* 173). The journalist (his name, we've now learned, is Burhan, or "proof" in Arabic) has told al-Tantawi that al-Rahimi married nearly all his companions, that he "practiced love in all its forms, from the sexual to the platonic (*al-jinsī wa-l-ʿudhrī*), with every kind of woman, old or young, married, widowed, or divorced, poor or rich . . . he even made love to servants, garbage collectors, and beggars!" (*Ṭ* 173–74). Even more significantly, al-Rahimi endlessly travels "from town to town and continent to continent," never remaining in a single place for more than a few days (*Ṭ* 174). Al-Rahimi's caution even drives him "to adopt a number of different names and identities" in the course of his travels, to avoid being tracked down by any of his jilted lovers or, more importantly, by "the laws of the state" (*Ṭ* 174–75).[74] When Sabir asks about al-Rahimi's family, al-Tantawi tells him the man has "no family in Egypt" and that his father was "an emigrant from India" who made his millions "selling spiritual beverages" (*Ṭ* 175). The last al-Tantawi has heard, al-Rahimi was "on his way to India, and he gave my friend the book *How to Keep Your Youth for a Hundred Years* and an elegant case of aged wine" (*Ṭ* 178).

In conversation, al-Rahimi apparently told Burhan, "I roam from continent to continent as your fingers roam across your moustache . . . You haven't lived until you've circled the world practicing love." He then drank to the point of intoxication and "sang a love song he had learned from a tribe in the Congo" (*Ṭ* 178–79).

In these passages describing al-Rahimi, Mahfouz's Arabic is once again alive and fluid with Islamic polysemy. Although *mukhaḍram*—the adjective with which al-Tantawi's journalist friend signed his anonymous articles—can simply mean "old" or "aged" in Arabic, it more commonly refers to a person who lived both before and after the advent of Islam, in other words, in both the pagan and the early Islamic eras (hence my imperfect rendering, "age-crossing," in "the Age-Crossing Journalist"). That al-Rahimi is both *mukhaḍram* and has familial ties to India tells us he is perhaps not necessarily the embodiment of the monotheistic God, but a figure for *darshan*, a word from the Sanskrit *drish*, "to see," meaning "the eye-to-eye contact between an iconic divinity or divine personage and the devotee or worshipper" that "can by itself confer grace upon a seeker and result in a spiritual benefit."[75] Rabindra Ray calls *darshan* "a point of departure, not a form of encyclopedic ultimate knowledge"; its practice names "a process that continually amends its viewpoint in order to illuminate the path of action"[76]—an apt description for the stubborn, futile search for "respect, dignity, and peace" dramatized in *The Search*. Likewise, when al-Tantawi claims, of al-Rahimi's many love affairs, that "it is impossible to know who was the one leaving, and who was the one left behind," the Arabic—man al-hājir wa man al-mahjūr—plays on subject-object permutations of the same root, *h-j-r*, "to leave," implying that it is impossible to know whether al-Rahimi is the subject or the object of any action, impossible to fix him into "a proper name."[77] *H-j-r* is also the verb from which *hijrah*, the Prophet Muhammad's journey from Mecca to Medina, is derived, implying that al-Rahimi the *mukhaḍram* might have sided with the pagans of Mecca who derided and persecuted Muhammad, but that he might also have followed the companions who adopted the Prophet's monotheism. Furthermore, in translating the "different kinds of love" that al-Rahimi is said to have practiced into English, "sexual" certainly captures the Arabic of *jinsī*, but "platonic" utterly fails to translate the multiple historical and poetic resonances of *ʿudhrī*, the word Mahfouz uses here. ʿUdhrī poetry is associated with the Arabian tribe of ʿUdhrah, who, in the Umayyad period, became famous for their elegiac amatory verse, which "expressed passionate desire for an unattainable beloved, chastity and faithfulness until death."[78] For its variations on the theme of endless, impossible approaches to the beloved, ʿUdhrī love poetry is also widely understood to have influenced Islamic philosophy and mysticism.[79] We might thus say that al-Rahimi practiced both "worldly" and "otherworldly" forms of love, love of attainment and love whose passion derives from nonattainment, nonfulfillment—that is, *shawq*. With this surrounding context, it also matters that al-Rahimi is said to have made his millions selling not "alcohol"—Mahfouz could very easily have written *al-kuḥūl*—but "spiritual beverages," *mashrūbāt rūḥiyyah*, and that the last we see of him, he is drunk and singing a love song from a Congolese tribe, the Congo as this Cairene author's admittedly problematic figure for remoteness and difference. Unlike Sabir, who denies even the "foretaste" (*dhawq*) of "divine presence" (*wajd*) offered to him by Ilham's "inspiration" (the translation of *ilhām*), al-Rahimi has passed the Sufi waystation of "tasting" and entered the realm of "drinking," *shurb*, which, for the philosopher al-Sarraj, was that much closer to "drinking to one's fill" (*rayy*).[80] As in "Zaabalawi," drunkenness enables the mystical loss of the self or ego and its dissolution into all-encompassing love, which Mahfouz literalizes by characterizing al-Rahimi as a world-traveling lover, fathering more children than he can keep track of. Similarly, the only man to "see" or know anything about al-Rahimi, in the end, is Burhan—"proof"—who is, ironically, blind.

The form of these passages thus mirrors their content: just as al-Rahimi himself, like Zaabalawi, exceeds the bounds of fixed, mortal identities, so too Mahfouz's Arabic crosses this isthmus, a property embodied in *mukhaḍram*, in *hājir/mahjūr*, in *ʿudhrī*, in *mashrūbāt rūḥiyyah*.[81] Mahfouz's fiction consistently plays with Arabic as the language of the divine in the world of men, always overspilling the bounds of fixity and identity. Sayyid Sayyid al-Rahimi eludes the very limiting notions of self and subject to which Sabir makes himself a prisoner.

From "Culprit Unknown" to "Zaabalawi" and *al-Tariq*, Mahfouz's novels from the 1960s consistently depict modern subjectivity as a kind of imprisonment, linking the search for missing persons to the search for the self's annihilation, and using the dark, gritty tropes of noir and crime fiction to set the scene for a mystery that proves more metaphysical than empirical. But while the style of these later novels certainly separates them from the *Trilogy*, their narrative arcs as endless searches inextricably link them with the earlier tome, and specifically with its second volume, *Palace of Desire*. Both sets of work play with the Arabic language, as Mahfouz deliberately and conspicuously uses key terms from the metaphysical and epistemological lexicon of Sufism to characterize these twentieth-century philosophical searches not as secular-scientific divergences from the paradox-laden "way" or "path" followed by the friends of God but as continuations of it.

Already, the title of the *Trilogy*'s second volume, *Qaṣr al-Shawq* (*Palace of Desire*), tells us we are entering the world of a lover's asymptotic pursuit for a beloved who remains unattainable by definition. The "desire" in *Palace of Desire* loses a good deal of *shawq*'s layered Islamic and mystical history. In the tradition of speculative Sufism, *shawq* "expressed both a longing for the beatific vision in the Hereafter and a psycho-spiritual sentiment of yearning as part of a complex mystical love theory . . . concerned with the interiorization of piety . . . a focus on the *bāṭin*, the life of the soul, rather than on the *ẓāhir* of public faith."[82] *Shawq* is characterized by "introspectiveness and total absorption in the object of love. The lover turns away from reality towards an idealized form of his imagination, which occupies his mind to such an extent that even the presence of his real beloved cannot gain his attention. He prefers death to fulfillment."[83] It is difficult to think of a better description for

Kamal, the protagonist of the *Trilogy*, in the midst of his love for Aïda Shaddad, the sister of his good friend Husayn and the radiant light around which all of Kamal's experiences hover in the second volume of the *Trilogy*.

To understand the shawq that saturates *Qaṣr al-Shawq*, however, we need to take a brief detour to examine another love object and "missing person" at the heart of the previous volume in the *Trilogy, Bayn al-Qaṣrayn* (*Palace Walk*). If Jesus is the "missing person" around whom Jabra builds *In Search of Walid Masoud*, al-Husayn ibn ʿAli is the hollow core around which the entirety of Mahfouz's *Trilogy* revolves. A grandson of the prophet Muhammad famously martyred in the Battle of Karbala in 680 CE, al-Husayn is revered by Muslims all over the world, but particularly in Cairo, where the mosque, mausoleum, and square bearing his name and sometimes said to house his decapitated head are still the bustling center of the area around al-Azhar Mosque and University. In the eighth chapter of *Palace Walk*—the first for which Kamal serves as focalizer—Mahfouz describes the very particular place al-Husayn occupies both in Kamal's young heart and in his day-to-day life, as one of many sights (and sites) he passes on his way home from school. For the young Kamal, al-Husayn is the possibility of infinity and immortality in a finite, mortal world. Kamal's "youth and upbringing," we are told, "had fated al-Husayn to be an inexhaustible stimulus for the imagination and emotions of his heart" (*MK* 2:350). The young Kamal is not "taught to revere" al-Husayn, as the English translators of *Palace Walk* have it;[84] rather, this Muslim saint is the locus, the "stimulus" (*mīthār*) of his imaginative and emotive capacities. It is not the saint's status in the Prophet's bloodline that grants him a special place in the boy's "heart," however (and the "heart," *qalb*, is key to this and every other passage pertaining to al-Husayn over the 1,300-page course of the *Trilogy*). "Kamal's knowledge of the Prophet and his life . . . did not explain his soul's constant hunger to hear that life story repeated and embellished with the noblest stories and the deepest faith." Rather, something else—some other mysterious force—is at work here. "It reached the point where al-Husayn's story, across the centuries, found in Kamal a loving, passionate, faithful, sad, tearful listener" (*MK* 2:350). It is the shawq—the "longing for beatific vision in the hereafter"—of piety that saturates Kamal's relationship with al-Husayn. The only thing that comforts the boy is knowing "what was said about the martyr's head after it was separated from his pure body: no dwelling on earth would satisfy it except for Egypt, so it arrived there, pure and praising God, then laid to rest where his shrine now stands" (*MK* 2:350). No matter how many times Kamal hears the tale of this Islamic saint's martyrdom, his soul hungers for yet more repetitions, yet more embellishments; no matter how many times he passes by al-Husayn's shrine in a single day, going to or coming from school, the sight of its walls and minaret still call out to his soul and bring harmony to his heart:

> How often he stood near the shrine, dreaming and thinking, wishing his vision could penetrate the depths to gaze upon the beautiful face which, his mother assured him,

> had resisted the vicissitudes of fate with its divine secret, preserving its health and beauty to illuminate the tomb's darkness with the light of its blaze. When he couldn't find a way to realize his wish, he contented himself with the secret conversations he carried on during his long pauses there, eloquently expressing his love, complaining to al-Husayn about his young worries . . . Although his habit of passing by the mosque morning and evening had somewhat lessened the strength of its effect on him, still, as soon as his eye fell on the shrine, Kamal would recite the fatiha for it, even if he did so multiple times in one day. Indeed, custom could not uproot the joy of dreams from his breast; the sight of the lofty walls still harmonized with his heart, and its high minaret still emitted a call that his soul was quick to obey. (*MK* 2:350)

For young Kamal, truth lives here, in the mysterious, secret impenetrability of this shrine, and in the impossibility of verifying, through empirical knowledge, whether al-Husayn's head has truly remained young and beautiful through some "divine secret." Infinite and unverifiable, an "inexhaustible resource" of stories, emotions, wishes, and dreams, communicating not with the rational mind but with the soul and heart, al-Husayn seals and verifies truth by withholding (rather than explaining) mystery. Just as the story of al-Husayn's courage, faith, and martyrdom inspires the same level of fervent emotion no matter how many times Kamal hears it, so too the presence of al-Husayn's shrine in his neighborhood offers a constant, daily reminder of the interpenetration of worlds and times, the coexistence of local drink sellers and sweet shops with infinity and magic.

*Qaṣr al-Shawq*, by contrast, introduces us to a very different Kamal. The magic and infinity of al-Husayn have completely departed from his heart. In the fifth chapter of this second volume, he recalls his reaction upon first learning, from his Islamic history teacher, that "the shrine of al-Husayn is a symbol, nothing more" (*MK* 2:618). Whereas his commonsensical friend Fuʾad al-Hamzawi took this news with equanimity and ease, Kamal

> was like someone staggering from the shock of the blow that had struck at the core of his heart; he cried for a specter that had vanished and a dream that had disappeared. Al-Husayn was no longer their neighbor, and in fact had never been their neighbor, not for a single day. What had become of the kisses he'd imprinted with such trust and passion on the door of that shrine? What would become of his pride in proximity, his pleasure in propinquity? Nothing, nothing had come of all that, nothing remained but a symbol in the mosque and a desolation, a disappointment in his heart. That night he cried until his pillow was soaked through. (*MK* 2:618)

The "heart" (*al-qalb*) is once again central to this passage. Much of Kamal's identity is built on his family's proximity to that mosque and mausoleum. To lose al-Husayn is to lose the sense of otherworldly, inaccessible meaning and truth that has anchored his young life; it is a loss of innocence common to every coming-of-age story yet given a Cairene twist in Mahfouz's novel, which anchors this fall from grace both in the specificity of Islamic piety and in the physical space of the ancient quarter al-Gamaliyya, which—like Kamal—finds its heart anchored in al-Husayn's shrine.

Despite this disillusionment, however, Kamal has not entirely lost his penchant for worshipful devotion in *Palace of Desire*; he has simply replaced one object of veneration with another, and one Cairo neighborhood with another. When the reader first encounters him in this volume, he is lying in bed, addressing a lyrical six-page inner monologue to a young woman we later learn is Aïda, sister to the significantly named Husayn Shaddad (one Husayn gives way to another). That Aïda has replaced al-Husayn as the object of Kamal's worship is evident from the very first time the novel describes Kamal visiting her family's mansion (*qaṣr*, literally "palace") in Abbasiya. Kamal feels both "pleasure" (*iʿjāb*) in this quarter of Cairo, owing to the bourgeois neighborhood's "cleanliness, its layout, and the relaxing quiet that reigned over its residences, all qualities unknown to his bustling old neighborhood," as well as "a love and esteem that bordered on worship [*al-taqdīs*]," because Abbasiya was "the homeland of his heart, the dwelling place for his love's inspiration, and the abode of his beloved's palace [*qaṣr maʿbūdathihi*]" (*MK* 2:655). Where once Gamaliyya housed both mundane and otherworldly sites, now Abbasiya embodies both civilized modernity (cleanliness, quiet, an orderly layout) and "worship"—Aïda is not only Kamal's *maḥbūbah* (object of love) but his *maʿbūdah* (object of worship). The word *ʿābid*, "worshipper," also figures prominently in the lexicon of Ibn al-ʿArabi, where it signifies "everything other than God, that is, the cosmos," while the "worshipped," *al-maʿbūd*, is "that which is named God."[85] "All of this quarter's landmarks, sights, and roads," the narrator of the *Trilogy* informs us, "were connected, in [Kamal's] mind, with thoughts, emotions, and fantasies that, taken as a whole, had become the core of his life and the juncture of his dreams. Wherever he turned his face, there was something calling his heart to prayerful prostration [*sujūd*]" (*MK* 2:655–66). Kamal's pious heart, once so anchored in al-Husayn's quarter, has a new locus in Aïda, her mansion, and the aristocratic quarter named for the khedive. Lest we miss the implications of Kamal's very literal change of heart, Mahfouz offers us this explicit parallel, in Kamal's description of the Shaddad family mansion:

> With its two floors, the palace seemed from the outside like a great, lofty building . . . This view was printed on the page of [Kamal']s soul; its greatness held him prisoner, and the signs [*āyy*] of its stateliness enraptured him; he saw its grandeur as but a trivial token of its owner's worth; its windows appeared in his eyes, some closed, others with wide-open drapes, and he saw in their aloofness and concealment that which symbolized the value, modesty, abstinence, and mystery of his beloved; they were meanings [*maʿānin*] confirmed by the extensive garden and the desert stretching out to the horizon, presenting here or there a distant palm tree, a hyacinth vine climbing a wall, braids of jasmine scaling another, challenging his heart with memories that tangled over their heads like fruits, assailing him with words of love, pain, and worship. They all became appearances of the beloved [*ṭallan li-l-ḥabīb*], a breath

> of her spirit and a reflection of her features, all of them emitting—since he knew the palace's family had lived abroad in Paris—an atmosphere of beauty and dreaminess that harmonized with his love's loftiness, sanctity, and splendor, its anticipation of the unknown . . .
>
> It was no small thing for his fluttering heart to walk through this great mihrab, to tread on a surface her feet had trod before him; he almost stopped out of reverence or extended his hand to the wall of the house to seek its blessing, just as he once had at the tomb of al-Husayn, before learning that it was nothing but a symbol. (*MK* 2:656–57)

Kamal reads Aïda's posh Abbasiya palace as one might read a holy text: its outward signs (*ṭulūl, ẓawāhir*) are tokens or hints of its ineffable inner meanings (*maʿānī, bawāṭin*), especially the transcendent qualities of his beloved and her family.[86] Here again, as in the description of Amina in her rooftop garden, Mahfouz plays on the inherent polysemy of Arabic as both the language of men and that of the Qurʾan. The palace's "greatness" (*jalāl*) is also a frequent descriptor for God ("held dear and revered," ʿazza wa jalla); its stateliness is revealed in "signs," or *āyy*, also the word used for "verses" of the Qurʾan; and these signs "enrapture" Kamal—*taftinuhu*—literally testing his faith with temptations. Most importantly, Kamal views the entire property as a "mihrab"—a prayer-niche facing toward Mecca that is a feature of every mosque—and he has to catch himself not to perform the same rites of worship he once did at the tomb of al-Husayn.[87] The Shaddad mansion, a figure for the ineffable Aïda herself, literally reorients (or rather, *de*-orients) his desire, his shawq, his longing for and enslavement to the divine. This passage also notably embeds many of the terms and figures first associated with Amina in her garden of pious, affective knowledge—jasmine and hyacinth, worship and love, mystery and the unknown—with Kamal circumambulating the Shaddad mansion.

Kamal is most certainly a "seeker" in *Palace of Desire*, then, even if the person he is after shifts from the Muslim saint whose shrine finds its home in Islamic Cairo to the French-educated young woman whose palace sits stately in Abbasiya. He is the seeker who, like Detective Muhsin, Sabir al-Rahimi, and the narrator of "Zaabalawi," is bound by shawq, by impossible love. We soon learn that this love entails much more than mere attainment of its nominal object, Aïda. His love for her is explicitly bound up with his educational pursuit of what he calls "knowledge," "truth," and "the cultivation of thought." In a famous and much studied scene ten chapters earlier in *Palace of Desire*, Kamal's father—the domineering, fear-inducing al-Sayyid Ahmad Abd al-Jawad—confronts him about what college he plans to enter and what he wants to do with his life. He is dismayed when Kamal declares his intention to enter the Teachers' Training College and, fearful for his son's future, suggests Kamal consider law school instead. Here Kamal is forced to admit to himself that "there were desires in his soul which required careful scrutiny if their aims were to be made plain," and that "he wasn't even convinced he would grasp them at the Teachers' Training College, but still thought this institution the shortest path to understanding them." That the word Kamal uses for "desires" here is the plural of *shawq, ashwāq*, gives us a hint to what follows these comments in the same, lengthy passage of free indirect discourse. In part, yes, these desires had been stirred by "scattered readings" in literary criticism, sociology, and religion, as well as popular sources like the epic of ʿAntar and the *Thousand and One Nights*.

> But it was also true that he delighted at the presence of a strong bond connecting the [Teachers' Training] College to his heart and, more precisely, to his love. How? There was no cord tying his "beloved" [*maʿbūdah*] to law or economics, but there were cords—however thin and invisible—between her and religion, spirit, creation, philosophy, and other related forms of knowledge that tempted him to drink from their springs, in the same way that she was linked to song and music, through secrets he might glimpse in a moment of musical transport and the munificence of ecstasy. He found all of this within himself and believed in it ardently, but what could he say to his father? (*MK* 2:607)

Although much critical attention has focused on Kamal's election of the humanities and liberal arts over a more practical education in law or economics, this passage makes apparent for the first time in this volume how integrally Kamal's pursuit of "knowledge" and "thought" is linked to his pursuit of Aïda. Both love objects are substitutes for the martyr al-Husayn and all the significance he once embodied for Kamal—that taste of divinity and ineffability, of "religion, spirit, creation, philosophy," living and breathing in the everyday world of Gamaliyya. Aïda, in short, has become Kamal's religion. He is a shaykh pursuing the *fiqh* of Romantic love.

But just as Amina's epistemological panorama was edged with *majhūl* in *Palace Walk*, so too Kamal's reverence for Aïda and the "mysterious world of thought" he wishes to pursue in his studies is laced with fateful blindness. Mahfouz hints at Kamal's impending fall with a brief glimpse inside al-Sayyid Ahmad's head. As Kamal is speaking, his father examines his appearance, and suddenly, as the narrator jumps from Kamal's to al-Sayyid Ahmad's mind, the father sees his son, "as if for the first time," noticing his abnormally large head and nose, his thin build and his absurdly long neck. "Isn't it likely," he thinks, "that he'll fall prey to someone like me who searches for defects to make the butt of his jokes?" (*MK* 2:608; *CT* 590). This is precisely what comes to pass fourteen chapters later, when Kamal finds himself alone for the first time with Aïda in the Shaddad mansion gazebo. Whereas Kamal "took great pains to study his beloved as though seeking to fathom her secrets and print her features and symbols upon the page of his imagination" (*MK* 2:689), Aïda chides him for not having started to grow out his hair. "Don't you realize that your head is very large?" she says (*MK* 2:691). Soon she is staring at his nose and laughing. "I've just remembered some hilarious things I read in a famous French play," she tells him with haughty cruelty. "Have you read *Cyrano de Bergerac*?" (*MK* 2:691). Kamal's father has foreseen precisely the derision to which his son's absurd appearance and penchant for romantic worship (even in supposedly secular love) will subject him.

Yet despite this cruel treatment at Aïda's hands, Kamal does not revere her any less. On the contrary, her derision only makes him a more devoted worshipper, and it is in the terms of Islamic worship that Mahfouz describes the boy's reaction to her cruel words. "He had to accept this pain with Sufi resignation [*taslīm Ṣūfī*], just as a worshipper accepts divine decree with the utmost belief in its justice, no matter how harsh, knowing that it issues from a perfect, complete beloved [*ma'būd*] with no suspicion in any of his attributes or acts" (*MK* 2:691; *CT* 754). Like a Sufi, Kamal has dedicated himself to chronicling and naming the many types of pain to which his love has subjected him, including "the pain of separation, the pain of forbearance, the pain of leave-taking, the pain of doubt, the pain of despair," as well as "pains that can be borne, pains that are even sweet, and pains that won't rest no matter how many sighs and tears he offers up to them" (*MK* 2:692), a list that reads almost like the table of contents for a manual of Sufi practice in asceticism. Mahfouz even refers to Kamal's experience in love as a form of religious education. "It was as though he had loved in order to study the encyclopedic *fiqh* of pain [li-yatafaqqah fī ma'jam al-alam]" (*MK* 2:692). Kamal may have chosen to study the liberal arts at school, and to socialize with the aristocracy in the palaces of Abbasiya rather than with the working class in the coffeehouses around al-Husayn Square, but his heart is still grounded in al-Gamaliyya, with its rich history of Islamic scholarship, its human interpretation (*fiqh*) of divine law (*sharī'ah*). Kamal depends on this unattainable love for his very existence, as he once built his world on the inaccessible "divine secret" of al-Husayn's magically preserved and holy head.

Immediately following their meeting in the gazebo, however, Kamal's ultimate disappointment in love begins. In the very next chapter, Hasan Salim, a member of Kamal's friend group with an even higher class status than Husayn Shaddad, reveals to Kamal that Aïda is "in love" and, specifically, is in love with him, Hasan Salim. What's worse, Aïda has begun ignoring Kamal, sometimes acting outright hostile toward him. When Kamal confronts her in the gazebo about this harsh treatment, he discovers that Hasan Salim has twisted the words from their conversation about Aïda into scandalous lies about Kamal, and try as he might, he cannot convince her of their untruth. Still, even after yet more cruel treatment, Kamal continues to worship his "beloved." Three chapters later, he still makes a "pilgrimage" (*yaḥajj*) to visit Abbasiya every evening at sunset, and he still "circumambulates the mansion" (*yaṭūf bi-l-qaṣr*) as one might circumambulate the Kaaba in Mecca, "temporarily sated with contemplation of the shrine (*maqam*) and reviewing his memories" (*MK* 2:714). In this same chapter, he is surprised, after a long separation, to see Aïda leaving the house. He follows her and, now having nothing left to lose, breathlessly confesses his love. But, as in the conversation with his father nineteen chapters earlier, Aïda brings his lofty aspirations crashing back down to earth when she asks him "what comes next?" (*MK* 2:717). Although Mahfouz's narration has followed Kamal for almost eight hundred pages at this point, making us sympathetic to his view of things, now, seeing him momentarily through Aïda's eyes, we glimpse the absurdity of his romantic reverence. She asks him "what he wants"; out loud, he stammers, "I want . . . I want you to give me permission to love you." Aïda can't help but laugh at this response. "You bewilder me. It seems to me that you even bewilder yourself [*tuḥayyir nafsaka*]." For the first time, Aïda is not wrong or cruel; Kamal does exist in a perpetual state of "bewilderment," or *ḥayra*, another term from Ibn al-ʿArabi's Sufi lexicon that Mahfouz reanimates in this all-important scene. "To find God is to fall into bewilderment [*ḥayra*], not the bewilderment of being lost and unable to find one's way, but the bewilderment of finding and knowing God and of not-finding and not-knowing Him at the same time."[88] In the passage above, Aïda speaks more truthfully than either she or Kamal realizes. As a "seeker," Kamal truly does live in a state of "bewilderment" when it comes to his love, his quest, which for now has taken a divinized version of Aïda as its object. His very name embeds the idea that he moves beyond mere "completion" as a creation of God (*tamām*), toward "perfection" through worship and revelation" (*kamāl*)[89]—a "perfection" we glimpsed several hundred pages earlier, when the *Trilogy's* narrator described Amina's world as one whose "merits . . . were not confined to the melodies of life," but were "supplemented and perfected by worship [*yukammiluhā bi-l-ʿibādah*]" (*MK* 2:343).

Forced to consider "what he wants," then, Kamal reflects on Aïda's question: "He hadn't answered because he doesn't know what he wants. Would it be wrong to say he longs for communion in love [*wiṣāl*], the communion of spirit with spirit, and to rap on the secret's locked door with an embrace or a kiss?" (*MK* 2:718). What Kamal seeks is *wiṣāl*, yet another "technical term of Sufism" borrowed from early love poetry and signifying "an amorous relationship which one accuses the other of not respecting, rather than union as such."[90] As this term passes from love poetry into the writing of Sufi thinkers, it carries the traces of unrequited love to the quest for divine union.[91] Kamal is often considered in opposition to Mahfouz's later protagonists, all of them mystic-type figures questing after truths that remain just out of their reach. Here, and throughout the passages chronicling the nature and saga of his love for Aïda, however, we can see that Kamal too is a "seeker" after divine union, tragically confusing the divine with the worldly, replacing al-Husayn ibn ʿAli with Husayn and Aïda Shaddad.

One final mention of al-Husayn's shrine, and its loss, is worth mentioning here. On the night of Aïda's marriage to Hasan Salim, after the main celebrations have ended, Kamal and his friend Ismaʿil Latif walk and converse on the street outside the mansion. In response to Kamal's offhand question about how much longer the festivities are likely to go on, Ismaʿil notes that they will have to wind down soon, so the newlyweds can get some sleep before departing for their honeymoon, then corrects himself. "But who's ever slept on their wedding night? . . . Don't let Hasan's reserve mislead you. He'll be leaping and bouncing like a stallion until dawn" (*MK* 2:752). At this, Kamal marvels at yet a new, distilled form of pain, "the essence of pain, the pain of pains," "not from losing your lover, for you never aspired to possess her, but because she has descended from the heights of her heaven, because she has dirtied herself in the mud after a rich life led above the clouds, because she allows her cheek to be kissed and her blood to flow! And her body to be degraded, worn out in common service" (*MK* 2:752; *CT* 872). Rather than enlighten Kamal or soften the blow of this confrontation with Aïda's humanity and susceptibility to sexual desire and possession, Isma'il Latif's words only deepen Kamal's despair, his sense of the emptiness at the heart of an existence he once believed to be enchanted by contact with infinity, unknowability. And once again, al-Husayn surfaces as the central figure for this emptiness: "Behind the veil of sacrality before which you've always prostrated yourself, your whole life, they'll be cavorting like children. Why does everything seem so empty! Mother . . . father . . . Aïda . . . al-Husayn's tomb as well . . . ah, what fierce pain!" (*MK* 2:753; *CT* 873). Kamal simultaneously longs to confront the reality of bodies having sexual intercourse and recoils from the thought of such a confrontation, clinging to the idealized, holy image of Aïda that he has created for himself (much as Sabir clung to the prison of the criminal identity he also built for himself). When Kamal and Isma'il go their separate ways, Kamal only advances a few yards before turning around. He slips into the darkness of the desert that surrounds the Shaddad mansion—an appropriate place for a mystical worshipper to contemplate the light and mystery of his spiritual beloved:

> Worship won't be of any use tonight, since it knows nothing of selfish desires. He had never aimed for Aïda; as for Hasan Salim, he was from a different sect for whom worship was not required. Thus Kamal stood, tormenting himself in the desert, while over there kisses like any others known to human beings were exchanged, and sighs overflowing with sweat and swooning caused blood to trickle out and a nightgown to fall away from a mortal body, like this mortal world with its empty hopes and frivolous dreams. Go ahead and cry over what seems to you the abasement of the gods, and may your heart be filled with the tragedy. But where will the beautiful, amazing feelings that illuminated his heart for four full years go? They were not a delusion or the echo of a delusion; they were life's life, and even if circumstances control the body, what power can take possession of the spirit? Let the beloved [*al-ma'būdah*] remain his object of worship [*ma'būdatih*]; let love remain his torture and his refuge, bewilderment his diversion, until he stood before the Creator one day and asked Him about the enigmas of things that perplexed him . . . Ah, if only he could contemplate what was behind that window, if only he could uncover the secret to the secrets of his existence. (*MK* 2:755; *CT* 876–77)

Kamal's contemplation of Aïda is saturated with both the figures and the technical lexicon of Sufism. Kamal is torn between the infinity of worship (*al-'ibādah*)—which, as we have seen, he wholly identifies with love—and the hateful worldliness of the self, the ego (*al-nafs*, in the phrase "worship knows nothing of selfish desires," wa khalā al-ʿibādah min maṭālib al-nafs). Kamal recognizes that he never wanted to marry or possess Aïda; what he wanted was to worship her, preserve her place in the inaccessible, lofty "sky" with which she is consistently associated throughout *Palace of Desire*.[92] His desire is not lust, but longing—shawq. Just as in this passage Kamal stands in a dark desert contemplating a light behind a window, light and radiance as figures for divine illumination also saturate early Sufi works dealing with shawq.[93] What Kamal wants is not union in marriage, but communion in "arrival"—*wiṣāl*—the dissolution of the ego which, paradoxically, leads to its eternal presence (*baqāʾ*). In a state of shawq, to attain the object of one's love is to evaporate, to lose the defining relationship of one's existence. It is not the possession of the love object but the yearning for it that teaches piety and the abnegation of the "self" or *nafs*, also a key term in this passage. Similarly, given that Kamal associates his quest for Aïda with his search for knowledge, truth, and beauty, it is not in the attainment of, but rather in the endless questing after, truth that Kamal's life—and the lives of Mahfouz's other protagonists, and Jabra's characters—comes to have any meaning. Hasan Salim knows nothing of these mystical paradoxes, for he comes from a different "sect" that does not require worship as one of its tenets. Kamal, by contrast, holds to his "standing"—his *mawqif*—in the desert, clinging to the infinity of his lover's passion even as he mourns its worldly demise, a pious moth circling the lamp in the niche of Aïda's palace.

This scene in the desert is the often overlooked backdrop to a more famous scene from *Palace of Desire*—one in which al-Sayyid Ahmad confronts Kamal about the article he's written on Darwin's theory of evolution.[94] Mahfouz makes Kamal's disillusionment with religion inextricable from his disappointment in love: his heart is said to be "filled to bursting with pains—the pain of disappointed love, the pain of doubt, the pain of a dying faith" (*MK* 2:762). At the prompting of his father's questions, Kamal is forced to ask himself why he had written his article on Darwin's theory of evolution in the first place. "It was as if he wanted to announce the death of his faith to everyone," the narrator tells us. "But I am not an unbeliever, I still believe in God; as for religion . . . where is religion? It's gone! Just as the head of al-Husayn is gone, just as Aïda is gone, just as my self-confidence is gone" (*MK* 2:762). The successive losses of Kamal's young adult life here, again, all gesture back to the original loss of al-Husayn. Having overcome what he here calls "legends and fables," there is a recurring emptiness, a void at the center of Kamal's existence. "Our father Adam!" he laughs to himself. "He's no father of mine. Let my father be an ape, if that is truth's will [*in shāʾa al-ḥaqīqah*]" (*MK* 2:763). Here "truth" (*al-ḥaqīqah*) has quite literally replaced "God" (*Allāh*) in the Arabic expression *in shāʾa Allāh* ("if it is God's will"), reflecting in miniature Kamal's disillusionment with the imaginative stories of his youth and his turn to science as the optimal path to truth. Significantly, though, these are both linked to Aïda's cruelty: "If I were really from a prophetic bloodline, she would not have mocked me so murderously!" (*MK* 2:763).

While it might seem that Kamal's idealistic piety will die with this relinquishing of religion and embrace of science, this change later proves merely to be a further permutation of that idealism. "Truth"—*al-ḥaqīqah*—has now replaced al-Husayn ibn ʿAli and Aïda as the object of Kamal's material and metaphysical pursuits. "He secretly promised his mother that he would dedicate his life to spreading God's light, for wasn't it identical with truth's light? Of course it was, and with his liberation from religion, he would be closer to God than he had been when he believed in Him, for what is true religion if not science? . . . If prophets were sent forth today, they would choose science as their message" (*MK* 2:764). Kamal "still believes in God," but God is now to be embodied only as "truth," and specifically as "scientific truth," the prophecy of the present, the rupture leading from a "superstitious past" to an "enlightened future" (*MK* 2:764). Later, Kamal's friend Ismaʿil Latif points out the hypocrisy in this view: "Even after your conversion to atheism, you still believe in 'truth, goodness, and beauty,' and you wish to dedicate your life to them. Isn't this what religion calls for?" (*MK* 2:767). Nevertheless, Kamal still affirms—in his mind—that the choice between Aïda and living an exalted life (*al-ḥayāt al-sāmiyyah*, literally a "heavenly life") is false, because "behind every ideal, I always see a glimmer of Aïda" (*MK* 2:767). Kamal's life leaps from idealism to idealism, from Islamic piety to romantic reverence, and now to a new faith—one in science itself. Yet every idealism is buffeted by winds of disappointment: as Yaseen Noorani writes, he "lives the fall of Aïda all of his life."[95]

Having passed through a series of stations on his journey to knowledge and completeness, including "love communion" (*wiṣāl*), "bewilderment" (*ḥayrah*), and "impossible longing" (shawq), it seems inevitable that Kamal should end up seeking drunkenness in a tavern on the Cairo street Wajh al-Birka, just as the narrator had to drink to "find" Zaabalawi in "Zaabalawi," and Sayyid Sayyid al-Rahimi made his fortune selling "spirit beverages." Rather than using alcohol to muster the courage to "investigate woman"—that is, to have sex with a prostitute and thereby confront the reality of his own body and of Aïda's, the stated goal of this journey—Kamal searches instead for a new ideal. "Aïda is gone," he thinks, "so I must create another Aïda embodying all of the meanings she symbolized" (*MK* 2:770).

Three major paragraphs chronicle Kamal's drunkenness (*MK* 2:771–72), and their tone once again mimics Sufi style, seeking figurative language to capture the essence of this drunkenness: "an inner music played by the spirit, to which ordinary music was, by comparison, like the peel of the apple compared to its fruit" (*MK* 2:771). No single metaphor can encapsulate this sensation; drunkenness is a form of music so transcendent that it itself needs a figurative explanation (the apple and its peel). Concatenated metaphors lead to beautiful bewilderment; again, Kamal could be writing a treatise on Sufi practice: "What could be the secret of this golden liquid that creates such a miracle in only a few moments? Perhaps it purifies life's stream of all foam and sediment, releasing its suppressed current, just as the first time it released complete freedom and pure ecstasy; this is the natural feeling of life's thrust when it is liberated from the body's noose, society's shackles, history's memories, and fears for the future: a pure, clear music dripping with delight and inspiring delight" (*MK* 2:771). The "secret" of drunkenness, in other words, is a glimpse of the infinite—a music that is both saturated with and generating "delight" or "rapture" (*ṭarab*). Here, Kamal returns to the question he posed earlier, and the narration subtly slips in a first-person possessive pronoun for the first time: "Something like it has visited my spirit [*rūḥī*] before, but when, how, and where? Ah . . . I remember . . . it was love! The day she said my name, 'Hey Kamal.'" But again, this feeling cannot be contained either in a single metaphor or in a single narrative voice, as we shift from first to second person: "You were drunk without knowing what drunkenness is; admit that you're a longtime drunkard, that you've spent lifetimes kicking up a racket on the path of wine-drunk love, paved with flowers and sweet herbs" (*MK* 2:771–72). Kamal has come to the tavern trying to forget Aïda, but earthly wine has only called her simultaneous status as his "beloved" and his "enslaver" (*maʿbūdah*) to his mind all the more forcefully—indeed, it has almost put him through a reversion, as he rewinds through all the pain she inflicted to find his love as a pure "dewdrop," not yet muddied by reality. "Love and get drunk, or get drunk and love"—this could easily be the motto of Zaabalawi or Sayyid Sayyid al-Rahimi in *al-Ṭarīq*.

The language of this passage grows increasingly recondite as Kamal's drunkenness progresses. It is difficult to say who speaks, and of what, in these lines, but a familiar image draws us back from drunken abstraction to Kamal's memories: "As for the strands of black hair hanging over her forehead, they were a Kaaba toward which all the drunkards in all the taverns of love and divine presence [*wajd*] oriented themselves" (*MK* 2:772). Earlier in this volume, when Kamal roamed the desert outside the Shaddad family mansion, he felt the place itself to be holy—a "great mihrab" where he was tempted to prostrate himself in prayer, to graze a door with his hand or his lips. Here, however, Aïda herself has become a Kaaba, the focal point not only for Kamal's prayers, but for all love-drunk worshippers. If Aïda's house is a "mihrab," it points to Aïda herself, who here becomes the Kaaba in Mecca.

In a highfalutin philosophical speech he subsequently makes to Ismaʿil—this time speaking out loud rather than in internal monologue—Kamal affirms that

> this ecstasy is the secret of life and its lofty goal; wine is nothing but its harbinger, the tangible example we've been given for it. How can we make life a form of perpetual ecstasy, like the ecstasy of wine but without resorting to wine? We won't find the answer in debate, productivity, fighting, or exertion, all of those are means but not ends. Happiness won't be achieved until we free ourselves from using all means and allow ourselves to live a rational, spiritual, pure life, unmuddied by any troubles; this is the happiness for which wine gives us a model [*mithāl*]; all work is a means to reach this happiness, but as for the happiness itself, it is not a means to anything . . . (*MK* 2:772; *CT* 911)

No matter how many hundreds of pages of life, history, and generational change transpire in the *Trilogy*, Kamal cannot relinquish either the "idealism," *ʿālam al-mithāl* (*MK* 2:606), or the language of inner and outer meanings, *ẓāhiriyyah* and *bāṭiniyyah*, in which he was raised. Wine is a signifier whose referent is happiness, yet it is perpetually absent so long as wine remains the means. Only in transcending the logic of means and ends, Kamal asserts here, does happiness arrive. Of course, this is all framed in dialogue, and Ismaʿil laments Kamal's speech as a terrible buzzkill. "You're the worst . . . I was hoping you'd be a charming, witty conversationalist in your drunken ecstasy, but you're like a sick man who only gets worse the more he drinks" (*MK* 2:772).[96]

Ismaʿil's comment illustrates the extent to which Kamal's journey is not a path Mahfouz prescribes, not a tale of secular liberalism triumphing over first-order religious and political desires, but a cautionary tale of spiritual "sickness" like the narrator's in "Zaabalawi," or Sabir's in *al-Ṭarīq*, of endless torment and encyclopedic pains, inescapable wandering in a vortex of retreating truths. From this relatively early point in his career, Mahfouz seems to recognize liberalism's negative liberty as painful atomization—the misery of subjective isolation from any form of social, political, or familial collectivity. My reading of *Qaṣr al-Shawq* thus diverges from the critical consensus that Kamal Abd al-Jawad, the *Trilogy's* protagonist, is the "embodiment of liberal progressivism," leading "a promethean struggle against family, faith and ignorance in a quest to achieve freedom and independence from social constraint."[97] While certainly supported by abundant evidence both from the text itself and from Mahfouz's nonfictional writings on liberal politics and philosophy, such a characterization of the *Trilogy*'s protagonist neglects a key feature of Kamal's story: it follows the mode of tragedy, rather than that of liberal individualist romance. It is, in David Scott's terms, not a story of "overcoming, of vindication," of "salvation and redemption . . . depending upon a certain (utopian) horizon toward which the emancipationist history is imagined to be moving," but of "a man . . . obliged to act in a world in which values are unstable and ambiguous . . . and the relationship between past, present, and future is . . . a broken series of paradoxes and reversals."[98] These paradoxes and reversals are as concatenated in Kamal's life as in that of any colonized subject. Although Kamal's mind does triumph over the religious and political commitments that might have ensnared him, the price of this victory is endless wandering and incurable loss, as the flipside of "freedom from" commitments turns out to be endless loneliness, and an inability to descend from the world of ideals.

Shawq is Mahfouz's distinctly Islamic-Arabic-Egyptian figure for what Scott, borrowing from Northrop Frye and Hayden White, calls tragedy. Lest we forget the disillusionments and losses that have engendered this transformation, Kamal's imaginative childhood relationship with al-Husayn ibn ʿAli resurfaces—yet again—in this chapter chronicling his first experience drinking alcohol. Ismaʿil Latif wishes their old friend Husayn Shaddad, long since departed for Europe, were there in the bar with the two of them, to witness the pious Muslim Kamal

ʿAbd al-Jawad's first glass of whiskey. "Where is Husayn to witness this scene for himself?" Ismaʿil asks. In Kamal's mind, however, the question echoes with double meaning: "Where is Husayn? Where?" (*MK* 2:770).

## THE LIMITS OF SUFI SOCIALISM

With these admittedly voluminous readings under our belts, let me clarify: I am not arguing that the "true" or "real" meanings of Mahfouz's works reside only in their Islamic resonances; nor should reading these books become merely a process of sleuthing out, identifying, and compiling the Sufi terms and passages therein. To read in such a way would be to miss the alternative methods of seeking truth—and, for our purposes, the alternative ways of reading—which Mahfouz dramatizes, again and again, in all his works, from the epic realism of the *Trilogy* to the condensed mysteries of "Zaabalawi," "Culprit Unknown," and *al-Ṭarīq*. Rather, the readings above, focused on the "missing persons" at the heart of these selected texts by Mahfouz, illustrate two seemingly obvious but previously unremarked features of the author's poetics. First, Mahfouz consciously and deliberately played with the thematic, formal, and epistemological conventions of detective fiction in much the same way as writers like Poe, Borges, and Auster did, using the genre as a way to "ask questions about mysteries of being and knowing which transcend the mere machinations of the mystery plot."[99] Stories like "Culprit Unknown" and "Zaabalawi" blur the roles of detective, criminal, and victim, for example, thereby interrogating the boundedness of subjectivity on which modern modes of identification and policing depend. *Al-Ṭarīq* also questions "the epistemological method of discovering truth by questioning sources of knowledge."[100]

In many ways, however, Mahfouz's interest in these epistemological and hermeneutic questions transcends the conceits of the detective plot alone. His "metaphysical detective stories" are, in many ways, more metaphysical than detective stories, and this brings me to my second point. These readings from "Culprit Unknown," "Zaabalawi," *al-Ṭarīq*, and *Palace of Desire* also illustrate how subtly, cunningly, and persistently Mahfouz, like Jabra, plays on the expansive polyvalence of key Arabic terms, making the double nature of the Arabic language itself both the recurrent theme and the formal conceit of his works. Mahfouz's Arabic keeps the (metaphysical, Islamic) past alive in the (scientific, "enlightened") present, creating unlikely and surprising juxtapositions, as between detective fiction and Sufi parable, police investigation and mystical seeking. Whatever the writer himself may have said about his literary creations or what was meant therein (and I acknowledge his voluminous essays on the importance of political liberalism), the references to *shawq* and *dhawq*, *ittiṣāl* and *infiṣāl*, *al-ṭarīq* and *al-wujūd*, together summon a world of seeking that these novels and short stories simultaneously deem "past" and at the same time mine for epistemological resources distinct from those bequeathed by science and empiricism. In a 1960 interview, Mahfouz once clarified that, in *Children of the Alley* and other works, he was calling for "Sufi socialism"—that is, "looking to God" (al-taṭalluʿ ilā Allāh, also "waiting for" or "anticipating God"). "As long as profit exists," he says, "the profiteer will be evil, the profited-from will be miserable, and the relation between them will be one of hatred and resentment. In such a relationship, there can be no looking to God."[101]

Mahfouz's coupling of Sufism with socialism is curious, however, particularly in light of the alienation and atomization suffered by all his protagonists who "seek" in these short stories and novels. Kamal's passionate shawq for truth and beauty alienates him from every possible form of collectivity and community, including family, marriage, political organizing, and organized religion. Sabir, too, in *al-Ṭarīq*, turns away from the revelations and inspirations offered by Ilham—the model of how to live life without a father, the offer of a small amount of capital with which to start a business—to pursue the impossible dream of his father. The narrator of "Zaabalawi" is also, in a sense, self-absorbed, trapped in an identity he wishes to overcome, but not by banding together with others. These Sufi characters have very little "sociality," let alone "socialism." Mahfouz offers us many things: a critique of liberal individualism not as triumph but as tragedy, a dismantling of "science" as yet another religious credo of which to be skeptical, an emotional geography of Cairo that takes al-Husayn's shrine as its beating heart and Abbasiya as its mysterious undoing, and a reanimation of the Arabic language as a model for transcendence and plenitude, in opposition to the strict lines and bounded identities of modernity. But, in the absence of any real communitarianism or collectivity, he does not give us socialism, Sufi or otherwise.

Like Jabra, then, Mahfouz also fails to write his characters out of their own vertiginous subjectivities, giving them only fleeting, paradoxical moments of mystical self-loss and union with the world. The detectives, investigators, and "seekers" in these works either remain prisoners of their own minds, continue to be baffled by the mysteries of existence, or succumb to a liberating (but temporary) annihilation. But they are never given over to others. Despite their fascination with the promise and potentiality of the mystical, then, neither Mahfouz nor Jabra ever fully arrived at a narrative erasure of the modern, liberal subject. The task of imagining other voices, devising new literary forms for representing new collectivities and social struggles, was taken up by other authors hoping to meld the Arabic novel with popular genres like the *Thousand and One Nights* and the "narrative ballad," or *mawwāl*. Writing both before and after Mahfouz and Jabra, the Egyptian Fathi Ghanim and the Lebanese Elias Khoury used the conventions of metaphysical detective fiction in a different way: not to stage an individualized, endlessly deferred, cyclical quest for meaning, but to eclipse the literary detective's relevance entirely, giving voice instead to the "nonliterary" others who would otherwise have fallen under his critical, private "I."

4

# Effacing the Author, or the Detective as Medium

## *Fathi Ghanim and Elias Khoury*

In a 1980 essay for the weekly literary supplement to the Lebanese daily *al-Safīr*, the prominent Lebanese author and critic Elias Khoury argued that, while Arab modernism has "managed to adapt all the forms of Western modernism, from the nation-state to the police and modernist art," still "one particular art form has remained impossible to borrow: the detective novel [*al-riwāyah al-būlīsiyyah*]."[1] Khoury backs up his claim by highlighting the ideological role detective fiction plays in Western capitalist society. In the West, Khoury writes, the bourgeois class exercises power through a "complex network of state apparatuses" that allow the capitalist order to "reaffirm its 'logical, rational' nature . . . as one that defends against the baser social instincts and impulses it must suppress." The police officer emerges as the epitome of this nature ("law incarnate," in Khoury's phrase), a hero figure rather like G. K. Chesterton's "unsleeping sentinels," who guard civilization from barbarous criminality.[2] In the Arab world, however, the mystification by which the police are transformed into heroic defenders of civilization has yet to occur. "Power is an apparatus *outside* society and its relations" in these countries, Khoury writes, "and for this reason . . . it doesn't have any ideological justification for its legality." The "good cop," according to Khoury, remains a foreign figure to Arab readers; Arab modernism simply declined to import the "detective novel."[3]

Around the same time that Elias Khoury the literary critic was asserting the impossibility of "detective stories" in Arabic, however, Elias Khoury the novelist was experimenting with a new "poetics of prose" adapted from the *Thousand and One Nights*. In "The Death of the Author" (*Mawt al-Mu'allif*) an essay published in *al-Safīr* only eight months after "On the Police and the Police Story," Khoury criticized a prevailing tendency in Arabic letters to view poetry as the "true mouthpiece of the people" and to dismiss prose as a mere "medium of communication." Against this tendency, Khoury upheld the *Nights* as "the only text that voluntarily renounces the power of text."[4] Crucially, for Khoury, the *Nights* offer contemporary Arab authors a model of prose writing in which "there is no longer an author, and the need for a single individual to summarize the experiences of others disappears," unlike in premodern Arabic poetry, where the poet serves as the spokesman for the tribe. The "poetics of prose" that Khoury adapts from the *Nights* thus "erases its author," transforming him into "the first absentee and the first victim, a figure who only appears in order to disappear inside a world that cannot be controlled, a world into which he dissolves, and in which the words alone flourish, the victims flourish when their faces and their language are revealed in a never-ending series of secrets."[5] "The Death of the Author," in short, uses the *Nights* to outline a new relationship of power between the author and his narrative materials, between the narrative subject and the objects of his representation.[6] Here authorship is decoupled from authority, just as the *muʾallif*—literally, the "arranger" or "composer" of words, thoughts, and ideas—is transformed from a puppet master into a mere "medium" through whom others, particularly disenfranchised or "victimized" others, might speak.[7]

Curiously, however, to put this new poetics into practice in his 1981 novel *White Masks* (*al-Wujūh al-Bayḍāʾ*, literally "The White Faces"), Khoury uses the premise of a murder mystery. That is, to effect the reconfiguration of narrative power he deems so necessary in "The Death of the Author," Khoury takes his cue from the detective fiction whose impossibility in Arabic he had announced in the same publication a mere eight months earlier. Although *White Masks* may not follow all the rules of the classic detective story, it still shares many features with crime fiction.[8] How else are we to understand a novel that begins with the discovery of a man's corpse in a Beirut trash pile and proceeds as a search for his killer, passing through a series of interviews, court testimonies, and forensic reports in the process? Despite his own pronouncement regarding the impossibility of Arabic detective stories, then, even Khoury himself dabbled in detection.

In the last chapter, we saw how Mahfouz and Jabra experimented with metaphysical detection as a way beyond the limits of the subject but ultimately ended up only with individuals engaged in infinite, atomized searches. This chapter remains with the topic of metaphysical detection in Arabic, but it focuses on two works that use the premise of baḥth somewhat differently. As in the works by Mahfouz and Jabra examined in the last chapter, both Khoury's *White Masks* and Fathi Ghanim's *al-Jabal* (The Mountain, 1959) feature detective-like characters who set out in pursuit of answers, immersing themselves in worlds and communities about which they know next to nothing. Yet in these novels, the detective character serves as a fictional stand-in for the author himself, and his voice is ultimately silenced as the suspected criminals gradually, communally assume control of the novel's narration. These are investigations that, far from solving the original mystery, only end up erasing the investigator's voice, language, and subjectivity.

The effect of this structure, in the work of Ghanim and Khoury, is twofold. First, it allows each author to interrogate and dismantle a specific, official or quasi-official ideological discourse used, at the time of his writing, as a justification for state violence. In Ghanim's case, this was the Egyptian discourse of "reformism" or *iṣlāḥ*, and specifically the 1947 project to relocate the people of al-Gurna (al-Qurnah), a small Upper Egyptian village, from their homes in the antiquities-laden Valley of the Kings to a "model village" designed by renowned Egyptian architect Hassan Fathy, thus transforming them from criminal "tomb robbers" into "model peasants."[9] In Khoury's case, the discourse in question was the wartime Lebanese one lionizing the figure of the "martyr" or *shahīd* while ignoring or erasing the everyday suffering, violence, dislocation, and death suffered by Beirut's most marginalized civilian communities. Second, the effacement of the detective—and, by extension, of the author—allows each writer to open up the novel as a communal and social form, rather than a metropolitan, individualist one. Ghanim's interruption of *al-Jabal* with the popularly sung Egyptian "narrative ballad" or *mawwāl* of Bahiyyah and Yasin gives a hopeful glimpse of what the novel as a narrative form might become, of how to transform the solitary, detective-like act of reading into a performance of radical empathy, a communal act rather like listening to a mawwāl. Khoury's novel also places its faith in the possibilities that the communal, associative poetics of the *Nights* make available to authors of Arabic fiction. Although they are responding to very different conjunctures of social and material conditions, both *al-Jabal* and *White Masks* use "investigation" to model a form of unlearning, of erasure, of opening the supposedly fixed borders of the modern self to the voices and experiences of others. They craft a new epistemology of fiction, a poetics of investigation that destabilizes the self-assurance of the all-knowing narrative subject and, by extension, that of the reader herself.

## LITERARY COUNTERPOINT, AL-GURNA TO BEIRUT

Despite the different historical periods and national contexts in which they were writing, both Elias Khoury and Fathi Ghanim found themselves surrounded by political discourses whose rigidity and reductionism left little room for negotiating what were, in their view, complex social and material conditions. They therefore turned to fiction as a contrapuntal space, and the form of their novels as open, unsolved investigations represents a turn away from the prescriptivism and triumphalism that saturated public discourse in both post-1952 Egypt and wartime Beirut. Understanding the political and historical significance of the narrative structure to which they both turned, however, requires greater familiarity with the nonliterary discourses in which each work was embedded and to which it was responding. Let me first address the context of *al-Jabal* before linking Ghanim's disillusionment and narrative experimentation with Khoury's in *White Masks*.

Before he became better known as a journalist and novelist, Ghanim, like Tawfiq al-Hakim before him, worked as a government functionary—an "investigations inspector" (*mufattish li-l-taḥqīqāt*), to be precise—with the Egyptian Ministry of Education.[10] It was in this capacity that he was sent, in 1947, to investigate a case of vandalism and theft in the recently constructed model village of New Gurna, and this real-life trip forms the heart of *al-Jabal*'s fictional investigative narrative. The actual history of the Egyptian village of al-Gurna, its people, and their relationship to the model village of New Gurna, has been told and retold many times, as historians, anthropologists, architects, and Egyptologists alike have inscribed this small, local space within a web of national and international relations and concerns. Located on the west bank of the Nile, across the river from Luxor, al-Gurna's inhabitants—the Gurnawis—live among the tombs and funerary temples known to archaeologists as the Theban Necropolis and to visitors as the Valley of the Kings. For the better part of al-Gurna's modern history, the Gurnawis made their living through the antiquities trade, both as laborers on European-managed archaeological digs and as traders themselves in the illicit international market for ancient Egyptian artefacts.[11] In 1945, following a case in which an entire bas-relief wall was removed from one of these tombs and sold to a private buyer, the Egyptian Antiquities Department decided that the Gurnawis' trade in "tomb robbing" had gone too far.[12] The villagers were to be forcibly uprooted from the Theban Necropolis and relocated to a model village built on the farmland in the valley below. To design the village, the Antiquities Department commissioned Hassan Fathy, a Cairo-based architect who had previous success with "rural rehabilitation" in the model village of Bahtim, just north of Cairo.[13] For Fathy, New Gurna represented an opportunity to experiment with the "vernacular modernist" style for which he had become internationally renowned. Against the homogenizing, industrial style of modernist architecture in the United States and Europe, Fathy's designs used local Egyptian materials such as mud brick and straw (rather than imported red brick and concrete), and they integrated features from Islamic architecture that were much maligned among Europhilic Egyptian architects, such as the dome as a form of air conditioning, the inner courtyard, and the windcatcher.[14]

But the Gurnawis' relocation to New Gurna did not go as planned. In addition to the bureaucratic and logistical difficulties Fathy faced, the villagers' resistance to being forcibly removed from their homes was perhaps the biggest and—for Fathy—the most puzzling problem of all. "They had no intention of giving up their nice, profitable, squalid houses in the cemetery with treasure waiting to be mined under their floors to move to a new, hygienic, beautiful village away from the tombs," Fathy wrote in his memoir of the project.[15] Two years after construction began, villagers cut the dikes that protected New Gurna from seasonal flooding and inundated the better part of the model village. In the frenzy to identify the culprits, many local and metropolitan inspectors were sent to New Gurna, among them a young Fathi Ghanim. For his part, Hassan Fathy was underwhelmed with the investigations. "While all this [repair work on the dikes] was being done," he writes, "the district attorney descended upon us to make an investigation into the flooding. He and his assistants went round asking every villager in turn: 'Did you pierce the dike?' Every villager in turn replied 'No,' and when the attorney had filled three sheets of legal-sized paper with these answers, he went home satisfied that the affair had been investigated."[16] It is as if Fathy has borrowed the scene (and his own disdainful, condescending attitude) from Tawfiq al-Hakim's *Diary of a Country Prosecutor*.

Ghanim, by contrast, sought to transform his own investigations in New Gurna into something other than a useless bureaucratic report. *al-Jabal* chronicles the journey of its first-person narrator (also named "Fathi Ghanim") from Cairo to Luxor to New Gurna, and eventually to the village of (old) al-Gurna itself. On his way, the investigator moves from a world of government functionaries in Cairo to local officials such as his friend, the deputy prosecutor in Luxor, to the European-trained "architect" (Hassan Fathy's fictional stand-in) and his entourage of French artists in New Gurna.[17] Each stratum of upper-class Egyptian society proposes its own solution to the "problem" of the countryside and its inhabitants, the impoverished peasant masses who must be civilized before they can be considered part of the emergent nation.[18] Eventually, the narrator ends up among the "people of the mountain" (*ahl al-jabal*) themselves, who, after some resistance, agree to confide in this government representative, telling him stories of the violence and exploitation they have endured both as excavators of antiquities for insatiable European collectors and as the subjects of governmental "rural rehabilitation" projects like New Gurna itself. Neither fully committed to the authorities' projects of relocation and reform, which he correctly understands to be laced with violence, nor satisfied with the life-threatening conditions in which the Gurnawis are forced to make their living, the detective-narrator of *al-Jabal* represents a rare medium between the people and the state. Whereas Hassan Fathy laments being "in an unhappy in-between situation, neither properly of the government nor of the village," and thus "suffering from both sides,"[19] this "in-between situation" is precisely what Ghanim cultivates for himself and his fictional detective stand-in in *al-Jabal*.

In its focus on al-Gurna, *al-Jabal* takes part in a long tradition of writing about the Valley of the Kings, both as an archaeological site, in nineteenth-century accounts of Egyptological excavation (for example, in the memoirs of Howard Carter, the famed uncoverer of Tutankhamun's tomb in 1922),[20] and as a space, in twentieth-century accounts, where questions of modern national sovereignty are negotiated in conjunction with archaeology, tourism, and state power.[21] For the most part, as Kees van der Spek points out, nineteenth- and early twentieth-century European accounts of al-Gurna took scant interest in the lives and livelihoods of the modern residents of the Nile's west bank, granting pride of place instead to the reconstructed histories of ancient nobles. When modern Gurnawis are depicted in these accounts, it is usually as lawless "tomb robbers" with no understanding of or respect for the art-historical significance of ancient valuables.[22] "The silence that surrounds the cultural specificity of west bank villagers," van der Spek notes, "stands in sharp contrast with the epigraphic and archaeological activities of Egyptologists whose many annual research projects seek to shed light on all aspects of life and death in ancient Egypt."[23] This privileging of ancient history over modern socioeconomic realities has served both to attract increasingly wealthy foreign tourists to Upper Egypt and to bolster local "political objectives that center on the construction of a national identity and its associated tourism-industry revenue base."[24] The marginalization of the Gurnawis through the veneration of the pharaohs thus changes from a strategy of colonial-archaeological labor exploitation, in the late nineteenth and early twentieth centuries,[25] to one by which a new national bourgeoisie, in the second half of the twentieth century, neutralizes an unruly local populace threatening its financial interests. These interests lie specifically in the tourism industry, with all its power to attract foreign capital. Both van der Spek and Timothy Mitchell amply chronicle the social and economic dimensions of this "enclave tourism" with its emphasis on "minimizing unregulated contact . . . and increasing [tourists'] physical separation from the local community," as well as on the production of a "heritage consumption" industry.[26]

In its simultaneous focus on the "model village" project at New Gurna, furthermore, and on Hassan Fathy's architectural project more generally, *al-Jabal* also converses with another discourse: that of rural reform and social improvement (iṣlāḥ) as it was envisioned by Egyptian social scientists, intellectuals, and statesmen at two crucial periods of anticolonial nationalism. The first period followed the mass protests of March 1919 and the rise of the anticolonial Wafd Party with populist hero Saad Zaghloul as its figurehead. The second period followed the Officers' Revolt of July 1952, when the postcolonial Egyptian state was reorganized around what Omnia El Shakry calls a "social-welfare mode of regulation," which aimed at "containing radical social change through piecemeal social reform and amelioration of the conditions of the working poor."[27] In both of these historical moments, El Shakry argues, rural Egyptians like the Gurnawis formed the "central contradiction of national identity within Egyptian colonial society—at the same time that they were localized by the nationalist elite as the repository of cultural authenticity, they were also demarcated as a locus of backwardness to be reformed and reconstituted as modern moral subjects of the nation-state."[28] The project of resettling the "lawless" and "thieving" residents of al-Gurna in a model village designed by a "modern" architect thus also aimed at recreating the Gurnawis in the mode of "model peasants," changing not only their physical location but also "reconstructing bodies and minds."[29]

Ghanim's novel simultaneously participates in these discourses and stands apart from them, criticizing while refusing to counter one form of prescriptivism with another. On one level, the narrator's distance from the "model village" project allows him to criticize the aestheticizing tendency in the architect's language and design, its emphasis on form and appearance over function. While leading the narrator of *al-Jabal* on a tour of the new village's mosque, for example, the architect explains to him "how the holes where light came in were meant to harmonize with the lines of the building and the movements of the people praying—as though they weren't people praying at all, but rather ballet dancers on a stage with the most modern theatrical lighting."[30] It quickly becomes clear to the narrator that the "model village" is less a project to improve the lives of the Gurnawis and more, in the words of Mohamed Elshahed, "a reactionary response to modernism as a style and a project," an architecture "less about authenticity and more about romanticism . . . primitivism, and revivalism."[31] Indeed, Ghanim's fictionalized version of Hassan Fathy is willing to marshal any means necessary to increase his international renown. "We'll make [the project] succeed by force!" the architect exclaims to a visiting official from the Ministry of Education later in the novel. "The people of the mountain are ignorant and don't understand . . . People won't be civilized except through the force of the whip. Fine, if that's what they want, then let's whip them!" (*J* 161). Hidden beneath the rhetoric of reform, modernism, and nation making, both in Ghanim's novel and in Hasan Fathy's own accounts, there still lingers the whip—the *courbage* or *kurbāj*—that enduring symbol of colonial coercion, conscription, and violence in Egypt.

The narrator of *al-Jabal* soon takes issue not only with the architect's project in New Gurna, but with all the flashy, high-minded reform projects that "wear the mask of reform" but "were undertaken for reasons unconnected to true reform," including "personal interest and glory, false ideas, or naïve attempts to imitate Europe or America." These thoughts lead to the culmination of the novel's moral message: through creative tautology, and through a play on the Arabic root *ṣ-l-ḥ*, both narrator and author attempt to reclaim the term "reform" (iṣlāḥ) from the overuse and stagnation to which it has been subjected. "'Reform,'" the narrator affirms, "must be in the interest of improvement ('al-iṣlāḥ' yajib an yakūn li-l-iṣlāḥ). It should be done in the interest of (*li-maṣlaḥat*) those for whom the reformist project was intended" (*J* 166).

The moment is admittedly heavy-handed. Ghanim would later express regret about being so direct. "Perhaps it would have been better," he said in a 1995 interview, "to let the characters and events in the novel express the conflict for themselves and not rely so much on theoretical discussions about the city and the country."[32] Still, the passage raises an important question: if "reform" is to be more than mere "sloganeering" or "fashion," what would it look like? How is "true reform" to be achieved? On this point, Ghanim is less prescriptive. After the narrator spends a night among the Gurnawis in *al-Jabal*, listening to their stories in their own words, he returns to the model village "between waking and sleep" with his head "full of vague and delirious words" and promptly collapses into bed (*J* 155). While asleep, he dreams of the mountain dwellers uncovering a new tomb filled with treasures. But instead of selling the artifacts to foreign collectors for a quick profit, as they have done for nearly a hundred years, the Gurnawis alert the Egyptian Antiquities Department of their discovery. Soon al-Gurna is teeming with archaeologists and tourists, who begin buying the "beautiful straw platters" woven by the village's women and the limestone statuettes carved in the ancient style by its men. "This is the real treasure that the people of the mountain discovered," the narrator thinks in between waking and sleep. "The statuettes that they make with their own two hands are the real treasure. They're not fakes, because . . . they are the product of their labor, and they symbolize labor itself. Labor is the real treasure" (*J* 156). He subsequently envisions the government building statuette-manufacturing factories in al-Gurna, to be cooperatively owned by the people of the mountain.

The fantasy is short-lived, however. "What is this nonsense running through my mind?" the narrator thinks. "To the people of the mountain, the government is the police who want to uproot them from their caves by force and toss them into houses roofed with domes like tombs. The government is not *their* government. All it ever thinks about is how to control them" (*J* 156–57). The villagers, in other words, are right not to trust government officials like him, since all these officials ever seem to bring with them are violent, coercive, and thoroughly useless forms of control. That the narrator of the novel shares his name with its author, furthermore, reveals Ghanim's recognition of the potential for the author to become yet another exploitative agent of the state, yet another essentializing social reformer whose representations of village "backwardness" will be mobilized as a justification for state violence.

If the narrator's dream vision of cooperative statuette-manufacturing factories is not the answer to the question of "true reform," then what is? In the same 1995 interview I cited earlier, Ghanim suggested that the novel was a "caution" to the Nasser regime against mere "sloganeering" on the question of reform. "Reform," he noted, "is an abstract issue that cannot be resolved overnight. It is a process of studying psychological customs that can only change slowly, over a long period, on the condition that there is real conviction on the part of the people that what is happening is in their best interests. They cannot be convinced through mere words."[33] But there is another answer to the above question embedded in the form of Ghanim's novel itself. Maybe the first step in "true reform," Ghanim seems to imply, would look something like the narrative of *al-Jabal*: the erasure of the detective's voice, and of all official, metropolitan voices weighing in on the lives and livelihoods of the Gurnawis—from the Antiquities Department and Hassan Fathy all the way to the author-*cum*-government-inspector Ghanim himself, and the amplification of the stories told by *ahl al-jabal*, the people of the mountain, in their own words and their own dialect.

I will return to the form of Ghanim's novel in a moment, to illustrate how its commentary on al-Gurna serves also as a metafictional lesson in learning to read and seek knowledge differently. For now, however, let me turn to Khoury's *White Masks* to show how it also struggles with political language, and with words whose meaning seems to have been lost, distorted, or calcified through overuse. Khoury's concern is not with the Egyptian rhetoric of iṣlāḥ, however, but with the figure of the shahīd or "martyr" in the historically and politically intertwined contexts of the Palestinian Revolution and the Lebanese Civil War. The Palestinian Revolution is usually dated from the Cairo Accords of 1969 to the Israeli invasion of Beirut in 1982, when the Palestine Liberation Organization (PLO) held political control of the Palestinian refugee camps in Lebanon, transforming them into what Laleh Khalili has called "the central node of the transnational Palestinian national movement and the primary base of Palestinian military operations against Israel."[34] Khalili also notes the centrality of "commemorative practices" to the articulation of Palestinian national identity in the camps both during and after the revolution, stressing in particular the historical dynamism and rhetorical contestation enacted through these practices, which reflect "transformations in the character, affinities, values, and mobilizing strategies of the Palestinian national movement."[35] Where the figure of the guerilla-fedayee armed with Kalashnikov and keffiyeh was central to the PLO's iconography of resistance during the period of the revolution, after 1982 the shahīd or "martyr" gradually assumed the fedayee's place as emblem of heroic sacrifice.[36] This shift was the consequence of numerous historical developments on the local, regional, and international levels, chief among them the replacement of the ethos of anticolonial liberationist heroism with the "liberal discourse of rights and development at the end of the Cold War."[37]

Though intertwined with these Palestinian histories of commemoration, martyrdom as public discourse in Lebanon has its own specific history, as Lucia Volk has shown. Against the predominant tendency to associate martyrdom with "Islamic radicalism," Volk notes the long-standing use of martyr discourse by "political elites of different ethno-religious backgrounds" who sought to "give concrete shape to, and win political legitimacy through championing, a unifying national idea" by "sketching faces, sculpting bodies, carving texts, and circulating photographs and banners that show Lebanon as a place where Muslims and Christians struggle and die together."[38] The intersection of martyr culture with the rise of mass media during the years of the Lebanese Civil War, however, arguably transformed the commemoration of martyrs from the grave business of political elites and national publics into a practice hotly contested among various parties, groups, and factions.[39] That the designation "martyr" often came with material compensation from these factions also played a significant role in this contested semantic and iconographic terrain.[40]

Khoury's *White Masks* is, in many ways, a literary response to this complex, ever-shifting discourse surrounding both the freedom fighter and the martyr. Formed as he was in the crucible of the Palestinian liberation struggle,[41] Khoury has long been concerned with the "question" of Palestine (*al-qaḍiyyah*) in both his literary and his critical work. Yet the many interwoven stories that comprise the text of *White Masks* are deeply—if obliquely—critical of these iconic figures. In particular, the novel questions the politics by which certain stories of death are granted added significance through their designation as "martyrdom," while others are engulfed in a generalized sea of forgetting. At one point, for example, Khoury stages a conversation between a humble building caretaker, Mahmud Fakhro, and an idealistic fighter with one of the local cadres, who used to be a university student. "We're fighting for the revolution," the young man tells Mahmud, "for the sake of the poor . . . for people like you who have nothing and live in poverty and misery."[42] Yet, even as the young man's comrades in arms later declare him a shahīd after his body is torn up by sniper fire on the street, Mahmud is acutely aware that, despite his rhetoric, the young man's sacrifice has done nothing to transform his own social, economic, and personal situation. How can the fighter be called a martyr if his death changes nothing in the lives of "the poor" for whom he claims to fight and die? "He's a martyr, and I'm a martyr," Mahmud ultimately notes with a mixture of sadness and irony (*WM* 103; *WB* 112).

Elsewhere in *White Masks*, the story of Imm Mohammad also questions the ethics of awarding some deaths not only the political significance but also the economic compensation that comes with the designation of "martyrdom," at the expense of others. In a first-person testimony tucked into the novel's "Provisional Epilogue," Imm Mohammad tells the narrator how her husband, on returning to work as a longshoreman after a preliminary end to hostilities in 1978, was killed not by a sniper's bullet but by a refrigerator, which fell on him while he was unloading it from a truck. "He wasn't hit by a bullet or a shell," Imm Mohammad tells the narrator. "No one abducted him, so that we could say he died as a servant of God, no, he just dropped dead" (*WB* 330). A poor mother of eight, Imm Mohammad tries to register her husband as a martyr to get a monthly compensatory stipend from a local militia. But the militiamen reject her plea because her husband was not a fighter. "But he *is* a *shahīd*," she protests. "Say that he died in the line of duty, for his country, for the port . . . for whatever the devil you like, but please consider him a *shahīd* of *something!*" (*WB* 331). Though martyrdom is meant to function symbolically as a "struggle for life" and a "heroic resistance which redeems suffering and overcomes tyranny,"[43] here Khoury criticizes the mundane calculus, the everyday social and economic discriminations that, far from being obliterated by the martyr's sacrifice, are in reality only further entrenched by it.

Khoury's critique is perhaps at its most cutting, however, in the chapter narrated by Fahd Badreddin, a "retired" fedayee with the leftist Lebanese National Movement (LNM). The entire chapter, in fact, is dedicated to highlighting the distance between the idealistic rhetoric of heroic sacrifice used by the fedayeen and the actual, embodied fact of death as Fahd experienced it in the war. Fahd describes feelings of invincibility and limitlessness in the early days of his enlistment, a desire to "hold up the sky," to "reach the sky and carry it in my hands, just as I've read about in books" (*WB* 197, 202). Yet this transcendence quickly disintegrates in a series of encounters Fahd has with death on the battlefield. After being forced to leave a dying comrade in arms behind during a retreat on snowy Mount Sannine, for example,[44] Fahd asks his commanding officer to send a search party back for the young man. The officer refuses. "It's simple," the officer says with surprising calm, "We'll call him a martyr" (*WB* 223). Here the designation of martyrdom, like a philosopher's stone, is used to transform meaningless death into sacrificial significance. Fahd, however, has seen the real circumstances surrounding his comrade's demise: the young man did not "rush off into the sky" but was torn apart in an explosion of flesh and blood, dragged through the snow, burning with fever, delirious and on the edge of death, begging Fahd to leave him behind and save himself. In another scene, Fahd watches as his commanding officer murders an eight-year-old Christian boy in cold blood, simply because the boy wandered into enemy territory in the mountains. "Do you think that if he'd arrested *you* he'd have left *you* alive?" the officer asks Fahd. "No one has nothing to do with it . . . This is a war, they kill us, and we kill them" (*WB* 235). A few days later, Fahd collides with "something hard like an inflated tire," while crawling across the battlefield on his stomach. "Then the worms started crawling over my hand and my arm," he remembers in horror, "on my waist and the lower part of my chest, on my cartridge belt, and there was that smell . . ." (*WB* 236). The object turns out to be the young boy's rotting corpse, and this sensation of worms crawling all over his body, combined with "that smell," haunts Fahd throughout the chapter he narrates, recurring in all the encounters he remembers with the murdered man at the heart of *White Masks*, Khalil Ahmad Jaber. Here again, we are far from the fantasy of the shahīd's heroic transcendence.

Khoury places Fahd between two irreconcilable positions. On the one hand, this retired fighter can no longer muster the kind of naïve dedication that he sees in the newly recruited young men, fueled by idealizations of death as martyrdom and of the shahīd as nationalist hero. "They don't know the meaning of the word death," Fahd writes of the new recruits. "Death is disgusting. They talk about it as though it were something beautiful, but it's disgusting. I tell them . . . but they don't believe me" (*WB* 210). On the other hand, as an adult, Fahd has never led any life outside the realm of the fedayeen. He left home, family, and university to enlist, and he now no longer knows how to live as a civilian. Throughout the many prolepses and analepses of his chapter, he constantly returns to his liminal status in the party offices of the LNM's Joint Forces. "Here I sit," he repeats. "I'm here . . . and I won't go anywhere else. I can't. Maybe they can, but as for me, I just can't" (*WB* 213). War has immobilized Fahd both spiritually and physically, and this immobility literalizes Khoury's own ambivalent position between passionate commitment to the cause of Palestinian liberation and rejection of the brutal tactics deployed by the PLO and the LNM in the name of that cause.

Khoury's ambivalence became particularly acute in the wake of the PLO's siege of the predominantly Christian coastal town of Damour in January 1976. In revenge for Christian Phalangists' massacres in the predominantly Palestinian camps of Karantina, Maslakh, and, most notably, Tell al-Zaatar, in which many thousands of Palestinians had been killed (often through extremely gruesome torture),[45] the PLO and LNM laid siege to Damour, killing hundreds of civilians, destroying homes, and even desecrating a centuries-old Christian cemetery.[46] In a cruel twist of irony, the PLO would subsequently resettle many survivors of the Tell al-Zaatar massacre in Damour.[47] "I was astonished," Khoury said in an interview several years later, "that the progressive Palestinian camp believed in al-Damur. It was the crucial moment for me to discover that our ideology did not protect us from behaving in a savage, fascist way. What is the meaning of all our discourse and all our ideology if we kill children, women, and men because they are Christians or Muslims or whatever?"[48] Before Damour, Khoury had hesitated to criticize the PLO. "Criticism was very difficult," he said, "because in our consciousness the Palestinian revolution was sacred."[49] Following Damour, however, Khoury began to use literary writing to work through the difficulties and intricacies of his position. His aim, as he wrote in an essay for *al-Safir*, was to work against the wartime situation in which the exchange of ideas was enacted not with "writing" but with "bodies," how "corpses had become a way of proclaiming a position, through shelling, kidnapping, or execution."[50]

The character of Fahd Badreddin in *White Masks* thus literalizes Khoury's sense of in-betweenness. Suspended between his continued belief in the cause and his unwillingness to perpetuate the endless cycle of killing and revenge, Fahd's tone oscillates between the self-righteousness of revolutionary commitment and the self-questioning of intellectual introspection. "I fought just like everyone else," he affirms, "and I stayed. Others left, but I stayed." Yet this claim to authenticity begins to ring hollow in the very next line: "Anyway how could I leave? Where would I go?" (*WB* 243). The world of Beirut at war has no place for a disillusioned fedayee, so scarred by his recurring memories of death that he cannot resume life either as a fighter or as a civilian. The party offices become the limbo between "rushing off into the sky" and colliding with decomposing corpses:

> I'm here in the office, I stay without budging, I remain here and I wait [*antaẓir*] . . . I'm waiting for my mother, I'm waiting to get married, I'm waiting to die, I'm waiting for the revolution, I'm waiting, I'm waiting for nothing, I'm here and I'm waiting for nothing, expecting nothing . . .

> I'm the one who waits, expecting nothing.
> I'm the one who waits, expecting everything. (*WB* 245)[51]

The ambivalence of the Arabic verb *intaẓara*—which can mean both to "wait" and to "expect"—semantically reproduces the hesitation between the teleological, historicist nature of revolutionary action and the existential uncertainty of mere waiting. Through Fahd, Khoury reconsiders his unquestioning embrace of heady nationalist rhetoric extolling heroism, self-sacrifice, and martyrdom earlier in his career. "Writing was very important," Khoury said of this time, "because it gave me the chance to rethink and to understand what was going on."[52] The PLO, however, did not take kindly to Khoury's "rethinking." *White Masks* was all but banned from distribution in the Lebanese camps until the PLO's withdrawal from Beirut in 1982.[53]

Where Fathi Ghanim's *al-Jabal* articulates a counterpoint to the state's empty rhetoric of "rural reform" (iṣlāḥ) and "model villagers," then, Khoury's *White Masks* reconsiders the language and iconography of martyrdom and heroism that were so central to the Palestinian Revolution. These are, admittedly, extremely different conjunctures of material, social, and political circumstances, but on the level of theme and content, both novels share a single purpose: they register a disillusionment with the uses of language—and of the Arabic language in particular—by official or semi-official bodies in contexts of national struggle, liberation, and postcolonial state building. They highlight how far terms like *reform* and *martyrdom* had been displaced and manipulated through their use in slogans, posters, and other public forums produced either by the state (as in Egypt) or by anticolonial nationalist organizations (as with the PLO in Lebanon). Within these contexts, both Khoury and Ghanim assumed the task of making language strange again, wresting words from the hands of sloganeers and reinvigorating them by returning (quite literally) to their roots. The plot-level investigations conducted by their frame narrators thus crystallize the authors' own metafictional quests for new languages and literary forms that might resist appropriation and manipulation.

At the same time, neither author was content merely to counter one form of triumphalist rhetoric with another. Ghanim's narrator's dream of cooperative ownership and government-supervised economic uplift under Gamal Abdel Nasser ultimately amounts only to so much "ranting and raving" in *al-Jabal*, and Khoury's murdered protagonist, Khalil Ahmad Jaber, only ever replaces the martyr posters he tears down with whiteness and erasure in *White Masks*. The alternatives that both Ghanim and Khoury offer their readers, I wish to suggest, must be excavated not from the content of these novels but from their form, their structure, and specifically from the way they sideline the voices of their central investigators (in both cases, frame narrators with autobiographical parallels to the authors themselves) to make room for the voices of others. In this way, both Khoury and Ghanim offer us lessons in how to read, see, seek, and know differently.

## IN SEARCH OF NEW LANGUAGE, FROM MATHAL TO MAWWĀL

One reading of Fathi Ghanim's *al-Jabal* views it as a parable about "the confrontation . . . between old and new; between backward village society and progressive urban society; between the traditional way of doing things and the wish to improve the living conditions of the mountain dwellers."[54] According to this reading, the novel is primarily significant for its "didactic . . . social and political message: namely, that social changes must grow from within and not be imposed from without, that a change inspired by personal interests and empty slogans is doomed to fail."[55] This is the reading I reviewed above, and it aptly ties Ghanim's novel to its political, historical, and social context in the debates around al-Gurna and the Gurnawis. Yet what interests me in *al-Jabal* is not so much its moral and pedagogical message (whose blatancy in the text its author later regretted) but rather its reflections on the practice of investigation itself, alternately expressed as *taftīsh* and *taḥqīq*. What interest me are the moments when the narrator comes up against the limits of his professional training and is forced to surrender his identity as an investigator to clear space, instead, for the voices of the mountain dwellers, in whom he finds a "human" alternative to his inhuman training as a government bureaucrat.

Two moments in *al-Jabal* encapsulate this confrontation particularly well. The first is a tale within a tale told to the narrator by the ʿumdah (mayor or leader) of al-Gurna. In this nested narrative, the ʿumdah recounts to the narrator a confrontation he had with a woman referred to only as "the princess" during the opening festivities for the model village organized by the architect.[56] Although the other Gurnawis took up arms to protest the party and the model village whose completion it was celebrating, the ʿumdah tells the narrator that he hoped to use the event as an opportunity to tell the princess his people's side of the story, in their own words. After finally gaining an audience with her, the ʿumdah urges the princess to prevent the mountain dwellers' forced relocation to the model village, and he does so in a long monologue that Ghanim writes in the Upper Egyptian dialect (substituting the letter *jīm* for the letter *qāf*, for example, and using several local turns of phrase).[57] A combination of intoxication, exoticization, and linguistic misunderstanding, however, comes between the ʿumdah and the princess, who likely speaks and understands English, French, and perhaps Turkish better than she does Arabic, let alone the ʿumdah's Upper Egyptian dialect. She and her American entourage "looked on the ʿumdah as he spoke and gestured with his hands as though he were a ballet dancer or an actor in an incomprehensible Chinese opera" (*J* 77). "I'm not afraid," she brags in English. "I don't think they are the kind that eat human flesh" (*J* 73). The Americans, meanwhile, ask if the ʿumdah is the "Chief" of their people, "just like the Indian Chiefs in our country. Bring us some beads and sweets to give him as presents!" (*J* 75).

On one level, the ʿumdah's tale is yet another in a series of instances in *al-Jabal* where Westernized city dwellers exoticize and tokenize the Gurnawis as enticing, charming, but ultimately backward savages in need of civilizing and sanitizing.[58] Yet, as a scene *about* understanding and its failure, the ʿumdah's story has an additional and, I would argue, more significant narrative function in *al-Jabal*. Not only does the narrator, "Fathi Ghanim," understand the ʿumdah's point of view in a way the princess never could, but hearing about the princess's attitude toward the ʿumdah forces the narrator to question his own presumptions as a state investigator. This passage immediately follows the ʿumdah's nestled tale within a tale:

> As the ʿumdah told me his story about the princess, and as I recreated what had happened in my mind, images and visions swirled in my head, and my respect for the man sitting next to me increased. I felt an awe for him that I had never felt for any other person in existence . . .
>
> I was engulfed by feelings of disgust with my mission. What was this nonsense for which I had been sent here? What can I do about a problem like this? What does the head of investigations want from me? In truth, he doesn't want anything at all; all he wants is for routine to run its course . . .
>
> My duty as a government employee and investigations inspector is to summon Husayn ʿAli and ask him those timeless questions that appear in every report—name? age? profession? nature of your complaint?—and after that, to appoint some other inspectors to form a committee that would take an inventory of the model village and report on whether there had been any misappropriation or not. If they didn't find any evidence, they'd close the investigation, and that would be that. The noise in our heads would be gone, but the real problem would remain unchanged.
>
> I realized that I was not carrying out an investigation [*taḥqīq*]. I was misrepresenting [*tazwīr*] the ʿumdah's feelings and the mountain dwellers' problems—the troubles they were suffering, the poverty they were enduring, and the hope they were searching for in the belly of the mountain.
>
> My mission as detective inspector [*mufattish li-l-taḥqīqāt*] is to suppress all of these truths [*ḥaqāʾiq*] and transform them into a few trivial questions. (*J* 79)

Once again, Ghanim revives worn out, overused Arabic words by playing and punning on their grammatical roots. The narrator affirms that his is not a true "investigation" or *taḥqīq* but merely "fabrication" and "misrepresentation"—*tazwīr*—which rhymes morphologically with its counterpart *taḥqīq*, yet has the opposite meaning. Ironically, as an inspector or, more literally, a "truth establisher"—*muḥaqqiq*—the narrator's job is to *suppress* the mountain dwellers' "truths" (*ḥaqāʾiq*), not reveal them. "It bothered me that I was disturbing the ʿumdah," he notes later on, "that my nature as an inspector still drove me to pose questions and insist on having them answered, until I seemed to be invading people's souls and feeding off their emotions . . . I still don't know how to get rid of this state bureaucrat, this investigator buried deep inside me" (*J* 81). The investigator's task in *al-Jabal* is much more than merely "finding the truth," it turns out. It is a question of overcoming the knowledge-seeking drive within himself, retraining his intellect and his senses in such a way that he can hear, understand, and ultimately transmit the Gurnawis' tales of immiseration and loss. Ghanim the author, in turn, trains his readers in the same.

The narrator surrenders narrative control a second time in *al-Jabal* on meeting Husayn ʿAli, the man whose official complaint served as the impetus for his deployment to al-Gurna. Husayn describes for the narrator how the drive to "scrape away" at the mountain (*al-kaḥt*, a keyword of the novel) in search of ancient treasures to sell in the absence of any other livelihood ultimately led to the deaths of both his sister and his father—the first by her own father, who mistook her, in the darkness of the cave, for an intruder out to steal the treasure he was about to uncover, and the second when he was later crushed by falling rocks. While Husayn's story itself offers a salient critique of the Orientalizing tendencies of foreigners and metropolitan Egyptians alike,[59] the narrative gesture through which it is introduced to the reader is—to me—even more central to Ghanim's narrative poetics of investigation and seeking. When questioned about his complaint, Husayn does not begin with himself or his own life's story but with a kind of moral lesson for the prosecutor, a prologue drawn from the oral archive of Egyptian folk literature. Specifically, he seats the narrator so that he can hear but not see a band of Gurnawis performing a "narrative ballad" or *mawwāl*, a form of sung poetry that, especially in Upper Egypt, often laments the injustice of the law (whether colonial or national) and celebrates the exploits of a rogue hero.[60] Beginning with an invocation to the upper-class "effendi" narrator, Husayn ʿAli sets the scene for his own story by invoking another, written in Upper Egyptian:

إسمع يا أفندي أبو ليلة بيجول ايه . . .

"*Listen, Effendi, to what Abu Laylah has to tell you!*"

The voice of Abu Laylah was strong, beautiful, and sad, monotonous in its melodies yet full of emotion and despair. It told the story of a crime . . .[61] [and] Husayn ʿAli sang along with it at some parts, whispering passionately: "*Oh Bahiyyah, tell me tell me, who killed Yasin?*" and growing quiet as the refrain rose:

*"Give us your sentence, oh lawyer, oh Bey*
*We've been wronged, and we stand here before you today!"*
*The Bey tilted his chic tarbush over one ear*
*And sentenced the man to no more than four years*
*"Two years in the prison," he said with refinement,*
*"and two more in the cells, solitary confinement."*

Husayn ʿAli grew quiet again, then his voice rose with that of Abu Laylah:

*I sing my lament, but you don't cry for me*
*To whom can I tell these tales of misery?*
*Lean to the left now, then lean to the right,*
*but no one around us can make things all right.*

> I realized that Husayn ʿAli had intended for me to hear this song, as though he wanted to show me the opinion the mountain dwellers have of the investigators and prosecutors who tilt their tarbushes over their ears and issue verdicts to the oppressed without ever understanding their problems . . .
>
> I was completely incapable of communicating these thoughts and feelings to Husayn ʿAli. I wanted to say something, but I found that ordinary speech was worn out and meaningless in comparison to this heightened, poetic language echoing and resonating off the mountain. (*J* 93–94)

By prefacing his own tale with the well-known mawwāl of Bahiyyah and Yasin,[62] Husayn is invoking a long tradition in Egyptian folk literature whereby the narrative ballad speaks truth to power, revealing the vast distance between the law as it has historically been practiced upon the bodies of Egyptian peasants and the notion of justice with which it is supposed to coincide. By including the narrator in the audience of the mawwāl, moreover, Husayn ʿAli invites his metropolitan interlocutor "not passively to listen, but to share in" a particular interpretation of events.[63]

This invitation, however, also extends beyond the pages of the novel to include the reader herself. Like the narrator, she too is being asked to look beyond the "worn out," "meaningless," and "trivial" words of the government case file and open herself to this poetry, transcribed in Upper Egyptian colloquial Arabic, which seems to "broadcast from a great radio in the sky," "echoing and resonating off the mountain" until it becomes one with the landscape, taking on the elemental qualities of air and rock.

In these scenes, to be an "investigator" seems like much more than merely a profession. It is a spiritual and bodily disposition, an ethics, a learned way of being in the world and interacting with others. It is as if the narrator of *al-Jabal* must battle against his own moral and intellectual education to fully connect with the mountain dwellers who are the objects of his search. Just as Husayn ʿAli commands the narrator, Fathi Ghanim, to "listen to what Abu Laylah has to say," so too Fathi Ghanim the author commands his refined, literary readers to absorb the vital language of the mawwāl in his novel. Ghanim forces his readers to confront their own resemblance to "detective inspectors," performing their status as powerful, knowing subjects by constituting the mountain dwellers as quaint, exoticized literary objects. Through this confrontation, Ghanim makes the Arabic novel a space in which to train readers in a different kind of reading, one that is less like investigating, excavating, or digging after treasure (*al-kaḥt*), and more like "getting rid of the state officer, the investigator buried deep inside us" by listening to and participating in a mawwāl, relating to other people "as human beings, rather than as state bureaucrats" (*J* 81).

This renunciation of narrative power enacts precisely the "death of the author" that Khoury theorized in his 1980 essay for *al-Safīr*, more than twenty years after the publication of *al-Jabal* in Egypt. It is also precisely the poetics of prose that Khoury puts into practice in *White Masks*. Both the prologue and the "provisional epilogue" of this novel dramatize its narrator's compulsive yet fruitless efforts to wrest the "truth" about Khalil Ahmad Jaber's murder from the information he has collected through his own interviews with people connected to the victim in various ways. In the prologue, the frame narrator enumerates several possible motives for the murder (money, women, mistaken identity, suicide), only to dismiss each one for a variety of reasons. The more he reads, the more distant the truth begins to seem. "I've searched, I've spent many months seeking, searching, and reading in order to know . . . but to no avail" (*WB* 303). In the end he decides to simply "let the documents speak for themselves" (atruk al-kalām li-l-wathāʾiq), and his use of the word *kalām* (strongly tied to spoken language in Arabic) presages the colloquial Arabic that will pepper the testimonies given in subsequent chapters. The stories of others, spoken in their everyday, familiar language, gradually erase the voice not only of *White Masks*' unnamed frame narrator, but also that of its author, Khoury himself.

Khoury thus "refuses to provide readers with any sort of ordering or reordering of the totally fractured world within which they find themselves living," perfecting instead "a craft of complete narrative uncertainty in which a 'speaker' is unable to explain much of the causality of what he endeavors to report."[64] This refusal is evident from the very first line of the novel: "This is not a story" (Hādhihi laysat qiṣṣah) (*WB* 9). The use of the Arabic *qiṣṣah* is important here, as the word simultaneously connotes not only cutting, trimming, or splicing together (*qaṣṣa, yaquṣṣu*), but also a notion of sequentiality. The thirteenth-century lexicographer and grammarian Ibn Manzur notes the following: "It is said *qaṣaṣta al-shayʾ* if you followed its traces sequentially, one after the other . . . And it is said 'the storyteller tells stories' because he links together one event after another and utters his words in an orderly fashion."[65] Orderliness and sequence are thus inherent to the definition of *qiṣṣah* (story) in Arabic and persist even into modern usage. The purpose of a conventional story, then—including the detective story—is to lead the reader from a mysterious or puzzling situation to a logical, cathartic, and instructive conclusion.

In the history of Arabic letters in particular, such conclusions have often been articulated as aphorisms or proverbs (*amthāl*, sing. *mathal*). Derived partly from Hellenistic letters and partly from the "wisdom literature" of ancient Near Eastern cultures, the proverb is one of Arabic's oldest and most esteemed modes of cultural transmission.[66] The Qurʾan itself often assumes an aphoristic tone, just as it emphasizes the importance of proverbs derived from illustrative parables.[67] The hadith too—the sayings of the Prophet Muhammad—assume the form of aphorisms meant to guide good behavior, and their condensed form facilitates both the mnemonic practice of the transmitters and the activation of this wisdom through the practice of the believers. Also central to the aphoristic tradition in Arabic are the sayings of ʿAli ibn Abi Talib, cousin and son-in-law of the Prophet Muhammad.[68] In the medieval period, knowledge of aphoristic literature was an indispensable skill for any poet, statesman, or other court official who hoped to better his fortunes with his patron through cunning displays of rhetorical skill.[69]

In contrast with this long and revered tradition, however, the narrator of *White Masks* concludes his failed detective story with an empty litany of aphorisms or *amthāl* dislodged from the stories that once gave them significance:[70]

> I've searched and seen, but I can't see anything. What you see is what I see: this Khalil Ahmad Jaber was killed. We must find a reason for his death.
>
> That is what we learned. For every cause, there is an effect, for every result, a cause, for every birth, a death.
>
> So we have learned and learned.
>
> What goes up must come down.
>
> He who digs a pit for his brother will fall into it himself.
>
> Contentment is an inexhaustible treasure.
>
> The best of speech is short and clear.
>
> Kiss the hand you cannot break and pray that it be broken.
>
> Whoever marries our mother becomes our stepfather.
>
> When regimes change, watch your back.
>
> Moderation in all things is the best policy.
>
> Even if it flies, it's still a goat!
>
> At a time when people are greatly concerned about other people, the cat is worried about giving birth.
>
> The funeral is elaborate, but the corpse is a dog.
>
> Your tongue is your horse: if you take care of it, it will take care of you.
>
> The defining features of Man are his heart and his tongue.
>
> When a secret becomes known to two, it becomes known to all.
>
> If speech is silver, then silence is golden.
>
> He who sets out on the path will eventually arrive.
>
> Et cetera, et cetera, et cetera, et cetera, et cetera, et cetera, et cetera, et cetera, et cetera, et cetera, et cetera, et c . . . e . . . t . . . e . . . r . . . a . . . (*WB* 334–35)

The first several sentences call to mind the parodies of cause and effect that we saw in Tawfiq al-Hakim's *Diary of a Country Prosecutor* and Naguib Mahfouz's "Culprit Unknown." What Khoury's frame narrator performs for the reader here is not only a search for answers but a search for the Arabic forms in which such answers have traditionally been articulated. As the words of his proverbs gradually fall to pieces,[71] however, war is reflected as a historical occurrence from which no tidy message or instruction can be distilled. Like a contemporary author himself, the frame narrator of *White Masks* must piece together a new mode for reckoning with history from the ruins of premodern modes of transmission.

If Khoury insists on renouncing the position of the "author" (the *mu᾿allif* or "arranger" of knowledge) and the twinned premises of the *qiṣṣah* (the orderly, sequential "story") and the *mathal* (the instructive "aphorism") alike in *White Masks*, it is perhaps because he has seen how the cause-and-effect logic of the "story" has been used by political actors on all sides of the Lebanese Civil War to justify a seemingly endless series of atrocities. The PLO's massacre of Christian civilians at Damour in 1976 was justified as a retaliation for the Christian Phalangists' massacre of Palestinians at Tell al-Zaatar, just as the Phalangists' massacre of Palestinian civilians on a bus headed to the camps on April 13, 1975 was justified as a retaliation for the Ain El Remmaneh incident earlier that day, when a car of unidentified gunmen killed four men at a church gathering attended by several prominent Phalangist partisans.[72] The loss of Palestine and the aftermath of that loss in the Lebanese Civil War have laid waste to the delicate mechanics of reference, torn apart the tenuous cords that conventionally weave remembered experiences into morally instructive, chronological narratives. Revolutionary rhetoric, moreover, has perverted the language of liberation by using it to paper over atrocity. In response to this situation, a new language becomes necessary.

Khoury begins to assemble this experimental language in the fragmentary monologues spoken by Khalil Ahmad Jaber to Fatimah Fakhro, the wife of the building caretaker Mahmud Fakhro and narrator of the novel's third chapter. Fatimah subsequently remembers and relates these monologues to the narrator, who then transcribes them for his "investigation." These speeches are composed of "ruptures, fragmentations, a rhetorical piling up of incomplete sentences, syncopated questions, unfinished statements, hallucinatory and oneiric images, in short, ambiguities of all sorts which often baffle the reader."[73] Fatimah and Khalil meet as two survivors, each having lost a son either directly or indirectly to the war. Khalil's language articulates a series of "calamities" for which Fatimah previously had no words (*WB* 90–91):

> لا يبقى هناك شيء، كل شيء يختفي، أنت تختفين وأنا أختفي والمدينة تختفي والصور تختفي كل شيء يختفي ويصبح أبيض، أبيض مثل بياض البيضة، مثل بياض العيون، مثل الأبيض. كل شيء يمحّي، تسقط الأشياء هكذا كأنّها لا تسقط. كل شيء يموت، كأنّنا نموت، كأنّ كل شيء يموت، كأنّ كلّ شيء.

> There is nothing left, everything is disappearing, you disappear and I disappear and the city disappears and the pictures disappear, everything disappears and becomes white, white like the whiteness of egg white, white like the whites of your eyes, white like white. Everything is being erased, everything falling just like this, as though it weren't falling . . . Everything dies, as though we're dying, as though everything were dying, as though everything. (*WB* 139–40)

Arabic grammar and syntax themselves are shattered in this passage.[74] In contrast with the way newspapers, martyr posters, and documentary films lay claim to truth throughout *White Masks*, Khalil speaks a language that contains its own effacement, whose assertions and descriptions trail off into senselessness ("white like white," "as though everything") but never claim authority or singularity. For Fatimah, as for other parents forced to grieve their children in this novel, Khalil's defiance of sense making offers a palliative to the martyr posters and missives that hasten to exploit an unthinkable occurrence by appropriating it for a singular, revolutionary purpose. The monologues fill in the negative space left by Khoury's parodic piling-up of proverbs.

## OVERCOMING THE INVESTIGATOR WITHIN

Faced with a crisis of language and authorship, both Khoury and Ghanim refract themselves and their voices through the novel as if through a prism, troubling the premise of detection from the very beginning. By staging their narrators' confusion and forcing them to relinquish control over their narrative materials, both authors use the structure of "investigation" to repaint the figure of the author not as an all-knowing cultural authority but as a self-questioning investigator in search of new literary languages. Where Ghanim calls on the musical Upper-Egyptian language and communal function of the mawwāl in contradistinction to the state-controlled rhetoric of "reform" (iṣlāḥ), Khoury takes apart the martyr-poster, the qiṣṣah, and the mathal alike to play instead with the dream language of a madman. In both cases, the premise of the detective narrative allows the author to experiment with a new epistemology of fiction, one that relinquishes detection's often unspoken ties to authority, knowledge, and—by extension—to colonial, imperial, and state power. These shifting narrative poetics marked important transformations in the politics of literary representation in both national contexts. Ghanim's experiments with voice, language, and structure formed part of a generalized shift away from earlier Egyptian litterateurs' romantic depictions of rural space and people,[75] yet his narrator's uncertainty about the future of étatist reform projects maintains a reticence about Nasserist triumphalism notably absent from other Egyptian works of Soviet-inspired socialist realism. Khoury's antiheroic depiction of the fedayee and the shahīd alike, meanwhile, contrasts sharply and self-consciously with the heroic tones surrounding these figures in earlier works by Ghassan Kanafani, Mahmoud Darwish, Fadwa Tuqan, Nizar Qabbani, and others.[76]

The most important link between Ghanim's fictional meditation on al-Gurna and Khoury's imaginative critical reflection on the Lebanese Civil War, however, is their shared meditation on reading itself. In both books, reading, like detection, is no longer a process of objective, dispassionate observation, deduction, and instructive conclusion. Rather, the reader, like the narrator in each case, must relinquish her obsessive drive to know (the "investigator within," in Ghanim's formulation) and instead listen to the voices, languages, and experiences of others, even if these seem to defy the rules of the novel as a literary form, as well as the logic of sense and grammar themselves. Distinctions between narrative subjects and narrated objects are thus not fixed but permeable and ever-shifting in *al-Jabal* and *White Masks*. Through their narrators' struggle with and eventual overcoming of their learned investigative drives, Khoury and Ghanim model a new reading practice for those encountering their novels. As the narrators renounce their authority to observe, deduce, and ultimately speak for the disenfranchised people whom they've been sent to investigate, so the reader is invited to relinquish her impulses to "make sense" of postrevolutionary Egypt and Civil War-era Lebanon to ultimately transform them into objects of her knowledge. The texts thus offer lessons in method not only to their respective Arabic readerships but also to contemporary scholars in Middle East studies and comparative literature alike.

Still, there is a utopian bent to *al-Jabal* and *White Masks*: both seem to hope that by dramatizing the narrative subject's eclipse in fiction, that subject's domineering, official, "investigative" voice can be replaced with forms of communal narration excavated from the archive of Arab folk literature, on the one hand, and from the everyday, colloquial speech of Upper Egyptians, southern Lebanese, doormen, maids, and garbage collectors, on the other. While readers of these novels may yet learn the lessons they have to offer—about how to read less like a "truth establisher" and more like a mawwāl-listener—their anticolonial poetics remain relatively marginal to the literary establishments in both contexts. The significance of *White Masks* has been largely eclipsed by *Gate of the Sun*, Khoury's later and more sweeping tome of the Nakba and the Palestinian resistance struggle, and few contemporary Egyptian writers cite Fathi Ghanim as any sort of influence. Where *al-Jabal* and *White Masks* articulate their new "ways of seeking" in this positive, even utopian register, the texts in the next chapter—Sonallah Ibrahim's *The Committee* and *Zaat*—work negatively, first staging the failure and futility of "seeking" when undertaken in the isolation of a neoliberal economy and society, and then transforming the process of baḥth into a principle of composition that calls on readers to redefine, reclaim, and reinhabit the notion of a "public."

5

# Epic Fails

## *Sonallah Ibrahim's Modern Myths of Seeking*

> I was hoping I could write a modern myth, with a character that would overcome all the existing deteriorating circumstances. But when I started writing . . . the character was transformed into a completely crushed one.
>
> —SONALLAH IBRAHIM[1]

The Egyptian author Sonallah Ibrahim has been called many things, including a "rebel with a pen,"[2] "a novelist of lost causes,"[3] "Egypt's oracular novelist,"[4] and "the Arab world's preeminent bard of dashed hope and disillusionment."[5] Yet, as several recent interviews have made clear, Ibrahim's work is also deeply indebted to detective fiction, and specifically to Raymond Chandler's noir. Ibrahim has named Chandler's protagonist Philip Marlowe as one of his all-time "favorite heroes in fiction,"[6] and he has cited the "modern, lively, simple . . . even poetic" style of Chandler's novels as one of the biggest influences on his own writing. For Ibrahim, Chandler and Ernest Hemingway belong together in an unconventional school of writing—a "school of simple exhibition which hides many meanings."[7] It's difficult to think of a better phrase to describe Ibrahim's own novels, narrated as they are in plain, often colloquial, language, yet always obliquely condemning the shadowy networks that sustain national, international, and capitalist power.

Like the author himself, the unnamed narrator of Ibrahim's 1981 novella *The Committee* (*al-Lajnah*) is, at one point, very explicit about distinguishing the kinds of detective novels he likes from those he doesn't. In the novel's fourth chapter, one of the members of the titular committee, referred to only as "the short man," notices the absence of "even one work by Agatha Christie" among the many procedurals piled in the narrator's hallway. "I actually only like a specific kind of detective fiction," the narrator explains,

> the kind built on action and movement. My favorites are the ones where a hero chases down criminals and gangsters, undergoing every kind of hardship and misery

> in the process and—as is the case in most of these novels—confronting society and its ruling classes in defense of someone from among the weak and disenfranchised . . . These novels don't require much mental effort from the reader because they are built on action, but that doesn't mean that Agatha Christie's novels are somehow more intellectual. Her fictions are constructed around simplistic, imaginary puzzles that no one should waste his mental energies deciphering, especially since reality itself is full of actual puzzles interesting enough to require all one's faculties.[8]

Indeed, much of the action of *The Committee* is dedicated to identifying, researching, and laying out the "hidden meanings" behind these "real puzzles"—for example, connecting Coca-Cola's penetration into Egyptian markets with the declining quality of tap water, the decrease in public housing projects, the disappearance of local cigarettes, the rise in cases of depression, and the higher doses of foreign-produced pharmaceuticals prescribed in the country.[9] In fact, the novella lays out a "method" of seeking that has been called "conspiracist,"[10] but that I will argue is in fact akin to "confronting the ruling classes in defense of someone from among the weak and disenfranchised," in other words, to Marxist critique. It is a method for writing a people's history, a complex practice veiled in simple language, or, in Ibrahim's own words, a form of "simple exhibition which hides many meanings."[11]

In what follows, I first lay out the features of the "way of seeking" Ibrahim pioneers in *The Committee*, then turn to *Zaat* (1992) to show how the later novel solicits the reader to perform the complex labor of investigation shouldered by the earlier novel's first-person narrator. I illustrate how Egypt's "oracular novelist," this "bard of dashed hope and disillusionment," turns reading into a training in historical-materialist investigation, as well as an invitation to form community and solidarity through the negative image of the isolated, defeated, yet still morally crusading individual.[12] The way of seeking dramatized in *The Committee* and transformed into a way of reading in *Zaat* thus stands in sharp contrast with the ways of seeking dramatized in the previous chapter. Ghanim and Khoury destabilized the rhythms of their narratives with unexpected voices, forms, and registers of speech in the hopes of democratizing or popularizing the novel, making it a social as opposed to an individual form. Ibrahim, meanwhile, takes the opposite tack, plumbing the depths of his era's isolation, alienation, and despair—the misery of neoliberal atomization—as the negative image of possible future communalisms. His novels offer us not so much "the dream of a world in which things would be different," as the nightmare that makes such a transformed world thinkable.[13]

## TOTALITY, FUTURITY, AND THE INVESTIGATIVE POETICS OF THE COMMITTEE

Given Sonallah Ibrahim's repeated expressions of admiration for Chandler (and, it's worth noting, Maurice Leblanc's Arsène Lupin),[14] we should not be surprised that the narrator's views on detective fiction in *The Committee* jibe almost perfectly with Chandler's in his 1944 essay "The Simple Art of Murder." Mocking the improbable intricacies and contrivances of "classic" British clue puzzles and their even more far-fetched American progeny, Chandler also asks why any reader should be interested in "the same utterly incomprehensible trick of how somebody stabbed Mrs. Pottington Postlethwaite III with the solid platinum poignard just as she flatted on the top note of the 'Bell Song' from *Lakmé* in the presence of fifteen ill-assorted guests."[15] Like the narrator of *The Committee*, Chandler argues that clue puzzles like Christie's "are too contrived, and too little aware of what goes on in the world."[16] His concern throughout the essay is with realism, not as a rigid set of formal principles but as a question of authenticity, stretching from a novel's plot to its language.

But more than this, Chandler—like Ibrahim's narrator—is also concerned with the *moral* quality of detective fiction, its ability, when it "takes murder out of the Venetian vase and drops it into the alley,"[17] to expose the hypocrisies of modern law and order, causing its readers to notice, perhaps for the first time, the oft-obscured injustices in the societies around them: "The realist in murder writes of a world in which gangsters can rule nations and almost rule cities . . . a world where a judge with a cellar full of bootleg liquor can send a man to jail for having a pint in his pocket . . . because law and order are things we talk about but refrain from practicing . . ."[18] In Chandler's view, the world of the detective story should be one in which there is some measure of "redemption" for the poor and disenfranchised, a redemption achieved through the actions of the detective himself.[19] Most importantly for the narrator of *The Committee*, the detective story, in Chandler's hands, is "this man's adventure *in search of a hidden truth*."[20] There is no need, Chandler and our narrator assert, to invent elaborate settings, plots, and murders when the real injustices and crimes around us are so widespread, so complex, so deliberately and carefully obscured by those in power. Even that arch conservative G. K. Chesterton reminds us that "morality is the most dark and daring of conspiracies," and detection a modern form of "knight-errantry."[21]

The narrator's preference for this "specific kind of detective fiction" in *The Committee* also explains the seemingly random assortment of biographies he's collected in his home library—ranging from the Prophet Muhammad, Ibn Rushd, Abu Dharr al-Ghifari, and Abu Sa'id al-Jannabi, to Karl Marx, Marie Curie, Albert Schweitzer, Ho Chi Minh, Fidel Castro, Che Guevara, Patrice Lumumba, Mehdi Ben Barka, Ahmed Ben Bella, Farajallah el-Helou, Shuhdi Atiya, and many others.[22] Each was either a religious outcast, (proto)socialist, communist, anti-imperial nationalist, or some combination of these.[23] The narrator of *The Committee*, in other words, has assembled a library of outcasts, renegades, communists, and heretics in which Arsène Lupin and Philip Marlowe make sense, but Hercule Poirot—famed dispeller of crime from respectable British social circles—does not. Once again, Ibrahim subtly clues us into his narrator's simultaneously moral, Marxist, and anti-imperialist sensibilities. The narrator—at least, before his encounter with the Committee—hopes to be yet another crusader for the poor and disenfranchised against the "ruling classes." Yet because they occur in isolation from any kind of public, the narrator of *The Committee* will be sorely disappointed in his quests for justice. His Infitah-era "adventure to expose a hidden truth" will end in nothing more than disillusionment, frustration, and ultimately self-destruction.

Communicating through telegram, the Committee asks the narrator to prepare a study of the "greatest contemporary Arab luminary." To respond to their call, the narrator goes through a lengthy process of selection, research, and preparation which he later refers to as his "method" or "methodology" (*minhāj*) (*L* 96). Although he never uses any explicitly Marxist terms, there are two aspects to his method, I argue, that make it a form of Marxist critique. First, it is concerned with "totality"—that is, with considering the connections between the subjective experiences of alienated individuals and the objective social realities that condition these experiences.[24] For Western Marxists like Georg Lukács, it was necessary to "abandon the view that objects are rigidly opposed to each other" and "elevate their interrelatedness and the interaction between those 'relations' and the 'objects' to the same plane of reality" in order to dispel alienation and apprehend historical change.[25] Like Lukács, the narrator of *The Committee* is concerned with "interrelatedness" (*irtibāṭāt mutasha*ʿʿ*ibah*) (*L* 47), and he seeks to explain the "mysterious puzzles and strange phenomena" that structure his life by stitching them into a larger fabric of material and social circumstances. He quickly realizes that he must find the methodology appropriate to explaining "every phenomenon in itself, and all of the phenomena in their relationships with one another" (*L* 96).

The narrator spends long hours in the archives of state newspapers, ladies' journals, and the American embassy, tracing the involvement of his chosen subject—a man referred to only as "the Doctor"—in numerous realms of Egyptian life. These include the entertainment industry, the nationalization of foreign companies following the Tripartite Aggression of 1956 (referred to as "Egyptification," or *tamṣīr*), the propaganda efforts surrounding Nasserist pan-Arabism, and subsequently, after Sadat's rise to power, securing government subcontracts for the private firms in which he holds large stakes, marrying the daughter of a Gulf-based "oil king," and serving as a middleman between foreign financiers and local consumers. By refusing to consider any of the Doctor's endeavors in isolation from the others, the narrator of *The Committee* sees how this mysterious figure has continually milked the political system for his own profit, turning on a dime from pan-Arab socialist to neoliberal Egyptian capitalist. Given his disempowered position with respect to the Committee, the narrator is—according to Lukács—uniquely positioned to see these "connections" because, unlike the capitalist, he already understands himself as an object, rather than a subject, of history.[26]

The narrator's method can be characterized as Marxist for another reason: it is focused on the future, and on the inevitable, inexorable movement of history in favor of the disempowered. At the end of the novel, after a second official interview with the Committee during which he once again fails to confront them as he might have liked, the narrator makes one last attempt at vindication. He puts a blank cassette into his tape recorder, places it atop a pile of books, and begins addressing it "as though it were a committee." After affirming to this imaginary committee that "every noble intention in this world must be directed at getting rid of you," he affirms that he is "not so innocent as to believe that if this goal were achieved, it would be the end of the journey, for it is only natural that a new committee would replace you, and no matter how good its intentions or how high-minded its goals, sooner or later corruption would infiltrate it too," and it, in turn, would be fated for dissolution. Yet the narrator, by studying history, has learned that "through this very process—the process of change and repeated dissolution—your group will lose its influence, while the power of *those like me* to confront and resist it will rise." Though he regrets having failed to truly confront the Committee (owing, in part, to his "infatuated pursuit of knowledge"), still the narrator is comforted by his "conviction about what *will* come to pass, however long it takes, for *this is the logic of history* and the way of life" (*L* 120, emphases added).

In the narrator's invocation of "the logic of history," it is hard not to hear an echo of the idea that "the history of all hitherto existing society is the history of class struggles."[27] The Committee's power, it seems, will inevitably be superseded by the "lower classes" or, in the narrator's phrase, "those like him" (*L* 87, 120) through the sheer force of history and struggle. This emphasis on posterity explains the otherwise puzzling citation of Russian Marxist poet Vladimir Mayakovsky in the novella's last chapter. As he prepares to carry out the Committee's bizarre sentence of "self-consumption" (literally, eating himself), the narrator comes across

> these lines from Mayakovsky, which he said shortly before his tragic end:
>
> *I swear, from this moment forward, to never speak with the shameful tongue of reason and common sense . . .*
>
> *Now a person can stand up and speak, and his words will resonate across the ages, all history, all creation.*
>
> The fate of the man who had spoken them reminded me of my own tragedy. (*L* 118–19; *C* 154)[28]

In his commitment to the political and social ideals of communism, on the one hand, and his continued clashes with Soviet state authorities, on the other, Mayakovsky's "fate" does indeed seem to resemble that of the narrator in *The Committee*, as well as that of Ibrahim himself. A committed Leninist and supporter of the October Revolution from very early on, Mayakovsky denounced the bureaucratic entrenchment and state-enforced cultural standards of the Stalin regime in the 1920s and through the end of his life.[29] The lines Ibrahim cites come from a series of late fragments found among Mayakovsky's papers after his suicide in 1930, apparently written as a second prologue to a never-written poem about Stalin's first Five-Year Plan (with the more famous poem "At the Top of My

Voice" serving as the first.)[30] Central to both fragments—and to Ibrahim's invocation of them—is the renunciation of "common sense," "being reasonable," and "convention." Like Ibrahim's narrator, the poetic speaker in Mayakovsky's fragments seems aware that his life is essentially over, that there is nothing left for him to do but address his plea to posterity, letting his voice resonate through various levels of time, from the cosmic ("the ages"), to the secular ("history"), to the divine ("all creation"). Following the "wild torment of his life," Mayakovsky implicitly addresses the readers of an ideal future—the "planet's proletariat," living in the "far communist future"—who may discover these fragments in the wake of his self-inflicted death.[31] Given that Mayakovsky composed the lines less than a year before his suicide, it makes sense that the narrator of Ibrahim's *The Committee*, who is just sitting down to destroy himself, would equate Mayakovsky's "fate" with his own "tragedy" (*L* 118–19).

The narrator in *The Committee*, then, is not "uninteresting, and therefore disinterested."[32] His "way of seeking" is more Marxist than it is "suspicious," in Rita Felski's pejorative sense of this term, "paranoid," in Eve Kosofsky Sedgwick's,[33] or even "conspiracist," as Benjamin Koerber has argued.[34] Rather, he seems driven by a Marxist concern with totality, on the one hand, and futurity, on the other. Moreover, it is difficult to think of the narrator as a delusional conspiracy theorist when the "connections" he uncovers are, for the most part, real. At one point, for example, he notes that "since tap water now represents Coca-Cola's only competitor, we can see why it would invest in a project to desalinate seawater carried out by the Aqua-Chem company, which Coca-Cola acquired several years ago, in 1970, to be exact" (*L* 97). This is no conspiracy theory: in his 1986 address to Coca-Cola Company shareholders in Atlanta, then-president Roberto C. Goizueta noted that "at this point in the U.S., people consume more soft drinks than any other liquid, *including ordinary tap water*. If we take full advantage of our opportunities, we will see the same wave catching on in market after market, until eventually the number one beverage on earth will not be tea or coffee or wine or beer; it will be soft drinks, our soft drinks."[35] Coca-Cola executives like Goizueta *did* view tap water as their number one competitor in the world, and they *did* in fact acquire the Milwaukee-based Aqua-Chem water filtration company in a "blundering attempt at diversification," with the reasoning that "this would be a tool for getting into the Arab countries, which refused to deal with Coca-Cola because the company did business with Israel."[36] The move was ultimately a failure, but the importance of this business history is very clear: in order to become "the number one beverage on earth," Coke had to not only redefine the specific food and drink cultures of the countries where it wished to penetrate, but indeed, reconfigure human thirst itself.

The narrator's problem, in a nutshell, is that he's a Marxist thinker in an era of neoliberalization—an Egyptian subject atomized, against his will, in a political climate that has scrapped collective action and sold it for parts. When we follow the paper trail of the other "phenomena" he so intricately weaves together, we learn that he was correct about other elements of his research as well. John Trotter, the Texas-based CEO of a Coca-Cola bottling plant in Guatemala, *did* collaborate with local conservative politicians, military officers, and police to threaten, intimidate, and ultimately kill workers associated with unionization efforts at the Embotelladora Guatemalteca S. A. in starting in 1975.[37] The Coca-Cola Company also *did* "present a huge grant to the Brooklyn Museum in 1977 to rescue Egyptian pharaonic antiquities from collapse" (*L* 96–97; *C* 124–25), providing more than four hundred thousand dollars for a Museum-led project to conserve and record the monuments of ancient Thebes.[38] And while the company hasn't exactly financed "an entire university budget," as the narrator also claims (*L* 97; *C* 125), still Coca-Cola's founder, Asa Chandler—a devoted Methodist—*was* instrumental in the founding of Emory University near Coca-Cola's headquarters in Atlanta. Coca-Cola's second president, Robert W. Woodruff, "bequeathed gifts to Emory that surpassed $150 million, much of it in Coke stock."[39]

Furthermore, the Coca-Cola Company *was* responsible for the mistreatment of migrant farmworkers in the Florida orange groves of its subsidiary, Minute Maid, throughout the 1960s. It took the intervention of César Chavez's United Farmworkers union in 1970 to bring these workers marginal improvements to their wages and working conditions,[40] as well as the summoning of then-CEO of Coca-Cola, J. Paul Austin, before a Senate Subcommittee on Migratory Labor headed by Walter Mondale, the Minnesota senator who would go on to be vice president under Jimmy Carter.[41] Austin admitted before Mondale and the rest of the Senate "committee" that labor and living conditions in the Minute Maid orange groves were indeed "deplorable," but "his solution was to start more worker motivation programs, accompanied by lots of publicity, books, and films on Coca-Cola's rehabilitation efforts . . . a media solution to a real problem."[42] Only two years after the hearings, Mondale himself, when asked what gains his campaign had won the migrant workers, would answer "not much."[43] Meanwhile, as the narrator of *The Committee* also reminds us, Mondale *was* indeed invited to become a member of the Trilateral Commission, a nongovernmental policy-shaping group founded by billionaire David Rockefeller, shortly after its establishment in 1973. Like the Committee, whose quasi-military, quasi-civilian status Ibrahim captures with the neologism *madan ʿaskariyyah*, or "civilitary" (*L* 87), the Trilateral Commission unites private interests and public figures from the United States, Western Europe, and Japan to "foster cooperation" between these three regions. Mondale accepted the offer, and thereby stood, as a private citizen, alongside the same Coca-Cola president he had battled as a public servant, speaking on behalf of impoverished migrant laborers, only three years earlier (*L* 96–97; *C* 124–25).[44]

We might thus be inclined to forgive Ibrahim's narrator for arguing that "this slender bottle . . . played a decisive role in the choice of our mode of life, the inclinations of our tastes, the presidents and kings of our countries, the wars we participated in, and the treaties we entered into" (*L* 23; *C* 23). Coca-Cola may well have served as "a method devised by Arab Spring revolutionaries to mitigate the effects of tear-gas," yet this isolated fact alone should not excuse the company's decades of monopoly law avoidance, labor abuses at home and abroad, and political and cultural manipulation on a global scale, nor does it make the beverage a "method . . . for overthrowing dictators."[45] Rather, as the narrator of *The Committee* also points out, Coca-Cola has often indirectly helped to *enforce* dictatorial rule: this "slender bottle" purposefully modeled after a "girl with an hourglass figure" has, for the past several decades, also been used by militias and secret police across the Middle East as an instrument of rape and torture (*C* 20).[46] Given the "homosexuality test" to which the narrator is subjected in the very first chapter of *The Committee*, such methods of torture are never far from the reader's mind.

By undertaking his economic, historical-materialist research, then, the narrator aims to be like Chandler's Marlowe, Leblanc's Lupin, even an Arab popular hero like ʿAntarah or l'Adham al-Sharqawi, locating and calling out the corruptions of the "ruling classes" on behalf of the country's masses ("me and others like me"). However, when he returns to the real world, after spending months holed up with his "study" of the Doctor, the narrator's actual quest for justice inevitably fails, in large part because he cannot find a public of grateful admirers to cheer him on. Indeed, it is the deterioration of the "public"—understood as both audience and shared social infrastructure—that ultimately undoes the narrator over the course of three encounters.

The first occurs on the street, amid crowds of sweaty, thirsty civilians clamoring for ice-cold Coca-Cola from a vendor who has doubled the price of his stock "on the premise of . . . illusory ice," while the curvy glass bottles swim in open-faced coolers filled with murky, lukewarm water. The vendor "seemed to be in a state of ecstasy as he . . . ministered to [his customers] with the warm bottles,"[47] and as they "sip the magic liquid," they "gulp down the contents in a state of surrender" (*L* 106–7). By the decree of private enterprise and dismantled public infrastructure, which together have allowed tap water to deteriorate to a brown sludge, Egyptian thirst will now be quenched exclusively by Coca-Cola, and the vendor in this scene has taken advantage of this new economic situation. Inducing the "surrender" (*istislām*) of its consumers and the "ecstasy" (*nashwah*) of its purveyor, Coca-Cola has become a kind of religion for these crowds, who pay the unjust price "in a frozen daze," hypnotized by the power of the bottle, the "magic liquid" (*L* 107). Before the narrator realizes what's happening, the vendor has placed an open bottle in his hand, too, forcing him, like the others, to pay the unjust price and sip the lukewarm Coke "unconsciously, automatically" (*L* 107).

The second confrontation occurs as the narrator is riding the "Carter" bus. Bearing images of two hands clasped in friendship superimposed over an American flag, these public buses were meant to be "heralds of the prosperity promised" by Egypt's new US-friendly economic policy under Sadat and, after him, Hosni

Mubarak. Nevertheless, the buses are falling apart, and whereas "early in the buses' service, the dancing motion they caused had called forth a shy smile from all the riders" (thus fostering a sense of social collectivity), today, even though the buses' "dancing" has increased dramatically, the riders' enjoyment has disappeared completely. "It seemed to me," the narrator notes, "like they were busy with other things, staring gravely at the billboards adorning the streets, the advertisements for the latest inventions from around the world, in every arena, and at the latest makes and models of private cars, furnished with numerous mechanisms for protecting their riders from noise, pollution, heat, cold, and the eyes of others, like tiny tanks" (*L* 110).[48] Moreover, when he tries to confront a man who has been silently fondling a woman beside him, the narrator draws courage from the idea that the other passengers "would take my side, drawing on religious or moral principles to condemn the giant's sexual behavior, to disapprove of his striking a defenseless woman, or simply choosing to stand by the truth." He is sorely disappointed, however: every one of the passengers simply "looks the other way, some at things along the route, others simply turning their backs" (*L* 113; *C* 146). The man, meanwhile, lunges at the narrator, knocking him to the ground and fracturing his arm. The ʿAntarah-like confrontation the narrator had imagined—in which the grateful passengers would cheer the righteous hero on—in reality leaves him feeling even more alienated than before. The broken arm is not the only wound he sustains; the utter fragmentation, atomization, and monadization of Egyptian social life shatters him as well.

A third and final failed confrontation with Egypt's new neoliberal economic system happens at the private medical clinic where the narrator goes to seek treatment for his wounded arm. After paying five pounds for a service his government technically guarantees its citizens for free, his first appointment with the medical doctor goes off without a hitch; but, after a few hours at home, he realizes the prescribed painkillers aren't working. He returns to the clinic for a follow-up appointment, where he is asked to pay a "consultation fee" yet again. "This is profiteering, pure and simple!" he exclaims. Yet, where he expects the other patients in the waiting room to cheer him on, they merely follow the discussion in silence, "their poker faces betraying no shadow of their thoughts" (*C* 150). The narrator then makes one last attempt at confronting the system. When the doctor stakes the necessity of his clinic on the claim that "there's no [public] hospital whose services you can trust," the narrator exasperatedly points out that it's the doctor and others like him who have ruined the public health system by opening their own private clinics. "I'm entitled to free treatment from you," the narrator concludes, gesturing to include the doctor and his furniture, air conditioner, sound system, and medical equipment:

> None of this has resulted from your unique genius. You and others like you benefit from a system of inherited privileges that have been stolen from me and others like

> me, from my parents and my grandparents, and the parents and grandparents of others like me over time. Above and beyond this, you are from the generation that had a free education, a free ride on me and others like me. (*L* 116)

For yet a third time, the narrator has confronted the superstructure where, even though his investigations have struck at the base, simply being right about the structures of wage theft and crumbling public infrastructure that have enabled the doctor's private gain does nothing to actually change those structures. With every confrontation, the narrator is met not with the support of the cheering masses—"me and others like me"—but only with embarrassment, alienation, and isolation. Like Mayakovsky, he is caught between his utopian visions of communist collectivity and the realities of self-interested social atomization. He has nothing left to do but dream of a "far communist future"[49] or, in the narrator's case, an inexorable "logic of history" that will eventually erode the power of the Committee, of all committees.

However, in this very concern for the future, there is also a deep—and, for Ibrahim, a centrally important—ambivalence. Mayakovsky's political disillusionment, psychological dissolution, and suicide give his impassioned addresses to future generations of proletarians a note of futility. The arrival of the future he describes is uncertain, to say the least, and thus "At the Top of My Voice" seems to be screaming into the void more than it is addressing a community to come. So, too, the narrator of *The Committee* is at his most confrontational and optimistic only when he is narrating to the void, his only audience the hissing of an audiocassette tape set to record. The audiocassette itself, in the final scene of *The Committee*, becomes a figure of the uncertain future: the reader is given no guarantee that any listener will ever hear and act on the narrator's words. Just as there is nothing to guarantee the coming of the "far communist future" prophesied by Mayakovsky's poetic speaker, so the narrator's conviction about the "logic of history" working against the Committee (and all committees) is rendered uncertain by the very medium that records it. This uncertainty becomes a principle of composition in *Zaat*.

## EPIC FAILURE AND THE SUMMONING OF A PUBLIC IN *ZAAT*

> *If there is something comforting—religious, if you want—about paranoia, there is still also anti-paranoia, where nothing is connected to anything, a condition not any of us can bear for long.*
>
> —THOMAS PYNCHON, *GRAVITY'S RAINBOW*

Published eleven years after *The Committee*, and nearly three times as long, Ibrahim's 1992 novel *Zaat* strikes a very different note from the earlier novella. Where *The Committee* is structured, in large part, around the investigation carried out by its first-person narrator, *Zaat* features an omniscient narrator and chapters that alternate between the wry and sardonic telling of its titular protagonist's story and the compilation of headlines and news items that tumble over each other, bold and sometimes offset into boxes, in the novel's even-numbered chapters. As in *The Committee*, each headline in *Zaat* is caught in a tangled web of relationships: to other headlines within the same chapter, to headlines in the other docufictional chapters, and to the events that take place in the life of Zaat, her family, her neighbors, and her coworkers.[50] Through these connections, the macrocosms of Egypt's Americanization, Islamicization, and neoliberalization are shown to have their effects in the microcosms of everyday life. The two works might seem to have very little to do with each other on the level of form or content; my aim, however, will be to connect *Zaat*'s focus on everyday alienation, loneliness, and corruption in the era of Hosni Mubarak with the more explicit investigative poetics of *The Committee.*

Specifically, I argue that by alternating the narration of Zaat's life with the compilation of headlines and news items (many of them "directly cited from government and opposition newspapers," as a note from the publisher affirms in the novel's frontmatter),[51] *Zaat* the novel places its reader directly into the position once occupied by the narrator of *The Committee*. Whereas *The Committee* chronicles its narrator's process of search and discovery in the newspaper archives, *Zaat* brings the archive to the reader, forcing them to connect the docufictional chapters' reports of political corruption, public mismanagement, economic liberalization, and cultural Islamicization with the narrative chapters' tales of polluted food, sexual frustrations, social climbing, and alienation. In *The Committee*, the unnamed narrator does all the work required to understand the totality of the Egyptian present; in *Zaat*, the burden of this work, this "research" (baḥth), falls to the reader.

Moreover, if the narrator of *The Committee* was concerned with totality and futurity—that is, with a Marxist way of seeking—so the reader of *Zaat*, by being indirectly placed into that narrator's position, is summoned into a similar way of reading. To read *Zaat* is to read "as a Marxist," then, in the sense that the structure of the novel forces one to connect the individual feelings of alienation, loneliness, and defeat described in its narrative chapters with the collective historical, economic, and political occurrences reported in its docufictional chapters. Ibrahim exploits the linear nature of narrative to reveal (without explicitly asserting) connections between the powers of Egypt's Mubarak-era military government and the immiseration of everyday Egyptian citizens.[52] If, in *The Committee*, the labor of critique fell to the narrator alone, in *Zaat* the absence of these connections is transformed into a negative principle of composition whose positive image is a practice of reading, seeking, and seeing that it summons into being.[53]

To achieve this authorial conjuring trick, Ibrahim continues *The Committee*'s interest in totality by sowing connections between the novel's docufictional chapters and its narrative ones, leaving it to the reader-detective to connect these clues into branching tales of injustice. Healthcare, housing, the construction industry, waste management, transportation, police violence, labor organizing, food production—the privatization of these and other formerly public sectors is reported in the novel's headlines, and the effects of this privatization trickle down into Zaat's personal life. One of the central failed adventures in *Zaat* is built around the disintegration of water treatment systems and public electrical lines in the rural village of Zifta, combined with the local authorities' corrupt collusion to cover up their mismanagement. The novel's docufictional chapters report on "little Farag," for example, who drowned in "an open sewage manhole near the Republic Palace in Kobba" (which one general writes off as "an act of fate and completely unavoidable"),[54] and on "two hundred cases of hepatitis in the village of al-Nagila . . . after sewage contaminated the drinking water" (*Z* 178). Then, in one of the novel's narrative chapters, we are told about Jihan, the eleven-year-old niece of Zaat's neighbor—ironically named after first lady Jihan al-Sadat—who was electrocuted on her way to school after slipping in the mud and grabbing onto a faulty lamppost, during a rainstorm that left the village's streets flooded with sewage. Power lines, these very literal images of connectivity and technological progress, here lead not to the modernization of the countryside but to the death of innocent and unsuspecting children.

As if this story weren't bad enough, however, the police who respond to Jihan's electrocution want to avoid the blame they know should fall on them for the accident. They manipulate Jihan's parents, asserting that the postmortem examination required to substantiate the family's claims of public negligence would constitute a "gruesome fate" for their daughter's body. Yet, even after the parents sign a death certificate falsely attesting to their daughter's death from "chronic heart problems," the police still accuse the father of forgery and compel him, with the threat of his daughter's autopsy, to produce two witnesses who can testify to Jihan's history of heart disease. "It's important to prove that there was no negligence involved," they inform Jihan's father. "What are the governor and the electricity officials supposed to do about a lamppost and an uncovered wire when it rains? It was her destiny . . ." (*Z* 130). Reports of failing public sewage systems in the novel's docufictional chapters, in other words, have simply flitted past Zaat's uncomprehending eyes with the daily headlines: she cannot connect Jihan's gruesome fate with that of "little Farag" or "al-Nagila." Whereas, in al-Hakim's 1937 *Diary of a Country Prosecutor*, autopsy was a "gruesome" imposition by the state on traditional practices of mourning and burial, as well as a crude, disillusioning, and ultimately failed penetration into the mysterious "interior" of a human being, here the authorities have coopted the rhetoric of tradition to counsel Jihan's father away from the autopsy that would reveal their culpability. And, rather than undertake a quest for justice in the countryside similar to those narrated in al-Hakim's novel, as well as in those of Yusuf al-Qaʿid and Yusuf Idris, Zaat travels to Zifta merely to collect more material for "transmission" among the "machines"—that is, her female colleagues—at the newspaper archive where she works. The task of "questing for justice," it is implied, now falls to the reader.

The connective tissue linking Zaat's many misadventures with the novel's newspaper headlines is only one aspect of a bigger historical reality narrated in *Zaat*—namely, the mixing, jumbling, and reshuffling of public and private that has resulted from Egypt's neoliberalization in the 1980s and 1990s. In the same way that "the words all climb on top of one another's backs and the phrases and meanings get mixed up" whenever Zaat tries to read or write (*Z* 7–8), so too *Zaat's* Egypt is a topsy-turvy world in which the privatization of public services has sown comic confusion among the novel's characters. The private language of love, tenderness, and romance, for example, has been replaced by the rhetoric of advertising and commercialism. During her first date with her future husband Abdel Meguid, Zaat offers the following flirtation: "Washing clothes is no longer a problem thanks to Omo. Just pour a splash into a plastic water bucket, mix until it foams, throw in your shirts or blouses, then make a tea or do the cooking. After that, just a scrub or two—no need to destroy your fingers or the washerwoman!" (*Dh* 13; *Z* 4)

Likewise, a number of the Nasser-era Arabic phrases coined to describe the promising new world of local, publicly owned Egyptian industrial production have been dislodged from their original meanings in *Zaat* and now refer to aspects of the private sphere. Egypt is no longer a country following the "march of progress" toward development, instituting sweeping social and economic reforms to fly in the face of Western democracies touting free market capitalism as the only path to modernity. Now, in the era of Sadat and the Infitah, the "march of social progress" has been replaced with the "march of demolition and construction"—that is, the improvement of private bathrooms and interior spaces rather than public works (*Dh* 54). There is also the "activation of Zaat's tear glands" (*Dh* 97) and the transformation of the bedroom into an industrial "hatchery" that can also be "operationalized" (*tashghīl al-mafrakhah*) (*Dh* 153). The economic "self-reliance" (*al-iʿtimād ʿalā al-nafs*), pronounced as an empowering strategy of anti-imperial industrial and agricultural production in the years of Nasser, is transformed into a euphemism for masturbation; so too mouths become "machines" (*mākīnāt*, the transliterated English word rather than the Arabic *ālāt*); conversation becomes "transmission" (*bathth*); and "boycott" (*muqāṭaʿah*) is no longer an economic strategy to resist Soviet-era US imperial interests but a social tactic of "cutting off" anyone who does not conform to the country's new social-climbing standards of conversation. The Nasser era's language of Third World, anti-colonial nationalism has been almost entirely repurposed, in *Zaat*, for the new world of individualism, consumerism, and social competition.

In line with the economic and political transformations of the Infitah, Egyptians like Zaat are no longer encouraged to improve the common, shared spaces of public life, nor is there any hope or purpose in seeking justice for those who have been wronged by those in power. Despite her sense of "professional duty,"

Zaat's attempt to convince her colleague to report on the scandal of Jihan's electrocution ends not only with defeat but also with mortal fear, when the reporter suggests she "should go to the opposition papers" with her story (*Dh* 166–67; *Z* 131). Meanwhile, Zaat's project to curb the number of cats, cat feces, and spilled garbage littering her apartment building's stairways—a quasi-public space—by encouraging her neighbors to adopt a new garbage collection system is also met with spectacular failure. Now the *inside* of one's home is all that matters.[55] Thus, when a private car in front of her taxi comes to a sudden stop on the October 6 bridge into Heliopolis, discharging a veiled woman who frantically runs out into the traffic, Zaat can only think of one explanation for why "a respectable-seeming woman with a family, children, and a private car" would do such a thing in the middle of the night: "'She must want moquette'" (*Dh* 159). As with Coca-Cola in *The Committee*, the Infitah has reconfigured not only the Egyptian economy but Egyptian desire itself, such that the craving for high-pile carpet, for many housewives, surpasses the will to live. Free market capitalism, ever questing after new markets, has completely reconfigured the Egyptian self—the nation's *dhāt*.

The plot-level failure of these and other attempts at public improvement and social justice in *Zaat* is also mirrored on the level of form in the novel—specifically, in the narrative structure of "transmission." Where the narrator's "method" of investigation and research (baḥth) in *The Committee* was governed by the logic of interconnection, development, and narrativization, the form of "transmission" (*bathth*) introduced in *Zaat* is governed by a logic of lists and enumeration. Here is a typical "transmission" from the machines at Zaat's workplace:

> Rabbit Face talked about the Betanoun fire: the fire brigade had taken an hour and a half to get there and then they discovered that their hoses were leaking; Broad Shoulders told them about the letter she had seen on the letters page in the newspaper about a young second wife who lost her sight after her husband's children prayed for her to go blind; and Black Mole reported how her husband had been asking her to wear the higab. Then the conversation moved on to how long was left before it was time to go home for the day, the days off they should be having, the raise and the next bonus, where they were going for their holidays next summer, the share of each individual in the compulsory scheme to pay off Egypt's debt, the plastic coating that you could stick on clear glass to make it look *fumée*, and the wife who cut up her husband with a knife. (*Dh* 164–65; *Z* 130)

According to the logic of transmission, the dysfunctional local fire department is of a piece with tabloid tales of witchcraft and magic, just as everyday watercooler complaints sit alongside violent murder and cheap, housewifely tricks for saving money while appearing wealthy. "Instead of analogy, we have enumeration."[56] The language of transmission assumes the grammatical illusion of progress in the same way that the country itself has taken on the outward signs of progress: new power lines, advanced medicine, elevated highways, sewage systems, and so on. Yet the infrastructure does not hold, and the miserable lives of the populace continue unchanged, and indeed, sometimes even worse than before.

In *Zaat*, changes in Egyptian economics have altered the very nature of social interaction itself, such that any "quest" or "search" (baḥth) for justice is inevitably transformed into nothing more than the "transmission" (*bathth*) of scandal. Zaat's narrative, however, struggles to continue following the narrative models that characterized the Nasser era—that is, those anticolonial forms of narrative that, as David Scott reminds us (writing in the Caribbean context), largely follow the topoi of romance: "narratives of overcoming . . . of vindication . . . telling stories of salvation and redemption," and "depending upon a certain (utopian) horizon toward which the emancipationist history is imagined to be moving."[57] Every misadventure Zaat undertakes (especially the journey to Zifta) could be told as one of "overcoming," "vindication," or "redemption." Yet everything around her comes into conflict with this romantic questing. The never-ending march of demolition and construction, the enumerative logic of "transmission," the repetitive circularity of her boss Aminophis's rotating daily reports—none of these forms is in sync with Zaat's sought-after narrative structure.

This clash of narrative forms peaks in the lengthy, nightmarish adventure of the olive tin. In addition to encapsulating the conflict between Zaat's romantic-epic narrative existence and the bureaucratic obstacles that frustrate it, the adventure of the olive tin also epitomizes the similarities between Ibrahim's novel and the oral Arab epic it obliquely references, the *Epic of the Commander Dhat al-Himmah* (*Sīrat al-Amīrah Dhāt al-Himmah*).[58] Like the *sīrah*, *Zaat* is the story of a life, but rather than focusing on an "exemplary life" like that of the legendary female Arab warrior, it focuses on the remarkable *un*exemplarity of Zaat and her tale. Both *Zaat* and the sīrah "include features of spoken Arabic" that often veer into "very base humor"; both "combine historic persons and events with imaginary characters and situations." *Zaat* also includes exclamations and asides on the part of its narrator that directly summon the participation of the reading public (usually in the form: "Did Zaat despair? Never!" [*Z* 163]), in the same way notations on the manuscript copies of the *Epic* and other sīrahs reminded storytellers of key moments in which to solicit audience participation. And like the sīrah, the numerous, piled-up episodes of *Zaat* "read like a storyteller's train of thought, frequently moving from one setting to another" without much connective narrative tissue.[59] (Indeed, one scholar has noted that the epic of Dhat al-Himmah in particular "exemplifies the narrators' technique of accumulating disasters," making it a particularly apt intertext for Ibrahim.)[60]

Yet it is the motivations that inspire Zaat to pursue the "case of the olive tin" that make this character most like her namesake Dhat al-Himmah—or at least, a clownish latter-day version of that namesake. One day, while washing a tin of imported Greek olives she has purchased from a local grocer, Zaat watches as the sticker specifying a future expiration date peels off to reveal another, older expiration stamp whose date has long passed. While her husband Abdel Meguid advises her to simply return to the shop and exchange the olives for something else, Zaat's daughter Doaa cites a saying of the Prophet Muhammad "calling the believer, if he witnesses an abomination, to right it with his sword, and, if he is unable to do that, then with his tongue, which is the least that should be expected of a good Muslim" (*Z* 190). Add to this pious motivation the more worldly concern with the "duties of a good citizen" instilled in Zaat thanks to the "glorious declaration of principles" made by Himmat, her colleague at the newspaper archives,[61] and Zaat is sufficiently motivated to "set off" on her next adventure—much like Arsène Lupin, Philip Marlowe, and the narrator of *The Committee* before her. Like Dhat al-Himmah, Zaat now hopes to become an "accomplished warrior [and] defender of her people," and thus she "ventures away from the familiarity and the structure of kin and society in order to . . . work for the benefit of her community."[62] However, unlike the princess from the sīrah, Zaat will eventually be crushed and demoralized in her battle with Egyptian bureaucracy.

The narration of the "adventure of the olive tin" so painstakingly recreates the frustration of bureaucratic headache that readers are likely to feel as demoralized as the protagonists by the end of its seventeen pages. Among the many stereotypically Egyptian obstacles Zaat and Himmat confront in their quest, perhaps the most excruciating is having to pinball between offices and buildings, as each government official passes the buck in turn. Carrying a folder of paperwork that grows fatter with each correction certificate, police stamp, carbon copy, and petition they accumulate along the way, the two women shuttle from the Office of Public Health to the police headquarters, the Public Prosecutor's Office, and the Health Ministry, and from officer, to sergeant, to secretary, to clerk. At one point, one of the sergeants even seems to enjoy the baroque procedures to which he's subjecting Himmat: "It's no use" (*Mayanfa'sh*), he says to her.

> Himmat was livid: "What do you mean, 'it's no use'?" . . .
> "I can't issue you a copy."
> "Why not?"
> "All I have is the correction certificate."
> "Great. That's what I want."
> "And the original report?"
> "I have a copy of it."
> "You don't understand. I can't give you a copy of the correction certificate on its own. You have to take both of them together."
> "Fair enough. Give me both of them. It's only a small fee, isn't it?"
> "The original report isn't here."
> "Where's it gone?"
> "The Public Prosecutor's office."
> "When will it come back?"
> "That's in God's hands, and even if it does come back . . ."

> "What do you mean?"
>
> "Didn't I just say that you have to take both of them together? When the first report comes back the correction certificate will have gone to the Prosecutor."
>
> "And when the correction certificate comes back from the Prosecutor the original will have . . ."
>
> The sergeant was beginning to enjoy himself and his face softened for the first time: "Gone to the Records Department."
>
> Himmat joined in the game: "And when it comes back from the Records Department the other one will have gone to the Archives." (*Dh* 243–44; *Z* 194–95)

Numerous other moments in this misadventure chronicle the delaying tactics, extortion, and sexual harassment to which Himmat is subjected at the hands of apathetic clerks, distracted secretaries, and other Egyptian public servants. At one point, she is shocked to see one of the "general supervisors" whose signatures she must obtain wearing, in addition to a woolen sweater over his colorful polyester shirt, "flip-flops—yes, I swear, *flip-flops*" (shibshib, ayy wallahi shibshib) (*Z* 200; *Dh* 251).

The adventure culminates at the Egyptian ministry of health, where Himmat has spent the better part of a day tracking down a series of Ustazes, Bashas, and Madames in quest of signatures, certificates, and stamps. At the very end of her quest, a clerk—noticing the absence of a signature from the general supervisor on her form—admonishes both her and his coworker, Mahmoud, who has accompanied Himmat on the better part of her journey: "We can't stamp a paper like this. It would mean that Muhiyy Bey wasn't here. You don't want one of our colleagues to get into trouble do you?" The only thing worse than each official's shirking his extremely easy duty in turn is their willingness to cover for their colleagues at the expense of the time and sanity of the citizens they nominally serve. At the prompting of Himmat's exasperated tears, however, the clerk comes up with a solution: he paints several layers of Wite-Out over the space where the supervisor's signature should be, then stamps the paper. "Now everything is 100 percent in order, *miyya miyya*" he tells her with a smile (*Dh* 253; *Z* 202).

The clerk's parting words are a statement of arch irony: absolutely nothing is "in order" (*salīmah*) at all. For Zaat and Himmat to be *salīmah* would imply being simultaneously "safe" from harmful expired foods; "undamaged" and "unhurt" by the experience of trying to get them off the market; and, most importantly, "healthy" in both body and mind.[63] Of course, Himmat and Zaat are anything but "safe," "undamaged," or "healthy," even if their file of olive tin-related papers now passes muster. (Meanwhile, the spoiled tin of imported Greek olives itself—along with the countless other shipments of spoiled meat, hormonally treated chicken, rancid processed cheese, and expired pharmaceuticals consumed by Egyptians throughout *Zaat*—is now nowhere in sight.) Yet another quest away from the private, domestic space and into the world of public life has yielded nothing for Zaat but further defeat and alienation. The linking of episodes in the "epic of the olive tin" mirrors the enumerative logic of transmission itself, and the epic, the sīrah, of the olive tin is shown to be an epic fail.

The final pages of the novel, in fact, are saturated with figures for this clash between aspiration and reality—moments that project Zaat's nightmarish and tragic reality against the scrim of her romantic dreams. At one point, Abdel Maguid is heading home from one of his long walks through the streets of Heliopolis, where he has been eagerly "watching women buy ice cream and observing the different ways they licked it." While riding on the tram, he begins "to make up one of his Antarian super-hero escapades for Zaat [*iḥdā ʿAntariyyātih*]," narrating how he gave three would-be muggers a run for their money (*Z* 166–67; *Dh* 208). But, like the narrator of *The Committee*, Abdel Maguid is no ʿAntara—he is a sad, sexually frustrated, middle-aged man, deriving his self-consciously perverted pleasure from observing the suggestive female arts of ice cream licking.

Perhaps the most remarkable of these figures, however, involves the chocolate cake Zaat's brother-in-law Dr. Fresh supplies for her son's birthday party, after Zaat's own "*chocolat ice*" (*shūkūlā ays*, a transliteration of this mixed French-English hybrid) based on a recipe excavated from the archives of *Ḥawāʾ* magazine, emerges from the freezer as a "brownish, sticky mass that . . . did not obtain the desired shape or taste" (*Dh* 346). Dr. Fresh's eighteen-inch-long, four-inch-high "gateau" (*ṭūrṭah*) seems—at first—to save the day. But at one point during the party, the doctor's Griffon dog Bousy absconds to the kitchen, and when Zaat follows him, she discovers that "Bousy had 'done it,' with extreme liberality, under the table bearing the doctor's cake" (*Dh* 348). Staring at the scene, Zaat is overcome by her worst vision yet:

> As she eyed in disgust Bousy's deed, which had taken the shape of a small coiled snake, or a pile of cream squeezed from an icing cone, it vanished in the blink of an eye and reemerged on top of the sumptuous gateau. Invisible hands spread it around until it had covered the entire surface, replacing the cake's pale color with its own brown hue, the color of the "dressing" that Zaat would have preferred in the first place . . . When they turned off the lights and lit the candles on the cake, she expected at any moment to see it with the brown coating, and she watched apprehensively as she sang Happy Birthday in English with the others: '*haaby bersday toooo yoo. Haaaby bersday tooo Amgad*' . . . When she saw them all greedily devouring their portions of cake, she rushed to the toilet and vomited. (*Z* 280–81; *Dh* 348)

Like many middle-class Egyptians in the late 1980s and early 1990s, Zaat dreams of nothing more than American-style suburban respectability, inspired by the pages of *Ḥawāʾ* magazine, the Nasser-era "Arab dream," and the "transmissions" of neighbors, work colleagues, and family members, who brag about their ability to acquire brand-name watches, washing machines, bathroom fixtures, and foods. Yet once again, as throughout the entirety of Ibrahim's novel, Zaat's Egyptian-style American Dream has—quite literally—gone to shit.

## HOW ZAAT'S SUBJECTIVITY BECOMES OBJECTIVITY

Unlike the narrator from *The Committee*, Zaat does not record herself giving a defiant final speech in the hopes that listeners in the "far communist future" might hear her cries. Her alienation culminates when she absconds to the bathroom, which Ibrahim calls the "cry-a-torium" (*mabkā*, a place-noun or *ism makān* derived from the verb "to cry," *bakā*), that most private of spaces. It is the readers of *Zaat* who must now form Zaat's "public," that collective tape recorder transmitting her cries to posterity. Through the medium of the novel, Ibrahim transforms Zaat's subjective alienation and disillusionment into a form of communal, objective experience, inviting readers into the investigative position once occupied by the narrator of *The Committee*. *Zaat* is certainly not a lyric poem, yet the extent of its protagonist's alienation, the exaggeratedly nightmarish quality of her existence, and her utter inability to connect her own miseries with those reported in the newspapers call to mind Theodor Adorno's remarks on lyric poetry. Adorno calls the lyric work "a subjectivity that turns into objectivity," because he understands the lyric subject's withdrawal from the objective, material world as something "not absolutely individual," but rather "socially motivated behind the author's back." "The work's distance from mere existence becomes the measure of what is false and bad in the latter. In its protest the poem expresses the dream of a world in which things would be different."[64]

Adorno's social poetics of the lyric seem a near-perfect negative image of the investigative poetics at work in *Zaat*. By taking away the audience (the public) in whose name "kindhearted Zaat's" crusades and adventures might have been carried out (*Z* 15), *Zaat* creates a vacuum that, it is hoped, might be filled by the novel's readers. "The less the work thematizes the relationship of 'I' and society, the more spontaneously [this relationship] crystallizes of its own accord."[65] Interspersing headlines with misadventures, soliciting our participation in the quasi-oral epic of Zaat, Ibrahim forces us to consider the extent to which the social and communal ideals of an admittedly utopian Arab dream have been banished from the life of the subject. At the same time, this nightmare is also, negatively, the dream of a world in which things would be different.

A glimpse of that world is visible in the character of Umm Wahid, one of a triumvirate of "Umms" whom Zaat employs as domestic workers. Unlike other lower-class characters in *Zaat* (for example, the doorman of Zaat's building, who will not sit down inside the home of any of its residents unless invited to do so) (*Z* 38), Umm Wahid

> left no doubt, from the beginning, as to her position vis-à-vis the social topography: she sat down immediately on the chair opposite Zaat without anyone asking her, took out a packet of Cleopatras, and lit one up. Before she had finished it she lit another one from the end of the first. She was a stout woman in her forties, good

> looking, extremely intelligent, hardworking, and widely cultured despite her illiteracy (thanks to numerous transmission channels). She wanted nothing to do with changes on the international scene, nor with the world order, new or old, nor with the fight between the doves and the hawks in Israel, nor who really held the most cards (El Sadat had always insisted that America held 99 percent of them). But she knew about the dangers of taking too many antibiotics and how AIDS was transmitted, how depression affects people, the benefits of arugula and lettuce, the price of the dollar and sterling in the currency exchange shops, and how important it was to skin chickens in order to reduce the effects of the hormones that are added to their feed, that the capital placement companies were a scam, the secret behind the construction work that had been underway at Cairo Airport since its inception, why Hussein Fahmy had divorced Mervat Amin, what exactly happened to ʿAdawiyya at the hands of the Kuwaiti prince, and the source of the money that Shaykh Shaʿrawi spent so lavishly (*Z* 269).

Umm Wahid embodies a kind of wiliness and street intelligence despite, or perhaps because of, her lower-class status—she is a typical Egyptian folk hero, plucked from the *mawwāl* and transplanted into the Mubarak era. In an Egypt where class stratifications seem to saturate every aspect of daily life, Umm Wahid's brazen disregard of the "social topography," combined with her preference for local Egyptian Cleopatra cigarettes over the imported American Marlboros favored by police officers (*Z* 191), make her simultaneously one of the book's most nonchalant characters and, consequently, its most important figure of resistance. To act in the name of the "responsibilities and duties of the good citizen," as Zaat and Himmat do in the adventure of the olive tin, is to be doomed to failure in a postcolonial era that values "transmission" over anticolonial romance. Yet to simply disregard the social topography is to be "cultured" (*muthaqqaf*) in a manner different from and more promising than the intellectualism typically associated with this word, in Arabic and in English.

Beyond her indifference to the global politics that obsess the nation's intellectuals and her knowledge of the secret truths behind the nation's latest tabloid scandals,[66] Umm Wahid knows through street smarts what it took the narrator of *The Committee* years of painstaking research to discover—namely, that, in an adage he attributes to Balzac, "behind every great fortune is a great crime" (*C* 94). She knows that the capital placement companies are a scam designed to take advantage of lower-class Egyptians in need of housing that was once publicly subsidized, and that there are corrupt "secrets" behind the country's construction boom, most likely linked to the real-life founder of the Arab Contractors Company, Osman Ahmed Osman, whose name litters the novel's headlines on political corruption. Like the narrator of *The Committee*, Umm Wahid also knows that the rise in depression among Egyptians is not a strange or isolated medical phenomenon but a product of the country's economic and agricultural transformations, which have brought a rise in the consumption of harmful, often spoiled, imported foods, a decline in the production of local, healthful goods, the overprescription of imported pharmaceuticals, and a widespread belief that wealth and material goods—unattainable to the vast majority of Egyptians—are the markers of true happiness.

With this intuitive grasp of Egyptian totality, Umm Wahid makes no bones about quietly stealing from her employers—including Zaat herself. When Zaat confronts Umm Wahid about these repeated thefts, the uneducated woman replies with the novel's most informed critique of the new economic order. Why shouldn't she enjoy life as others do? Why shouldn't she have new appliances and furnishings like those owned by the simple agricultural worker who lives next door to Zaat? "And don't tell me," Umm Wahid continues, "that it all comes from the sweat of his brow. The truth will out, and he's corrupt as they come." Umm Wahid then produces yet another convincing proof from her quiver: "If she had gone to school and been educated, she'd now be a doctor like the other women who were no better than her, and who had only been given such opportunities through chance" (*Dh* 343–44). Since providence and the government have not seen fit to distribute educational opportunities equally, Umm Wahid has taken the redistributive task of a "corrective revolution" (*thawrah taṣḥīḥiyyah*) into her own hands (*Dh* 344)—a phrase she repurposes, ironically, from Sadat, who gave this name to his 1971 campaign to eliminate high-ranking Nasserist officials from his newly minted government.[67]

Umm Wahid's "dialectics were not learned from Hegel," and she "did not have to read to make up [her] mind which side to join, which side to fight on."[68] Ibrahim presents readers with her irreverence, her frank and simple takedown of Egypt's newly imported bootstraps narrative, with a tone less of mockery than of deep respect. Where Mayakovsky spoke "at the top of his voice," and the narrator of *The Committee* firmly stated his faith in the "logic of history" to no one in particular, Umm Wahid simply plunks herself down on her boss's couch, chain-smokes Cleopatras, and holds forth with her socialist critique. She does not expend herself in investigations or quests; she knows intuitively that the premise of justice under capitalism is an illusion, and that simply exposing this truth will do nothing to change it. We might learn from Umm Wahid that there is little promise in the practice of baḥth alone. The conditions that immiserate us are on the surface of our experience, stitched into the stories that link headlines with transmissions, material circumstances with individual lives. *Zaat* trains us in a practice of investigation pioneered by the narrator of *The Committee*, but Umm Wahid teaches us the ultimate end of such investigations: that they yield not collective knowledge but collective action, that the Marlowe-esque "knight-errant" with a moral purpose is merely a premise for the unification of the crowds cheering him on.

# Epilogue

## *Monstrous Omniscience*

I began this study with Mahfouz's Amina in her rooftop garden, watering the flowers and jasmine vines, feeding the chickens and pigeons, and contemplating the "invisible cords" that link the visible with the invisible, the known with the unknown, and the world of her own home with the one bustling outside its walls. And here I have ended with yet another Egyptian mother, Umm Wahid, whose irreverence, melodramatic adventures, and instinctive grasp of social and economic injustices couldn't be further from Amina's practices of piety, cloistering, and care. Umm Wahid has been to prison ("*yooooh*, lots of times") (*Z* 273); Amina is terrified even at the prospect of her name being written in a police report. Amina has no grasp of the social totality of which she is a part (she is more concerned with divine totality and "completeness" or "perfection," *kamāl*); Umm Wahid seems all too aware of the various economic and political forces conspiring to immiserate lower-class Egyptians—and how to outsmart them. The two characters live in different Cairos, different worlds, yet each practices a way of seeing built from everyday experience rather than formal education and expertise. From them, and from many other characters in Arabic fictions of investigation, we can learn to see and seek in nonpanoptic ways.

This book has examined how fictions from the Arab world stage scenes of seeing, reading, and knowing—all acts with which the detective is stereotypically concerned. I have shown how these practices, when staged in fiction, offer counterpoints to state-sanctioned practices of knowledge production designed to identify, categorize, and thereby control. I have argued that, by observing the blind spots in these fictional investigators' ways of seeing, readers and critics of these novels can learn to recognize the social conditions determining their own ways of seeking and knowing. I have made the wager, finally, that Arab novels of investigation (*baḥth*) can train their readers in alternative, noncoercive practices of looking at "the other." Perhaps this has been the wager of a naïve Pollyanna insufficiently attentive to the social, economic, and political worlds in which literary texts come to matter (or not matter). As a corrective, let me clarify that not all Arabic novels that thematize investigation necessarily offer their readers such critical viewpoints. To illustrate, let me return briefly to the scene of the crime—omniscience as narrative point of view—this time as it has been staged in a more recent novel.

In 2013, the Iraqi novelist Ahmed Saadawi won the International Prize for Arabic Fiction (commonly known as the "Arabic Booker") for his novel *Frankenstein in Baghdad* (*Frānkishtāyin fī Baghdād*). The book stitches together the lives of numerous Iraqis of various backgrounds, including Elishva, an elderly Assyrian woman looking for her missing son Daniel (abducted by the Iraqi Baath party for mandatory conscription in the 1990s), Hadi, a junk collector fond of telling fantastical stories, and a coterie of journalists, documentarians, and photographers struggling to write and publish amid the chaos and corruption caused by the 2003 American invasion. The book also stitches together a Frankenstein-like monster, his body parts assembled by the junk dealer Hadi, and his spirit reanimated by Elishva, who addresses fervent prayers to an icon of Saint George, pleading for her son's safe return. Animated by the spirit of a guard killed in a suicide bombing on a hotel, this Iraqi Frankenstein's limbs continually call him to avenge the deaths of the people to whose bodies they once belonged. But as the monster—or the "Whatsitsname" (*al-Shismuh*), as he's referred to throughout—avenges each death, he also sheds body parts, requiring replacements that in turn call out for revenge, and so on ad infinitum. The cycle of violence and vengeance soon overwhelms monster and reader alike. "There are no innocents who are completely innocent or criminals who are completely criminal," the Whatsitsname thinks to himself. "This was the realization that would undermine his mission—because every criminal he killed was also a victim."[1]

Despite some metafictional gestures,[2] Saadawi's novel sutures its multiple storylines through omniscient narration and free indirect discourse. In a single scene, the reader is liable to be shuttled from the mind of a self-serving real-estate developer like Faraj, for example, to the consciousness of a beggar who's just witnessed a crime, then into the perspective of a corrupt police officer like Brigadier Sorour Mohamed Majid. The transitions can sometimes be jarringly awkward: "Faraj slowly took a sip of tea and looked with contempt at the old beggar. At the same moment, someone else was drinking his tea—Brigadier Sorour Mohamed Majid."[3] Where the other novels I have examined in this book play with narrative perspective as a commentary on power and knowledge production in colonial and authoritarian states, *Frankenstein in Baghdad* seems more interested in granting its readers an all-seeing perspective on post-2003 Iraq than in challenging them to think about who knows what, through which means, and when. Tawfiq al-Hakim's

*Diary of a Country Prosecutor* was replete with interjections and interruptions that frustrated the narrator's progress toward solving the murder of Qamar al-Dawla ʿAlwan, and it thereby mocked its *adīb*-like narrator's dismissive essentialisms about the countryside. The frame narrator of Elias Khoury's *White Masks*, meanwhile, threw up his hands from the very beginning of that novel, refusing to "make sense" of the narrative materials he had gathered and leaving the last word with "the documents themselves." *Frankenstein in Baghdad*, by contrast, flows "seamlessly" (ironically, given the novel's titular subject) from one chapter, character, and subjectivity into the next.

In particular, readers are granted access to a number of spaces, communities, and histories that are often suppressed or marginalized in writing on and from Iraq. The up-close glimpse at Iraqi Assyrians through Elishva, her priest, and her expat daughters in Australia; the memory of the Iraqi Jewish community uncovered when Hadi the junk dealer finds a Hebrew inscription concealed behind a statue of the Virgin Mary in his crumbling residence; the echo of ongoing tribal rivalries in the backstory of the journalist Mahmoud al-Sawadi, who was forced to leave his provincial hometown after a dispute with a man from a rival clan; these and other pat subplots read like introductions to Iraqi history intended as revelations for foreigners (perhaps specifically Americans), as though *Frankenstein in Baghdad* were "born translated."[4] The novel also has its requisite villain: Brigadier Sorour, a former Baath party member who used his army connections to resist de-Baathification and score a post as the head of the top-secret Tracking and Pursuit Department. This fictional department, we learn, is "a special information unit set up by the Americans" whose mission is "to monitor unusual crimes, urban legends, and superstitious rumors . . . and, more important, to make predictions about crimes that would take place in the future: car bombings and assassinations of officials and other important people" (*F* 75). When we learn that Brigadier Sorour has employed soothsayers, tarot card readers, astrologists, and various other kinds of seers and magicians to detect "pre-crimes" for his unit, the novel invites us to laugh at his superstitious backwardness and side with Mahmoud and the other journalists and photographers struggling to work amid the perilous terrain of the American occupation.

Yet the novel's representational strategies and form of narration are also, lest we forget, a form of politics. The reader who is invited to take an omniscient view of Iraqi society through the literary text has more in common with the brigadier's band of seers and soothsayers than she might like to believe. We may well laugh at the "great astrologer" with his "long white pointed beard, his tall conical hat, and his flowing robes," just as we laugh at the idea that he had "enslaved the djinn and the familiar spirits and used Babylonian astrological secrets and the sciences of the Sabeans and the Mandeans to find the aura of the name surrounding the body of the criminal." (Another chuckle arrives when that "name" is revealed: "It's . . . it's the One Who Has No Name") (*F* 112). The great astrologer strikes an absurd pose staring into a playing card "as if he could see in it a deep chasm or a door that opened onto a whole world only he could see" (*F* 211). Yet the forms of reading and understanding that *Frankenstein in Baghdad* solicits its readers to practice also open up "whole worlds" that "only we can see." Like the seers who deliver specialized knowledge derived from their visionary capabilities, Saadawi delivers a ready-made, multiconfessional Iraq for the reader's consumption, smoothing over the seams between one narrative perspective and the next.

The novel ends as it began—omnisciently. There is the rather confusing reappearance of the unnamed "author" from the prologue, who informs the reader that he has written a novel built from the testimonies of Mahmoud, Abu Salim, and the Whatsitsname itself, but that this novel was confiscated by the authorities and has not yet been returned to him. Yet, unlike most metafictional author-figures, whose role is usually to comment on the limitations and omissions structuring any act of narration, the author-character in *Frankenstein in Baghdad* continues to have unfettered, omniscient access to the characters' innermost thoughts and memories. Specifically, this "author" narrates experiences and monologues to which his interviews and the files leaked from the Tracking and Pursuit Department couldn't possibly have given him access—for example, the midnight scene in which Hadi the junk dealer encounters his now-horribly disfigured face in a hospital mirror,[5] or the Whatsitsname's inner reflections on death and vengeance the night he murdered the senior astrologer.[6] Where Jabra's Dr. Jawad, Khoury's unnamed frame narrator, and Ghanim's quasi-autobiographical first-person narrator invited their readers to meditate on the limits and blind spots structuring every "search" for truth, Saadawi's "author" (*muʾallif*)—true to his name—picks up the remaining pieces of the narrative and stitches them into their proper places, rather like Hercule Poirot tying up the loose ends that even the characters themselves might not have remembered.

Given *Frankenstein in Baghdad*'s continued use of free indirect discourse despite the presence of a metafictional author-figure, it is appropriate that the novel should end with a scene observed from a rooftop. The final chapter moves from the metafictional author-character's voice back into that of the novel's original third-person narrator, who describes the characters from Lane 7 as they celebrate the arrest of Hadi the storyteller, whom the police have misidentified as the Monster, the Whatitsname, Criminal X. "Everyone was happy," the reader is told, "tasting a kind of joy they had forgotten in the decades of disasters that had befallen their country . . . Reduced to a state of childlike elation, no one could see, or even tried to see, those timid eyes looking out from behind the balconies and windows of the abandoned Orouba Hotel." It is the monster, the Whatsitsname—now referred to only as "the specter of an unknown man"—looking down on the festivities from the hotel's third floor (*F* 280).

But of course, someone *does* see these eyes—none other than the sorcerer-like reader herself. Saadawi's omniscient narration plays the same role for the novel's form that the astrologers' magic plays for its plot: it allows the reader to glimpse the face and track the location of the "Whatsitsname," to "know" the man who "is not known" and "has no name." Although *Frankenstein in Baghdad* was written many decades after the novels I have read throughout this study, the "narrative subject" is still omnipresent in Saadawi's novel,[7] lurking in the background, on the rooftops, like the monster it describes. The only difference is that the viewing figure at the center of this Iraqi panorama is a *monster*—a terrifying figure sewn together from the body parts of an accumulating number of victims. If there is something to redeem Saadawi's otherwise unremarkable take on narrative perspective and "investigation" in *Frankenstein in Baghdad*, it is this subtle equation of omniscience with the monstrous.

We may well condemn Tawfiq al-Hakim's racist essentializations of rural Egyptians in *Diary of a Country Prosecutor* and dismiss the pat, utopian socialist endings of novels like Ghanim's *al-Jabal* and Idris' *The Sinners*. Yet these authors from the first half of the twentieth century give us something that even the most highly regarded authors of the early twenty-first do not: narrators who do not know, who have been frustrated in their quests for knowledge, and whose aspirations of omniscience are persistently foreclosed by such humble figures as peasant girls, mad shaykhs, landless migrant laborers, and "tomb-raiding" Gurnawis. The all-seeing and unseen eye is alive and well, by contrast, in Saadawi's *Frankenstein*. We are perhaps meant to be frightened of the still-living monster looking down on the celebrations, terrified that he will strike again in the sequel. But, if we look again, we might sense the parallels between this stitched-up monster on his third-story perch and the monstrous nature of our own worst reading impulses.

In reading the novels selected for this study, I have highlighted specific narrative forms and structures overlooked in most accounts of modern fiction from the Arab world, in the hopes of transforming these structures into new methodologies and ways of reading for scholars in disciplines ranging from history and comparative literature to anthropology and religious studies. Tawfiq al-Hakim and Driss Chraïbi taught us to look for the traces of past communalisms, buried myths, and critiques of objectivity in the experiences of native officers of the law seeking social status and economic advantage through employment in (post) colonial legal systems. Yusuf Idris and Yusuf al-Qaʿid showed us how to look on the secreted world of the Egyptian *ʿizbah* not with the eyes of an effendi, developer, or Cairo-based author, but with those of a migrant laborer, a landless, undocumented farmer, or a writer caught between the imperative to document exploitation in "the other Egypt" and the anxiety of making his living from "the corpses of the destitute."[8] Naguib Mahfouz and Jabra Ibrahim Jabra revealed the porosity of the border said to divide dispassionate investigation from mystical contemplation, as well as the perils of atomization involved in such isolated, personalized quests for fleeting, unknowable, ineffable others. Fathi Ghanim and Elias Khoury illustrated how a detective-like quest for the "truth" risks blinding one to the many stories that branch off from a single criminal investigation, some of which offer new languages and literary forms with which to challenge the authority of the official, and the officiality of the author. And Sonallah Ibrahim teaches us, once again, the importance of the public, communal, and collective as the necessary scaffolding for any critique of power. With every new reading (and yes, this is a book of many readings), I have felt called into a series of new methods for approaching Arabic language and literature, none of which aims to be exclusive, all of which question the gaze that claims to see and thereby understand all.

Most of all, I have been shown how quickly and easily any given method, any "way of seeing," can turn itself inside out, showing its blind spots. Just as the "criminals" in Idris's *The Sinners* and al-Qaʿid's *Yaḥduth* turned out to be a victims of larger social and economic injustices on the ʿizbah; just as Kamal's incorrigible idealism in the *Trilogy* caused him to displace his former faith in God onto his "beloved" (*maʿbūdah*, lit. "object of worship"), so too all the literary works examined in this study remind us of the conditions determining and limiting what we, as critics and readers, can see. They remind us to consider the many ways that surface and depth are related in any act of reading, such that "the object loses its determination and the critic recognizes the totality that constitutes both the object and her relation to it."[9]

The "poetics of investigation" invites the ongoing, unfixed, shape-shifting quality of baḥth into the houses of Middle East studies and comparative literature alike. For Middle East studies, a practice of baḥth encourages a form of research that is never content with a single meaning or reading but is rather constantly looking for new eyes with which to see, particularly when the literary and cultural objects under investigation deem these viewpoints antiquated or outdated, suspicious or superstitious, marginal or unimportant, colloquial or unofficial. For comparative literature, a practice of baḥth makes possible an attitude toward method as an evolving set of practices, ever building on new languages, idioms, histories, and materials, rather than a fixed set of operations or procedures performed by subject-readers on object-texts. To remain aware of the social and material circumstances limiting what and how we see is not to make ourselves irreducibly contingent or to fetishize indeterminacy, but rather to compel the—I think, enabling—recognition that all practices, including social, economic, and political ones, are contingent and determined in one way or another, and thus open to revision and remaking.[10]

To read a few Arabic novels about investigation, and to read them closely, might seem in retrospect like a somewhat trivial occupation for a book-length study, but I have tried, in Gayatri Spivak's words, "to work as hard as old-fashioned Comp. Lit. is known to be capable of doing," in an attempt to "reclaim the role of teaching literature as training the imagination—the great inbuilt instrument of othering." I have gathered texts that feature scholars, experts, investigators, and yes, detectives, to model a practice of methodological training, not only for myself, but also for others seeking to bridge area studies' emphasis on studying the languages of "the other" with comparative literature's attention to language as idiom, as "more than just a field language."[11] Sitting with the languages of these texts, paying attention to their idiomaticity and the way they record specific configurations of historical and social circumstances, I have learned how Arab authors in several national and historical contexts instinctively grasped the problem of colonial panopticism and spun it into narratives of tragicomic satire, sensational revelation, or vertiginous "seeking." Looking at these texts, I have seen myself reflected in figures like Jabra's sociologist-turned-mystic, Mahfouz's soul-sick wanderers, and Ghanim's state-trained investigator or "truth establisher" (*muḥaqqiq*). Following these detectives and seekers as they bumbled through their research, sometimes overtaken by the voices of the workers, peasants, and farmers under investigation, sometimes thrown back into the vortex of truth, I have tried to stay true to what Edward Said described, more than forty years ago, as "the most important task of all" in the wake of Orientalism: "to ask how one can study other cultures and peoples from . . . nonrepressive and nonmanipulative perspective[s]" by "rethinking the whole complex problem of knowledge and power."[12] Such a rethinking, I have wagered, can be excavated from the literary texts and practices of these "others" themselves, if only we know how to look.

# ACKNOWLEDGEMENTS

I have learned one thing for certain while writing this book: there really is no end to the search. Somehow, you learn to live with both the thrilling infinity of seeking and the imperfect finitude of writing. At times, this divide caused me great suffering. At others, mentors, colleagues, and friends convinced me that, in Naguib Mahfouz's words, "such suffering is part of the cure."

I am grateful to Margaret Larkin, who saw "a great Arabist" in a wandering comp lit grad, and who gave me the courage, inspiration, and training to follow this path. The traces of her philological and theoretical rigor are on every page of this book. Chana Kronfeld is still one of the best readers I have ever had; I thank her for nurturing the best parts of my writing and helping me let go of the rest. Stefania Pandolfo's seminars changed my own ways of seeking, thinking, and being more than once. Thanks, too, to Karl Britto for the questions that first shatter, then allow me to rebuild my arguments and readings, even still. At Berkeley, I was also lucky to be in the orbit of Anne-Lise François, Vicky Kahn, Rob Kaufman, and Niklaus Largier, with whom I am fortunate to still be in conversation.

This book would never have seen the light of day if Shahzad Bashir had not given it a home, in every sense of the word. I thank him for his calm and steady belief in this project, and in me. In a peak pandemic manuscript workshop, Hosam Aboul-Ela and Kamran Rastegar graciously offered comments and questions I am still pondering, and that I hope to have at least partly addressed. Ken Haynes was a mentor, friend, and supporter when my self-doubt was at its apex, and this project owes him an infinite debt. Heartiest thanks most of all to Elliott Colla, one-time teacher, full-time mentor, all-time friend. He is an inspiration in every way I can imagine, and in some ways I can't.

Research for this book began at UC Berkeley, where it was supported by a Jacob K. Javits Fellowship from the U.S. Department of Education, a Graduate Division Summer Research Fellowship, and the Sultan Program in Arab Studies Fellowship from Berkeley's Center for Middle Eastern Studies. My research, writing, and teaching continued at Brown

University, where I was honored to be in conversation with colleagues in the Department of Comparative Literature, especially Susan Bernstein, Tamara Chin, Michelle Clayton, Dore J. Levy, Ourida Mostefai, Marc Redfield, Jay Reed, Arnold Weinstein, and Esther Whitfield; and, elsewhere, Timothy Bewes, Leela Gandhi, and Thangam Ravindranathan. I thank Elias Muhanna in particular for his support, companionship, and advice—he makes it all look so easy. Beshara Doumani continues to inspire with his scholarship, commitment, and unflagging support for junior scholars; I am exceedingly lucky to know him. I also thank Michael Allan, Sinan Antoon, Qussay al-Attabi, Michael Cooperson, Dale J. Correa, Mansoura Ez-Eldin, Huda Fakhreddine, Nouri Gana, Amanda Hannoosh-Steinberg, Rebecca C. Johnson, Alexander Key, Amir Moosavi, Karla Nielsen, Jeffrey Sacks, Stephen Sheehi, Shaden Tageldin, and Anna Ziajka-Stanton.

I also benefitted immensely from a 2018–19 National Endowment for the Humanities Fellowship from the American Research Center in Egypt (ARCE). In Cairo, I was lucky to have the help of the indefatigable Djodi Deutsch at ARCE, and of Saleh Seoudi at the AUC Fifth Settlement campus library. The Netherlands-Flemish Institute Library was an oasis of books, quiet, coffee, and cats.

I am delighted to now call the University of Texas at Austin home, and to have such welcoming abodes in the Departments of Middle Eastern Studies, French and Italian Studies, and the Program in Comparative Literature. I am particularly grateful to Na'ama Pat-El and Paola Bonifazio—chairs extraordinaires—and to Kamran Ali, Samy Ayoub, Marc Bizer, Ben Brower, Yoav Di-Capua, Karen Grumberg, Heather Houser, Akbar Hyder, Jonathan Kaplan, Azfar Moin, and Hervé Picherit for their advice and knowledge.

Thanks to everyone who has ever taught me Arabic: my first teacher Mirena Christoff, Ustadh Fadil at the Institut Bourguiba des Langues Vivantes, my roommate Amina Ayari in Tunis, who welcomed me into her family in Hammam Sousse, and Anna Selma Senna, who taught me the Tunisian I loved but promptly forgot after arriving in Cairo three years later. In Cairo, the CASA and AUC dream team Dina Bashir, Nadia Harb, Heba Salem, Laila al-Sawi, Iman Soliman, and Shahira Yacout taught me that *illii yas 'al maa yatuhsh,* but getting lost is okay too.

At the University of California Press, Eric Schmidt shepherded this project to the greenest pastures, working tirelessly through a pandemic and remaining flexible despite all my deadline-altering life changes. I thank him as well as LeKeisha Hughes and Jyoti Arvey for guiding me through the publishing process. I am also grateful to Hala Halim and Dwight Reynolds for their perceptive responses to and suggestions for this manuscript; the book is stronger thanks to their efforts.

. . .

My friends are truly friends of God. Harris Feinsod devoted far more of his editorial genius to this book's introduction, chapters, and framing than I deserved. He is living proof that comp lit wins. Max Weiss offered pinch-hitting edits on a beast of a chapter at the zero hour, and so much else. His friendship means the world. Sam England will always be a quality product, and I am honored to have him in my entourage. Tristram Wolff and Corey Byrnes have sustained me in manifold ways over nearly fifteen years; wherever they are feels like home. Andrea Gadberry always knows what to say to keep us all going. I was and continue to be inspired by so many other brilliant friends: in and around Berkeley's orbit, Kareem

James Abu-Zeid, Paco Brito, Ashley Brock, Mandy Cohen, Kathryn Crim, Ayelet Even-Nur, Aria Fani, Amanda Goldstein, Katie Kadue, Tom McEnaney, Ramsey McGlazer, Elizabeth Saylor, Kris Trujillo, and Laura Wagner; and at UCLA, Shir Alon, Nasia Anam, Fatima Burney, Alexander Jabbari, Suleiman Hodali, Michelle Quay, Sahba Shayani, Duncan Yoon, and Omar Zahzah welcomed this interloper into their world.

Providence would not have been the same without the friendship and camaraderie of Leah Beeferman, Stephen Crocker, Bathsheba Demuth, Sasha-Mae Eccleston, Dennis Hogan, Jennifer Johnson, Paul Kohlbry, Brian Lander, Sreemati Mitter, Flannery Patton, Tom Roberge, Aliya Sabharwal, Sarah Thomas, and Alex Winder. I remember Elizabeth Lord every day.

To my family—a host of Gregorians, Safoyans, and Mirzabegians spread across the East and West coasts, and a few places in between—thank you for the love, the food, and the music. To my sister Carolyn Drumsta, for all the company and inside jokes over the years, and my mom, Vicky Gregorian, for literally everything. To Adam, actual angel, who humbles and amazes me more every minute. And to Levi, first and last reader, friend of God, guardian of time, labor, love—I owe you more than I can say.

# NOTES

## INTRODUCTION: TOWARD A POETICS OF INVESTIGATION

1. Rasheed El-Enany asserts that any missing information about Mahfouz's childhood can be found by looking at the fictional portrayal of Kamal in the *Trilogy*. See *Naguib Mahfouz: The Pursuit of Meaning* (London: Routledge, 1993), 73, 4–8.

2. Sasson Somekh, *The Changing Rhythm: A Study of Najīb Maḥfūẓ's Novels* (Leiden: E. J. Brill, 1973), 126.

3. Naguib Mahfouz, *al-Mu'allafāt al-Kāmilah*, vol. 2 (Beirut: Maktabat Lubnān, 1991), 344 (my translation). Hereafter, I cite from the Arabic volume parenthetically in-text, abbreviating as *MK* followed by volume and page numbers.

4. In Arabic: *Fa-l-saṭḥ huwa al-dunyā al-jadīdah . . . khalaqathu bi-rūḥihā khalqan jadīdan*. Mahfouz's use of the cognate object (*mafa'ūl muṭlaq*) intensifies the verb *kh-l-q*, "create," and its associations with divine creation.

5. Timothy Mitchell, *Colonising Egypt* (Berkeley: University of California Press, 1991), 1–13 passim.

6. El-Enany, *Naguib Mahfouz*, 83–84 (emphasis added).

7. Timothy Mitchell, *Rule of Experts: Egypt, Techno-Politics, Modernity* (Berkeley: University of California Press, 2002), 51–53.

8. *'Ibādah* is, properly, "worship," but it shares its root with *'abd*, "slave." In Islamic law (*fiqh*), the *'ibādāt*, "rules that lay out specific obligations to God," are often contrasted with *mu'āmalāt*, "those rules of Islamic law that govern the relationships of humans to one another." See Haider Hamoudi, "*Mu'āmalāt*," in *EI3*, ed. Kate Fleet, Gudrun Krämer, Denis Matringe, John Nawas, and Devin J. Stewart, https://referenceworks.brillonline.com/entries/encyclopaedia-of-islam-3/muamalat-COM_36548?s.num=0&s.f.s2_parent=s.f.book.encyclopaedia-of-islam-3&s.q=Mu%CA%BF%C4%81mal%C4%81t.

9. Mitchell, *Colonising Egypt*, 62.

10. On the history of this trope in the medieval period and its afterlife in the early Arabic press from Beirut and Damascus, see Elizabeth M. Holt, *Fictitious Capital: Silk, Cotton, and the Rise of the Arabic Novel* (New York: Fordham University Press, 2017), 18–39.

11. Fruma Zachs and Basilius Bawardi, "Arab Nation-Building Through Detective Stories in *al-Ḍiyā*ʾ: The Cultural Translations of Nasīb al-Mashʿalānī," *Die Welt des Islams* 60, no. 1 (2020): 79–101; Basilius Bawardi and Alif Faranesh, "Non-Canonical Arabic Detective Fiction: The Beginnings of the Genre," *Journal of Arabic and Islamic Studies* 18 (2018): 23–49; Samah Selim, *Popular Fiction, Translation, and the Nahda in Egypt* (Cham: Palgrave Macmillan, 2019); Mattiyahu Peled, "Creative Translation: Towards the Study of Arabic Translations of Western Literature Since the 19th Century," *Journal of Arabic Literature* 10 (1979): 128–50.

12. Peter Brooks, *Reading for the Plot: Design and Intention in Narrative* (Cambridge, MA: Harvard University Press, 1984), 24–25, 27.

13. In her study of legal reform and the binding of the human with the law in turn-of-the-century Egypt, Samera Esmeir turns, at one point, to what she calls a "counter-history" of the "lost human," an alternative to the mode of "juridical humanity" to which the bulk of her study is devoted. Articulated through reference to the writings of the Egyptian mystic and modernist Tantawi Jawhari, this alternative ethics of the human models itself "not as a concept but a quest" for knowledge. "The impossibility of knowing the atom," she writes of Jawhari, "does not stop the search. And the search, the impossible journey, is the way to live life." See Samera Esmeir, *Juridical Humanity: A Colonial History* (Stanford, CA: Stanford University Press, 2012), 95–104.

14. John Berger, *Ways of Seeing* (London: British Broadcasting Corporation and Penguin Books, 1972), 16.

15. Selim, *Popular Fiction*, 13–14.

16. The Arabic *adab*, as well as its derivative *adīb*, "man of culture and refined tastes," "man of letters," "writer, author," has a long history, but in its modern usage, it can mean either politeness, refinement, good upbringing, or "literature," as in the French (*littérature*) or English senses. See Boutros Hallaq, "Adab, e) Modern Usage," in *EI3*, ed. Kate Fleet, Gudrun Krämer, Denis Matringe, John Nawas, and Devin J. Stewart, https://referenceworks.brillonline.com/entries/encyclopaedia-of-islam-3/adab-e-modern-usage-COM_23653?s.num=0&s.f.s2_parent=s.f.book.encyclopaedia-of-islam-3&s.q=Adab%2C+e%29+Modern+Usage. On the long history of the English "literature" (as meaning also "refinement," "polite learning through reading"), see Raymond Williams, *Keywords: A Vocabulary of Culture and Society*, new ed. (Oxford: Oxford University Press, 2015), 134–38.

17. This approach, developed in the 1970s and 1980s, stands in contrast with an earlier, World War II-era generation of critics, who extolled the popularity of detective fiction in the West as the mark of a morally superior democratic rule's success over fascism, Nazism, and totalitarianism. See Howard Haycraft, "Dictators, Democrats, and Detectives," in *Murder for Pleasure: The Life and Times of the Detective Story*, 3rd ed. (New York: Biblio and Tannen, 1968); E. M. Wrong, "Crime and Detection," in *The Art of the Mystery Story: A Collection of Critical Essays* (New York: Simon & Schuster, 1946); Dorothy Sayers, "The Omnibus of Crime," in *The Art of the Mystery Story*.

18. Michel Foucault, *Discipline and Punish: The Birth of the Prison*, trans. Alan Sheridan (New York: Vintage, 1977), 69.

19. Franco Moretti, *Signs Taken for Wonders: On the Sociology of Literary Forms* (London: Verso, 2005), 143, 145.

20. D. A. Miller, *The Novel and the Police* (Berkeley: University of California Press, 1988), x.

21. Dennis Porter, *The Pursuit of Crime: Art and Ideology in Detective Fiction* (New Haven, CT: Yale University Press, 1981), 216. See also Stephen Knight, *Form and Ideology in Crime Fiction* (Bloomington: Indiana University Press, 1980).

22. Miller, *The Novel and the Police*, 27.

23. Part of the convention of veiling among middle- and upper-class women in Cairo throughout the nineteenth and twentieth centuries was to keep one's proper name concealed or unspoken. Veiling, a broad term for enclosure from public spaces, is both an "Islamic" practice and a Middle Eastern one with much older roots, and it has a long and complex history. See, for example, Leila Ahmed, *Women and Gender in Islam* (New Haven, CT: Yale University Press, 1992), 5, 53–56; Marilyn Booth, ed., *Harem Histories: Envisioning Places and Living Spaces* (Durham, NC: Duke University Press, 2010).

24. See Miller's assertion that "whenever the novel censures policing power, it has already reinvented it, in *the very practice of novelistic representation*" (20–21, emphasis in the original). My point is that the bureaucratic police file is not necessarily identical with the realist novel, which registers Amina's *fear* of this new form of power in a way that the report, *fiche*, or *maḥḍar* never could.

25. On Michel Zévaco's stories in Arabic, see Selim, *Popular Literature*, 28.

26. Saad Zaghloul was a populist hero and figurehead of the 1919 revolt against British rule in Egypt, a historical event central to the lives of both Mahfouz and his protagonist.

27. Founded by Iraqi theologian and jurist Ahmad ibn Hanbal (d. 855 CE), the Hanbali school of Sunni Islamic jurisprudence is widely considered the most traditionalist.

28. Mitchell also examines the social dimensions and economy of European tourists, writers, artists, and lithographers climbing the Great Pyramid for a panoramic "point of view." See Mitchell, *Colonising Egypt*, 25–28. On the many awkward affects associated with the transition to (Western) modernity among Arab writers and intellectuals, see Tarek El-Ariss, *Trials of Arab Modernity: Literary Affects and the New Political* (New York: Fordham University Press, 2013).

29. Richard J. McGregor, "Grave Visitation/Worship," in *EI3*, ed. Kate Fleet, Gudrun Krämer, Denis Matringe, John Nawas, and Devin J. Stewart, https://referenceworks.brillonline .com/entries/encyclopaedia-of-islam-3/grave-visitationworship-COM_27519?s.num=0&s .f.s2_parent=s.f.book.encyclopaedia-of-islam-3&s.q=Grave+Visitation%2FWorship.

30. See, for example, Stephen Sheehi, *Foundations of Modern Arab Identity* (Gainesville: University Press of Florida, 2004); Selim, *The Novel and the Rural Imaginary in Egypt, 1880–1985* (London: Routledge, 2004); Kamran Rastegar, *Literary Modernity Between the Middle East and Europe: Textual Transactions in Nineteenth-Century Arabic, English, and Persian Literatures* (London: Routledge, 2007); Shaden M. Tageldin, *Disarming Words: Empire and the Seductions of Translation in Egypt* (Berkeley: University of California Press, 2011); El-Ariss, *Trials of Arab Modernity*; Jeffrey Sacks, *Iterations of Loss: Mutilation and Aesthetic Form, al-Shidyaq to Darwish* (New York: Fordham University Press, 2015); Holt, *Fictitious Capital;* Tarek El-Ariss, ed., *The Arab Renaissance: A Bilingual Anthology of the Nahda* (New York: Modern Language Association, 2018), and Rebecca C. Johnson, *Stranger Fictions: A History of the Novel in Arabic Translation* (Ithaca, NY: Cornell University Press, 2021).

31. See, for example, Martina Censi, *Le corps dans le roman des écrivaines Syriennes contemporaines: dire, écrire, inscrire la différence* (Leiden: E. J. Brill, 2016); Zeina Halabi, *The Unmaking of the Arab Intellectual: Prophecy, Exile, and the Nation* (Edinburgh: Edinburgh University Press, 2017); Tarek El-Ariss, *Leaks, Hacks, and Scandals: Arab Culture in the Digital Age* (Princeton, NJ: Princeton University Press, 2018); Teresa Pepe, *Blogging From Egypt: Digital Literature, 2005–2016* (Edinburgh: Edinburgh University Press, 2019).

32. For an excellent account of popular fiction, pulp, and the role of translation and adaptation in early twentieth-century Egypt, see Selim, *Popular Fiction*.

33. Gayatri Spivak, *Death of a Discipline* (New York: Columbia University Press, 2003), 9.

34. Esmeir, *Juridical Humanity*, 201–2, 206.

35. Sonallah Ibrahim, *al-Lajnah*, 9th printing (Cairo: Dār al-Mustaqbal al-ʿArabī, 2004), 47.

36. I borrow the terms *docufictional* and *narrative* to describe the two types of chapters in *Zaat* from Samia Mehrez, "Sonallah Ibrahim's *Zaat*: The Ultimate Objectification of the Self," in *Egyptian Writers Between History and Fiction: Essays on Naguib Mahfouz, Sonallah Ibrahim, and Gamal al-Ghitani* (Cairo: American University in Cairo Press, 1994), 119–45.

37. Christopher Prendergast, "The World Republic of Letters," in *Debating World Literature*, ed. Christopher Prendergast (London: Verso, 2004), 1; Fadi A. Bardawil, *Revolution and Disenchantment: Arab Marxism and the Binds of Emancipation* (Durham, NC: Duke University Press, 2020), 3–24.

38. Jason M. Baskin, "Soft Eyes: Marxism, Surface, and Depth," *Mediations* 28, no. 2 (2015): 5–18.

39. Gayatri Chakravorty Spivak, *Death of a Discipline* (New York: Columbia University Press, 2003), 23.

## 1. THE DETECTIVE AS CONSCRIPT: TAWFIQ AL-HAKIM AND DRISS CHRAÏBI ON THE MARGINS OF THE LAW

1. Danielle Marx-Scouras, "A Literature of Departure: The Cross-Cultural Writing of Driss Chraïbi," *Research in African Literatures* 23, no. 2 (1992): 131.

2. Elliott Colla, "Anxious Advocacy: The Novel, the Law, and Extrajudicial Appeals in Egypt," *Public Culture* 17, no. 3 (2005): 417–44; Christopher Stone, "Tawfiq al-Hakim, Yusuf al-Qaʿid, and the 'Mature' Arabic Novel," in *Transforming Loss Into Beauty: Essays on Arabic Literature and Culture in Honor of Magda Al-Nowaihi*, ed. Marlé Hammond and Dana Sajdi (Cairo: American University in Cairo Press, 2008), 295–319.

3. The Anglo-Egyptian treaty of 1936 was negotiated by the prime minister, Mustafa al-Nahhas, in the wake of King Fuad I's death and the accession to the throne of King Farouk I, who was only sixteen years old at the time. It allowed the British to maintain military bases in the Suez Canal Zone, a stipulation that the Wafd had, in earlier years, stridently opposed.

4. James Whidden, *Monarchy and Modernity in Egypt: Politics, Islam, and Neo-Colonialism Between the Wars* (London: I. B. Tauris, 2013), 17.

5. Afaf Lutfi al-Sayyid Marsot, *A History of Egypt: From the Arab Conquest to the Present* (Cambridge: Cambridge University Press, 2007), 29.

6. ʿAbd al-Rahman al-Sharqawi's 1954 novel *The Land* (*al-Arḍ*) offers a tragicomic parody of these elections. See Desmond Stewart's much-abridged translation, *Egyptian Earth* (London: Saqi Books, 2005), 175–82.

7. Tawfiq al-Hakim was born in Alexandria in 1898, to a mother with Turkish origins from Egypt's bourgeois landowning class, and a father from a humbler background who went on to become a judge and own a good deal of agricultural land. After his well-to-do parents heard of their son's extracurricular interest in popular performance, they immediately sent him to France to study for a doctorate in law. This curative had the opposite of its intended effect: al-Hakim spent his time abroad immersed in French avant-garde theater. After failing to receive his doctorate, he returned to Egypt in 1928 and—through the intercessions of his father—was granted a series of legal posts over the course of six years, first in Alexandria, then in the provincial capitals of Tanta, Dusuq, and Damanhur. See M. M. Badawi, "A Passion for Experimentation: The Novels and Plays of Tawfiq Al-Hakim," *Third World Quarterly* 10, no. 2 (1988): 949–50.

8. Tawfiq al-Hakim, *Diary of a Country Prosecutor*, trans. Abba Eban (London: Saqi Books, 2005), 133; Tawfiq al-Hakim, *Yawmiyyāt Nāʾib fī al-Aryāf* (Beirut: Dār al-Kitāb al-Lubnānī, 1983) 191 (translation modified). Hereafter, I cite from these works parenthetically in text, abbreviating Eban's translation as *D* and the Arabic edition as *Y*. It is worth noting that the 1983 Dār al-Kitāb al-Lubnānī edition censored a famous courtroom scene involving a prostitute. For this scene, I rely on the original serialized publication of *Yawmiyyāt* in the Egyptian journal *al-Riwāyah* from February to August 1937.

9. Ghali Shukri, *Thawrat al-Muʿtazil: Dirāsah fī Adab Tawfīq al-Ḥakīm* (Cairo: Maktabat al-Anjlū, 1966), 234

10. See Susan Slymovics, *The Performance of Human Rights in Morocco* (Philadelphia: University of Pennsylvania Press, 2005), 2; Fadoua Loudiy, *Transitional Justice and Human Rights in Morocco* (New York: Routledge, 2014).

11. There is some debate as to where this "dark period" in Morocco's postindependence history begins and ends. See Slymovics, *Performance*, 43, 50.

12. Slymovics, *Performance*, 2.

13. C. R. Pennell, *Morocco: From Empire to Independence* (Oxford: Oneworld, 2003), 202–3. The best known of these accounts is certainly Tahar Ben Jelloun's *This Blinding Absence of Light*, trans. Linda Coverdale (New York: Penguin, 2006).

14. Slymovics, "Disappearances" and "Prisons" in *Performance*.

15. On the "ontological split" between narrating/seeing subject and world-as-object, see Mitchell, *Colonising Egypt*, 5 passim, and Selim, *Rural Imaginary*, 14–15.

16. Driss Chraïbi, *Flutes of Death*, trans. Robin Roosevelt (Boulder: Lynne Rienner, 1996).

17. From *Le Grand Robert de la langue française*, a *pays* is "a territory inhabited by a collectivity (nation, region, province, canton, commune), and constituting, with its population, a named geographical reality."

18. Lucie Ryzova clarifies that "the efendi should never be understood as simply a class position," but is rather "first and foremost a cultural concept signifying a stance toward modernity in a particular historical context . . . a social category marked by a number of socially recognized signs." That is, "empirically speaking, there were rich efendis, poor efendis, and there were 'middle class' efendis." Lucie Ryzova, *The Age of the Efendiyya: Passages to Modernity in National-Colonial Egypt* (Oxford: Oxford University Press, 2014), 8–9.

19. See Ryzova's reading of Yahya Haqqi's "The Lamp of Umm Hashim" (*Qindīl Umm Hāshim*), *The Age of the Efendiyya*, 1–5.

20. Driss Chraïbi, *Une enquête au pays* (Paris: Seuil, 1981), 131, my translation; hereafter abbreviated *E* and cited parenthetically in-text. I offer my own translations from French throughout.

21. Ryzova, *The Age of the Efendiyya*, 3.

22. Stanley Diamond, *In Search of the Primitive: A Critique of Civilization* (New Brunswick, NJ: E. P. Dutton/Transaction Books, 1974). Quoted in Talal Asad, "Conscripts of Western Civilization," in *Dialectical Anthropology: Essays in Honor of Stanley Diamond*, vol. 1 *Civilization in Crisis*, ed. Christine Gailey (Gainesville: University Press of Florida, 1992), 333; David Scott, *Conscripts of Modernity: The Tragedy of Colonial Enlightenment* (Durham, NC: Duke University Press, 2004).

23. Asad, "Conscripts of Western Civilization," 339; Scott, *Conscripts of Modernity*, 101–7.

24. Diamond, *In Search of the Primitive* (quoted in Asad, "Conscripts of Western Civilization," 333).

25. Scott, *Conscripts of Modernity*, 106–7.

26. Scott, *Conscripts of Modernity*, 129.

27. Miller, *The Novel and the Police*, 2.

28. As in much Egyptian fiction dealing with rural bureaucracy, the prosecutor and other government officials remain nameless, referred to only by their official titles ("the Prosecutor," "the Police Chief" [*ma ʾmūr*], "the Doctor," etc.). This is also true in the novels of Yusuf al-Qaʿid, Fathi Ghanim, and Yusuf Idris, examined in chapters 2 and 3. Regarding this tendency in Egyptian fiction of the "sixties generation," see Sabry Hafez, "The Egyptian Novel in the Sixties," *JAL* 7 (1976): 68.

29. I alter Abba Eban's transliteration of this name from "Kamar al-Dawla" to "Qamar al-Dawla."

30. "A friend of God (*walī Allāh*) is one tied to God through piety, love, and obedience, a holy person, often a paragon of virtue and a miracle worker, memorialized in hagiography and shrine visitation." See Richard J. McGregor, "Friend of God," in *EI3*, ed. Kate Fleet, Gudrun Krämer, Denis Matringe, John Nawas, and Devin J. Stewart, https://referenceworks.brillonline.com/entries/encyclopaedia-of-islam-3/friend-of-god-COM_27194?s.num=0&s.f.s2_parent=s.f.book.encyclopaedia-of-islam-3&s.q=friend+of+god.

31. Pierre Cachia, "Idealism and Ideology: The Case of Tawfiq Al-Ḥakīm," *Journal of the American Oriental Society* 100, no. 3 (1980): 225–35; Hilary Kilpatrick, "Tradition and Innovation in the Fiction of Ghassān Kanafānī," *JAL* 7 (1976): 53–64.

32. See, for example, Badawi, "A Passion for Experimentation," 949; Roger Allen, *The Arabic Novel: An Historical and Critical Introduction*, 2nd ed. (Syracuse, NY: Syracuse University Press, 1995), 41; and Omnia El Shakry, *The Great Social Laboratory: Subjects of Knowledge in Colonial and Postcolonial Egypt* (Stanford, CA: Stanford University Press, 2007), 102. By contrast, both Kilpatrick and Samah Selim offer readings that take the novel's status as fiction into account. See Hilary Kilpatrick, *The Modern Egyptian Novel: A Study in Social Criticism* (London: Ithaca Press, 1974), 46; Selim, *Rural Imaginary*, 117–26.

33. On "pharaonic nationalism" generally, and in *Return of the Spirit* specifically, see Elliott Colla, *Conflicted Antiquities: Egyptology, Egyptomania, Egyptian Modernity* (Durham, NC: Duke University Press, 2007), 159–62 and 268.

34. For a history of social improvement projects in Egypt from the late nineteenth century through the era of twentieth-century nationalism, see El Shakry, *The Great Social Laboratory*.

35. Agatha Christie, *Death on the Nile* (New York: Dodd, Mead, 1970), 110.

36. On "parodic stylization," see Mikhail Bakhtin, *The Dialogic Imagination*, trans. Caryl Emerson and Michael Holquist (Austin: University of Texas Press, 1981), 292.

37. Selim, *Rural Imaginary*, 121–22.

38. Judith Butler, *Gender Trouble: Feminism and the Subversion of Identity* (New York: Routledge, 2006), 186–89.

39. Mohamed Elshahed offers the most thorough exploration of *radaḥ* I have come across, including several examples from Egyptian film: "An art form of insult . . . a quick use of spontaneous poetic lines hurled between two women, usually . . . with musical rhythm. Sometimes infused with various cultural references, proverbs, metaphors, and insinuations . . . or with insult to appearances, family, traits, profession, and insulting a man's masculinity, mocking the class of the other in cases when it is a bourgeois vs. a 'baladi' woman." See Mohamed Elshahed (@cairobserver), "An art form of insult, ردح . . ." Instagram, August 19, 2022, https://www.instagram.com/p/ChcsSCBLsI9/?utm_source=ig_web_copy_link.

40. *Rubaabakyaa*, from the Italian "roba vecchia," in Arabic means a rag-and-bone man, a junk dealer.

41. The entire exchange between the two women is written in colloquial Egyptian Arabic, reconfirming Ghali Shukri's argument that al-Hakim's *Yawmiyyāt*, with its rural heteroglossia, was a key precursor to Yusuf Idris's work, especially *The Sinners* (*al-Ḥarām*), examined in the next chapter.

42. Butler, *Gender Trouble*, 187.

43. Butler, "1999 Preface" to *Gender Trouble*, xxiv.

44. Elsewhere, Chraïbi describes "officialité" as "something special, undefinable, which impregnated his voice, his glance, his stance and even his clothes with a kind of oil hyperconcentrated with immateriality," and government officials (especially the police) as "bathed in officiality" (*E* 155–56).

45. Roosevelt translates "des divers degrés de la colère ou de la coprolalie" as "the many stages between rage and despondency," leaving out the significance of coprolalia, "the involuntary and repetitive use of obscene language as a symptom of mental illness or organic brain disease," or, etymologically, "shit speech."

46. As Marx-Scouras writes, "For Chraïbi, there are no pure civilizations. Any search for original purity implies intolerance" ("Literature of Departure," 141).

47. See, for example, the word *baragouiner*, one of the chief's favorite insults for Ali's mongrel language (*Enquête*, 36 and 43). A xenophobic insult for incorrect or incomprehensible speech, the word is probably derived from the Breton "bara" (bread) and "gwin" (wine), words often used by speakers of this language at inns frequented by speakers of Parisian French. See *Dictionnaire étymologique du français* (1994), s.v. "baragouiner."

48. *Le Grand Robert de la langue française*, s.v. "charabia," accessed February 28, 2019, https://gr-bvdep-com.revproxy.brown.edu/robert.asp.

49. The Egyptian critic Fakhri Salih notes that al-Hakim's heteroglossia in *Diary* "begins in the language of reportage dripping with sarcasm, then moves to the language of telephone revelations by country ʿumdahs, opening the novel to a complex world of varied, adjacent languages and dialects used by professionals and people from the city and the countryside, as well as different classes of society." See Fakhri Salih, "Aʿmāl Tawfīq

al-Ḥakīm al-Riwā'iyyah: I'ādat Qirā'ah," in *Tawfīq al-Ḥakīm: Ḥuḍūr Mutajaddid*, ed. Gaber Asfour (Cairo: al-Majlis al-A'lā li-l-Thaqāfah, 1998), 787.

50. Max Horkheimer and Theodor Adorno, *Dialectic of Enlightenment: Philosophical Fragments*, trans. Edmund Jephcott (Stanford, CA: Stanford University Press, 2002), 6.

51. Horkheimer and Adorno, *Dialectic of Enlightenment*, 4, 9.

52. Mitchell, *Colonising Egypt*, 5.

53. Khaled Fahmy, "The Anatomy of Justice: Forensic Medicine and Criminal Law in Nineteenth-Century Egypt," *Islamic Law and Society* 6, no. 2 (1999): 268.

54. On the question of "language choice" in Maghrebi writing, see Anne Armitage, "The Debate Over Literary Writing in a Foreign Language: An Overview of Francophonie in the Maghreb," *Alif: Journal of Comparative Poetics* 20 (2000): 39–67.

55. For a more detailed examination of these glimmers of recognition, see Emily Drumsta, "An Epic of the Body and of Memory: Atavism and the Critique of Enlightenment in Driss Chraïbi's *Une Enquête au pays*," *Research in African Literatures* 50, no. 2 (2019): 198–218.

56. Chraïbi once again melds languages here. In French, "Jews" would be "les juifs"; in Arabic, *al-yahūd* (and "Jewish" would be *yahūdī*). He transcribes the Arabic *yahūdī* as "des Youdis." Likewise, in Arabic, *naṣrānī* (pl. *naṣārā*) is a common way to refer to Christians as a group (as opposed to the French *Chrétiens*).

57. Part of Chraïbi's affirmation of autochthonous alterity is also typographical: he italicizes the entire mother's tale, setting it off from the rest of the novel both linguistically and visually.

58. Here I part from Anjali Prabhu's claim that "it is through his advantage in language that Ali saves himself . . . Language, which he produces endlessly through the night much like Sheherazade does in the *Arabian Nights*, saves his life." See Anjali Prabhu, "Theorizing the Role of the Intermediary in Postcolonial (Con)Text: Driss Chraïbi's *Une Enquête Au Pays*," *Studies in 20th & 21st Century Literature* 27, no. 1 (2003): 185–86. Even though Ali does talk through the night in this scene, we cannot be sure that the content of his speech matches the content of the narration.

59. Here I am building once again on Miller's reading of *Nana*: "[Nana's] greatest anxiety is apparently inspired by the prospect of being 'mise en carte': put on a police list entailing obligatory medical examination . . . Yet the police procedures that are censured in the story reappear less corruptibly in Zola's method of telling it. What is *Nana* but an extended *mise-en-carte* of a prostitute?" See Miller, *The Novel and the Police*, 21.

60. On *Miramar* as national romance, see Elliott Colla, "Miramar and Postcolonial Melancholia" in *Approaches to Teaching the Works of Naguib Mahfouz*, ed. Waïl S. Hassan and Susan Muaddi Darraj (New York: MLA Press, 2012), 173–75. See also Selim, *Rural Imaginary*, 123–24.

61. J. M. Coetzee, *Waiting for the Barbarians* (New York: Penguin, 1982), 81. This comparison is inspired by Gayatri Spivak's reading of Coetzee's novel in *Death of a Discipline* (New York: Columbia University Press, 2004), 21–23.

62. Mohammad Salama, "The Aesthetics of 'Pygmalion' in G. B. Shaw and Tawfīq Al-Ḥakīm: A Study of Transcendence and Decadence," *JAL* 31, no. 3 (2000): 236.

63. The sentence "I am Asfur" could also be translated "I am a bird," further explaining the image of "gleaning grains" or "gathering seeds" in the second sentence.

64. Shukri, *Thawrat al-Muʿtazil*, 246 (emphasis in the original).

65. Pierre Cachia, *An Overview of Arabic Literature* (Edinburgh: Edinburgh University Press, 1990), 172.

66. Scott, *Conscripts of Modernity*, 129.

67. This is the opposite of the conventional view in detective fiction criticism, which tends to equate the figure of the detective with that of the reader. See, for example, Peter Hühn, "The Detective as Reader: Narrativity and Reading Concepts in Detective Fiction," *Modern Fiction Studies* 33, no. 3 (2009): 451–66.

## 2. MURDER ON THE *ʿIZBAH*: SPECTRAL LEGALITY AND EGYPTIAN SENSATION FICTION—YUSUF IDRIS TO YUSUF AL-QAʿID

1. Martin Priestman, *Detective Fiction and Literature: The Figure on the Carpet* (New York: St. Martin's Press, 1991), 6.

2. El Shakry, *The Great Social Laboratory*, 198, 202–3.

3. "From the 1950s onwards, the village novel begins explicitly to interrogate the relationship between power and ideology in Egyptian society and to foreground the coercive nature of this alliance" (Selim, *Rural Imaginary*, 127).

4. Martin Hinds and El-Said Badawi, *A Dictionary of Egyptian Arabic*, s.v. "ʿizbah," 575, http://ejtaal.net.

5. Mitchell, *Rule of Experts*, 70.

6. On the formation and consolidation of large farming estates in the nineteenth century, see Gabriel Baer, *A History of Landownership in Modern Egypt 1800–1950* (Oxford: Oxford University Press, 1962), 13–70; on the shift from subsistence to monoculture farming in conjunction with shifting relations of production and global flows of capital, see Mitchell, *Rule of Experts*, 59–79 and *Colonising Egypt*, 34–44. On the failure of Nasser-era land reform laws, see Doreen Warriner, *Land Reform and Development in the Middle East: A Study of Egypt, Syria, and Iraq*, 2nd ed. (London: Oxford University Press, 1962), 31–35, and Mitchell, *Rule of Experts*, 43, 154–59, 165–72.

7. Esmeir, *Juridical Humanity*, 201–2.

8. Esmeir, *Juridical Humanity*, 202 (emphasis in the original).

9. Esmeir, *Juridical Humanity*, 231.

10. Esmeir, *Juridical Humanity*, 224–28.

11. For the most part, as Esmeir insists, state investigations of criminal activity on the estates during this time "recorded the evidence of estate managers, inspectors, or owners who abused estate peasants in their search for evidence about individuals most interested in killing inspectors," rather than documenting peasants' own testimonies about conditions on the ʿizbah (220).

12. On Nasserist "étatism," see El Shakry, *The Great Social Laboratory*, 197–218. Mitchell notes how, during Sadat's presidency, "the state managerial class and their rural allies used the military and political defeat of 1967, the economic crisis it accelerated . . . and the resulting pressure upon the regime to begin accommodating itself within American regional interests, to reassert their influence over government policy" (*Rule of Experts*, 166).

13. See El Shakry, *The Great Social Laboratory*, 119–23.

14. Fu'ad Tulbah, *Yūsuf Idrīs wa-l-Tābū* (Cairo: Maktabat Miṣr, 1985), 33.

15. Caroline Reitz illustrates how these twinned purposes shaped Victorian fictions of detective and colonial adventure both. See Caroline Reitz, *Detecting the Nation: Fictions of Detection and the Imperial Venture* (Columbus: Ohio State University Press, 2004).

16. ʿAbd al-Rahman Abu ʿAwf, *Yūsuf Idrīs wa ʿĀlamuhu fī al-Qiṣṣah al-Qaṣīrah wa-l-Riwāyah* (Cairo: al-Hayʾah al-Miṣriyyah li-l-Kitāb, 1994), 44.

17. Tulbah, *Yūsuf Idrīs*, 12.

18. Izyad Bih Wuld Muhammad Bashir, *Tajdīd al-Riwāyah al-ʿArabiyyah: Yūsuf al-Qaʿīd Namūdhajan*, 1st printing (Cairo: al-Hayʾah al-ʿĀmmah li-Quṣūr al-Thaqāfah, 2006), 415.

19. Esmeir, *Juridical Humanity*, 219–20.

20. Mitchell, *Colonising Egypt*, 34.

21. Mitchell, *Rule of Experts*, 59–62; *Colonising Egypt*, 40.

22. Yusuf al-Qaʿid, *News from the Meneisi Farm*, trans. Marie-Therese F. Abdel-Messih (Cairo: General Egyptian Book Organization, 1987), 33 (translation modified); Yusuf al-Qaʿid, *Akhbār ʿIzbat al-Manīsī* (Cairo: Dār al-Hilāl, 1985), 16.

23. Esmeir, *Juridical Humanity*, 225.

24. Mitchell, *Rule of Experts*, 70.

25. Throughout *The Sinners*, Idris mostly refers to the estate farm as a *taftīsh*, an administrative term meaning "irrigation area." Here, however, he reveals the continuance of "spectral legality" on the estate farm by citing a number of historical terms for such farms. *Abʿādiyyah* or *ibʿādiyyah* (literally, "land set aside") is a nineteenth-century term referring to "uncultivated land surveyed but not included in Muhammad ʿAli's [1812–1814] cadaster," which the Pasha would later grant to certain notables and high officials in his government. Though at first they were more like tenants, in time these officials would become the de facto owners of the land, enjoying rights of sale and transfer. The tradition of granting lands to officials and notables would continue under Khedive Ismaʿil, and thus the concept of the *ibʿādiyyah* was "divested of its original meaning" such that "to this day *Ibʿādīyah* is a common place name (mainly in the northern part of the Delta)" (Baer, *History of Landownership*, 16–17, 233). "*Daayirah*," meanwhile (a colloquial elision of *dāʾirah*), when used in a general sense, does mean "a large landholding, usually including several estates" (Hinds and Badawi, *Dictionary of Colloquial Egyptian*, 310), but *Dāʾirah Saniyyah* was also the specific phrase used to refer to the agricultural lands consolidated and owned by Khedive Ismaʿil starting in the 1860s, and later sold to pay off his debts to European creditors, thus accelerating the rise of private property and facilitating British colonial control. See Esmeir, *Juridical Humanity*, 207–19; Baer, *History of Landownership in Egypt*, 41–43 passim.

26. Yusuf Idris, *The Sinners*, trans. Kristin Peterson-Ishaq (Boulder, CO: Lynne Rienner, 2009), 26–27; Yusuf Idris, *al-Ḥarām*, in *Yūsuf Idrīs: al-Riwāyāt* (Cairo: Dār al-Shurūq, 1987), 34–35. Both are hereafter cited in-text, *The Sinners* is abbreviated *S* and *al-Ḥarām* is abbreviated *Ḥ*.

27. Esmeir, *Juridical Humanity*, 211, 218.

28. al-Qaʿid, *News*, 30–31 (translation modified).

29. al-Qaʿid, *News*, 33.

30. Shukri, *Thawrat al-Muʿtazil*, 240–45.

31. Yusuf al-Qaʿid, *Yaḥduth fī Miṣr al-Ān* (Cairo: Dār Usāmah li-l-Ṭabaʿ wa-l-Nashr, 1977), 9 (hereafter abbreviated *YMA* in parenthetical citations). Al-Qaʿid also published a short story collection with the title *Man Yahdkur Miṣr al-Ukhrā?* [Who remembers the other Egypt?] (Damascus: al-Jumhuriyyah al-ʿArabiyyah al-Sūriyyah, Wizārat al-Thaqāfah, 1984). The text of *Yaḥduth* that I work with in this chapter is the first edition, which, according to the front material of the fourth edition, was published "at the author's expense" in 1977, the year Sadat officially lifted the policy of advance censorship for all novels by the Ministry of Culture. See Yusuf al-Qaʿid, preface to *Yaḥduth fī Miṣr al-Ān*, 4th ed. (Cairo: Dār al-Mustaqbal al-ʿArabī, 1986), 4. This statement is corroborated by a footnote on the title page of the first edition: "It is worth mentioning that it was not possible to publish this novel, which was written at the end of 1974 and the beginning of 1975, until Egyptian censorship regulations on books were lifted [in 1977]. The censors confiscated the novel during this time" (3). For similar reasons, the second and third editions of the novel were published outside Egypt: the second in Beirut by Dār Ibn Rushd in 1977, and the third in Acre, in the Occupied Palestinian Territories, by Dār al-Aswār in 1979.

32. Gérard Genette, *Narrative Discourse: An Essay in Method*, trans. Jane E. Lewin (Ithaca, NY: Cornell University Press, 1980), 188–89.

33. Esmeir notes that seasonal migrant workers were "the most exploited by estate owners" because, lacking stable residency and employment, they could be hired for very low wages. Around the turn of the century, their numbers reached approximately 659,000, and they were paid only three piasters per day. See Esmeir, *Juridical Humanity*, 218–19. Mitchell also notes that "the landless were as much a part of the arrangement as the workers tied to the estate. Their role lay not just in the discipline they helped enforce among estate workers by their availability to replace them, but in the provision of extra labor at harvest and other periods of peak demand . . . There developed mobile brigades of workers, controlled by labor contractors and overseers, resulting in a dual labor force" (*Rule of Experts* 65).

34. To render the speech of the Gharabwa, here Idris writes in the unconventional dialect of the western Delta: "*l-ashyaaḥ [al-ashyāʾ] tibʾaa maʿdan*" ("Everything's going to be perfect!").

35. On the rhetoric against the cotton worm in British-colonial Egypt as one of "warfare" and "battles," see Esmeir, *Juridical Humanity*, 149–96.

36. Idris, *The Sinners*, 29. On the failure of the police lineup as a tactic in *Diary of a Country Prosecutor*, see Colla, "Anxious Advocacy," 441–42.

37. Idris is well-known—sometimes praised, sometimes derided—for using colloquial Egyptian Arabic in his short stories, novels, and plays, not only for dialogue, as in many writers' works, but also in narration and description themselves. In the introduction he wrote for the 1956 Dār Rūz al-Yūsuf edition of Idris's play *Farahat's Republic (Jumhūriyyat Faraḥāt)*, Taha Hussein famously criticized Idris's use of Egyptian Arabic in his literary works. For an overview of Idris's style and use of language, see Sasson Somekh, "Language and Theme in the Short Stories of Yūsuf Idrīs," *JAL* 6, no. 1 (1975): 89–100. For interviews in which Idris speaks about his use of language, register, and style, see Ghali Shukri, *Duktūr Yūsuf Idrīs: Farfūr Khārij al-Sūr* (Cairo: al-Hayʾah al-ʿĀmmah li-l-Istiʿlāmāt, 1992).

38. Yusuf Idris, *Mālik al-Quṭn* (The king of cotton) *wa Jumhūriyyat Faraḥāt: Masraḥīyatān* (Cairo: al-Muʾassasah al-Qawmiyyah li-l-Nashr wa-l-Tawzīʿ, 1963).

39. Idris was born and raised in the rural Egyptian town of al-Bayrum (in Sharqiya province), then graduated from Cairo University in 1951, later obtaining credentials in psychiatry and public health. He worked for a time at Qasr al-ʿAyni Hospital in Cairo and later as a health inspector for the Ministry of National Guidance, where he was appointed to one of the poorest neighborhoods in the city. See Arthur Goldschmidt, "Idris, Dr. Yusuf," in *Biographical Dictionary of Modern Egypt* (Boulder, CO: Lynne Rienner, 1999), 88–89. For an analysis of this scene as one designed to incite readers to action on behalf of migrant workers like Aziza, see Abu ʿAwf, *Yūsuf Idrīs wa ʿĀlamuh*, 57–61. Roger Allen notes the importance of Idris's medical training, rural upbringing, and commitment to the Egyptian Left (a commitment for which he was jailed on numerous occasions) in the shaping of his short stories throughout the 1950s and 60s. See Roger Allen, "The Artistry of Yūsuf Idrīs," *World Literature Today* 55, no. 1 (1981): 43–47.

40. Shukri, *Duktūr Yūsuf Idrīs*, 48–50.

41. On the breaking of taboo throughout Idris's literary works, see Tulbah, *Yūsuf Idrīs wa-l-Tābū*.

42. These changes are noted by Idris's English translator, Kristin Peterson-Ishaq. When Dār al-Shurūq printed Idris's complete works in 1987, they used the original, quasi-utopian version. For Idris's edits, see the 1977 edition printed by the Cairo publishing house Maktabat Gharīb.

43. Mitchell, *Rule of Experts*, 43.

44. See Sadiq Jalal al-ʿAzm's *al-Naqd al-Dhātī baʿda al-Hazīmah* (Beirut: Dār al-Talīʿah, 1968). The notion that this political and military event served as a kind of cultural, intellectual, and aesthetic rupture has been taken up by many scholars of Arabic literature and culture. See Roger Allen, *The Arabic Novel: An Historical and Critical Introduction* (Syracuse, NY: Syracuse University Press, 1995), 59; Idwar al-Kharrat, *al-Ḥassāsiyyah al-Jadīdah: Maqālāt fī al-Ẓāhirah al-Qiṣaṣiyyah*, 1st ed. (Beirut: Dār al-Ādāb, 1993), 11; Elias Khoury, *al-Dhākirah al-Mafqūdah: Dirāsāt Naqdiyyah*, 1st ed. (Beirut: Muʾassasat al-Abḥāth al-ʿArabiyyah, 1982), 41–42; Halim Barakat, *The Arab World: Society, Culture, and State* (Berkeley: University of California Press, 1993), 256. I am disloyal to this narrative of rupture, which I think invites politically overdetermined readings of literary texts.

45. Tulbah, *Yūsuf Idrīs wa-l-Tābū*, 36.

46. The following overview draws from Stone's synopsis in "'Mature' Arabic Novel."

47. In *Yaḥduth*, as in nearly all of al-Qaʿid's other novels, government officials are not given names, but only referred to by their (often lengthy) titles. Here I follow Stone's lead in referring to *raʾīs majlis al-qariyah* (literally "the chairman of the village council") as "the Chairman," *ḥaḍrat al-ḍābiṭ* ("the respected police officer") as "the Officer," and *ṭabīb al-wiḥdah* ("the region's doctor") as "the Doctor." See Stone, "'Mature' Arabic Novel," 297–98.

48. The doctor's dream of transferring from the public to the private sector is in line with the "cost-recovery programs" advised by the U.S. Agency for International Development (USAID) beginning in the late 1970s. See Mitchell, *Rule of Experts*, 229–30.

49. Bashir, *Tajdīd al-Riwāyah*, 415.

50. Rather than writing "no" (*lā* in formal Arabic; *laaʾa* or *maafeesh* in Egyptian), al-Qaʿid transliterates the English "no" (*nuu*) with multiple *waw*'s throughout this passage.

51. In a "culture of fear," Mitchell writes, "violence directed against people in a small community often relies on the power to impose silence," yet at the same time, "the silence imposed by local forms of violence is seldom total." Death, disappearance, physical abuse,

or torture must be "whispered about, recalled by its victims, and hinted at" if they are to function as tools of social and political control. Disappearance, then, "gains its force as an absence that is continually made present." See Mitchell, *Rule of Experts*, 127.

52. For more on the narrative ballad (*mawwāl*, pl. *mawāwīl*) in Egypt, see Pierre Cachia, *Popular Narrative Ballads of Modern Egypt* (Oxford and New York: Oxford University Press, 1989) and *Exploring Arab Folk Literature* (Edinburgh: Edinburgh University Press, 2011). Abu Zayd, unlike al-Sharqawi or al-Zanati Khalifah, is a hero from the Bani Hilal epic cycle. On the ballad of al-Adham al-Sharqawi in particular, see Margaret Larkin, "A Brigand Hero of Egyptian Colloquial Literature," *JAL* 23, no. 1 (1992): 49–64.

53. The saying "the mule is in the pitcher" is from a popular tale involving the folk hero and trickster Juha. It refers to getting away with something preposterous or ridiculous.

54. Salih Sulayman ʿAbd al-ʿAzim, *Sūsiyūlūjiyā al-Riwāyah al-Siyāsiyyah: Yūsuf al-Qaʿīd Namūdhajan* (Cairo: al-Hayʾah al-Miṣriyyah al-ʿĀmmah li-l-Kitāb, 1998) 130–35.

55. Samah Selim stresses the "empowering" and "challenging" aspects of colloquial Arabic as "subaltern discourse," suggesting "the possibility of a popular, folksy critique of all hegemonic discourse, including that of bourgeois narrative fiction" (123). See Selim, *Rural Imaginary*, 92, 101, 173–74. In al-Qaʿid's novel, by contrast, the most dehumanizing, official rhetoric is often given to the reader in colloquial Egyptian.

56. The word originates in Arabic (*ʿaraḍa* = to present, *ḥāl* = a condition or state), migrates into Turkish and Persian, and then returns to colloquial Egyptian in rural areas via Ottoman Turkish, the language of the state for many centuries. The need for such an official in Ottoman times makes sense, given that the local language of everyday life in the provinces (colloquial Arabic) was completely different from that of the state (Turkish), and given that very few villagers and farmers could read and write the latter. The presence of such an official in al-Qaʿid's novel of the 1970s, however, reveals the continuing disconnect between the central government and the people, the city and the country.

57. In Egyptian Arabic: *Min ṭaʾṭaʾ lis-salaam ʿaleeku.*

58. Mitchell, *Rule of Experts*, 181–86.

59. Mitchell, *Rule of Experts*, 184.

60. ʿAbd al-ʿAzim, *Sūsiyūlujīyā*, 192.

61. "*Khiṭābān li-l-Raʾīsayn fī Ḥafl al-ʿAshāʾ*," *al-Ahrām*, June 13, 1974, 3.

62. al-Qaʿid, preface to *Yaḥduth fī Miṣr al-Ān*, 4th ed., 6.

63. Mustafa Bayyumi, *al-Fallāḥ wa Muʾassasāt al-Sulṭah: Dirāsah fī Adab Yūsuf al-Qaʿīd* (Cairo: Dār al-Hudā, 2001), 135.

64. Mitchell, *Rule of Experts*, 209.

## 3. BUREAU OF MISSING PERSONS: METAPHYSICAL DETECTION AND THE SUBJECT IN JABRA IBRAHIM JABRA AND NAGUIB MAHFOUZ

1. I am using "metaphysical detection" in the sense theorized by Patricia Merivale and Susan Elizabeth Sweeney in their edited volume *Detecting Texts: The Metaphysical Detective Story from Poe to Postmodernism* (Philadelphia: University of Pennsylvania Press, 1999).

2. Merivale and Sweeney, introduction to *Detecting Texts*, 2.

3. Jeanne C. Ewert, "'A Thousand Other Mysteries': Metaphysical Detection, Ontological Quests," in *Detecting Texts: The Metaphysical Detective Story from Poe to Postmodernism*,

ed. Patricia Merivale and Susan Elizabeth Sweeney (Philadelphia: University of Pennsylvania Press), 179.

4. When exercising his analytical faculties, Dupin's manner becomes "frigid and abstract, his eyes vacant in expression." See Edgar Allan Poe, "The Murders in the Rue Morgue," in *Complete Stories and Poems of Edgar Allan Poe* (New York: Doubleday, n.d.), 5.

5. Roger Allen, "The Happy Traitor: Tales of Translation," *Comparative Literature Studies* 47, no. 4 (2010): 477–79.

6. Somekh, *The Changing Rhythm*, 185; Naguib Mahfouz, *Ataḥaddath Ilaykum* (Beirut: Dār al-ʿAwdah, 1977), 93. See also Trevor Le Gassick, introduction to *The Thief and the Dogs*, by Naguib Mahfouz, trans. Trevor Le Gassick and M. M. Badawi, revised by John Rodenbeck (New York: Anchor Books 2008), 8; Naguib Mahfouz, *Fountain and Tomb*, trans. Soad Sobhy, Essam Fattouh, and James Kenneson (Washington, DC: Three Continents Press, 1988), 43–44.

7. Ziad Elmarsafy, *Sufism in the Contemporary Arabic Novel* (Edinburgh: Edinburgh University Press, 2012), 23–51; El-Enany, *Naguib Mahfouz*, 15–16 passim; Latifa al-Zayyat, *Najīb Maḥfūẓ: al-Ṣūrah wa-l-Mithāl* (Cairo: Kitāb al-Ahālī, 1989); Georges Tarabichi, *Allāh fī Riḥlat Najīb Maḥfūẓ al-Ramziyyah* (Beirut: Dār al-Ṭalīʿah, 1973), 36–83; Michael Beard, "Homage to Ibn al-Fârid: Nostalgia in 'Zaabalawi,'" in *Approaches to Teaching the Works of Naguib Mahfouz*, ed. Waïl Hassan and Susan Muaddi Darraj (New York: Modern Language Association of America, 2012), 164–71. Pierre Cachia notes how "a dissatisfaction with Science and Reason as the ultimate keys to reality" transformed the later novels of Naguib Mahfouz into works marked by "questing." See Cachia, *Overview*, 24.

8. Muhsin Jasim al-Musawi, *The Postcolonial Arabic Novel: Debating Ambivalence* (Leiden: E. J. Brill, 2003), 156; Mattiyahu Peled, "Sexuality in Jabra's Novel, *The Search for Walīd Masʿūd*," in *Love and Sexuality in Modern Arabic Literature*, ed. Roger Allen, Hilary Kilpatrick, and Ed de Moor (London: Saqi Books, 1995).

9. Jabra Ibrahim Jabra, *al-Baḥth ʿan Walīd Masʿūd*, 4th printing (Beirut: Dār al-Adāb), hereafter cited parenthetically in-text as *B*. Jabra Ibrahim Jabra, *In Search of Walid Masoud*, trans. Roger Allen and Adnan Haydar (Syracuse, NY: Syracuse University Press, 2000), hereafter cited parenthetically in-text as *ISWM*. When referring to the novel, I hereafter shorten its English title to *Walid Masoud* (distinguished from the character himself, whose name I do not italicize).

10. Tzvetan Todorov, "The Typology of Detective Fiction," in *The Poetics of Prose*, trans. Richard Howard (Ithaca, NY: Cornell University Press, 1977), 44–45.

11. al-Musawi, *Postcolonial Arabic Novel*, 156; Johnson, "Politics of Reading."

12. Stefan G. Meyer, *The Experimental Arabic Novel: Postcolonial Literary Modernism in the Levant* (Albany: State University of New York Press, 2001), 52, 54; Issa J. Boullata, "Living with the Tigress and the Muses: An Essay on Jabra Ibrahim Jabra," *World Literature Today* 75, no. 2 (2001): 219.

13. Patricia Merivale, "Gumshoe Gothics: Poe's 'Man of the Crowd' and His Followers," in *Detecting Texts*, ed. Merivale and Sweeney (Philadelphia: University of Pennsylvania Press, 1999), 105.

14. Merivale, "Gumshoe Gothics," 107.

15. Stephan Guth, "Novel, Arabic," in *EI3*, ed. Kate Fleet, Gudrun Krämer, Denis Matringe, John Nawas, Devin J. Stewart, https://referenceworks.brillonline.com/entries/encyclopaedia-of-islam-3/novel-arabic-COM_27115?s.num=0&s.f.s2_parent=s.f.book.encyclopaedia-of-islam-3&s.q=Novel%2C+Arabic.

16. Poe, "Man of the Crowd," 219.

17. See *Walid Masoud* 86; *Baḥth*, 116–17.

18. Poe, "Man of the Crowd," 215.

19. Friedrich Nietzsche, "On Truth and Lies in a Nonmoral Sense," in *The Nietzsche Reader*, ed. Keith Ansell Pearson and Duncan Large (Malden: Blackwell, 2006), 117.

20. Paul de Man, "Anthropomorphism and Trope in the Lyric," in *The Rhetoric of Romanticism* (New York: Columbia University Press, 1984), 240–42.

21. de Man, "Anthropomorphism," 242.

22. de Man, "Anthropomorphism," 241.

23. Michael Cooperson, introduction to al-Hariri, *Impostures*, trans. Michael Cooperson (New York: New York University Press, 2020), xxv.

24. Cooperson, introduction, xxiii.

25. Cooperson, introduction, xxvi.

26. Georg Lukács, *The Theory of the Novel*, trans. Anna Bostock (Cambridge, MA: MIT Press, 1971), 88.

27. This is the phrase used by Dr. Jawad Husni, the frame narrator of Jabra's novel. See Jabra, *Walid Masoud*, 279.

28. Jabra chronicles his childhood in the first volume of his autobiography, *The First Well: A Bethlehem Boyhood*, trans. Issa J. Boullata (Fayetteville: University of Arkansas Press, 1995). In a recent article, William Tamplin identifies Adana as Jabra's actual birthplace and asks why Jabra "deliberately hides" his Assyrian origins throughout his autobiographical and fictional works. There is no evidence in the sources that Jabra in fact *intended* to conceal his birthplace and Assyrian ancestry, but even if he did, these supposed "concealments" (30, 32, 33, 34, 36, 37, 48, 49, 51) certainly do not "compel" readers to analyze Jabra's works in any particular way, as Tamplin argues (49). See William Tamplin, "The Other Wells: Family History and the Self-Creation of Jabra Ibrahim Jabra," *Jerusalem Quarterly* 85 (2021): 30–60.

29. Boullata, "Living with the Tigress," 214–23.

30. Elias Khoury, *Bāb al-Shams*, 7th printing (Beirut: Dār al-Ādāb, 2017), 99. Though *nukhbawiyyah* does mean "well-chosen," it also resonates with the word *nukhbah*, the "elite."

31. For Jabra's essays on Romanticism, see "Jūn Kīts wa-l-Jamāl wa-l-Mawt," *al-Adīb* 16, no. 10 (1949): 14–16; "Bayrūn wa-l-Shayṭāniyyah," *al-Adīb* 21, no. 4 (1952): 33–40; "Maʿ Kīts ʿAlā al-Rābiyah," *al-Adīb* 23, no. 3 (1953): 45–46; and "'Amthāl al-Jaḥīm' li-Wilyim Blayik," *al-Adīb* 23, no. 4 (1953): 3–5; among others. Muhammad ʿAsfur has assembled the most authoritative bibliography of Jabra's work to date (corrected by Jabra himself). See his *Narjis wa-l-marāyā: Dirāsah li-kitābāt Jabrā Ibrāhīm Jabrā al-Ibdāʿiyyah* (Beirut: al-Muʾassasah al-ʿArabiyyah li-l-Dirāsāt wa-l-Nashr, 2009), 273. On American Modernist poetry, see Jabra, "al-Shiʿr al-Amrīkī al-Ḥadīth," *al-Ādāb* 3, no. 1 (1955): 110–15, as well as the critical introductions he wrote to his translations of poems from the English, including Dylan Thomas's "In My Craft, or Sullen Art" ("Fī Ṣanʿatī aw Fannī al-Zaʿūl"), *al-Adīb* 27, no. 5 (1955): 13; Edith Sitwell's "Serenade" and "Street Songs" ("Sarānādā wa Ughniyyāt

al-Shāriʿ"), *Shiʿr* 3 (1957): 69–72; and Ezra Pound's "From Sextus to Cynthia" ("Min Sakstūs ilā Sinthīyā"), *al-Adīb* 27, no. 6 (1955): 19.

32. Jabra, "al-Shiʿr wa-l-Naqd al-Jāhil" (Poetry and ignorant criticism), *Adab* 2, no. 1 (1963): 74–82. This was republished as "al-Shiʿr al-Ḥurr wa-l-Naqd al-Khāṭiʾ" (Free verse and false criticism) in *al-Riḥlah al-Thaminah: Dirāsāt Naqdiyyah* (Sidon: al-Maktabah al-ʿAṣriyyah, 1967), 7–19.

33. Collected in Jabra, *al-Fann wa al-Fannān: Kitābāt fī al-Naqd al-Tashkīlī* (Beirut: al-Muʾassasah al-ʿArabiyyah li-l-Dirāsāt wa-l-Nashr, 2000) and Jabra, *al-Fann al-Muʿaṣir fī al-ʿIrāq* (Baghdad: Wizārat al-Thaqāfah wa-l-Iʿlām, 1970).

34. See William Faulkner, *al-Ṣakhab wa-l-ʿUnf*, trans. Jabra Ibrahim Jabra (Beirut: al-Muʾassasah al-ʿArabiyyah li-l-Dirāsāt wa-l-Nashr, 1983); William Shakespeare, *Hāmlit*, trans. Jabra Ibrahim Jabra (Beirut: Dār Majallat Shiʿr, 1960); and Walt Whitman, "'*Ughniyyat Nafsī*,' *li-l-Shāʿir Wālt Wītmān*," trans. Jabra Ibrahim Jabra, in *al-Adīb* 23, no. 5 (May 1953): 3–9.

35. Jabra Ibrahim Jabra, "al-Ḥurriyyah wa-l-Ṭūfān" (Freedom and the flood), in *al-Ḥurriyyah wa-l-Ṭūfān: Dirāsāt Naqdiyyah*, 3rd printing (Beirut: al-Muʾassasah al-ʿArabiyyah li-l-Dirāsāt wa-l-Nashr, 1979), 20.

36. Robyn Creswell, *City of Beginnings: Poetic Modernism in Beirut* (Princeton, NJ: Princeton University Press, 2019), 18–19. See also the chapter "The Genealogy of Arabic Modernism," which gives a more detailed history of Malik's intellectual formation and its effects among the philosophies and poetries of the *Shiʿr* magazine poets in Lebanon.

37. Creswell, *City of Beginnings*, 9.

38. In distinguishing "explicit poetics" (what a writer says about their art in critical essays, introductions, and the like) from "implicit poetics" (the artistic principles, philosophical ideas, and political positions "reconstructed from the poets' actual works"), I follow Chana Kronfeld in her article "Beyond Thematicism in the Historiography of Post-1948 Political Poetry," *Jewish Social Studies* 18, no. 3 (2012): 180–96, and her book *On the Margins of Modernism: Decentering Literary Dynamics* (Berkeley: University of California Press, 1996).

39. Jabra Ibrahim Jabra, *Hunters in a Narrow Street* (Boulder, CO: Lynne Rienner, 1997), hereafter abbreviated as *H* in parenthetical in-text citations.

40. Jabra Ibrahim Jabra, "The Palestinian Exile as Writer," *Journal of Palestine Studies* 8, no. 2 (1979): 77. See also Zeina Halabi's reading of this essay in "The Day the Wandering Dreamer Became a Fidaʾi: Jabra Ibrahim Jabra and the Fashioning of Political Commitment," in *Commitment and Beyond: Reflections on/of the Political in Arabic Literature Since the 1940s*, ed. Friederike Pannewick and Georges Khalil (Wiesbaden: Reichert Verlag, 2015), 157–70.

41. Creswell, *City of Beginnings*, 72

42. See chapters 3 and 10 of *Walid Masoud*, respectively. The name "Issa Nasser" is significant for a carpenter character from Bethlehem: it literally means "Jesus the Helper," a close extension of "Jesus the Nazarene" (*al-Nāṣirī*). At every turn, Jabra works to dispel the abstract idealization of Jesus and to transform him into an everyday Bethlehemite.

43. Each chapter of *Walid Masoud* could, in fact, be read as a selection from the various primary documents Jawad collects in his "research" (*baḥth*), including love poems (pp. 202–4), correspondence (pp. 143–44), journal entries (pp. 110–13), and short stories

based on real events (pp. 31–46). Likewise, we are told that after Walid's disappearance, all Jawad has left of him is an "accumulation of his papers, stuffed into huge envelopes," which he plans to use as primary sources for his study (6), and that Wisal gives Jawad "several bundles of folded papers and a large collection of small blue pages all the same size" before leaving Baghdad to join the Fedayeen in Beirut (288).

44. For variations on this interpretation, see Boullata, "Living with the Tigress," 219; Meyer, *Experimental Arabic Novel*, 54; and Peled, "Sexuality," 143.

45. Rebecca Carol Johnson, "The Politics of Reading: Revolution and Recognition in Jabra Ibrahim Jabra's *In Search of Walid Masoud*," in *Recognition: The Poetics of Narrative, Interdisciplinary Studies on Anagnorisis*, ed. Philip F. Kennedy and Marilyn Lawrence (New York: Peter Lang, 2009), 178–92.

46. Vladimir Nabokov, *The Real Life of Sebastian Knight* (New York: Vintage, 1992), 50.

47. See, for example, Halabi, "Wandering Dreamer" and Halabi, *The Unmaking of the Arab Intellectual*, 65–108; al-Musawi, *The Postcolonial Arabic Novel*, 156.

48. de Man, "Anthropomorphism," 241.

49. Here I think of Jorge Luis Borges's verdict on translation that "there can only be drafts. The concept of the 'definitive text' corresponds only to religion or exhaustion." See Jorge Luis Borges, "The Homeric Versions," in *Selected Non-Fictions*, trans. Eliot Weinberger (New York: Penguin, 2000), 69.

50. Samir Fawzi Hajj analyzes at length what he calls Jabra's "mirror-style" and use of "reflective characters" in *Walid Masoud*. See Samir Fawzi Hajj, *Marāyā Jabrā Ibrāhīm Jabrā wa-l-Fann al-Riwāʾī*, 1st printing (Beirut: al-Muʾassasah al-ʿArabiyyah li-l-Dirāsāt wa-l-Nashr, 2005), 110–21. Meyer also notes that "in their *reflections* on Walid, the other characters are merely *reflecting* on aspects of themselves," and thus "Walid simply serves as a *mirror* in which these characters see themselves." See Meyer, *Experimental Arabic Novel*, 52 and 54 (emphases added). Likewise, Isa Boullata claims that, "in the process of their attempt to unravel the garbled utterances of the tape recording, [Walīd's] friends—as though looking in a mirror—reveal more of themselves than of him." See Boullata, "Living with the Tigress," 219.

51. For two readings of masculine identity, sexuality, and their relations to post-1967 politics in *Walid Masoud*, see Samira Aghacy, *Masculine Identity in the Fiction of the Arab East Since 1967* (Syracuse, NY: Syracuse University Press, 2009), 59–68; and Peled, "Sexuality."

52. Jabra Ibrahim Jabra, *The Ship*, trans. Roger Allen and Adnan Haydar (Boulder, CO: Three Continents Press, 1985), 52–54.

53. de Man, "Anthropomorphism," 241.

54. Jabra, *The Ship*, 106.

55. An English translation of this novel by Mohamed Islam, edited by Magdi Wahba, was published as *The Search* by The American University in Cairo Press in 1987, and subsequently republished by Anchor Books in the United States, in 1991. I offer a more literal translation of its original Arabic title as *The Way*, and I give my own translations from the Arabic when citing from the novel throughout this chapter.

56. Naguib Mahfouz, *al-Muʾallafāt al-Kāmilah* (Beirut: Maktabat Lubnān, 1991), vol. 3, 142. See also Naguib Mahfouz, "Culprit Unknown," trans. Emily Drumsta, *Asymptote*, July 2019, https://www.asymptotejournal.com/fiction/naguib-mahfouz-culprit-unknown/;

al-Hakim, *Diary*, 121–22; *Yawmiyyāt*, 170–71. Hereafter, I cite Mahfouz's "Complete Works" in parentheses (*MK*) followed by volume and page number (3:142).

57. Cooperson, introduction, xxvi.

58. William C. Chittick, *The Sufi Path of Knowledge: Ibn al-ʿArabi's Metaphysics of Imagination* (Albany: State University of New York Press, 1989), 79.

59. Chittick, *Sufi Path*, 79–80.

60. Peter Adamson, "Existence in Philosophy and Theology," in *EI3*, ed. Kate Fleet, Gudrun Krämer, Denis Matringe, John Nawas, Devin J. Stewart, https://referenceworks.brillonline.com/entries/encyclopaedia-of-islam-3/existence-in-philosophy-and-theology-COM_26265?s.num=0&s.f.s2_parent=s.f.book.encyclopaedia-of-islam-3&s.q=Existence+in+Philosophy+and+Theolog.

61. Adamson, "Existence."

62. Adamson, "Existence."

63. McGregor, "Friend of God."

64. G. K. Chesterton, "A Defence of Detective Stories," in *The Art of the Mystery Story: A Collection of Critical Essays*, ed. Howard Haycraft (New York: Simon & Schuster, 1946), 6.

65. Atif Khalil calls the *ḥāl* "a positive but fleeting psychological state born of the aspirant's relationship with God." See "Ḥāl in Sufism," in *EI3*, ed. Kate Fleet, Gudrun Krämer, Denis Matringe, John Nawas, Devin J. Stewart, https://referenceworks.brillonline.com/entries/encyclopaedia-of-islam-3/hal-in-sufism-COM_30219?s.num=0&s.f.s2_parent=s.f.book.encyclopaedia-of-islam-3&s.q=%E1%B8%A4%C4%81l+in+Sufism.

66. Roger Allen, "Teaching Mahfouz's 'Zaabalawi,'" 159, 161; and Michael Beard, "Homage to Ibn al-Fârid: Nostalgia in 'Zaabalawi,'" 165. Both these essays are in *Approaches to Teaching the Works of Naguib Mahfouz*, ed. Waïl S. Hassan and Susan Muaddi Darraj (New York: Modern Language Association of America, 2012).

67. Naguib Mahfouz, *al-Ṭarīq* (Cairo: Maktabat Maṣr, n.d.), hereafter abbreviated *Ṭ* and cited parenthetically in-text.

68. Chittick, *Sufi Path*, 79–80.

69. Chittick, *Sufi Path*, 220.

70. Denis Gril, "Dhawq," in *EI3*, ed. Kate Fleet, Gudrun Krämer, Denis Matringe, John Nawas, Devin J. Stewart, https://referenceworks.brillonline.com/entries/encyclopaedia-of-islam-3/dhawq-COM_26001?s.num=0&s.f.s2_parent=s.f.book.encyclopaedia-of-islam-3&s.q=Dhawq.

71. El-Enany, *Naguib Mahfouz*, 107. miriam cooke points out the shortcomings of this reading in her review of *The Search*: "This novel has been compared to Mahfouz's other writings of the 1960s in which the analogy between the search for a father figure and the search for God is transparent. Mahfouz's almost flippant interjections at the end of the novel . . . would seem, however, to indicate that the author wishes to deflect such simplistic interpretations." See miriam cooke, "Naguib Mahfouz: Review Article," review of *The Search* and *Fountain and Tomb* by Naguib Mahfouz, *Middle East Journal* 43, no. 3 (1989): 508.

72. Mahmud al-Rabiʿi, *Qirāʾāt al-Riwāyah: Namādhij min Najīb Maḥfūẓ* (Cairo: Dār al-Maʿārif, 1974).

73. Chittick, *Sufi Path*, 81.

74. Not only does al-Rahimi resemble Zaabalawi in his elusive refusal to be pinned down; he is also much like the clever thief Arsène Lupin, in Samah Selim's reading, "master of disguise and evasion . . . impossible to identify (and hence to capture)," and thus "the

order that he challenges and continually outwits is that of personhood itself" in the modern, liberal state. See Samah Selim, "Fiction and Colonial Identities: Arsène Lupin in Arabic," *Middle Eastern Studies* 13, no. 2 (2020): 202.

75. Constance A. Jones and James D. Ryan, "Darshan," *Encyclopedia of Hinduism* (New York: Facts on File, 2007), 119.

76. Rabindra Ray, "The Teaching of *Darshan* and Its Purpose," trans. Satish Deshpande, *Contributions to Indian Sociology* 53, no. 3 (2019): 422–23.

77. de Man, "Anthropomorphism," 242.

78. Renate Jacobi, "ʿ*Udhrī*," in *EI2*, ed. P. Bearman, Th. Bianquis, C. E. Bosworth, E. van Donzel, and W. P. Heinrichs, https://referenceworks.brillonline.com/entries/encyclopaedia-of-islam-2/udhri-SIM_7679?s.num=0&s.f.s2_parent=s.f.book.encyclopaedia-of-islam-2&s.q=%CA%BFUdhr%C4%AB.

79. Jacobi, "ʿ*Udhrī*."

80. In al-Sarraj's Sufi treatise *al-Lumaʿ*, "with regard to love [*wajd*], *dhawq* precedes *shurb* (drink) and *rayy* (drinking to one's fill)." See Gril, "*Dhawq*."

81. It is also a property of before-ness. "Sabir knew the name of God," we are told at one point in *The Way*, "but it had never occupied his mind. He had no relationship to religion worth mentioning, and [his home on] al-Nabi Daniyal Street had never witnessed a single religions tradition. He lived in an age before religion" (*T* 46).

82. L. Lewisohn, "Shawk," in *EI2*, ed. P. Bearman, Th. Bianquis, C. E. Bosworth, E. van Donzel, and W. P. Heinrichs, https://referenceworks.brillonline.com/entries/encyclopaedia-of-islam-2/shawk-SIM_6874?s.num=0&s.f.s2_parent=s.f.book.encyclopaedia-of-islam-2&s.q=Shawk.

83. Jacobi, "ʿ*Udhrī*."

84. Naguib Mahfouz, *The Cairo Trilogy: Palace Walk, Palace of Desire, Sugar Street*, trans. William Maynard Hutchins, Olive E. Kenny, Lorne M. Kenny, and Angele Botros Samaan (New York: Alfred A. Knopf, 2001), 53.

85. Chittick, *Sufi Path*, 311.

86. On the tradition of *bāṭiniyyah*, or allegorical interpretations of the Qurʾan, particularly among the Ismaʿilis in medieval times, see M. G. S. Hodgson, "Bāṭiniyya," in *EI2*, ed. P. Bearman, Th. Bianquis, C. E. Bosworth, E. van Donzel, and W. P. Heinrichs, https://referenceworks.brillonline.com/entries/encyclopaedia-of-islam-2/batiniyya-SIM_1284?s.num=0&s.f.s2_parent=s.f.book.encyclopaedia-of-islam-2&s.q=B%C4%81%E1%B9%ADiniyya.

87. The published English translation reads as follows: "The walk through these sacred precincts was an ordeal for his pounding heart" (687).

88. Chittick, *Sufi Path*, 4.

89. Chittick, *Sufi Path*, 297.

90. Denis Gril, "Wiṣāl," in *EI2*, ed. P. Bearman, Th. Bianquis, C. E. Bosworth, E. van Donzel, and W. P. Heinrichs, https://referenceworks.brillonline.com/entries/encyclopaedia-of-islam-2/wisal-SIM_8932?s.num=0&s.f.s2_parent=s.f.book.encyclopaedia-of-islam-2&s.q=Wi%E1%B9%A3%C4%81l.

91. Gril, "Wiṣāl."

92. Yaseen Noorani, *Culture and Hegemony in the Colonial Middle East* (New York: Palgrave Macmillan, 2010), 191–92.

93. Lewisohn, "Shawk."

94. See Michael Allan, "Re-Reading the Arab Darwin: The Lewis Affair and Naguib Mahfouz's *Palace of Desire*," *Modernism/Modernity* 23, no. 2 (2016): 319–40.

95. Noorani, *Culture and Hegemony*, 191.

96. I've rendered as "You're the worst" the Arabic phrase, *Allāh yakhrab baytak*, which literally means "may God destroy your house."

97. Ken Seigneurie, "Modern Nihilism and Naguib Mahfouz's Faith in Liberalism," *Middle Eastern Literatures* 24, no. 3 (2022): 173.

98. Scott, *Conscripts*, 8, 13.

99. Merivale and Sweeney, introduction, 2

100. Ewert, "A Thousand Other Mysteries," 179

101. Quoted in Hamdi Sakkut, "Najīb Maḥfūẓ wa-l-Ḥall al-Ṣūfī," *Alif: Journal of Comparative Poetics* 5 (1985): 44. The word Mahfouz uses for "profit" and its permutations is *istighlāl*.

## 4. EFFACING THE AUTHOR, OR THE DETECTIVE AS MEDIUM: FATHI GHANIM AND ELIAS KHOURY

1. Elias Khoury, "ʿAn al-Būlīs wa-l-Riwāyah al-Būlīsiyyah," reprinted in *al-Dhākirah al-Mafqūdah: Dirāsāt Naqdiyyah* (Beirut: Muʾassasat al-Abḥāth al-ʿArabiyyah, 1982), 350–53. Originally published in *al-Safīr*, February 24, 1980.

2. Chesterton, "Defence," 6.

3. There is a key terminological problem in Khoury's essay and nearly every recent study engaging the question of "detective fiction" in the Arab world: by rendering this term as *al-riwāyah al-būlīsiyyah* (literally, "the police novel"), Khoury and others limit their analysis to the subgenre of the police procedural, to the exclusion of the many other subgenres of detection that, more often than not, criticize and deride the police as obtuse bunglers (Poe, Conan Doyle) or corrupt villains (Chandler). See the essays in *Fuṣūl* 76 (2009); Bawardi and Faranesh, "Non-Canonical Arabic Detective Fiction"; Jonathan Smolin, *Moroccan Noir: Police, Crime, and Politics in Popular Culture* (Bloomington: Indiana University Press, 2013).

4. Elias Khoury, "Mawt al-Muʾallif" (The death of the author), in *al-Dhākirah al-Mafqūdah*, 74.

5. Khoury, "Mawt al-Muʾallif," 75.

6. Khoury makes no reference to Roland Barthes's essay of the same title.

7. On the author as "medium," see Elias Khoury, "Conversations with Ilyās Khūrī," interview by Sonja Mejcher, in *Geschichten über Geschichten: Errinerung im Romanwerk von Ilyās Khūrī* (Wiesbaden: Reichert Verlag, 2001), 141.

8. Sonja Mejcher-Atassi notes that Khoury's *White Masks* "sets out like a detective story," while Mona Takieddine Amyuni notes that "a detective story technique is often used" in Khoury's early novels, from *Little Mountain* through *The Journey of Little Gandhi* and *City Gates*. See Sonja Mejcher-Atassi, "The Martyr and His Image: Ilyās Khūrī's Novel *al-Wujūh al-Bayḍāʾ* (*The White Faces*, Beirut 1981)," in *Martyrdom in Literature: Visions of Death and Meaningful Suffering in Europe and the Middle East from Antiquity to Modernity*, ed. Friederike Pannewick (Wiesbaden: Reichert Verlag, 2004), 346; and Mona Takieddine Amyuni, "Between Reality and Myth: Ilyās Khūrī's Wounded Beirut," in *Myths, Historical Archetypes and Symbolic Figures in Arabic Literature: Towards a New Hermeneutic*

*Approach*, Proceedings of the International Symposium in Beirut, June 25–30, 1996, Orient-Institut der Deutschen Morgenländischen Gesellschaft (Stuttgart: Steiner, 1999), 609.

9. I borrow the phrase "model peasants" from Omnia El Shakry, *The Great Social Laboratory* (Stanford, CA: Stanford University Press, 2007), 123–32.

10. Goldschmidt, "Ghanim, Fathi," in *Biographical Dictionary of Modern Egypt*, 63; Ami Elad, "Ideology and Structure in Fatḥī Ghānim's 'Al-Jabal,'" *Journal of Arabic Literature* 20, no. 2 (1989): 168.

11. Kees van der Spek, *The Modern Neighbors of Tutankhamun: History, Life, and Work in the Villages of the Theban West Bank* (Cairo: American University in Cairo Press, 2011).

12. James Steele, *An Architecture for the People: The Complete Works of Hassan Fathy* (New York: Whitney Library of Design, 1997), 61–62. For a critique of the portrait of the Gurnawis as lawless "tomb robbers"—a portrait that the Egyptian architect Hassan Fathy paints and that his sympathetic critics (including Steele) repeat—see van der Spek, *Modern Neighbors*, 20–23 passim; and Mitchell, *Rule of Experts*, 200–203.

13. On Bahtim village as rural rehabilitation, see El Shakry, *The Great Social Laboratory*, 125–32.

14. Fathy chronicles the origins, plans, and ultimate failure of the model village at New Gurna in his book *Architecture for the Poor: An Experiment in Rural Egypt* (Chicago: University of Chicago Press, 1979), originally published as *Gourna: A Tale of Two Villages* by the Egyptian Ministry of Culture in 1969. For largely sympathetic accounts of Fathy's life and work from art and architecture historians in the 1980s, see James Steele, *Architecture for the People*, 61–89, and *Hassan Fathy* (London: Academy Editions, 1988); and J. M. Richards, Ismail Serageldin, and Darl Rastorfer, *Hassan Fathy* (London: Mimar, 1985). For a history of Fathy's reception and his legacy, see Panayiota Pyla, "The Many Lives of New Gourna: Alternative Histories of a Model Community and Their Current Significance," *Journal of Architecture* 14, no. 6 (2009): 715–30. For three critical historical accounts, see El Shakry, *Social Laboratory*, 123–32; Mitchell, *Rule of Experts*, 179–205; and Mohamed Elshahed, "Hassan Fathy: Architecture for the Rich," *Cairobserver*, January 6, 2013, http://cairobserver.com/post/39866891829/hassan-fathy-architecture-for-the-rich.

15. Fathy, *Architecture for the Poor*, 176.

16. Fathy, *Architecture for the Poor*, 178.

17. I translate Ghanim's *muhandis* (literally, "engineer") as "architect," because it is more in line with this character's actual role and with Hassan Fathy's real-life career. As in other works of Egyptian village fiction, representatives of the government—including the deputy prosecutor, the princess, the architect, and the investigations director at the Ministry of Education—remain unnamed in *al-Jabal*.

18. "The performing of the nation required that every one of its rural inhabitants be declared outside the nation, uncivilized and unhygienic, so that in rendering them civilized and clean, the nation could be made" (Mitchell, *Rule of Experts*, 192).

19. Fathy, *Architecture for the Poor*, 187.

20. Howard Carter and A. C. Mace, *The Tomb of Tut.Ankh.Amen, Discovered by the Late Earl of Carnarvon and Howard Carter* (London: Cassell, 1923–33).

21. See Colla, *Conflicted Antiquities*, 15–16, 35–41; van der Spek, *Modern Neighbors of Tutankhamun;* Mitchell, "Heritage and Violence," in *Rule of Experts*, 147–67; El Shakry, *The Great Social Laboratory*, 131–32.

22. van der Spek, *Modern Neighbors*, 20–25.

23. van der Spek, *Modern Neighbors*, 30–31.

24. van der Spek, *Modern Neighbors*, 35.

25. Colla, *Conflicted Antiquities*, 15–16, 37–40.

26. van der Spek, *Modern Neighbors;* Mitchell, *Rule of Experts*, 196–205.

27. El Shakry, *The Great Social Laboratory*, 198.

28. El Shakry, *The Great Social Laboratory*, 91.

29. El Shakry, *The Great Social Laboratory*, 125.

30. Fathi Ghanim, *al-Jabal* (Cairo: Riwayāt al-Hilāl), 37, hereafter cited parenthetically in-text with the abbreviation *J* followed by page number(s).

31. Elshahed, "Architecture for the Rich."

32. Husayn ʿId, *Fatḥī Ghānim, al-Ḥayāt wa-l-Ibdāʿ* (Cairo: al-Hayʾah al-ʿĀmmah li-Quṣūr al-Thaqāfah, 1995), 28–29.

33. ʿId, *Fatḥī Ghānim*, 15–16.

34. Laleh Khalili, "Heroic and Tragic Pasts: Mnemonic Narratives in the Palestinian Refugee Camps," *Critical Sociology* 33 (2007): 735. On the dating and social history of the Palestinian Revolution or *Thawrah*, see also Laleh Khalili, *Heroes and Martyrs of Palestine: The Politics of National Commemoration* (Cambridge: Cambridge University Press, 2009), 7; and Rosemary Sayigh, *The Palestinians: From Peasants to Revolutionaries, a People's History* (London: Zed Press, 1979).

35. Khalili, *Heroes and Martyrs*, 2.

36. Khalili, *Heroes and Martyrs*, 112–49.

37. Khalili, *Heroes and Martyrs*, 39.

38. Lucia Volk, *Memorials and Martyrs in Modern Lebanon* (Bloomington: Indiana University Press, 2010), 8.

39. Several studies have examined the processes by which slain political leaders such as Rafiq al-Hariri, Bashir al-Gemayel, and others have been transformed into martyrs, as well as the effects of this transformation on postwar Lebanese public discourse. See, for example, Are John Knudsen, "Death of a Statesman—Birth of a Martyr: Martyrdom and Memorials in Post-Civil War Lebanon," *Anthropology of the Middle East* 11, no. 2 (2016): 1–17; Sune Haugbolle, "The Secular Saint: Iconography and Ideology in the Cult of Bashir Jumayil," in *Politics of Worship in the Contemporary Middle East*, ed. A. Bandak and M. Bille (Leiden: E. J. Brill, 2013): 191–212; and Ward Vloeberghs, "Worshipping the Martyr-President: The *darīh* of Rafiq Hariri in Beirut," in *Ethnographies of Islam: Ritual Performances and Everyday Practices*, ed. P. G. Pinto, B. Dupre, and K. Spellman-Poots (Edinburgh: Edinburgh University Press, 2012), 80–93. Khalili also notes how Palestinian cultural figures such as Ghassan Kanafani and Naji al-ʿAli were granted martyr status in the context of Lebanese Palestinian refugee camps. See *Heroes and Martyrs*, 131–40.

40. Khalili points out that, "whether explicitly or not, the celebration of heroic figures—the fida'iyyin and martyrs—was woven into the infrastructure of service-provision" by the PLO (*Heroes and Martyrs*, 48).

41. Khoury enlisted with the PLO in Jordan in 1967 but left the ranks of the fedayeen and returned to Beirut following the events of Black September. After completing a dissertation on the 1860 Lebanese conflict in Paris, he worked alongside Mahmoud Darwish as an editor with the journal *Shuʾūn Filasṭīniyyah*.

42. Elias Khoury, *White Masks*, trans. Maia Tabet (Brooklyn: Archipelago Books, 2010), 101; Khoury, *al-Wujūh al-Bayḍā*ʾ, 3rd ed. (Beirut: Dār al-Ādāb, 2003), 110. Hereafter, I will give in-text parenthetical citations for Tabet's translation and Khoury's Arabic original as *WM* and *WB*, respectively, followed by page number(s).

43. Khalili, *Heroes and Martyrs*, 31.

44. The story parallels a tragedy Khoury himself suffered on Mount Sannine while fighting with the students' battalion of Fatah. "On Sannin one of my closest friends Muhammad Shbaru died. I dedicated my novel *al-Jabal al-Ṣaghīr* (*The Little Mountain*) to his memory. In my novel, I gave him the name Talal. And Talal became the name of my son, who was born a few months after his death" (Khoury, "Conversations," 132). Talal is also the name of Fahd's closest friend and comrade-in-arms in *White Masks*; he frequently visits his grave, and converses with him even after death. See Khoury, *Wujūh*, 243–45.

45. Robert Fisk, *Pity the Nation: The Abduction of Lebanon* (New York: Nation Books, 2002), 85–86.

46. Of this incident, Fisk writes: "They lay there for days, the long dead, skeletons and withered cadavers still dressed in the nineteenth-century Sunday best in which they had been buried before mandate Palestine even existed" (Fisk, *Pity the Nation*, 100).

47. Fisk, *Pity the Nation*, 99–100; Fawwaz Traboulsi, *A History of Modern Lebanon* (London: Pluto Press, 2007), 192–93.

48. Khoury, "Conversations," 133.

49. Khoury, "Conversations," 134.

50. Khoury, "al-Kitābah wa-l-Mawt" (Writing and death), in *Zaman al-Iḥtilāl* (The time of occupation) (Beirut: Muʾassasat al-Abḥāth al-ʿArabiyyah, 1985), 253.

51. In Arabic: Anā huwa alladhī yantaẓir lā shayʾ. Anā huwa alladhī yantaẓir kull shayʾ.

52. Khoury, "Conversations," 134.

53. Mejcher-Atassi, "The Martyr and his Image," 353.

54. Elad, "Ideology and Structure," 170.

55. Elad, "Ideology and Structure," 185.

56. Ghanim does not specify to which exact princess of Egypt the text refers. If we follow Elad's reading and presume that the novel is set in 1947, the princess is most likely one of the daughters of King Fuʾad I, either Faʾizah, Faʾiqah, Fathiyyah, Fawziyyah, or Fawqiyyah. Ghanim does mention that she is the "sister of the King" (69), i.e., King Faruq.

57. The ʿUmdah's speech is only one in a series of instances, throughout the novel, where Ghanim interrupts literary Arabic with specifically Ṣaʿīdī (Upper Egyptian) dialect. See Elad, "Ideology and Structure," 183.

58. Elad, "Ideology and Structure," 173

59. The Khawagayya, the wife of a French archaeologist who uses her exploitative romantic relationship with Husayn to secure antiquities for her own private collection, stands as an interesting counterpoint to the figure of the architect in the novel. The Architect, though Egyptian, wants to bring modernity, progress, and development (albeit his own "vernacular" version of these things) to the villagers; the Khawagayya, though European, wants to preserve the villagers as they are, pristine and untouched by the corrupting forces of civilization. See Elad, "Ideology and Structure," 177.

60. See the following works by Pierre Cachia: *Popular Narrative Ballads*, 29–30; "The Egyptian 'Mawwāl': Its Ancestry, Its Development, and its Present Forms," *JAL* 8 (1977): 77–103; and *Exploring Arab Folk Literature* (Edinburgh: Edinburgh University Press, 2011).

61. In the part I have redacted here, Ghanim relates to the reader in formal Arabic the story which Abu Laylah (the Gurnawi singer) is about to tell the narrator in Upper Egyptian Arabic (italicized in the citation). He translates, in other words, the colloquial Upper Egyptian of the poem into literary prose for the reader.

62. The ballad, from around the turn of the twentieth century, tells of a peasant woman, Bahiyyah, whose lover Yasin was killed by camel-riding Sudanese warriors while serving as an Egyptian conscript in Lord Kitchener's 1898 campaign in the Sudan. Bahiyyah must bear witness to the murder in court, but she is distressed at the miscarriage of justice when her lover's murderers receive such a light sentence (only four years in prison). See Cachia, *Exploring Arab Folk Literature*, 205. The *mawwāl* of Bahiyyah and Yasin has had a long afterlife. In the mid-1960s, the playwright Najib Surur turned it into a verse novel and series of plays in the Egyptian dialect. See Najib Surur, *Yāsīn wa Bahiyyah: Riwāyah Shiʿriyyah* (Cairo: Majallat al-Masraḥ, 1965) and Cachia, "Folk Themes in the Works of Najib Surur," in *Exploring Arab Folk Literature*, 203–13. It has also been sung by the famous and prolific folk performer Muhammad Taha. See, for example, "Yā Bahiyyah wa-Khabbirīnī . . . Muḥammad Ṭāhā," Hani Farid, July 13, 2021, YouTube video, 3:45, https://www.youtube.com/watch?v=nFa8h9tQU84.

63. Larkin, "Brigand Hero," 49.

64. Roger Allen, "Literary History and the Arabic Novel," *World Literature Today* 75, no. 2 (2001): 212.

65. Ibn Manzur, *Lisān al-ʿArab*, s.v. *q-ṣ-ṣ*, https://ejtaal.net/.

66. Lutz Berger, "Aphorism," in *EI3*, ed. Kate Fleet, Gudrun Krämer, Denis Matringe, John Nawas, and Devin J. Stewart, http://dx.doi.org/10.1163/1573-3912_ei3_COM_22773.

67. See, for example, the frequently repeated phrase: "We have propounded for men, in this Qurʾan, every kind of parable. [Wa la-qad ḍarabnā li-l-nās fī hādhā al-Qurʾān min kull mathal]" (Qurʾan 17:89, 18:54, 30:58, 39:27).

68. For an introduction to and translation of many of these deeply revered sayings, see ʿAli ibn Abi Talib, al-Jahiz, and al-Qadi al-Qudaʿi, *A Treasury of Virtues: Sayings, Sermons, and Teachings of ʿAlī Al-Qāḍī al-Quḍāʿi: With the One Hundred Proverbs Attributed to Al-Jāḥiẓ*, trans. Tahera Qutbuddin, Library of Arabic Literature (New York: New York University Press, 2013).

69. Berger, "Aphorism," *EI3*.

70. Here I offer a rather clunky literal translation of this passage that contrasts with Maia Tabet's sleeker version in *White Masks*. Tabet's translation leaves out the proverbs that do not have a clear English equivalent, and it does not retain Khoury's line breaks, instead grouping the proverbs into a single paragraph. My retranslation is meant to illustrate the plodding, repetitive, almost comic effect of Khoury's piled-up proverbs. I relied heavily on Anis Freyha's *Dictionary of Modern Lebanese Proverbs* (Beirut: Librairie du Liban, 1974).

71. This is as true in the Arabic script as in my English translation above:

وإلى آخره، إلى آخره، إلى آخره، إلى آخره، إلى آخره، إلى آخره، إلى آخره، إلى آخره، إلى آخره، إلى
آخره، إلى آ . . . خـ . . . ر . . . ه . . .

72. Traboulsi, *A History of Modern Lebanon*, 183.

73. Amyuni, "Between Reality and Myth," 607.

74. I have drastically excerpted the passage, which spans an entire page.

75. Selim, *Rural Imaginary*, 127–58.

76. On heroic literary portrayals of the fedayee in Palestinian literature around 1967, see Halabi, "The Day the Wandering Dreamer Became a Fida'i," 164–66; and Khalid A. Sulaiman, *Palestine and Modern Arab Poetry* (London: Zed, 1984), 139–48.

## 5. EPIC FAILS: SONALLAH IBRAHIM'S MODERN MYTHS OF SEEKING

1. Quoted in Mehrez, "Sonallah Ibrahim's *Dhat*," 130.

2. Paul Starkey, *Sonallah Ibrahim: Rebel With a Pen* (Edinburgh: Edinburgh University Press, 2016).

3. Elliott Colla, "Revolution on Ice," review of *al-Jalīd*, by Sonallah Ibrahim, *Jadaliyya*, January 6, 2014, https://www.jadaliyya.com/Details/30039/Revolution-on-Ice.

4. Creswell, "Sonallah Ibrahim: Egypt's Oracular Novelist," *New Yorker*, August 20, 2013.

5. Negar Azimi, "Curb Your Enthusiasm: Sonallah Ibrahim's Cranky Elegy for the Left," review of *Ice*, by Sonallah Ibrahim, trans. Margaret Litvin, *Bookforum*, December/January 2020, https://www.bookforum.com/print/2604/sonallah-ibrahim-s-cranky-elegy-for-the-left-23739.

6. Ursula Lindsey, "Sonallah Ibrahim, Taking Stock," *Arabist*, June 25, 2010, https://arabist.net/blog/2010/6/25/sonallah-ibrahim-taking-stock.html.

7. Jonathan Guyer, *The Strange Case of the Arab Whodunit*, produced by Sean Glynn and David Waters, BBC Radio 4, November 16, 2017, https://www.bbc.co.uk/sounds/play/b09f2cxy.

8. Sonallah Ibrahim, *al-Lajnah*, 9th printing (Cairo: Dār al-Mustaqbal al-ʿArabī, 2004), 77 (hereafter abbreviated *L* and cited in-text).

9. Sonallah Ibrahim, *The Committee*, trans. Mary St. Germain and Charlene Constable (Syracuse, NY: Syracuse University Press, 2001), 127–30 (hereafter abbreviated *C* and cited in-text).

10. Benjamin Koerber, *Conspiracy in Modern Egyptian Literature* (Edinburgh: Edinburgh University Press, 2018), 100, 107, 115.

11. Ibrahim, quoted in Guyer, *Strange Case*.

12. By "historical-materialist investigation," I mean an approach to history that prioritizes the relations of production, which are necessarily social, as the ultimate (but not the only) determining factor of historical change. See Friedrich Engels, "Letter to J. Bloch, In Königsberg," https://www.marxists.org/archive/marx/works/1890/letters/90_09_21.htm; and Karl Marx, "Preface to A Contribution to the Critique of Political Economy," https://www.marxists.org/archive/marx/works/1859/critique-pol-economy/preface.htm#eb1.

13. Theodor Adorno, "On Lyric Poetry and Society," in *Notes to Literature*, vol. 1, ed. Rolf Tiedemann, trans. Shierry Weber Nicholsen (New York: Columbia University Press, 1991), 39.

14. See the short story "Arsīn Lūbīn" in Ibrahim's collection *Tilka al-Rāʾiḥah*, 4th printing (Minyā: Dār al-Hudā li-l-Nashr wa-l-Tawzīʿ, 2009), 91–98, and my translation of this story in *ArabLit Quarterly* 3, no. 2 (2020): 68–71.

15. Raymond Chandler, "The Simple Art of Murder," in *The Simple Art of Murder* (New York: Vintage Books, 1988), 10.

16. Chandler, "Simple Art of Murder," 11.

17. Chandler, "Simple Art of Murder," 14.

18. Chandler, "Simple Art of Murder," 17. The last sentence bears a striking resemblance to the narrator's impassioned denunciation of the Egyptian legal system in Tawfiq al-Hakim's *Diary of a Country Prosecutor*.

19. The private eye is, indeed, always a "he" in Chandler, as in many works of classic American noir. On the rise of female detectives in American and British noir in the nineteen-eighties, see Sally Munt, *Murder by the Book? Feminism and the Crime Novel* (London: Routledge, 1994); and Priscilla L. Walton and Manina Jones, *Detective Agency: Women Rewriting the Hard-Boiled Tradition* (Berkeley: University of California Press, 1999).

20. Chandler, "Simple Art of Murder," 18 (emphasis added).

21. Chesterton, "Defense."

22. For the full list, see Ibrahim, *al-Lajnah*, 81. Note that in their translation, St. Germain and Constable leave out Ho Chi Minh, as well the prominent anti-imperialist Arab figures Mehdi Ben Barka (head of the left-wing Moroccan National Union of Popular Forces, who was disappeared in 1965; they render the name as "Ibn Baraka"), Ahmed Ben Bella (the Algerian nationalist fighter who became that country's first president after it won independence from the French), and Farajallah el-Helou (the onetime leader of the Lebanese Communist Party).

23. Before he was recognized as the Prophet, Muhammad was seen as an eccentric challenging the religiously premised political power of the Meccan elite. The early Islamic figures Abu Dharr al-Ghifari and Abu Saʿid al-Jannabi have both been read by modern thinkers (especially Ali Shariati) as early proponents of socialist governance, and Ho Chi Minh, Fidel Castro, Che Guevara, and Patrice Lumumba are some of the most well-recognized Third-World anticolonial inheritors of Karl Marx and Vladimir Lenin. Ibn Rushd (a.k.a. Averroes) was a renegade proponent of Aristotelian logic and philosophy in an Andalusian world dominated by the theology of al-Ghazali, just as the Alsatian reverend Albert Schweitzer revealed the fictionality of "life-of-Jesus" narratives by historicizing them. The Moroccan Mehdi Ben Barka, the Algerian Ahmed Ben Bella, the Lebanese Farajallah el-Helou, and the Egyptian Shuhdi Atiya, were all prominent Arab leftists or communists.

24. On the history of "totality" as a concept and its relation to continental philosophy generally, see Martin Jay, *Marxism and Totality: The Adventures of a Concept from Lukács to Habermas* (Berkeley: University of California Press, 1984).

25. Georg Lukács, "The Standpoint of the Proletariat," in *History and Class Consciousness*, https://www.marxists.org/archive/lukacs/works/history/hcc07_1.htm.

26. Lukács, "The Standpoint of the Proletariat." While the narrator of *The Committee* does not refer directly either to "capitalists" or "the proletariat," he nevertheless notes that the Committee members "belong to worlds different from my own, and their lives run along independent courses completely unaffected by the result of the encounter taking place between me and them—the complete opposite of what is true for me" (*L* 119).

27. This is the first line of chapter 1 in Karl Marx and Friedrich Engels's *Manifesto of the Communist Party*, https://www.marxists.org/archive/marx/works/1848/communist-manifesto/ch01.htm#a2.

28. Here I give a literal translation of Mayakovsky from Ibrahim's Arabic into English, rather than the published English translation of Mayakovsky's lines that Mary St. Germain and Charlene Constable include in their translation.

29. This denunciation is especially evident in late plays such as *The Bedbug* and *The Bathhouse* (both from 1929). See Edward J. Brown, *Mayakovsky: A Poet in the Revolution* (Princeton, NJ: Princeton University Press, 1973).

30. See Brown's analysis of these lines in *Mayakovsky*, 352–57.

31. Brown, *Mayakovsky*, 357; Vladimir Mayakovsky, "At the Top of My Voice," trans. Max Hayward and George Reavey (New York: Meridian Books, 1960), https://www.marxists.org/subject/art/literature/mayakovsky/1930/at-top-my-voice.htm. Yuri Slezkine also notes that "the future was best described by Mayakovsky" in *The Bedbug* and *The Bathhouse*. See Yuri Slezkine, *The House of Government* (Princeton, NJ: Princeton University Press, 2017), 271.

32. For this reading of Ibrahim's novella, see Koerber, *Conspiracy*, 97.

33. If it is possible to view the narrator's method as "paranoid," in accordance with Sedgwick's use of this term, I believe it is the positive, "enabling," and "energizing" force of paranoia highlighted by Heather Love at work here. See Heather Love, "Truth and Consequences: On Paranoid Reading and Reparative Reading," *Criticism* 52, no. 2 (2010): 235–41.

34. See Rita Felski, *The Limits of Critique* (Chicago: University of Chicago Press, 2015) (especially chapter 3, "An Inspector Calls"); Eve Sedgwick, "Paranoid Reading and Reparative Reading, or You're So Paranoid, You Probably Think This Essay is About You," in *Touching Feeling: Affect, Pedagogy, Performativity* (Durham, NC: Duke University Press, 2003); and Koerber, *Conspiracy*.

35. Irene Angelico, dir. *The Cola Conquest, 2: How Coca-Cola Took over the World.* (London: TV Choice Limited; Infobase, 2016) (emphasis added).

36. Thomas Oliver, *The Real Coke, the Real Story* (New York: Random House, 1986), 37, 59 (emphasis added). See also "Coca-Cola may buy Aqua-Chem," *Chemical and Engineering News*, February 2, 1970, https://pubs.acs.org/doi/abs/10.1021/cen-v048n005.p017.

37. Henry J. Frundt, *Refreshing Pauses: Coca-Cola and Human Rights in Guatemala* (New York: Praeger, 1987).

38. "Coca-Cola Aids Egyptian Project," *Jewish Telegraphic Agency*, November 16, 1977, https://www.jta.org/1977/11/16/archive/coca-cola-aids-egyptian-project. See also Jessica Mitford, "Egyptomania: Tut, Mut, and the Rest of the Gang," in *Poison Penmanship: The Gentle Art of Muckraking* (New York: Knopf, 1979), 247. Mitford writes of her travels to Upper Egypt with James Manning, an archaeologist involved in "the Brooklyn Museum expedition financed by the Coca-Cola Company, excavating the precinct of Mut at Luxor."

39. Frundt, *Refreshing Pauses*, 30.

40. See "Chavez Signs Florida's First Farm Pact," *New York Times*, March 1, 1972; and Philip Shabecoff, "Life Improves for Florida's Orange Harvesters," *New York Times*, March 19, 1973. See also Edward R. Murrow, 1960: "Harvest of Shame," produced by David Lowe, CBS Reports, CBS News, uploaded November 24, 2010, YouTube video, 52:05, https://www.youtube.com/watch?v=yJTVF_dya7E.

41. The formation of this Senate committee was spurred, in part, by Murrow's "Harvest of Shame."

42. Frundt, *Refreshing Pauses*, 30.

43. "Mondale Says Migrant Labor Gained Little Through Congress," *New York Times*, March 22, 1971.

44. On Austin and Mondale as members of the Trilateral Commission, see Holly Sklar, ed. *Trilateralism: The Trilateral Commission and Elite Planning for World Management* (Boston: South End Press, 1980).

45. Koerber, *Conspiracy*, 106–7.

46. One harrowing (albeit fictionalized) account of the Coca-Cola bottle as instrument of rape in the torture of detainees can be found in Elias Khoury, *Yalo*, trans. Peter Theroux (New York: Picador, 2008).

47. A more literal translation would be that the vendor "heals" them with the bottles (*yu ʿālijuhum*), but the religious undertones of St. Germain and Constable's "minister" feel appropriate here, given the mystical "state" (*ḥāl*) in which the vendor finds himself. See Ibrahim, *The Committee*, 137.

48. Here too Ibrahim is connecting large-scale economic and political transformations with the everyday lives of ordinary Egyptians: Zeinab Abul-Magd has noted how, during the 1980s, the Egyptian military repurposed the national automotive sector for quasi-private, quasi-military enterprise. Owning a private vehicle had become "another mark of social mobility and prestige," and thus private cars like those the narrator describes "flooded the already overcrowded streets of Cairo," in the seventies and eighties, "rushing against cheap and decaying public transportation inherited from socialist times." See Zeinab Abul-Magd, *Militarizing the Nation: The Army, Business, and Revolution in Egypt* (New York: Columbia University Press, 2017), 98.

49. Mayakovsky, "At the Top of My Voice."

50. Here I borrow from Mehrez in referring to the novel's even-numbered chapters as "docufictional" and its odd-numbered ones as "narrative."

51. Sonallah Ibrahim, *Dhāt*, 4th printing (Cairo: Dar al-Mustaqbal al-ʿArabiyy, 2003), 7 (hereafter cited parenthetically in text, abbreviated *Dh*).

52. On the inexorable linearity of reading, Gérard Genette writes: "One can run a film backwards, image by image, but one cannot read a text backwards, letter by letter, or even word by word, or even sentence by sentence, without its ceasing to be a text" (Genette, *Narrative Discourse*, 34).

53. Here I am diverging slightly from Yoav Di-Capua's argument that "by exiling the cynical, cruel, and overall traumatic circumstances of his protagonists to sealed chapters where they lie beyond the reach of these events, Ibrāhīm blocks the possibility of historical being" (87). Though it may be true that historical being is blocked for the novel's characters, the position into which the novel's structure summons its reader makes precisely this form of being possible. See Yoav Di-Capua, "The Traumatic Subjectivity of Ṣunʿ Āllāh Ibrāhīm's Dhāt," *JAL* 43, no. 1 (2012): 80–101.

54. Sonallah Ibrahim, *Zaat*, trans. Anthony Calderbank (Cairo: American University in Cairo Press, 2001), 153 (hereafter cited in text with the abbreviation *Z*).

55. Ibrahim obliquely references a 1980s-era television advertisement for ceramic bathroom fixtures that made a strong impression on many Egyptians by encouraging them to "destroy your old bathroom!" (Insif ḥammaamak al-ʾadeemah) over footage of a bathroom being exploded with dynamite. The expression entered the colloquial Egyptian lexicon and

is still used in conversations about reform and modernization. See Dina Hussein, "'Zaat' and her Bathroom—and Television," *Mada Masr*, August 7, 2013, https://madamasr.com/en/2013/08/07/feature/culture/zaat-and-her-bathroom-and-television/.

56. de Man, "Anthropomorphism," 250.

57. Scott, *Conscripts*, 8.

58. The *sīrah* (pl. *siyar*) is an oral Arabic folk genre that combines qualities of Greek "epic," Old Norse "sagas," and medieval European "romance." See Melanie Magidow, "Epic of the Commander Dhat al-Himma," *Medieval Feminist Forum: A Journal of Gender and Sexuality* 9 (2018): 5. For more on the genre, see Dwight Reynolds, *Heroic Poets, Poetic Heroes: The Ethnography of Performance in an Arabic Oral Epic Tradition* (Ithaca, NY: Cornell University Press, 1995); Faruq Khurshid, *al-Siyar al-Shaʿbiyyah* (Cairo: Dār al-Maʿārif, 1978); M. C. Lyons, *The Arabian Epic: Heroic and Oral Storytelling*, (Cambridge: Cambridge University Press, 1995).

59. For all these generic and performance characteristics of the *sīrah* genre, see Magidow, "Epic," 5–14.

60. Lyons, *The Arabian Epic*, 1:62.

61. "Himmat" is also the other half of the folk heroine's name, Dhāt al-Himmah—literally, "a woman on a mission."

62. Magidow, "Epic," 11–12.

63. These are all possible connotations of *salīmah*.

64. Adorno, "Lyric Poetry," 43, 40.

65. Adorno, "Lyric Poetry," 42.

66. The scandal of "what happened to Adawiya at the hands of the Kuwaiti prince" refers to a story involving the Egyptian popular music icon Ahmad ʿAdawiyyah, who, on June 30, 1989, was found in a coma at the Marriott Hotel in Zamalek, in the room of Talal ibn Nasir al-Sabah, a Kuwaiti prince. Medical and police reports later found that ʿAdawiyyah (who was not the picture of health to begin with) had apparently overdosed on heroin, morphine, and codeine. (Sabah was arrested on drug trafficking charges many years later.) But, as the tabloids reported for several days on his mysterious coma, popular gossip quickly created the juiciest possible explanation: ʿAdawiyyah had been having an affair with one of the Kuwaiti prince's relatives, and in revenge the Prince had drugged ʿAdawiyyah to castrate him in his sleep. Regardless of its truth or untruth, that the Egyptian public could imagine a Kuwaiti prince being simultaneously so brutal and so completely above the law reveals the role of the Gulf States and Gulf money in Egypt around this time. See "Arshīf ʿAdawiyyah," Medina Portal, accessed July 14, 2023, https://www.medinaportal.com/series_cat/adw/.

67. Arthur Goldschmidt, *Modern Egypt: The Formation of a Nation-State*, 2nd ed. (New York: Routledge, 2018), 154–61.

68. Mayakovsky, "At the Top of My Voice."

## EPILOGUE: MONSTROUS OMNISCIENCE

1. Ahmed Saadawi, *Frankenstein in Baghdad*, trans. Jonathan Wright (New York: Penguin Books, 2018), 214, hereafter cited in-text with the abbreviation *F*.

2. The novel's prologue and concluding chapters suggest that the narrative we are about to read was composed by a man referred to only as "the author" (*al-muʾallif*) based on

"material contained in documents belonging to the Tracking and Pursuit Department," a fictional branch of the Iraqi secret police. The description of the narrative found in the author's possession—"about 250 pages long, divided into seventeen chapters"—almost matches the structure of *Frankenstein in Baghdad* itself. Nevertheless, with a few exceptions (e.g., the Whatsitsname's tape-recorded monologue in chapter 10), the chapters that follow are not compiled like reports in a police file or research dossier (as in Jabra's *Walid Masoud*, Khoury's *White Masks*, or al-Qaʿid's *Yaḥduth*) but told from the perspective of an omniscient narrator, darting in and out of the various characters' minds.

3. Saadawi, *Frankenstein*, 71.

4. Rebecca Walkowitz, *Born Translated: The Contemporary Novel in an Age of World Literature* (New York: Columbia University Press, 2015).

5. The transition into Hadi's perspective is also typical of Saadawi's omniscient style: "Abu Salim may have left the hospital, but someone else from Lane 7 had to stay rather longer—Hadi the junk dealer" (Saadawi, *Frankenstein*, 266–67).

6. "[The Whatsitsname] didn't want to perish without understanding why he was dying and where he would go after death, so he clung to life, maybe even more than others . . ." (Saadawi, *Frankenstein*, 267–68).

7. Selim, *The Novel and the Rural Imaginary in Egypt*, 10–16.

8. al-Qaʿid, *Yaḥduth*, 9, 170.

9. Jason M. Baskin, "Soft Eyes: Marxism, Surface, Depth," in *Mediations: Journal of the Marxist Literary Group* 28, no. 2 (2015): 13.

10. I am again building on Baskin's claims in "Soft Eyes" here, 13–14.

11. Spivak, *Death of a Discipline*, 15.

12. Edward Said, *Orientalism*, 25th anniversary edition (New York: Vintage, 1994), 24.

# BIBLIOGRAPHY

ʿAbd al-ʿAzim, Salih Sulayman. *Sūsiyūlūjiyā al-Riwāyah al-Siyāsiyyah: Yūsuf al-Qaʿīd Namūdhajan*. Cairo: al-Hayʾah al-Miṣriyyah al-ʿĀmmah li-l-Kitāb, 1998.

Abu ʿAwf, ʿAbd al-Rahman. *Yūsuf Idrīs wa ʿĀlamuhu fī al-Qiṣṣah al-Qaṣīrah wa-l-Riwāyah*. Cairo: al-Hayʾah al-Miṣriyyah li-l-Kitāb, 1994.

Abul-Magd, Zeinab. *Militarizing the Nation: The Army, Business, and Revolution in Egypt*. New York: Columbia University Press, 2017.

Adamson, Peter. "Existence in Philosophy and Theology." In *Encyclopaedia of Islam*, Edited by Kate Fleet, Gudrun Krämer, Denis Matringe, John Nawas, and Devin J. Stewart. 3rd ed.; online ed., 2017. https://referenceworks.brillonline.com/entries/encyclopaedia-of-islam-3/existence-in-philosophy-and-theology-COM_26265?s.num=0&s.f.s2_parent=s.f.book.encyclopaedia-of-islam-3&s.q=Existence+in+Philosophy+and+Theology.

Adorno, Theodor. "On Lyric Poetry and Society." In *Notes to Literature*, edited by Rolf Tiedemann, translated by Shierry Weber Nicholsen, 37–54. Vol. 1. New York: Columbia University Press, 1991.

Aghacy, Samira. *Masculine Identity in the Fiction of the Arab East Since 1967*. Syracuse, NY: Syracuse University Press, 2009.

Ahmed, Leila. *Women and Gender in Islam*. New Haven, CT: Yale University Press, 1992.

Allan, Michael. "Re-Reading the Arab Darwin: The Lewis Affair and Naguib Mahfouz's *Palace of Desire*." *Modernism/Modernity* 23, no. 2 (2016): 319–40.

Allen, Roger. *The Arabic Novel: An Historical and Critical Introduction*. 2nd ed. Syracuse, NY: Syracuse University Press, 1995.

———. "The Artistry of Yūsuf Idrīs." *World Literature Today* 55, no. 1 (1981): 43–47.

———. "The Happy Traitor: Tales of Translation." *Comparative Literature Studies* 47, no. 4 (2010): 472–86.

———. "Literary History and the Arabic Novel." *World Literature Today* 75, no. 2 (2001): 205–13.

———. "The Novels of Jabra and the Art of Translation." *Jusur* 7–8 (1996): 91–101.

———. "Teaching Mahfouz's 'Zaabalawi.'" In *Approaches to Teaching the Works of Naguib Mahfouz*, edited by Waïl S. Hassan and Susan Muaddi Darraj, 156–63. New York: Modern Language Association, 2012.

Amyuni, Mona Takieddine. "Between Reality and Myth: Ilyās Khūrī's Wounded Beirut." In *Myths, Historical Archetypes and Symbolic Figures in Arabic Literature: Towards a New Hermeneutic Approach*, 605–15. Proceedings of the International Symposium in Beirut, June 25–30, 1996. Orient-Institut der Deutschen Morgenländischen Gesellschaft. Stuttgart: Steiner, 1999.

Angelico, Irene, dir. *The Cola Conquest, 2: How Coca-Cola Took Over the World*. London: TV Choice Limited. Infobase, 2016.

Armitage, Anne. "The Debate Over Literary Writing in a Foreign Language: An Overview of Francophonie in the Maghreb." *Alif: Journal of Comparative Poetics* 20 (2000): 39–67.

"Arshīf ʿAdawiyyah." Medina Portal. Accessed July 14, 2023. https://www.medinaportal.com/series_cat/adw/.

Asad, Talal. "Conscripts of Western Civilization." In *Civilization in Crisis: Anthropological Perspectives*, vol. 1 of *Dialectical Anthropology: Essays in Honour of Stanley Diamond*, edited by Christine Ward Gailey, 334–351. Gainesville: University Press of Florida, 1992.

ʿAsfur, Muhammad. *Narjis wa-l-Marāyā: Dirāsah li-Kitābāt Jabrā Ibrāhīm Jabrā al-Ibdāʿiyyah*. Beirut: al-Muʾassasah al-ʿArabiyyah li-l-Dirāsāt wa-l-Nashr, 2009.

Azimi, Negar. "Curb Your Enthusiasm: Sonallah Ibrahim's Cranky Elegy for the Left." Review of *Ice*, by Sonallah Ibrahim. Translated by Margaret Litvin. *Bookforum*, December/January 2020. https://www.bookforum.com/print/2604/sonallah-ibrahim-s-cranky-elegy-for-the-left-23739.

al-ʿAzm, Sadiq Jalal. *al-Naqd al-Dhātī Baʿd al-Hazīmah*. Beirut: Dār al-Talīʿah, 1968.

Badawi, M. M. "A Passion for Experimentation: The Novels and Plays of Tawfiq al-Hakim." *Third World Quarterly* 10, no. 2 (1988): 949–60.

Baer, Gabriel. *A History of Landownership in Modern Egypt, 1800–1950*. Oxford: Oxford University Press, 1962.

Bakhtin, Mikhail. *The Dialogic Imagination*. Translated by Caryl Emerson and Michael Holquist. Austin: University of Texas Press, 1981.

Barakat, Halim. *The Arab World: Society, Culture, and State*. Berkeley: University of California Press, 1993.

Bardawil, Fadi. *Revolution and Disenchantment: Arab Marxism and the Binds of Emancipation.*, NC: Duke University Press, 2020.

Bashir, Izyad Bih Wuld Muhammad. *Tajdīd al-Riwāyah al-ʿArabiyyah: Yūsuf al-Qaʿīd Namūdhajan*. 1st printing. Cairo: al-Hayʾah al-ʿĀmmah li-Quṣūr al-Thaqāfah, 2006.

Baskin, Jason M. "Soft Eyes: Marxism, Surface, and Depth." *Mediations* 28, no. 2 (Spring 2015): 5–18.

Bawardi, Basilius and Alif Faranesh, "Non-Canonical Arabic Detective Fiction: The Beginnings of the Genre." *Journal of Arabic and Islamic Studies* 18 (2018): 23–49.

Bayyumi, Mustafa. *Al-Fallāḥ wa Muʾassasāt al-Sulṭah: Dirāsah fī Adab Yūsuf al-Qaʿīd*. Cairo: Dār al-Hudā, 2001.

Beard, Michael. "Homage to Ibn al-Fârid: Nostalgia in 'Zaabalawi.'" In *Approaches to Teaching the Works of Naguib Mahfouz*, edited by Waïl S. Hassan and Susan Muaddi Darraj, 164–70. New York: Modern Language Association of America, 2012.

Ben Jelloun, Tahar. *This Blinding Absence of Light*. Translated by Linda Coverdale. New York: Penguin, 2006.

Benjamin, Walter. "The Flâneur." In *Charles Baudelaire: A Lyric Poet in the Era of High Capitalism*, 35–66. Translated by Harry Zohn. London: New Left Books, 1973.

Berger, John. *Ways of Seeing*. London: BBC and Penguin Books, 1972.

Berger, Lutz. "Aphorism." In *Encyclopaedia of Islam*, edited by Kate Fleet, Gudrun Krämer, Denis Matringe, John Nawas, and Devin J. Stewart. 3rd ed.; online ed., 2009. http://dx.doi.org.ezproxy.lib.utexas.edu/10.1163/1573-3912_ei3_COM_22773>.

Booth, Marilyn, ed. *Harem Histories: Envisioning Places and Living Spaces*. Durham, NC: Duke University Press, 2010.

Borges, Jorge Luis. "The Homeric Versions." Translated by Eliot Weinberger. In *Selected Non-Fictions*, 69–74. New York: Penguin Books, 2000.

Boullata, Issa J. "Living with the Tigress and the Muses: An Essay on Jabra Ibrahim Jabra." *World Literature Today* 75, no. 2 (2001): 214–23.

Bray, Julia. "Al Mu'tasim's 'Bridge of Toil' and Abu Tammam's Amorium Qasida." In *Studies in Islamic and Middle Eastern Texts and Traditions in Memory of Norman Calder*, edited by G. R. Hawting, J. A. Mojaddedi, and A. Samely, 31–73. Oxford.: Oxford University Press, 2000.

Brooks, Peter. *Reading for the Plot: Design and Intention in Narrative*. Cambridge, MA: Harvard University Press, 1984.

Brown, Edward J. *Mayakovsky: A Poet in the Revolution*. Princeton, NJ: Princeton University Press, 1973.

Butler, Judith. *Gender Trouble: Feminism and the Subversion of Identity*. New York: Routledge, 2006.

Cachia, Pierre. "The Egyptian 'Mawwāl': Its Ancestry, Its Development, and Its Present Forms." *Journal of Arabic Literature* 8 (1977): 77–103.

———. *Exploring Arab Folk Literature*. Edinburgh: Edinburgh University Press, 2011.

———. "Idealism and Ideology: The Case of Tawfiq al-Ḥakīm." *Journal of the American Oriental Society* 100, no. 3 (1980): 225–35.

———. *An Overview of Arabic Literature*. Edinburgh: Edinburgh University Press, 1990.

———. *Popular Narrative Ballads of Modern Egypt*. Oxford and New York: Oxford University Press, 1989.

Carter, Howard, and A. C. Mace. *The Tomb of Tut.Ankh.Amen, Discovered by the Late Earl of Carnarvon and Howard Carter*. London: Cassell, 1923–33.

Censi, Martina. *Le corps dans le roman des écrivaines Syriennes contemporaines: dire, écrire, inscrire la différence*. Leiden: E. J. Brill, 2016.

Chandler, Raymond. "The Simple Art of Murder." In *The Simple Art of Murder*. 1–18. New York: Vintage, 1988.

Chesterton, G. K. "A Defence of Detective Stories." In *The Art of the Mystery Story: A Collection of Critical Essays*, edited by Howard Haycraft, 3–6. New York: Simon & Schuster, 1946.

Chittick, William C. *The Sufi Path of Knowledge: Ibn al-'Arabi's Metaphysics of the Imagination*. Albany, NY: State University of New York Press, 1989.

Chraïbi, Driss. *Une enquête au pays*. Paris: Seuil, 1981.

Chraïbi, Driss. *Flutes of Death*. Translated by Robin Roosevelt. Boulder, CO: Lynne Rienner, 1996.

Christie, Agatha. *Death on the Nile*. New York: Dodd, Mead, 1970.

"Coca-Cola Aids Egyptian Project." *Jewish Telegraphic Agency*, November 16, 1977. https://www.jta.org/1977/11/16/archive/coca-cola-aids-egyptian-project.

"Coca-Cola May Buy Aqua-Chem." *Chemical and Engineering News*, February 2, 1970. https://pubs.acs.org/doi/abs/10.1021/cen-v048n005.p017.

Coetzee, J. M. *Waiting for the Barbarians*. New York: Penguin Books, 1982.

Colla, Elliott. "Anxious Advocacy: The Novel, the Law, and Extrajudicial Appeals in Egypt." *Public Culture* 17, no. 3 (2005): 417–44.

———. *Conflicted Antiquities: Egyptology, Egyptomania, Egyptian Modernity*. Durham, NC: Duke University Press, 2007.

———. "Miramar and Postcolonial Melancholia." In *Approaches to Teaching the Works of Naguib Mahfouz*, edited by Waïl S. Hassan and Susan Muaddi Darraj, 171–83. New York: Modern Language Association Press, 2012.

———. "Revolution on Ice." Review of *al-Jalīd*, by Sonallah Ibrahim. *Jadaliyya*, January 6, 2014. https://www.jadaliyya.com/Details/30039/Revolution-on-Ice.

cooke, miriam. "Men Constructed in the Mirror of Prostitution." In *Naguib Mahfouz: From Regional Fame to Global Recognition*, edited by Michael Beard and Adnan Haydar, 106–25. Syracuse, NY: Syracuse University Press, 1993.

———. "Naguib Mahfouz: Review Article." Review of *The Search* and *Fountain and Tomb* by Naguib Mahfouz. *Middle East Journal* 43, no. 3 (1989): 507–11.

Cooperson, Michael. Introduction to al-Hariri, *Impostures*, xix–xxvii. Translated by Michael Cooperson. New York: New York University Press, 2020.

Creswell, Robyn. *City of Beginnings: Poetic Modernism in Beirut*. Princeton, NJ: Princeton University Press, 2019.

———. "Sonallah Ibrahim: Egypt's Oracular Novelist." *New Yorker*, August 20, 2013.

Crozier, Michel, Samuel P. Huntington, and Joji Watanuki. *The Crisis of Democracy: Report On the Governability of Democracies to the Trilateral Commission*. New York: New York University Press, 1975.

de Man, Paul. "Anthropomorphism and Trope in the Lyric." In *The Rhetoric of Romanticism*, 239–62. New York: Columbia University Press, 1984.

Di-Capua, Yoav. "The Traumatic Subjectivity of Ṣunʿ Allāh Ibrāhīm's Dhāt." *Journal of Arabic Literature* 43, no. 1 (2012): 80–101.

Diamond, Stanley. *In Search of the Primitive: A Critique of Civilization*. New Brunswick, NJ: E. P. Dutton/Transaction Books, 1974.

Drumsta, Emily. "An Epic of the Body and of Memory: Atavism and the Critique of Enlightenment in Driss Chraïbi's *Une Enquête au pays*." *Research in African Literatures* 50, no. 2 (2019): 198–218.

Elad, Ami. "Ideology and Structure in Fatḥī Ghānim's 'Al-Jabal." *Journal of Arabic Literature* 20, no. 2 (1989): 168–86.

El-Ariss, Tarek. *Trials of Arab Modernity: Literary Affects and the New Political*. New York: Fordham University Press, 2013.

———, ed. *The Arab Renaissance: A Bilingual Anthology of the Nahda*. New York: Modern Language Association, 2018.

———. *Leaks, Hacks, and Scandals: Arab Culture in the Digital Age*. Princeton, NJ: Princeton University Press, 2018.

El-Enany, Rasheed. *Naguib Mahfouz: The Pursuit of Meaning*. London: Routledge, 1993.

Elmarsafy, Ziad. *Sufism in the Contemporary Arabic Novel*. Edinburgh: Edinburgh University Press, 2012.

Elshahed, Mohamed (@cairobserver). "An art form of insult, *radaḥ* . . ." Instagram, August 19, 2022. https://www.instagram.com/p/ChcsSCBLsI9/?utm_source=ig_web_copy_link.

———. "Hassan Fathy: Architecture for the Rich." *Cairobserver*. January 6, 2013. http://cairobserver.com/post/39866891829/hassan-fathy-architecture-for-the-rich.

El Shakry, Omnia. *The Great Social Laboratory: Subjects of Knowledge in Colonial and Postcolonial Egypt*. Stanford, CA: Stanford University Press, 2007.

Engels, Friedrich. "Letter to J. Bloch, In Königsberg." https://www.marxists.org/archive/marx/works/1890/letters/90_09_21.htm.

Esmeir, Samera. *Juridical Humanity: A Colonial History*. Stanford, CA: Stanford University Press, 2012.

Ewert, Jeanne C. "'A Thousand Other Mysteries': Metaphysical Detection, Ontological Quests." In *Detecting Texts: The Metaphysical Detective Story from Poe to Postmodernism*, edited by Patricia Merivale and Susan Elizabeth Sweeney, 179–98. Philadelphia: University of Pennsylvania Press, 1999.

Fahmy, Khaled. *All the Pasha's Men: Mehmed Ali, His Army, and the Making of Modern Egypt*. Cairo: American University in Cairo Press, 1997.

———. "The Anatomy of Justice: Forensic Medicine and Criminal Law in Nineteenth-Century Egypt." *Islamic Law and Society* 6, no. 2 (1999): 224–71.

Fathy, Hassan. *Architecture for the Poor: An Experiment in Rural Egypt*. Chicago: University of Chicago Press, 1979.

Faulkner, William. *al-Ṣakhab wa-l-ʿUnf*. Translated by Jabra Ibrahim Jabra. Beirut: al-Muʾassasah al-ʿArabiyyah li-l-Dirāsāt wa-l-Nashr, 1983.

Felski, Rita. *The Limits of Critique*. Chicago: University of Chicago Press, 2015.

Fisk, Robert. *Pity the Nation: The Abduction of Lebanon*. New York: Nation Books, 2002.

Foucault, Michel. *Discipline and Punish: The Birth of the Prison*. Translated by Alan Sheridan. New York: Vintage, 1977.

Freyha, Anis. *Dictionary of Modern Lebanese Proverbs*. Beirut: Librairie du Liban, 1974.

*Fuṣūl: Majallat al-Naqd al-Adabī* 76: *al-Riwāyah al-Būlīsiyyah*. Cairo: al-Hayʾah al-Miṣriyyah al-ʿĀmmah li-l-Kitāb, 2009.

Frundt, Henry J. *Refreshing Pauses: Coca-Cola and Human Rights in Guatemala*. New York: Praeger, 1987.

Genette, Gérard. *Narrative Discourse: An Essay in Method*. Translated by Jane E. Lewin. Ithaca, NY: Cornell University Press, 1980.

Ghanim, Fathi. *al-Jabal*. Cairo: Riwāyāt al-Hilāl, 1965.

Goldschmidt, Arthur. "Ghanim, Fathi." In *Biographical Dictionary of Modern Egypt*, 63. Boulder, CO: Lynne Rienner, 1999.

———. "Idris, Dr. Yusuf" In *Biographical Dictionary of Modern Egypt*, 88. Boulder, CO: Lynne Rienner, 1999.

———. *Modern Egypt: The Formation of a Nation-State*. 2nd ed. New York: Routledge, 2018.

Greenberg, Nathaniel. *The Aesthetic of Revolution in the Film and Literature of Naguib Mahfouz (1952–1967)*. Lanham, MD: Lexington Books, 2014.

Gril, Denis. "Dhawq." In *Encyclopaedia of Islam*, edited by Kate Fleet, Gudrun Krämer, Denis Matringe, John Nawas, and Devin J. Stewart. 3rd ed.; online ed., 2015. http://dx.doi.org.ezproxy.lib.utexas.edu/10.1163/1573-3912_ei3_COM_26001.

———. "Wiṣāl." In *Encyclopaedia of Islam*, edited by P. Bearman, Th. Bianquis, C. E. Bosworth, E. van Donzel, and W. P. Heinrichs. 2nd ed.; online ed., 2012. https://referenceworks.brillonline.com/entries/encyclopaedia-of-islam-3/dhawq-COM_26001?s.num=0&s.f.s2_parent=s.f.book.encyclopaedia-of-islam-3&s.q=Dhawq.

Guth, Stephan. "Novel, Arabic." In *Encyclopaedia of Islam*, edited by Kate Fleet, Gudrun Krämer, Denis Matringe, John Nawas, and Devin J. Stewart. 3rd ed.; online ed., 2014. https://referenceworks.brillonline.com/entries/encyclopaedia-of-islam-2/wisal-SIM_8932?s.num=0&s.f.s2_parent=s.f.book.encyclopaedia-of-islam-2&s.q=Wi%E1%B9%A3%C4%81l.

Guyer, Jonathan. *The Strange Case of the Arab Whodunit*. Produced by Sean Glynn and David Waters. BBC Radio 4, November 16, 2017. https://www.bbc.co.uk/sounds/play/b09f2cxy.

Hafez, Sabry. "The Egyptian Novel in the Sixties." *Journal of Arabic Literature* 7 (1976): 68–84.

Hajj, Samir Fawzi. *Marāyā Jabrā Ibrāhīm Jabrā wa-l-Fann al-Riwāʾī*. 1st printing. Beirut: al-Muʾassasah al-ʿArabiyyah li-l-Dirāsāt wa-l-Nashr, 2005.

al-Hakim, Tawfiq. *Diary of a Country Prosecutor*. Translated by Abba Eban. London: Saqi Books, 2005.

———. *Return of the Spirit*. Translated by William Maynard Hutchins. Boulder: Lynne Rienner, 2012.

———. *Yawmiyyāt Nāʾib fi-l-Aryāf*. Beirut: Dār al-Kitāb al-Lubnānī, 1983.

Halabi, Zeina. "The Day the Wandering Dreamer Became a Fidaʾi: Jabra Ibrahim Jabra and the Fashioning of Political Commitment." In *Commitment and Beyond: Reflections on/of the Political in Arabic Literature Since the 1940s*, edited by Friederike Pannewick and Georges Khalil, 157–70. Wiesbaden: Reichert Verlag, 2015.

———. *The Unmaking of the Arab Intellectual: Prophecy, Exile, and the Nation*. Edinburgh: Edinburgh University Press, 2017.

Hallaq, Boutros. "Adab, e) Modern Usage." In *Encyclopaedia of Islam*, edited by Kate Fleet, Gudrun Krämer, Denis Matringe, John Nawas, and Devin J. Stewart. 3rd ed.; online ed., 2014. https://referenceworks.brillonline.com/entries/encyclopaedia-of-islam-3/adab-e-modern-usage-COM_23653?s.num=0&s.f.s2_parent=s.f.book.encyclopaedia-of-islam-3&s.q=Adab%2C+e%29+Modern+Usage.

———. "La littérature selon Manfalūṭī." *Arabica: Journal of Arabic and Islamic Studies* 50, no. 2 (2003): 131–76.

Hamoudi, Haider. "Muʿāmalāt." In *Encyclopaedia of Islam*, edited by Kate Fleet, Gudrun Krämer, Denis Matringe, John Nawas, and Devin J. Stewart. 3rd ed.; online ed., 2014. https://referenceworks.brillonline.com/entries/encyclopaedia-of-islam-3/muamalat-COM_36548?s.num=0&s.f.s2_parent=s.f.book.encyclopaedia-of-islam-3&s.q=Mu%CA%BF%C4%81mal%C4%81t.

Hartman, Michelle. "Re-Reading Women in/to Naguib Mahfouz's 'Al-Liss Wa'l Kilab (The Thief and the Dogs).'" *Research in African Literatures* 28, no. 3 (1997): 5–16.

Haugbolle, Sune. "The Secular Saint: Iconography and Ideology in the Cult of Bashir Jumayil." In *Politics of Worship in the Contemporary Middle East*, edited by A. Bandak and M. Bille, 191–212. Leiden: E. J. Brill, 2013.

Haycraft, Howard. *Murder for Pleasure: The Life and Times of the Detective Story*. 3rd ed. New York: Biblio and Tannen, 1968.

Heath, Peter. *The Thirsty Sword: Sirat ʿAntar and the Arabic Popular Epic*. Salt Lake City: University of Utah Press, 1996.

Heidegger, Martin. "The Age of the World Picture." In *The Question Concerning Technology and Other Essays*, 115–54. Translated by William Lovitt. New York: Harper and Row, 1977.

Hinds, Martin and El-Said Badawi. *A Dictionary of Egyptian Arabic*. Beirut: Librarie du Liban, 1986.

Hodgson, M. G. S. "Bāṭiniyya." In *Encyclopaedia of Islam*, edited by P. Bearman, Th. Bianquis, C. E. Bosworth, E. van Donzel, and W. P. Heinrichs. 2nd ed; online ed. 2012. https://referenceworks.brillonline.com/entries/encyclopaedia-of-islam-2/batiniyya-SIM_1284?s.num=0&s.f.s2_parent=s.f.book.encyclopaedia-of-islam-2&s.q=B%C4%81%E1%B9%ADiniyya.

Holt, Elizabeth M. *Fictitious Capital: Silk, Cotton, and the Rise of the Arabic Novel*. New York: Fordham University Press, 2018.

Horkheimer, Max, and Theodor Adorno. *Dialectic of Enlightenment: Philosophical Fragments*. Translated by Edmund Jephcott. Stanford, CA: Stanford University Press, 2002.

Hühn, Peter. "The Detective as Reader: Narrativity and Reading Concepts in Detective Fiction." *Modern Fiction Studies* 33, no. 3 (2009): 451–66.

Hunter, Robert. *Egypt Under the Khedives, 1805–1879: From Household Government to Modern Bureaucracy*. Pittsburgh: University of Pittsburgh Press, 1984.

Hussein, Dina. "'Zaat' and her Bathroom—and Television." *Mada Masr*, August 7, 2013. https://madamasr.com/en/2013/08/07/feature/culture/zaat-and-her-bathroom-and-television/.

Ibn Abi Talib, ʿAli, al-Jahiz, and al-Qadi al-Qudaʿi. *A Treasury of Virtues: Sayings, Sermons, and Teachings of ʿAlī, With the One Hundred Proverbs Attributed to al-Jāḥiẓ*. Translated by Tahera Qutbuddin. Library of Arabic Literature. New York: New York University Press, 2013.

Ibrahim, Sonallah. "Arsène Lupin." Translated by Emily Drumsta. *ArabLit Quarterly* 3, no. 2 (2020): 68–71.

———. "Arsīn Lūbīn." In *Tilka al-Rāʾiḥah*, 73–80. 1st ed. Cairo: Dār Shuhdī, 1986.

———. *The Committee*. Translated by Mary St. Germain and Charlene Constable. Syracuse, NY: Syracuse University Press, 2001.

———. *Dhāt*. 4th ed. Cairo: Dār al-Mustaqbal al-ʿArabī, 2004.

———. *al-Lajnah*. 9th Printing. Cairo: Dār al-Mustaqbal al-ʿArabī, 2004.

———. *Zaat*. Translated by Anthony Calderbank. Cairo: American University in Cairo Press, 2001.

ʿId, Husayn. *Fatḥī Ghānim, al-Ḥayāt wa-l-Ibdāʿ*. Cairo: al-Hayʾah al-ʿĀmmah li-Quṣūr al-Thaqāfah, 1995.

Idris, Yusuf. *Mālik al-Quṭn wa-Jumhūriyyat Faraḥāt: Masraḥiyyatān*. Cairo: al-Muʾassasah al-Qawmiyyah li-l-Nashr wa-l-Tawzīʿ, 1963.

———. *The Sinners*. Translated by Kristin Peterson-Ishaq. Boulder: Lynne Rienner, 2009.

———. *Yūsuf Idrīs: al-Riwāyāt*. Cairo: Dār al-Shurūq, 1987.

Irwin, John T. "Mysteries We Reread, Mysteries of Rereading: Poe, Borges, and the Analytical Detective Story." In *Detecting Texts: The Metaphysical Detective Story from Poe to Postmodernism*, edited by Patricia Merivale and Susan Elizabeth Sweeney, 27–54. Philadelphia: University of Pennsylvania Press, 1999.

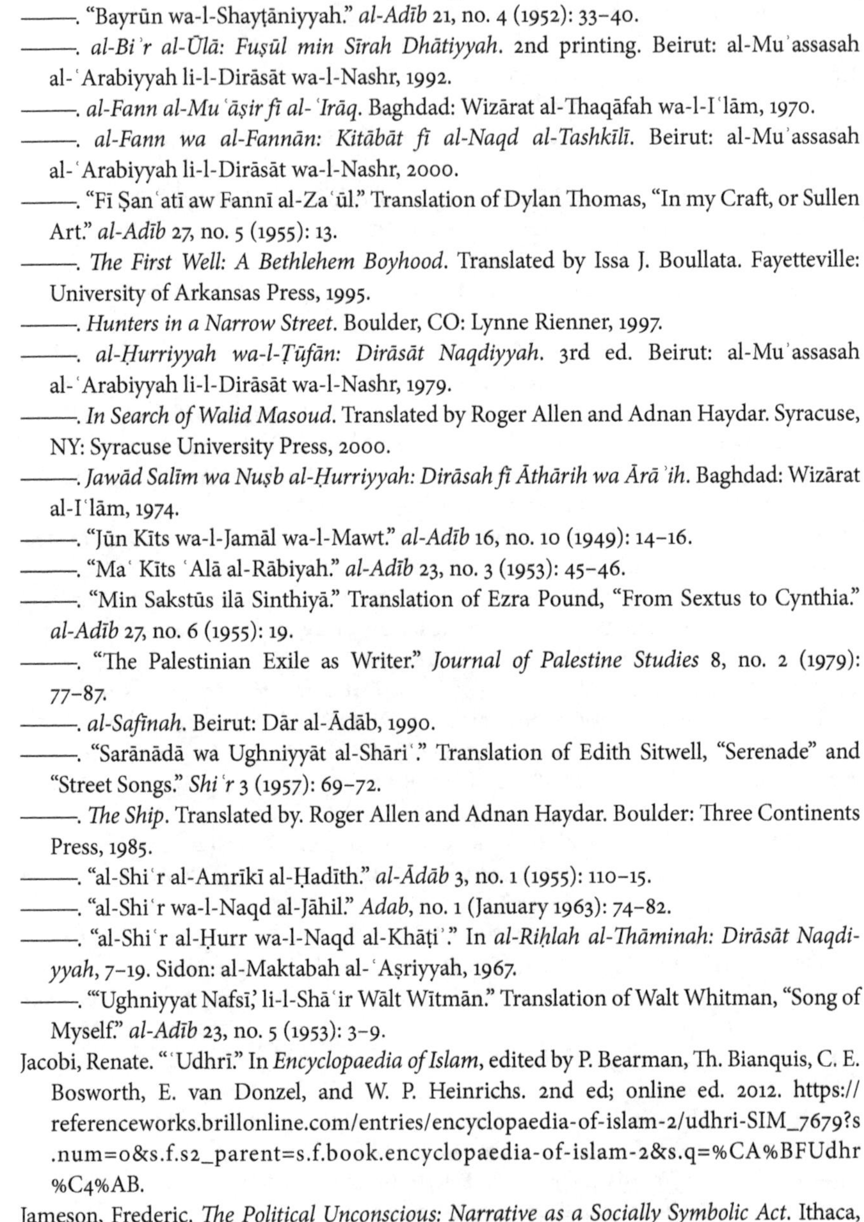

Jabra, Jabra Ibrahim. "Amthāl al-Jaḥīm li-Wilyim Blayik." *al-Adīb* 23, no. 4 (1953): 3–5.

———. *al-Baḥth ʿan Walīd Masʿūd*. 4th printing. Beirut: Dār al-Ādāb, 1990.

———. "Bayrūn wa-l-Shayṭāniyyah." *al-Adīb* 21, no. 4 (1952): 33–40.

———. *al-Biʾr al-Ūlā: Fuṣūl min Sīrah Dhātiyyah*. 2nd printing. Beirut: al-Muʾassasah al-ʿArabiyyah li-l-Dirāsāt wa-l-Nashr, 1992.

———. *al-Fann al-Muʿāṣir fī al-ʿIrāq*. Baghdad: Wizārat al-Thaqāfah wa-l-Iʿlām, 1970.

———. *al-Fann wa al-Fannān: Kitābāt fī al-Naqd al-Tashkīlī*. Beirut: al-Muʾassasah al-ʿArabiyyah li-l-Dirāsāt wa-l-Nashr, 2000.

———. "Fī Ṣanʿatī aw Fannī al-Zaʿūl." Translation of Dylan Thomas, "In my Craft, or Sullen Art." *al-Adīb* 27, no. 5 (1955): 13.

———. *The First Well: A Bethlehem Boyhood*. Translated by Issa J. Boullata. Fayetteville: University of Arkansas Press, 1995.

———. *Hunters in a Narrow Street*. Boulder, CO: Lynne Rienner, 1997.

———. *al-Ḥurriyyah wa-l-Ṭūfān: Dirāsāt Naqdiyyah*. 3rd ed. Beirut: al-Muʾassasah al-ʿArabiyyah li-l-Dirāsāt wa-l-Nashr, 1979.

———. *In Search of Walid Masoud*. Translated by Roger Allen and Adnan Haydar. Syracuse, NY: Syracuse University Press, 2000.

———. *Jawād Salīm wa Nuṣb al-Ḥurriyyah: Dirāsah fī Āthārih wa Ārāʾih*. Baghdad: Wizārat al-Iʿlām, 1974.

———. "Jūn Kīts wa-l-Jamāl wa-l-Mawt." *al-Adīb* 16, no. 10 (1949): 14–16.

———. "Maʿ Kīts ʿAlā al-Rābiyah." *al-Adīb* 23, no. 3 (1953): 45–46.

———. "Min Sakstūs ilā Sinthiyā." Translation of Ezra Pound, "From Sextus to Cynthia." *al-Adīb* 27, no. 6 (1955): 19.

———. "The Palestinian Exile as Writer." *Journal of Palestine Studies* 8, no. 2 (1979): 77–87.

———. *al-Safīnah*. Beirut: Dār al-Ādāb, 1990.

———. "Sarānādā wa Ughniyyāt al-Shāriʿ." Translation of Edith Sitwell, "Serenade" and "Street Songs." *Shiʿr* 3 (1957): 69–72.

———. *The Ship*. Translated by. Roger Allen and Adnan Haydar. Boulder: Three Continents Press, 1985.

———. "al-Shiʿr al-Amrīkī al-Ḥadīth." *al-Ādāb* 3, no. 1 (1955): 110–15.

———. "al-Shiʿr wa-l-Naqd al-Jāhil." *Adab*, no. 1 (January 1963): 74–82.

———. "al-Shiʿr al-Ḥurr wa-l-Naqd al-Khāṭiʾ." In *al-Riḥlah al-Thāminah: Dirāsāt Naqdiyyah*, 7–19. Sidon: al-Maktabah al-ʿAṣriyyah, 1967.

———. "'Ughniyyat Nafsī,' li-l-Shāʿir Wālt Wītmān." Translation of Walt Whitman, "Song of Myself." *al-Adīb* 23, no. 5 (1953): 3–9.

Jacobi, Renate. "ʿUdhrī." In *Encyclopaedia of Islam*, edited by P. Bearman, Th. Bianquis, C. E. Bosworth, E. van Donzel, and W. P. Heinrichs. 2nd ed; online ed. 2012. https://referenceworks.brillonline.com/entries/encyclopaedia-of-islam-2/udhri-SIM_7679?s.num=0&s.f.s2_parent=s.f.book.encyclopaedia-of-islam-2&s.q=%CA%BFUdhr%C4%AB.

Jameson, Frederic. *The Political Unconscious: Narrative as a Socially Symbolic Act*. Ithaca, NY: Cornell University Press, 1981.

———. *Raymond Chandler: The Detections of Totality*. London: Verso, 2016.

Jay, Martin. *Marxism and Totality: The Adventures of a Concept from Lukács to Habermas*. Berkeley: The University of California Press, 1984.

Johnson, Rebecca Carol. "The Politics of Reading: Revolution and Recognition in Jabra Ibrahim Jabra's *In Search of Walid Masoud*." In *Recognition: The Poetics of Narrative, Interdisciplinary Studies on Anagnorisis*, edited by Philip F. Kennedy and Marilyn Lawrence, 178–92. New York: Peter Lang, 2009.

Johnstone, Diana. "Une stratégie 'trilaterale.'" *Le Monde Diplomatique* 23, no. 272 (November 1976): 1, 13–14.

Jones, Constance A., and James D. Ryan. "Darshan." In *Encyclopedia of Hinduism*. New York: Facts on File, 2007.

Khalil, Atif. "Ḥāl in Sufism." In *Encyclopaedia of Islam*, edited by Kate Fleet, Gudrun Krämer, Denis Matringe, John Nawas, and Devin J. Stewart. 3rd ed.; online ed. 2022. https://referenceworks.brillonline.com/entries/encyclopaedia-of-islam-3/hal-in-sufism-COM_30219?s.num=0&s.f.s2_parent=s.f.book.encyclopaedia-of-islam-3&s.q=%E1%B8%A4%C4%81l+in+Sufism.

Khalili, Laleh. *Heroes and Martyrs of Palestine: The Politics of National Commemoration*. Cambridge: Cambridge University Press, 2009.

———. "Heroic and Tragic Pasts: Mnemonic Narratives in the Palestinian Refugee Camps." *Critical Sociology* 33 (2007): 731–59.

Kharrat, Idwar. *al-Ḥassāsiyyah al-Jadīdah: Maqālāt fi-l-Ẓāhirah al-Qiṣaṣiyyah*. 1st ed. Beirut: Dār al-Ādāb, 1993.

"Khiṭabān li-l-Ra'īsayn fī Ḥafl al-'Ashā'." *al-Ahrām* (Cairo), June 13, 1974.

Khoury, Elias. "'An al-būlīs wa-l-Qiṣṣah al-Būlīsiyyah." In *al-Dhākirah al-Mafqūdah*, 350–53. 1st ed. Beirut: Mu'assasat al-Abḥāth al-'Arabiyyah, 1982.

———. *Bāb al-Shams*. 7th printing. Beirut: Dār al-Ādāb, 2017.

———. "Conversations with Ilyās Khūrī." Interview by Sonja Mejcher. In *Geschichten über Geschichten: Errinerung im Romanwerk von Ilyās Khūrī*. Weisbaden: Reichert Verlag, 2001.

———. "al-Dhākirah al-Mafqūdah." In *al-Dhākirah al-Mafqūdah: Dirāsāt Naqdiyyah*, 25–43. Beirut: Mu'assasat al-Abḥāth al-'Arabiyyah, 1982.

———. "al-Kitābah wa-l-Mawt." In *Zaman al-Iḥtilāl*, 251–55. Beirut: Mu'assasat al-Abḥāth al-'Arabiyyah, 1985.

———. "Mawt al-Mu'allif." In *al-Dhākirah al-Mafqūdah: Dirāsāt Naqdiyyah*, 72–76. 1st ed. Beirut: Mu'assasat al-Abḥāth al-'Arabiyyah, 1982.

———. *White Masks*. Translated by Maia Tabet. Brooklyn: Archipelago Books, 2010.

———. *al-Wujūh al-Bayḍā'*. 3rd ed. Beirut: Dār al-Ādāb, 2003.

———. *Yalo*. Translated by Peter Theroux. New York: Picador, 2008.

Khurshid, Faruq. *al-Siyar al-Sha'biyyah*. Cairo: Dār al-Ma'ārif, 1978.

Kilpatrick, Hilary. *The Modern Egyptian Novel: A Study in Social Criticism*. London: Ithaca Press, 1974.

———. "Tradition and Innovation in the Fiction of Ghassān Kanafānī." *Journal of Arabic Literature* 7 (1976): 53–64.

Knight, Stephen. *Form and Ideology in Crime Fiction*. Bloomington: Indiana University Press, 1980.

Knudsen, Are John. "Death of a Statesman—Birth of a Martyr: Martyrdom and Memorials in Post-Civil War Lebanon." *Anthropology of the Middle East* 11, no. 2 (2016): 1–17.

Koerber, Benjamin. *Conspiracy in Modern Egyptian Literature*. Edinburgh: Edinburgh University Press, 2018.

Kronfeld, Chana. "Beyond Thematicism in the Historiography of Post-1948 Political Poetry." *Jewish Social Studies* 18, no. 3 (2012): 180–96.

———. *On the Margins of Modernism: Decentering Literary Dynamics*. Berkeley: University of California Press, 1996.

Larkin, Margaret. "A Brigand Hero of Egyptian Colloquial Literature." *Journal of Arabic Literature* 23, no. 1 (1992): 49–64.

Le Gassick, Trevor. Introduction to *The Thief and the Dogs*, by Naguib Mahfouz, 5–9. New York: Anchor Books, 2008.

Lewisohn, L. "Shawk." In *Encyclopaedia of Islam*, edited by P. Bearman, Th. Bianquis, C. E. Bosworth, E. van Donzel, and W. P. Heinrichs. 2nd ed; online ed. 2012. https://referenceworks.brillonline.com/entries/encyclopaedia-of-islam-2/shawk-SIM_6874?s.num=0&s.f.s2_parent=s.f.book.encyclopaedia-of-islam-2&s.q=Shawk.

Lindsey, Ursula. "Sonallah Ibrahim, Taking Stock." *Arabist*, June 25, 2010. https://arabist.net/blog/2010/6/25/sonallah-ibrahim-taking-stock.html.

Litvin, Margaret. *Hamlet's Arab Journey: Shakespeare's Prince and Nasser's Ghost*. Princeton, NJ: Princeton University Press, 2011.

Love, Heather. "Truth and Consequences: On Paranoid Reading and Reparative Reading." *Criticism* 52, no. 2 (2010): 235–41.

Loudiy, Fadoua. *Transitional Justice and Human Rights in Morocco*. London: Routledge, 2014.

Lukács, Georg. "The Standpoint of the Proletariat." In *History and Class Consciousness*. https://www.marxists.org/archive/lukacs/works/history/hcc07_1.htm.

———. *The Theory of the Novel*. Translated by Anna Bostock. Cambridge, MA: MIT Press, 1971.

Lyons, M. C. *The Arabian Epic: Heroic and Oral Storytelling*. Cambridge: Cambridge University Press, 1995.

Magidow, Melanie. "Epic of the Commander Dhat al-Himma." *Medieval Feminist Forum: A Journal of Gender and Sexuality* 9 (2018): 3–62.

Mahfouz, Naguib. *Ataḥaddath Ilaykum*. Beirut: Dār al-ʿAwdah, 1977.

———. *Autumn Quail*. Translated by Roger Allen. In *The Beggar, The Thief and the Dogs, Autumn Quail*. New York: Anchor Books, 2000.

———. *The Cairo Trilogy: Palace Walk, Palace of Desire, Sugar Street*. Translated by William Maynard Hutchins, Olive E. Kenny, Lorne M. Kenny, and Angele Botros Samaan. New York: Alfred A. Knopf, 2001.

———. "Culprit Unknown." Translated by Emily Drumsta. *Asymptote*, July 2019. https://www.asymptotejournal.com/fiction/naguib-mahfouz-culprit-unknown/.

———. *Fountain and Tomb*. Translated by Soad Sobhy, Essam Fattouh, and James Kenneson. Washington, DC: Three Continents Press, 1988.

———. *al-Muʾallafāt al-Kāmilah*. 5 vols. Beirut: Maktabat Lubnān, 1991.

———. *Naguib Mahfouz at Sidi Gaber: Reflections of a Nobel Laureate, 1994–2001*. Cairo: The American University in Cairo Press, 2001.

———. *The Search*. Translated by Mohamed Islam. Edited by Magdi Wahba. In *Respected Sir, Wedding Song, The Search*. New York: Anchor Books, 2001.

———. *al-Ṭarīq*. Cairo: Maktabat Miṣr, n.d.

———. *The Thief and the Dogs*. In *The Beggar, The Thief and the Dogs, Autumn Quail*. New York: Anchor Books, 2000.

———. "Zaabalawi." Translated by Denys Johnson-Davies. In *The Essential Naguib Mahfouz*, edited by Denys Johnson-Davies, 267–78. Cairo: American University in Cairo Press, 2011.

Marcus, Laura. "Detection and Literary Fiction." In *The Cambridge Companion to Crime Fiction*, edited by Martin Priestman, 245–68. Cambridge: Cambridge University Press, 2003.

Marsot, Afaf Lutfi al-Sayyid. *A History of Egypt: From the Arab Conquest to the Present*. Cambridge: Cambridge University Press, 2007.

Marx, Karl. "Preface." In *A Contribution to the Critique of Political Economy*. https://www.marxists.org/archive/marx/works/1859/critique-pol-economy/preface.htm#eb1.

Marx, Karl, and Friedrich Engels. *Manifesto of the Communist Party*. https://www.marxists.org/archive/marx/works/1848/communist-manifesto/ch01.htm#a2.

Marx-Scouras, Danielle. "A Literature of Departure: The Cross-Cultural Writing of Driss Chraïbi." *Research in African Literatures* 23, no. 2 (1992): 131–44.

Mayakovsky, Vladimir. "At the Top of My Voice." In *The Bedbug and Selected Poetry*. Translated by Max Hayward and George Reavey. New York: Meridian Books, 1960. https://www.marxists.org/subject/art/literature/mayakovsky/1930/at-top-my-voice.htm.

McGregor, Richard J. "Friend of God." In *Encyclopaedia of Islam*, edited by Kate Fleet, Gudrun Krämer, Denis Matringe, John Nawas, and Devin J. Stewart. 3rd ed.; online ed., 2013. https://referenceworks.brillonline.com/entries/encyclopaedia-of-islam-3/friend-of-god-COM_27194?s.num=0&s.f.s2_parent=s.f.book.encyclopaedia-of-islam-3&s.q=friend+of+god.

———. "Grave Visitation/Worship." In *Encyclopaedia of Islam*, edited by Kate Fleet, Gudrun Krämer, Denis Matringe, John Nawas, and Devin J. Stewart. 3rd ed.; online ed., 2016. https://referenceworks.brillonline.com/entries/encyclopaedia-of-islam-3/grave-visitationworship-COM_27519?s.num=0&s.f.s2_parent=s.f.book.encyclopaedia-of-islam-3&s.q=Grave+Visitation%2FWorship.

Mehrez, Samia. "Sonallah Ibrahim's *Dhat*: The Ultimate Objectification of the Self." In *Egyptian Writers Between History and Fiction: Essays on Naguib Mahfouz, Sonallah Ibrahim, and Gamal al-Ghitani*, 119–45. Cairo: American University in Cairo Press, 1994.

Mejcher-Atassi, Sonja. "The Martyr and His Image: Ilyās Khūrī's Novel *al-Wujūh al-Bayḍāʾ* (*The White Faces*, Beirut 1981)." In *Martyrdom in Literature: Visions of Death and Meaningful Suffering in Europe and the Middle East from Antiquity to Modernity*, edited by Friederike Pannewick, 343–55. Weisbaden: Reichert Verlag, 2004.

Merivale, Patricia. "Gumshoe Gothics: Poe's 'Man of the Crowd' and his Followers." In *Detecting Texts: The Metaphysical Detective Story from Poe to Postmodernism*, edited by Patricia Merivale and Susan Elizabeth Sweeney, 101–16. Philadelphia: University of Pennsylvania Press, 1999.

Merivale, Patricia, and Susan Elizabeth Sweeney, ed. *Detecting Texts: The Metaphysical Detective Story from Poe to Postmodernism*. Philadelphia: University of Pennsylvania Press, 1999.

Meyer, Stefan G. *The Experimental Arabic Novel: Postcolonial Literary Modernism in the Levant*. Albany: State University of New York Press, 2001.

Miller, D. A. *The Novel and the Police*. Berkeley: University of California Press, 1988.

Mitchell, Timothy. *Colonising Egypt*. Berkeley: University of California Press, 1991.

———. *Rule of Experts: Egypt, Techno-Politics, Modernity*. Berkeley: University of California Press, 2002.

Mitford, Jessica. "Egyptomania: Tut, Mut, and the Rest of the Gang." In *Poison Penmanship: The Gentle Art of Muckraking*. New York: Knopf, 1979.

Moosa, Matti. *The Origins of Modern Arabic Fiction*. Washington, DC: Three Continents Press, 1983.

*New York Times*. "Chavez Signs Florida's First Farm Pact." March 1, 1972. https://nyti.ms/1iiKbkP.

———. "Mondale Says Migrant Labor Gained Little Through Congress." March 22, 1971. https://nyti.ms/1knM9Sz.

Moretti, Franco. *Signs Taken for Wonders: On the Sociology of Literary Forms*. London: Verso, 2005.

Munt, Sally. *Murder by the Book? Feminism and the Crime Novel*. London: Routledge, 1994.

Murrow, Edward R. 1960: "Harvest of Shame." Produced by David Lowe. CBS Reports, CBS News. Uploaded November 24, 2010. YouTube video, 52:05. https://www.youtube.com/watch?v=yJTVF_dya7E.

al-Musawi, Muhsin Jasim. *Infirāt al-ʿIqd al-Muqaddas: Munʿaṭafāt al-Riwāyah al-ʿArabiyyah Baʿd Maḥfūẓ*. Cairo: al-Hayʾah al-Miṣriyyah li-l-Kitāb, 1999.

———. *The Postcolonial Arabic Novel: Debating Ambivalence*. Leiden: E. J. Brill, 2003.

Nabokov, Vladimir. *The Real Life of Sebastian Knight*. New York: Vintage, 1992.

Nietzsche, Friedrich. "On Truth and Lies in a Nonmoral Sense." In *The Nietzsche Reader*, edited by Keith Ansell Pearson and Duncan Large, 114–23. Malden: Blackwell, 2006.

Noorani, Yaseen. *Culture and Hegemony in the Colonial Middle East*. New York: Palgrave Macmillan, 2010.

Oliver, Thomas. *The Real Coke, the Real Story*. New York: Random House, 1986.

Pearson, Nels, and Marc Singer, eds. *Detective Fiction in a Postcolonial and Transnational World*. Farnham, VT: Ashgate, 2009.

Peled, Mattiyahu. "Creative Translation: Towards the Study of Arabic Translations of Western Literature Since the 19th Century." *Journal of Arabic Literature* 10 (1979): 128–50.

———. "Sexuality in Jabra's Novel, *The Search for Walīd Masʿūd*." In *Love and Sexuality in Modern Arabic Literature*, edited by Roger Allen, Hilary Kilpatrick, and Ed de Moor, 140–53. London: Saqi Books, 1995.

Pennell, C. R. *Morocco: From Empire to Independence*. Oxford: Oneworld, 2003.

Pepe, Teresa. *Blogging From Egypt: Digital Literature, 2005–2016*. Edinburgh: Edinburgh University Press, 2019.

Pepper, Andrew. *The Contemporary American Crime Novel: Race, Ethnicity, Gender, Class*. Edinburgh: Edinburgh University Press, 2000.

Poe, Edgar Allan. "The Man of the Crowd." In *Complete Stories and Poems of Edgar Allan Poe*, 215–21. New York: Doubleday, n.d.

———. "The Murders in the Rue Morgue." In *Complete Stories and Poems of Edgar Allan Poe*. New York: Doubleday, n.d.

Porter, Dennis. *The Pursuit of Crime: Art and Ideology in Detective Fiction*. New Haven, CT: Yale University Press, 1981.

Prabhu, Anjali. "Theorizing the Role of the Intermediary in Postcolonial (Con)Text: Driss Chraïbi's *Une Enquête au pays*." *Studies in 20th & 21st Century Literature* 27, no. 1 (2003): 167–90.

Prendergast, Christopher. "The World Republic of Letters." In *Debating World Literature*, edited by Christopher Prendergast, 1–25. London: Verso, 2004.

Priestman, Martin. *Detective Fiction and Literature: The Figure on the Carpet*. New York: St. Martin's Press, 1991.

Pyla, Panayiota. "The Many Lives of New Gourna: Alternative Histories of a Model Community and Their Current Significance." *Journal of Architecture* 14, no. 6 (2009): 715–30.

Pynchon, Thomas. *Gravity's Rainbow*. New York: Penguin, 2006.

al-Qa'id, Yusuf. *Akhbār 'Izbat al-Manīsī*. Cairo: Dār al-Hilāl, 1985.

———. *Man Yadhkur Miṣr al-Ukhrā?* Damascus: al-Jumhūriyyah al-'Arabiyyah al-Sūriyyah, Wizārat al-Thaqāfah, 1984.

———. *News from the Meneisi Farm*. Translated by Marie-Therese F. Abdel-Messih. Cairo: General Egyptian Book Organization, 1987.

———. *Yaḥduth fī Miṣr al-Ān*. 1st ed. Cairo: Dār Usāmah li-l-Ṭaba' wa-l-Nashr, 1977.

———. *Yaḥduth fī Miṣr al-Ān*. 4th ed. Cairo: Dār al-Mustaqbal al-'Arabī, 1986.

al-Rabi'i, Mahmud. *Qirā'āt al-Riwāyah: Namādhij min Najīb Maḥfūẓ*. Cairo: Dār al-Ma'ārif, 1974.

Rastegar, Kamran. *Literary Modernity Between the Middle East and Europe: Textual Transactions in Nineteenth-Century Arabic, English, and Persian Literatures*. London: Routledge, 2007.

Ray, Rabindra. "The Teaching of *Darshan* and its Purpose." Translated by Satish Deshpande. *Contributions to Indian Sociology* 53, no. 3 (2019): 422–30.

Reitz, Caroline. *Detecting the Nation: Fictions of Detection and the Imperial Venture*. Columbus: Ohio State University Press, 2004.

Reynolds, Dwight. *Arab Folklore: A Handbook*. Westport, CT: Greenwood Press, 2004.

———. *Heroic Poets, Poetic Heroes: The Ethnography of Performance in an Arabic Oral Epic Tradition*. Ithaca, NY: Cornell University Press, 1995.

Richards, J. M., Ismail Serageldin, and Darl Rastorfer. *Hassan Fathy*. Architects of the Third World Series. London: Mimar, 1991.

Rooney, Ellen. "Live Free or Describe: The Reading Effect and the Persistence of Form." *Differences: A Journal of Feminist Cultural Studies* 21, no. 5 (2010): 112–39.

Ryzova, Lucie. *The Age of the Efendiyya: Passages to Modernity in National-Colonial Egypt*. Oxford: Oxford University Press, 2014.

Sacks, Jeffrey. *Iterations of Loss: Mutilation and Aesthetic Form, al-Shidyaq to Darwish*. New York: Fordham University Press, 2015.

Saadawi, Ahmad. *Frankenstein in Baghdad*. Translated by Jonathan Wright. New York: Penguin Books, 2018.

———. *Frankishtāyin fī Baghdād*. Beirut: Manshūrāt al-Jamal, 2013.

Said, Edward. *Orientalism*. 25th Anniversary Edition. New York: Vintage, 1994.

Sakkut, Hamdi. "Najīb Maḥfūẓ wa-l-Ḥall al-Ṣūfī." *Alif: A Journal of Comparative Poetics* 5 (1985): 39–48.

Salama, Mohammad. "The Aesthetics of 'Pygmalion' in G. B. Shaw and Tawfiq Al-Ḥakīm: A Study of Transcendence and Decadence." *Journal of Arabic Literature* 31, no. 3 (2000): 222–37.

Salih, Fakhri. "A'māl Tawfīq al-Ḥakīm al-Riwā'iyyah: I'ādat Qirā'ah." In *Tawfīq al-Ḥakīm: Ḥuḍūr Mutajaddid*, edited by Gaber Asfour. Cairo: al-Majlis al-A'lā li-l-Thaqāfah, 1998.

Sayers, Dorothy. "The Omnibus of Crime." In *The Art of the Mystery Story: A Collection of Critical Essays*, edited by Howard Haycraft, 71–127. New York: Simon & Schuster, 1946.

Sayigh, Rosemary. *The Palestinians: From Peasants to Revolutionaries, a People's History.* London: Zed Press, 1979.

Schine, Rachel. "On Blackness in Arabic Popular Literature: The Black Heroes of the Siyar Sha'biyya, Their Conceptions, Contests, and Contexts." PhD diss., University of Chicago, 2019.

Scott, David. *Conscripts of Modernity: The Tragedy of Colonial Enlightenment.* Durham, NC: Duke University Press, 2004.

Scott, James. *Seeing Like a State: How Certain Schemes to Improve the Human Condition Have Failed.* New Haven, CT: Yale University Press, 1998.

Sedgwick, Eve Kosofsky. "Paranoid Reading and Reparative Reading, or, You're So Paranoid, You Probably Think This Essay is About You." In *Touching Feeling: Affect, Pedagogy, Performativity,* 123–51. Durham, NC: Duke University Press, 2003.

Seigneurie, Ken. "Modern Nihilism and Naguib Mahfouz's Faith in Liberalism." *Middle Eastern Literatures* 24, no. 3 (2022): 167–89.

Selim, Samah. "Fiction and Colonial Identities: Arsène Lupin in Arabic." *Middle Eastern Studies* 13, no. 2 (2010): 191–210.

———. *The Novel and the Rural Imaginary in Egypt, 1880–1985.* London: Routledge, 2004.

———. *Popular Fiction, Translation, and the Nahda in Egypt.* Cham, Switzerland: Palgrave Macmillan, 2019.

Shabecoff, Philip. "Life Improves for Florida's Orange Harvesters." *New York Times,* March 19, 1973. https://nyti.ms/1PtxP6x.

Shadid, Anthony. "In Baghdad Ruins, Remains of a Cultural Bridge." *New York Times,* May 21, 2010. https://www.nytimes.com/2010/05/22/world/middleeast/22house.html.

Shakespeare, William. *Hāmlit.* Translated by Jabra Ibrahim Jabra. Beirut: Dār Majallat Shi'r, 1960.

al-Sharqawi, 'Abd al-Rahman. *Egyptian Earth.* Translated by Desmond Stewart. London: Saqi Books, 2005.

Sheehi, Stephen. *Foundations of Modern Arab Identity.* Gainesville: University Press of Florida, 2004.

Shukri, Ghali. *Duktūr Yūsuf Idrīs: Farfūr Khārij al-Sūr.* Cairo: al-Hay'ah al-'Āmmah li-l-Isti'lāmāt, 1992.

———. *Thawrat al-Mu'tazil: Dirāsah fī Adab Tawfīq al-Ḥakīm.* Cairo: Maktabat al-Anjlū, 1966.

Sklar, Holly, ed. *Trilateralism: The Trilateral Commission and Elite Planning for World Management.* Boston: South End Press, 1980.

Slezkine, Yuri. *The House of Government.* Princeton, NJ: Princeton University Press, 2017.

Slymovics, Susan. *The Performance of Human Rights in Morocco.* Philadelphia: University of Pennsylvania Press, 2005.

Smolin, Jonathan. *Moroccan Noir: Police, Crime, and Politics in Popular Culture.* Bloomington: Indiana University Press, 2013.

Somekh, Sasson. *The Changing Rhythm: A Study of Najīb Maḥfūẓ's Novels.* Leiden: E. J. Brill, 1973.

———. "Language and Theme in the Short Stories of Yūsuf Idrīs." *Journal of Arabic Literature* 6, no. 1 (1975): 89–100.

Spivak, Gayatri Chakravorty. *Death of a Discipline.* New York: Columbia University Press, 2003.

Starkey, Paul. *Sonallah Ibrahim: Rebel With a Pen*. Edinburgh: Edinburgh University Press, 2016.

Steele, James. *An Architecture for the People: The Complete Works of Hassan Fathy*. New York: Whitney Library of Design, 1997.

———. *Hassan Fathy*. London: Academy Editions, 1988.

Stone, Christopher. "Tawfiq al-Hakim, Yusuf al-Qa'id, and the 'Mature' Arabic Novel." In *Transforming Loss Into Beauty: Essays on Arabic Literature and Culture in Honor of Magda Al-Nowaihi*, edited by Marlé Hammond and Dana Sajdi, 295–319.Cairo: American University in Cairo Press, 2008.

Sulaiman, Khalid A. *Palestine and Modern Arab Poetry*. London: Zed, 1984.

Surur, Najib. *Yāsīn wa Bahiyyah: Riwāyah Shiʿriyyah*. Cairo: Majallat al-Masraḥ, 1965.

Tageldin, Shaden M. *Disarming Words: Empire and the Seductions of Translation in Egypt*. Berkeley: University of California Press, 2011.

Tamplin, William. "The Other Wells: Family History and the Self Creation of Jabra Ibrahim Jabra." *Jerusalem Quarterly* 85 (2021): 30–60.

Tarabichi, George. *Allāh fī Riḥlat Najīb Maḥfūẓ al-Ramziyyah*. Beirut: Dār al-Ṭalīʿah, 1973.

Todorov, Tzvetan. *The Poetics of Prose*. Translated by Richard Howard. Ithaca, NY: Cornell University Press, 1977.

Tulbah, Fuʾad. *Yūsuf Idrīs wa-l-Tābū*. Cairo: Maktabat Miṣr, 1985.

Traboulsi, Fawwaz. *A History of Modern Lebanon*. London: Pluto Press, 2007.

van der Spek, Kees. *The Modern Neighbors of Tutankhamun: History, Life, and Work in the Villages of the Theban West Bank*. Cairo: American University in Cairo Press, 2011.

Vloeberghs, Ward. "Worshipping the Martyr-President: The *darīh* of Rafiq Hariri in Beirut." In *Ethnographies of Islam: Ritual Performances and Everyday Practices*, edited by P. G. Pinto, B. Dupre, and K. Spellman-Poots, 80–93. Edinburgh: Edinburgh University Press, 2012.

Volk, Lucia. *Memorials and Martyrs in Modern Lebanon*. Bloomington: Indiana University Press, 2010.

Walkowitz, Rebecca. *Born Translated: The Contemporary Novel in an Age of World Literature*. New York: Columbia University Press, 2015.

Walton, Priscilla L., and Manina Jones. *Detective Agency: Women Rewriting the Hard-Boiled Tradition*. Berkeley: University of California Press, 1999.

Warriner, Doreen. *Land Reform and Development in the Middle East: A Study of Egypt, Syria, and Iraq*. 2nd ed. London: Oxford University Press, 1962.

Whidden, James. *Monarchy and Modernity in Egypt: Politics, Islam, and Neo-Colonialism Between the Wars*. London: I. B. Tauris, 2013.

Williams, Raymond. *Keywords: A Vocabulary of Culture and Society*. Oxford: Oxford University Press, 2015.

Wrong, E. M. "Crime and Detection." In *The Art of the Mystery Story: A Collection of Critical Essays*, edited by Howard Haycraft, 18–32. New York: Simon & Schuster, 1946.

"Yā Bahiyyah wa-Khabbirīnī . . . Muḥammad Ṭāhā." Hani Farid, July 13, 2021. YouTube video, 3:45. https://www.youtube.com/watch?v=nFa8h9tQU84.

Zachs, Fruma, and Basilius Bawardi. "Arab Nation-Building Through Detective Stories in *al-Ḍiyāʾ*: The Cultural Translations of Nasīb al-Mashʿalānī." *Die Welt des Islams* 60, no. 1 (2020): 79–101.

al-Zayyat, Latifa. *Najīb Maḥfūẓ: al-Ṣūrah wa-l-Mithāl*. Cairo: Kitāb al-Ahālī, 1989.

# INDEX

NOTE: Page numbers in italics refer to illustrations.

Founded in 1893,
UNIVERSITY OF CALIFORNIA PRESS
publishes bold, progressive books and journals on topics in the arts, humanities, social sciences, and natural sciences—with a focus on social justice issues—that inspire thought and action among readers worldwide.

The UC PRESS FOUNDATION
raises funds to uphold the press's vital role as an independent, nonprofit publisher, and receives philanthropic support from a wide range of individuals and institutions—and from committed readers like you. To learn more, visit ucpress.edu/supportus.

Printed in the USA
CPSIA information can be obtained
at www.ICGtesting.com
JSHW012037090224
57040JS00004B/47

9 780520 390195